INTO
ETERNITY

INTO ETERNITY

The Life of
➤➤➤ JAMES JONES ❮❮❮
American Writer

❧

Frank MacShane

HOUGHTON MIFFLIN COMPANY · BOSTON
➤➤➤ 1985 ❮❮❮

Library of Congress Cataloging in Publication Data

MacShane, Frank.
  Into eternity.

  Includes index.
  1. Jones, James, 1921-1977 — Biography. 2. Novelists, American — 20th century — Biography. I. Title.
PS3560.049Z78   1985   813'.54   85-11891
ISBN 0-395-35355-6

Printed in the United States of America

A 10 9 8 7 6 5 4 3 2 1

❧

The author is grateful for permission to quote from the following works:

Excerpt from "Harp Song of the Dane Women" from *Rudyard Kipling's Verse, Definitive Edition*. Copyright 1906 by Rudyard Kipling. Reprinted by permission of Doubleday & Company, Inc.

Lines from "The Lake Isle of Innisfree" are reprinted with permission of Macmillan Publishing Company, Michael B. Yeats and Macmillan London Ltd. from *The Poems of W. B. Yeats* edited by Richard J. Finneran (New York: Macmillan, 1983).

"Dirge Without Music," by Edna St. Vincent Millay, from her *Collected Poems* (Harper & Row). Copyright 1982, 1955 by Edna St. Vincent Millay and Norma Millay Ellis.

Photographs by Jill Krementz are used courtesy of the photographer.

Photograph of the 27th Infantry Regiment is used courtesy of SSgt Arthur S. Macedo, US Army (Ret.), Dighton, Massachusetts, and San Diego, California (service in the 27th Infantry Regiment, 1937–1939).

The publisher has made every effort to locate the owners of all photographs and to obtain permission to reprint them. Any errors or omissions are unintentional, and corrections will be made in future editions if necessary.

For Gloria, Jamie, and Kaylie

whose help

made all the difference

and for

my son, Nicholas

➤➤ CONTENTS ◄◄

→» PREFACE AND «←
ACKNOWLEDGMENTS

JAMES JONES'S story is American to the bone. Born in the heartland of the country, he was forced by the Depression to join the army, only to find himself trapped in military life for five years by the advent of World War II. His only escape was through literature, and he wrote in order to have some control over a world he both loved and hated. Once discharged, he devoted himself single-mindedly to writing *From Here to Eternity*, a book that catapulted him to international fame and recognition before he was even thirty.

The success of that novel was followed by another period of intense work, which produced his second, even more ambitious novel, *Some Came Running*. Shortly before this novel was published, Jones moved to New York and married. Expecting further acclaim for the new book, he was shocked by the critical failure of *Some Came Running* and by the violence of the attack against him, and he and his wife moved to France. He remained there for the next fifteen years, enjoying the good life and continuing to work, but most of his writing did not achieve the intensity of his earlier books. He grew away from the sources of his strength as a writer, until in the mid-1970s he decided to return to America. He was determined to finish *Whistle*, the book that would complete a trilogy of war novels that included *From Here to Eternity* and *The Thin Red Line*, but he died before finishing the work. Nevertheless, it was evident when the novel was published posthumously that Jones had completed his literary monument and that he deserved to stand in the first rank of American writers in the second half of the twentieth century.

Despite the ups and downs of his career, Jones believed in himself as a writer. Accordingly, he preserved all documents that might be of use to students of his life and work. The hundreds of boxes and cartons of paper that he collected are now safely deposited in university libraries, and they constitute the main source of written information about him. I am grateful to the following individuals and institutions for the help they provided as I went through this material: Decherd Turner and John Chalmers of the Humanities Research Center at the University of Texas in Austin; the staff of the Beinecke Library at Yale University; Richard Ludwig and the staff of the Rare Book Collection in the Princeton University Library, whose papers from Charles Scribner's Sons include important correspondence from Jones.

The National Personnel Records Center in St. Louis, Missouri, and the Veterans Administration office in St. Petersburg, Florida, provided complete copies of the records covering Jones's military service and hospitalization. The New York Office of the Chief of Public Affairs of the United States Army under Colonel Leo McMahon and Colonel John C. Grant also gave substantial help. I am also particularly grateful to Arthur S. Macedo, formerly a member of Jones's own 27th Regiment, the "Wolfhounds," who, throughout the time in which I was writing this book, supplied me with an extraordinary amount of useful information about military customs and about the history and movements of the 27th Regiment in Hawaii and, later, in the South Pacific.

In addition, I am indebted to Hilary Cummings and to the University of Oregon Library for its collection of the papers of Robert Cantwell, which includes correspondence and material relating to Jones, and to Sally and Richard Jones, James Jones's sister-in-law and nephew, who sent me copies of Jones's correspondence with his brother, Jeff, as well as early manuscript stories. I am also obliged to Shelby Foote for copies of his correspondence with Jones.

Though most of the written material by and about Jones is now in public institutions, an equally important source of information exists in the memory of his family and friends. First among these are Gloria, Jamie, and Kaylie Jones, who from the first gave me every possible assistance in this project, answering questions and introducing me to others who might be of help. Kaylie Jones also accompanied me when I visited Robinson, Illinois, to interview Jones's childhood friends. Although this biography is in no way authorized, it is no exaggeration to say that without the warm support and encouragement of the family, this book would not exist.

I have also interviewed well over a hundred other people who knew Jones during the course of his life. These include fellow writers and fellow soldiers, as well as casual neighbors and friends. From each, I have learned something, and from some I have learned a great deal. In the notes for the appropriate chapter I have listed the names of everyone I spoke to, but here I would like to list in a group the large number whose help I especially value and to acknowledge publicly my debt to them. They are Neil Abercrombie, Charles and Tee Addams, Ellen Adler, Ruth Aley, Harry Antrim, Judith Atwell, the late Alice Baber, Lauren Bacall, Rosemary Bahr, James Baldwin, Cecile Gray and Irwin Bazelon, Saul Bellow, Thomas Berger, Alain Bernheim, Gladys Berry, Simon Michael Bessie, Arnold Black, Vance Bourjaily, John Bowers, Eugène Braun-Munk, Cabell Bruce, Jamie Bruce, Beryl Buchholz, Charles Burke, Hortense Calisher, Sue Camacho, Everest Capra, Sydney Chaplin, the late Bernard Childs, Ross Claiborne, John Cloninger, Betty Comden, Sylvinie and Judith Continho, Terry Crawford, William Curran, Faith Dane, Ruda Dauphin, Ethel de Croisset, Dr. William Diefenbach, Elaine Dundy, Jack Egle, Walter Eytan, Judy Feiffer, Eileen Finletter, Jack Flam, Annis Skaggs Fleming, Elizabeth Fondaras, Shelby Foote, Bernard Frizell, Martin Gabel, David Gelsanliter, Paul Gitlin, Robert Gluckman, Jan Goenvic, Herman Gollob, Herbert Gold, Monique Gonthier, Arthur Goodfriend, Adolph Green and Phyllis Newman, Winston Groom, Georges Grüber, Thomas Guinzburg, Leslie Hannon, the Countess of Hardwicke, Jones Harris, Genta Hawkins, Major General Michael Healy, Joseph Heller, Addie Herder, Dr. Michael Herman, Henry Hyde, Paul Jarrico, Paul Jenkins, Elaine Kaufman, John Keasler, Percy Knauth, Robert Knittle, John Knowles, Micky Knox, Laura Schwartz Korn, Scoops Kreger, Seymour Krim, Hope Laresche, Irving Lazar, Allen Lewis, Katherine MacGregor, Norman Mailer, Robert Markel, John P. Marquand, Jr., Frank Marshall, Andrew Marton, Robert and Bobby Massie, Peter Matthiessen, Edgar May, Mary McCarthy, John McKuin, Michael Mewshaw, Helen Meyer, Hugh Milanese, Vincente Minnelli, Helen Mitchell, Edwin Morgan, Willie Morris, Muriel Murphy, Vera Newlin, Bodil Nielsen, Robert Parrish, Joan Patterson, David Pearce, Arthur Pearlroth, Henry Pillsbury, George Plimpton, Angelo Quattrocchi, Peter Rand, David Ray, Elmore Richmond, Norman Rosten, Harold Roth, Herbert Ruhm, Françoise Sagan, Tessa Sale, Budd and Betsy Schulberg, Charles Scribner, Jr., Katherine Shannon, Arthur Shay, the late Irwin Shaw, Wilfrid Sheed, Steve Sheppard, Sargent Shriver, Kate Mosolino Soterity, David Spicehandler, Elaine Steinbeck, Daniel Stern, Carl Stroven, Rose and William Styron, Daniel Taradash, Dr. Eugene Teich, John Thompson, Edward Trzcinski, Andy Turner, Earl and Belva Turner, Kathleen Tynan, Hélène Veret, Gore Vidal, Peter Viertel, Kurt Vonnegut, Jack

Warden, Kathryn Weissberger, Arthur Weithas, General Frederick Weyand, A. B. C. Whipple, Samuel White, William Wilson, Benjamin and Irma Wolstein, Clement and Jessie Wood, Robert Wool, Fred Zinnemann.

I also want to thank a number of people who helped me in various ways during the making of this book: Frances Apt, Patricia Blake, Allen Boyer, Carl Brandt, Jordan Brener, Ann Cornett, Nancy Crampton, Betty Friedan, Helen Handley, Jill Krementz, Mike Lennon, Roy Livengood, Paul Pinkosh, Linn Sage, Rogers Scudder, Liz Smith, William Jay Smith, John Unterecker, and Gregory Williams. I am also indebted to Sophie Consagra and the American Academy in Rome, where I was writer-in-residence during the early stages of this book, and to Ambassador Carlo de Ferrariis Salzano and to Fabrizia Pratesi and Valeria Beltrani, who together provided a marvelous setting in which the book could be written.

From the beginning, my editor, Nan Talese, has been painstaking and encouraging. Combining enthusiasm with her professional skills, she has been a great support. I also appreciate my son Nicholas' patience and good humor during the time this book was being written.

New York and Porto Santo Stefano
August 1, 1984

ONE

1

❧

ROBINSON

EVEN BEFORE he finished his most famous novel, *From Here to Eternity*, James Jones was aware of his mission and potential as a writer. After reading a history of his publishing house, Charles Scribner's Sons, sent him by his editor, Maxwell Perkins, he replied that it was hard for him to realize that he was also "one of the Olympians" mentioned by the author. Yet Jones was also nervous and apprehensive, claiming that he was in a state of perpetual anxiety, "which I know I shall never be free of as long as I keep on trying to write."

Vacillations of mood are common among artists, but with Jones they were on a grander scale than with most. Coming out of nowhere with his first novel, he became famous overnight as thousands upon thousands of copies of *From Here to Eternity* were bought and the book was translated and published all over the world. The almost mythic quality of his rise from obscurity was confirmed in the making of an exceptionally successful movie based on the book and by the critical praise that was ratified when in 1952 he received the National Book Award for fiction. He had appeared like a comet from the heart of America, and he wrote with a directness and truthfulness that recalled such distinctly American writers as Walt Whitman and Mark Twain.

No one before had quite expressed Jones's vision of America, as a country of people torn between optimism and cynicism. Their heritage led them to want to fulfill their hopes, but often they dropped out in disappointment or failure. Jones felt the naked and desperate energy this fundamental schism created in American life, and he was therefore able to evoke a response in his readers that few of his contemporaries could match.

Jones enjoyed his success and celebrity; he lived a public life and was extraordinarily candid in his opinions. He was short and muscular, with a protruding jaw that made him look aggressive, but in fact he was a gentle man. Although his language and manners were often crude, he was kind and intelligent. His success led him to change the kind of life he led, and the country boy from Illinois was gradually transformed into a man of the world. At ease at dinner parties in New York and Paris, still he never lost his intrinsic unpretentiousness.

Like most artists, Jones was subject to contradictory impulses, and the tensions created were in large part responsible for the quality of his art. A man with the most ordinary of names, he was interested in the most ordinary of people — soldiers, small-town shopkeepers, teen-age children. The intimacy of the provincial world in which he grew up made him see how intensely emotional human relations really are. In the small towns of his youth, no theaters, museums, or concert halls existed to distract the human heart.

Jones's literary legacy derives from his sensitivity to his early experiences, but he was not an untutored reporter. His whole life was an education in books, and in the work of such writers as Teilhard de Chardin, Stendhal, Conrad, and Yeats he searched for an understanding of life. His reading nurtured his philosophical nature, and without cant or illusion he confronted the nature of love, sex, and mortality. He sought answers even while realizing that none existed. As an artist, he considered that his job was to record the quest with intelligence and with an understanding of those who failed or lived without hope.

Although he died young, at fifty-five, Jones left a large enough body of work to ensure that he would be remembered. The vitality of his writing, especially in *From Here to Eternity, The Thin Red Line,* and *Whistle,* reflects his awareness that in warfare, the insane relationship between tenderness and brutality that affects life everywhere is most vividly revealed.

Robinson, Illinois, stands near the Wabash River on the eastern edge of the state. Approached from Terre Haute on the flat plain of Indiana, the land gradually begins to undulate; gentle hills and wooded groves rise along the river's edge and separate the wide fields where soy beans, corn, and wheat are grown.

The land was first occupied by the prehistoric Indian mound builders, a few of whose remnants can still be found. They were followed

by Shawnee and Delaware Indians driven west by European coloniz-
ers from the eastern part of the continent. The first foreigners to
set foot on what was to become Illinois were French explorers, led
by Marquette and La Salle, who were in search of an outlet to the
sea from their holdings in Canada. Most of them continued their
westward explorations until they discovered the Mississippi and
built a fort at St. Louis, but a small group stayed behind and settled in
a town they called Vincennes, on the Oubache (or Wabash) River,
thirty miles southeast of present-day Robinson. In 1763, at the conclusion of the Seven Years' War, France ceded many of her North
American possessions to the English, and the French settlers withdrew. The English victors, however, were not interested in coloniza-
tion. Later, during the American Revolution, when Fort Kaskasskia
on the Mississippi River was captured by militia from Virginia, the
land became American. But it was so distant and unreal that all of Illinois was considered a mere county of Virginia, as though it were a
colony.

By 1816, when most of the Indian population had been forced to
move farther west, the land began to attract white settlers. New
counties were laid out in what was then known as the Northwest Territory. Two years later, the state of Illinois was created, and Crawford
County, where Robinson is located, started to absorb some of the numerous settlers who came across the plains from Virginia and other
Southern states in search of better land and homesteads. Named after
a prominent local lawyer, Robinson became the judicial center of the
county in 1843, with a courthouse and log jail. Plots of land were sold
off and a simple market town gradually evolved. The newcomers
were of English, Welsh, Scottish, and German stock, and most of
them were Methodists or Baptists. Schools and churches were soon
built, and by 1857, with fifteen hundred people, Robinson had its first
newspaper. Illinois was split by controversy over slavery and the
Civil War, but both Grant and Lincoln were native sons, and it contributed heavily to the Northern victory.

The coming of the railroads increased the size of Robinson, but
what transformed it was the discovery, in 1907, of oil. The population
grew to seven thousand as the Ohio Oil Company built a refinery and
began to exploit the natural resources under the rich land of the countryside. Soon Robinson became a far wealthier town than its size and
isolation might have seemed to justify. A number of white-pillared
mansions in the style of the Old South were built along Main Street,

and other large houses and estates were laid out along leafy avenues in the neighborhood. These belonged to the managers of the refinery and to the professionals who served its interests, and gradually Robinson became dependent on the Ohio Oil Company.

Because it was the administrative center of the county, Robinson had a courthouse built in the main square of the town. A large brick structure with curved Romanesque arches and pointed Gothic dormer windows, the courthouse was originally topped by a lofty clock tower but when the tower was dismantled, the building appeared squat and ill proportioned, like the hulk of a ship without a mast.

The courthouse square is the hub of Robinson, as it is in so many American towns, with Main Street running across its northern side and Walnut along its southern. Around the square were located, in James Jones's youth, the law offices that served the court, the Woodworth Hotel, the Crawford County Bank, the Second National Bank, the Hollywood Department Store, the Palace Clothes Store, and the Sugar Bowl Restaurant, as well as a barber shop, a jewelry store, a saloon, and the offices of the *Robinson Daily News.* Today, some of the names have been changed and some of the original buildings have been replaced, but the newsstand where Jones worked as a delivery boy is the same as it was in the thirties.

Jones was born at 202 East Walnut Street, in a house just behind the large Southern-style mansion his grandfather occupied on Main Street. In his later years, Jones liked to boast that he was "always an aristocrat — on three sides," and the claim of early American roots is justified by family records. On his mother's side, his ancestry went back to a certain Thomas Fuller from the County of Norfolk in England, who came to America in 1620. By the ninth generation, the Fullers had moved to Guilderland, New York, a small town west of Albany. One of the daughters married into the Blessing family, which had originally come to Pennsylvania in 1767. Over the years, the Blessings became prominent in the state government as assemblymen or as members of the New York militia.

William Henry Blessing, the first child of the Blessing-Fuller alliance, married Elsie White; her lineage went back to Thomas White, who was born in England in 1599 and settled in Weymouth, Massachusetts, in 1636. Blessing moved with his bride to Vinton, Iowa, by train and covered wagon, and there he established a contracting and building business and became a leader of the Presbyterian church. Their fourth child, Ada, eventually became James Jones's mother.

The Jones family were farmers in the country west of Robinson along the Embarras River. They appear to have arrived from Virginia by way of Ohio, settling as early as 1815, when the country was still a wilderness. Their village, Honey Creek, had not yet even been given a name. The Joneses traced their line back to Wales, whence they had emigrated before the Revolution. Many in the family were doctors or lawyers, but Jones's great-grandfather was a farmer who took an Indian wife. His son, George W. Jones, was born in 1858 and was brought up in Robinson. He served as sheriff of Crawford County from 1886 to 1890, before entering the firm of Jones and Newlin as an apprentice lawyer. He was admitted to the bar two years later. By this time, he had married Euphemia Bales, daughter of another county sheriff, whose family were originally from Indiana. Jones had four sons by her, and in 1920 bought his mansion on Main Street.

George W. Jones was a Methodist and an active member of the Democratic Party. He was also an opinionated teetotaler. He had coal-black hair and always walked to and from his office. A man of exceptional energy, he was also a writer and in 1922 had a book privately printed called *The Trials of Christ: Were They Legal?* which endeavored to prove that the Romans broke their own laws in submitting Jesus to legal inquiry.

A gloomy and temperamental man, George Jones was given to fits of violence. One day at the dinner table, he took such a dislike to a cake that had just been served that he flung it at the ceiling of the dining room. There the icing stuck until it began to melt and drip onto the table, where the children sat in awed silence. Despite such outbursts, George Jones took great pride in his family line and insisted that his sons live up to it. He had built up the family fortune and intended his four sons to be worthy of their inheritance. He wanted them to be professionals — two doctors and two lawyers — and he sent them off to Northwestern University for this purpose, forcing them to follow the careers he had chosen for them. Paul and Charles were to be lawyers; Hanby and Ramon, doctors. Ramon, who was to become James Jones's father, obtained his father's permission to study dentistry instead, because, as his son recalled, "he wanted to get out of school quicker so he could get married quicker." He did not want to be a dentist, but he submitted to his father's wish that he become a professional. The fourth son, Hanby, committed suicide while at the university.

Ramon Jones, later known as "Doctor Ray," was a big man and at

Northwestern was captain of the football team. His popularity led a classmate to offer him a job in Australia, but he was so dominated by his father that he declined. All of the brothers resented their father's power over them, and their mother's early death left them unprotected. George Jones was married a second time, in 1895, to Christine Kern. She was kind and gentle, a seamstress and dressmaker, but there was little she could do to moderate the atmosphere. Ramon tried to escape his fate by writing poems, but he lacked the strength to combat his father's tyranny. Soon he took the easier road to alcoholism, as his elder brothers had done before him. The town's social organization, with men's clubs and saloons, made this an easy compromise, but it was an evasive solution and soon introduced new problems.

On July 15, 1908, Ramon Jones married Ada Blessing, who, according to her son James, was "considered a great beauty locally. She would have preferred to remain a great beauty." The young couple were deeply in love, but the unresolved relationship between Ramon and his father undermined the stability they needed for a successful marriage. To escape his influence, they settled first in Flatrock, a tiny community south of Robinson, and there Ramon opened his dental practice. Two years later, their first son, George W. Jones, known as Jeff, was born.

Living in Flatrock soon exacted too heavy a price for their freedom, so they returned to Robinson. The move suited Ada, who had come to put great value on social life and status. Soon she was deeply involved in the Minerva Club, whose members consisted of the thirty socially most prominent women in Robinson. One of many such women's clubs around the country, it combined good works with social activities. The members held regular meetings at one another's houses, where they drank tea and discussed such subjects as home life, public affairs, the arts, beautification, hospitality, and uplift.

Ramon and Ada lived in a middle-class neighborhood of small freestanding houses built in a row. On an adjoining lot but facing Main Street stood the Colonial mansion inhabited by Ramon's father. The house of the younger Joneses was far more modest, with a small porch overlooking the sidewalk, a living room and dining room on the ground floor, and bedrooms upstairs. The family rarely used the formal rooms, for Ada had remodeled the kitchen, and that is where they usually ate and lived.

Ada's devotion to the Minerva Club seems to have been increased by the disappointment and ill health she endured after the loss of her second child, a stillborn girl. During her pregnancy, she had become very fat and soon learned that she had diabetes. She complained bitterly about her illness and loss of looks.

For twelve years after the stillbirth, Ada Jones had no other children, and it seemed unlikely that she ever would. Her diabetes and excessive weight were pronounced incurable by local doctors, and she felt deeply frustrated by her life. Then she met a Christian Science reader who lived in the neighborhood and fell under his influence. Not long afterward, she was pregnant again; and when the doctor recommended an abortion, Ada turned to her new religion for support. One night she woke to find the bedroom filled with a strange light. She woke her husband, who also saw it. They took it as a sign of God's will, and on November 6, 1921, in her own bed at home, Ada Jones gave birth to her second son, James Ramon Jones. Four years later, in 1925, a daughter, Mary Ann, was born.

The arrival of these children should have brought joy to the household, but by the time they appeared, Ramon and Ada were in their mid-thirties, and their ways were settled. Amiable and sociable, especially after a few drinks, Ramon regaled his children with stories, and the Jones household had some life as the neighborhood center for a jazz band that Jeff had organized. But the gulf between the parents had grown wide, and Ada began to resent the time she had to devote to her children's upbringing. Putting great stock in her lineage, which she considered more distinguished than her husband's, she chafed against her enforced domesticity. The proximity of her father-in-law, who lived in comparative opulence and grandeur, further irritated her, as did his habit of giving instructions for the rearing of his grandchildren. Inevitably, Ramon and Ada quarreled. She criticized his drinking and he, frustrated professionally because Robinson was too small to allow him to concentrate on his specialty, dental surgery, grew increasingly irritated by his wife's nagging and religiosity. James Jones later recalled that the atmosphere of the house was one of "hot emotions and broiling recriminations covered with a thin but resilient skin of gentility." The turmoil made him very much alone, and he learned that to survive, he would have to look out for himself.

He was a pretty child, with gentle features, blond curls, and a warm smile, but when he was about six, he became somewhat gawky, with a head too large for his spindly body. His ears suddenly seemed out of proportion, and his father said he looked like a car coming down the street with both doors open. One eye was weaker than the other, so his father had him fitted with glasses. Unlike his elder brother and his father, who were both large and athletic, Jones was frail, even delicate in appearance, with small hands. He was fond of his father, but soon learned to be wary of his mother, who was often violent and turned her frustrations against her son. Once, in the presence of a neighbor, she struck him hard on the face for something he had done. She even beat him with a broomstick. Like most small boys, he was active and often underfoot, which irritated his mother. When she had to cook or iron in the kitchen, she would take him out into the back yard, where she kept a chain to which he was attached so that she could go on with her work without fear of his running away. This treatment naturally frightened and puzzled him. In time, he learned that his mother had wanted a daughter as a second child and was disappointed in him. With Mary Ann's birth, he was relegated to the neglect suffered by many middle children whose parents favor either the eldest or the youngest.

As he grew up, Jones spent more and more time away from home, visiting the neighborhood children. He often played with Jim Lindsay, who lived on the same street and whose mother treated him kindly. Many of Jones's childhood games were played in a declivity that filled the space between his own house and that of Jimmy Buchanan, who lived next door. It was called the Hole and was a natural place for all sort of games, from snowball fights in the winter to the building of sand castles in the summer. Jones and the other neighborhood children also dressed up as soldiers, donning the helmets and duty belts their fathers had brought back as souvenirs from World War I. They would go out to the Hole and dig trenches and play war games.

Doctor Ray wanted his son to be tough enough to take care of himself, so he gave him boxing lessons. He pulled no punches in training the young boy and often knocked him down. Jones quickly found that the best defense was to be aggressive, and he began to abandon his natural gentleness for a more offensive attitude. He was helped by a certain innate courage that allowed him to cope with unexpected challenges. At thirteen, he was taken on a school visit to a slaughterhouse in the nearby town of Paris, Illinois. "We saw them kill the hogs and cut them up," he wrote to his favorite aunt, Mollie Haish, his mother's sister. "We watched them make wieners. Somebody bet me I couldn't eat a wiener while I watched them make them, well I did."

Often, however, Jones chose the easier route when faced with unpleasantness. He would climb up to the attic room that had been turned over to him after his brother grew up. There in solitude he built an imaginary world of his own, playing for hours on end with his toy soldiers and knights in armor. An even more beguiling escape route was reading. Because his father wrote poetry, the house was full of books. Jones took to them naturally and was soon an avid reader. When a guest came to the house, the young boy would demand to be read to, and if the guest skipped a passage, he would know it and correct him.

Later, when he was a student at the Lincoln Grade School, he visited the Carnegie Library, which was only two buildings away from his house. The librarian, Vera Newlin, introduced him to other books. Among his early favorites were P. C. Wren's *Beau Geste, Beau Sabreur,* and *Beau Ideal.* He read each one "at least twenty times; and I knew all of their characters, and each character's big scenes." Jones soon outgrew the children's section in the basement of the library, where he read stories and novels by Kipling, Stevenson, Scott, and Dickens, and he pestered Vera Newlin to allow him to browse through the adult books upstairs. There he found books by Galsworthy, Maugham, Conrad, and Maupassant, which he took home to his attic room. Years later, Jones paid tribute to the Carnegie Library by saying that "it had a great deal more to do with my becoming a writer than I had any concept of at the time I was reading there." Meanwhile, his reading had immediate benefits, for at Sunday school, which he was forced to attend, it was obvious that he was one of the few children who knew the Bible stories.

The Depression, which began in 1929 with the collapse of the stock market, was to have a disastrous effect on the Jones family, as it had on most Americans. George Jones had died in the summer, leaving his considerable holdings in the Samuel Insull utilities companies of Chicago to his wife and children. At first they were protected, but when the Insull empire suddenly foundered, the Joneses lost everything and overnight were robbed of their status as one of the most prominent families in Robinson. The big house on Main Street was sold, and heavy mortgages were taken on others owned by family members.

Because of his dental practice, for a while Ramon Jones was not as hard hit as others, but his income began to dwindle as people stopped going to the dentist. "Without dough you couldn't have a tooth pulled," John Dos Passos later recalled. Before long, Dr. Jones was forced to sell the house on Walnut Street and rent another nearby on King Street. But the family income continued to decline, and the Joneses were forced to move again, even farther from the center of Robinson. They finally took a small brick house on Ash Street near a playground that was literally across the tracks of the Illinois Central Railroad.

These moves were traumatic for everyone in the family and exacerbated the tensions that already existed. The shame of not having money often hit middle-class people harder than the poor, who were used to it. It was as though they had done something indecent, and few could admit what had happened. Ada Jones found it especially difficult to cope with the financial crisis. Accustomed to a relatively idle life, with servants to look after the cleaning and the children, she fell into a depressed state, punctuated by outbursts against her alcoholic husband. She remained religious, even though her faith gave her little support, and in general seemed paralyzed by events. James Jones later remembered her as "flipping pages of a magazine with a placid bored air" while his father tried to talk seriously to her. He described her as a person who "drinks coffee and smokes and just sits around and is a mother." If asked what she was thinking, she would reply, "Nothing."

Like many other middle-class women, Ada Jones lacked the resources to deal with economic and social changes over which she had no control. Increasingly, she blamed others for the misfortunes that had overwhelmed her. Her passivity may have helped Jones learn the lesson of self-sufficiency, for after her death he remembered her as one who was "totally selfish, totally self-centered, and totally whining and full of self-pity." He was eager to remove himself from her, perhaps fearful of habits that could be inherited. "She was also basically stupid in the very lowest human sense of the word," he wrote. "Whether she had any intelligence to begin with and later lost it or let it atrophy, I don't know. But she certainly showed no intelligence or sensitivity or sympathy toward Mary Ann and me, not from the first moment I can remember her." In later years, Jones went out of his way to make sure he did not emulate her in any way and occasionally blamed her for shortcomings in his own life. Undoubtedly she affected his attitude toward women, making him cautious and mistrustful.

Ada Jones was also a conniving woman; once she even asked her son to spy on his father, because she believed he was having an affair with another woman. Jones later told friends that his mother was not afraid of manipulating him in other ways. One day, discovering that he was masturbating, she told him that if he continued to do so, his hand would turn black. For a while he stopped, but as the fear of his hand turning black receded, he started again. After discovering him in the act one night, his mother waited until he fell asleep and then went into his room and rubbed black shoe polish into the palm of his hand.

Jones still cared for his father, however, for Ramon Jones read books and continued to try to write poetry. He was also proud and grateful for the support his father gave him. Jones once pushed another boy through the large plate glass window of a store and, afraid of the consequences, ran directly to a nearby bowling alley, where he knew he could find his father. He told him what had happened, and, even though "he was half tight, he got right up and went back across the street with me and took the whole thing on his shoulders and got it straightened out. I'll never forget that. It's a fine thing for a boy to have someone who is rather like a rock to his small intellect, someone who will always be there when needed." But gradually the strain of a failed marriage, a disappointing professional life, and loss of money became too much for the father to bear. He spent more and more time in bars and saloons and was no longer a man who could be depended on.

The collapse of his family deeply affected Jones, and though only ten, he became secretive and angry. He learned, he said, "never to tell anyone the truth about any of the things that were important to me." More and more, he wanted to escape: "I would sneak off and take refuge in my secret ambition to run away and join the Foreign Legion as an adventurer." Once, in fact, he set out for Chicago and walked two miles out of Robinson before he was discovered and brought back. On another occasion, while the family were living in the house by the playground, he was playing outside when a group of neighborhood children started to walk down the driveway, which they had been using as a short cut to the park. Jones was suddenly infuriated by their incursion on his property and shouted at them to go away. Afterward, he felt terrible remorse, realizing how petty he had been in his defense of family integrity. He saw that he had fallen into the same trap of smallness that had led others to ostracize his family because they had lost their money.

In September of 1935, James Jones entered Robinson Township High School. It should have been an event of some importance in his life, but it was overshadowed by financial and family difficulties. In order to help bring money into the family, he took a job at Si Seligman's news agency in the courthouse square. He was required to appear there at five o'clock in the morning with his bicycle, and after sorting the out-of-town newspapers from Terre Haute, Chicago, and Indianapolis, he would begin his delivery route. He also had to collect payment for the subscriptions, and he never missed a day, even in the coldest winter weather.

Seligman was a boxing enthusiast who trained boys in the back of his shop. Since Jones had already learned some boxing from his father and from his Uncle Charlie, who had bought back the family house on Main Street, Jones began to take part in these sessions. He was light but agile, and Seligman encouraged him to enter the Golden Gloves boxing tournament in Terre Haute. The first time he took part in this competition, where he was known as "Jeeper," he won by a decision in three rounds. On the second night he lost, even though he was better than his opponent. When Seligman asked him what went wrong, Jones simply replied, "I didn't feel like fighting." On another trip to Terre Haute, he reached the semifinals, but the sight of blood upset him. He disliked hurting people he knew.

Boxing wasn't officially recognized at Robinson High School, so Jones tried out for other sports. But he wasn't a naturally gifted athlete like his brother. He was too light for football, and because of his glasses, which made him insecure, he thought that the basketball players considered him unreliable. "I never made the squad," he told his brother. "Nobody would pass me the ball, sort of, in anything."

Failing in organized sports, Jones turned more and more to fighting, as distinct from boxing, though he professed to dislike it at first. Years later, he explained to Maxwell Perkins that he "was forced to fight for my pride from the time I first entered school." His small size made him an easy target for the jibes of his classmates, who knew of his family's social decline and his father's drunkenness. Unable to control the destructive influences of alcoholism and self-pity at home, Jones took out his frustration and anger in physical violence. He soon became notorious for striking out at anyone who crossed him. Not chosen to play on a school team, he would pick a fight with someone from the visiting school instead. "My teeth would be chattering, and my knees would be knocking, but rather than have people think I was a coward, I'd talk back."

Jones's rebelliousness also marred his academic performance. One of the brightest students in his class, he was bored by much of the curriculum and would frequently fall asleep in class. This behavior enraged the teachers, who would send him out into the hall as punishment. Inevitably, his marks were erratic. In his first year, his grades in English were A— and B; in algebra, C and C—; in Latin, B and D; in general science, B and C; in physical training, B and C. The falling-off noticeable in the second term was probably caused by his reaction to the teaching methods of the time. Normally, the instructor would deliver a lecture and the students would take notes. Little discussion was allowed. Jones complained that his weak eyes made it difficult for him to see the blackboard, but he was no more attentive when he was moved to a better seat. Although his parents were sent little blue slips calling attention to his shortcomings, his classmates recognized that he was far ahead of the other students.

Only in two courses did he come to life — the literature classes of his first and third years. Jones's freshman teacher, a young girl of twenty-four, had in fact been taken in as a boarder by his mother. "I of course was in love with her," Jones later recalled. "She liked me, and loyally set about to make a reader of me, only to find that with the exceptions of Shakespeare and Joyce I had very nearly read as much as she had (including Hemingway and Fitzgerald) without knowing any of these people were 'writers,' simply because my father had the books around. I would hang around the upstairs hall trying to catch a flash of thigh or panties or breast. She was very nice about this though I am sure it embarrassed her."

The teacher of English 3A, the junior year course, was Harriet Hodges, whose specialty was normally physical education. Unlike most of her colleagues, she encouraged discussion of literature by the students. Jones responded eagerly and became one of the leaders of the class, often reading a passage enthusiastically and without reticence, or beginning a discussion in which the others would join. Jones later remembered Harriet Hodges for her imaginative approach to what was considered suitable subject matter for class compositions. "I was at a peculiar stage of my life where I was getting a great charge and a great emotional release out of writing openly fictional themes (always derivative of some book I'd just read, naturally) for her English class. Attacked in class by what I now realize were several jealous straight-A plodders, I was defended by this lady who told me to keep right on and added that all writing was not necessarily the cataloguing of summer vacations."

Jones's social life was affected by the small-town quality of Robinson and by the prevailing uniformity of the population. Each neighborhood had its own primary school, but all of the young people went to the town's single high school. Walking or cycling along tree-lined streets, they would arrive at a red brick building that looked like a fort, with only a few trees to soften its appearance. Since there was little class distinction in the town among the young, the high school did not alter their social life. There was not much to do in any event. The high school football and basketball games were the principal social activities, augmented by the three movie houses, the Strand, the Grand, and the Lincoln, where one could attend a matinée for five cents. In a town so lacking in cultural diversion, without a theater or any live music except what was provided by the high school band, the young entertained one another at home. They held "pound parties," at which each guest was expected to bring a pound of salad or rolls or cookies.

The landscape itself was discouraging. In eastern Illinois, the towns were about twenty miles apart, and a trip from one to another offered little variety. Going to Chicago was a major undertaking, and even the closest city, Terre Haute, was forty miles away. Moreover, with its flatness, the countryside had a monotony that was exaggerated by its lack of color. It was green only in the summer; for the rest of the year it was either dusty or muddy, with a prevailing dun color. Jones later spoke of the evanescent light of Illinois, which brought vivid color only at dawn or at sunset and where the "summer-deep greens" of the countryside were a poignant reminder that "summer itself will not stay. School *must* begin again."

After the Saturday night movie, the young people could go to one of three places in town for a Coke and sandwich or for some chile. One of these was the Blue Castle, where there was a juke box for dancing. Two other spots to "hang out" were the Top Hat and Zook's Nook. Partly for financial reasons and partly because of his shyness, Jones rarely took a date to any of these places. The few times he did take a girl, he chose Mary Littlejohn or Evelyn Schaefer, because he "considered them more neighborhood friends than girl friends" and therefore unlikely to make it seem that he was getting involved. Exceptionally sensitive to social nuance, Jones later wrote that it was "all right for a guy to have a girl friend but if he ever seemed really hung up on her, he was looked at peculiarly." Quite the opposite was true of the girls, who thought that even straight A's were less important than having "a steady boy friend they could parade around."

Jones pretended not to care that he stood apart, mainly because he felt rejected by his contemporaries. "I like Robinson," said Vera Newlin, the librarian who helped him, "because when I walk down the street I like to see people I know. I smile when they smile." But from the time he was a small boy, Jones had little benign feeling for his fellows. Known for his energy and his scowling face, he would ride about on his tricycle with his jaw aggressively thrust out; later, he would walk along the street alone, with his shoulders hunched over.

In high school, Jones was unpopular with his classmates; he believed it was because he was always compared unfavorably with his brother. "Being class pres., Most Popular Boy, etc., you were an upstanding school citizen and a social success," he wrote Jeff in later years. "I, being considered class prick, most disliked boy in school, etc. have an entirely different view." Jones claimed that Jeff was remembered as "the guy that helped other kids out of jams. I was the guy that got in 'em." But he pretended he didn't mind. "The difference between you and me is that you like to have people like you. I don't give a fuck."

When he went to the Top Hat or the Blue Castle, almost always alone, he would make a nuisance of himself. He would pour salt into the sugar containers and throw firecrackers into the stove. These attempts to call attention to himself increased his unpopularity, and he would be asked to leave. He was considered a menace, a Peck's Bad Boy, certainly not a suitable boy friend for any of the girls in the town. His reputation as a roughneck led him into the company of the tough boys in Robinson, outcasts who hung about the pool room and who vented their feelings mainly through pranks and violence.

Eventually Jones began to feel at home in the raffish company that accepted him and to take a certain perverse pleasure in scrapping. Then one day, while fighting another boy, he found himself banging his opponent's head on the concrete pavement. Suddenly he realized what he was doing. Horrified by the ease with which he had slipped into violence, making him capable of nearly killing another person, he pulled back, stood up, and walked away.

Annis Skaggs, a classmate, was one of the few who recognized Jones's true nature, his underlying shyness and loneliness. She understood the claustrophobia caused by small towns, with their lack of privacy and fear of individualism. She knew that Jones, a reader, was curious about the world beyond the borders of Robinson and was full of romantic impulses and fresh ideas, which, as Vera Newlin also knew, "were always dangerous in a small town."

Jones responded to Annis' understanding and sympathy by trying to befriend her. After a party, he asked if he might walk her home. Annis replied that she had brothers to do that for her, and Jones took her reply as a rejection. Later, he tried to express his feelings for her less directly. On Valentine's Day, he bought a large box of chocolates and left it on her desk in the schoolroom. But the gift misfired, and all the children laughed at him and teased him. Years later, he wrote about the incident in a story called "The Valentine," which ends with the little boy standing in the corridor outside the classroom, knowing that he has made a fool of himself in trying to express his love. At the thought of going back inside to face renewed laughter, "sickness ran all through him, all over him, in long waves." He stands in the hall, waiting for the bell to ring, "clenching and unclenching his fists."

During his last year in high school, the excitement generated by Harriet Hodge in his junior year was quickly dissipated. He substituted public speaking for English and instead of difficult subjects like mathematics and foreign languages, he took geography and sociology. Even so, he earned only C's and D's. He later observed that learning to type was "probably the only thing of value that I garnered out of my high school career."

Jones also stopped participating in school activities. Whereas he had tried out for football and basketball in his early years, and had joined the Latin Club, the Mixed Chorus, and the operetta, and even been class secretary as a freshman, by the time he was a senior, his only contribution to school life was playing trombone in the band. In the June 1939 graduation issue of the school publication, "Notes 'n' Everything," Jones's photograph appeared above the legend "Jim is quite a scrapper. In his classes, he's a napper." The Class Prophecy read: "Well, well, Jim Jones got up here too! It says that he managed to stay out of mischief and live happily by suffering from sleeping sickness for 20 years." For his Last Will and Testament, the editors noted, Jones had left his sleeping sickness to another student.

The most dramatic event of Jones's school career took place on his graduation day. Before the ceremonies, he was helping fix some wires in the skylight of the auditorium when he slipped and fell through the glass, landing on the folding chairs, thirty feet below. He was badly injured, although he suffered no broken bones. Patched up and given a crutch so that he could graduate with his classmates, he sat with the school band and pretended to play, even though his swollen lip prevented him from doing so.

Jones's prospects for further education after high school were dim. The deepening Depression of the 1930s had brought intense hardship to many of his countrymen. By the middle of 1938, five million people had lost their jobs and fourteen percent of the population was on relief. A college education was not only expensive but to many seemed useless, since all over the country university graduates were unemployed. The American dream of college, marriage, and children was vanishing in the face of economic reality.

In the Jones household, money was tighter than ever, and sometimes when he was sent to the saloon to fetch his father, Jones would pour ketchup into a glass of water to make himself a kind of tomato soup, because there was nothing to eat at home. As for the social prestige of his family, Jones had by now learned that it was "very ephemeral" and not to be relied on in times of difficulty.

Every year, the graduating seniors from schools in the district traveled to a nearby town in order to learn about college and university prospects. In 1939, the meeting was held in Casey, and Jones went along in a bus with his classmates. He knew that his grades were too low for him to be accepted anywhere he might want to go, and he was too ill prepared for any of the university scholarships that had been made available through the National Youth Project, established by Franklin Roosevelt's administration. Discouraged and even indifferent to his future, Jones didn't bother to attend the meeting but with a group of his friends went to a bar instead. There, with the bravado that comes from exclusion and rejection, he proceeded to get drunk.

During the summer after his graduation, Jones went to Findlay, Ohio, where his brother lived, and there he got a temporary job in construction. Although Jeff was employed by the Ohio Oil Company, like so many members of the Jones family, he too had literary ambitions, and the two brothers talked about the possibility of writing a novel together. During the Depression many people thought of writing for magazines as a way of escaping the tedium of unemployment.

The brothers had higher literary goals in mind, and their talk sharpened Jones's own ambition for a literary career.

Realizing that the only permanent job he probably could find was as a day laborer at twenty-five cents an hour, working in a construction gang or hauling bags of cement, Jones decided to leave Findlay and bum his way to Canada. The trip would solve nothing, but it would be a change from the Middle West, where he had few prospects. He was too young for the Civilian Conservation Corps or for other jobs offered by the Works Progress Administration, but he knew that he had to get away from Robinson, which had come to represent nothing but incessant family nagging and personal loneliness. When he returned from Canada, he therefore decided, "in the death throes of the depression," to join the army. All over America, other young men were making the same decision, hoping that after a hitch with the military, they would come back to an economy that could make use of their talents.

Accordingly, on November 10, 1939, three days after his eighteenth birthday, Jones enlisted in the Army of the United States, often called the Regular Army. There was a certain relief in making the decision, but he felt like a "damned-fool kid," standing on the observation platform of the Illinois Central train in Robinson. Along with other recruits, he had been ordered to report to Chanute Field in Rantoul, Illinois. As the train drew away from the station, he "watched Mother and Dad grow smaller with distance." It was a dramatic moment: he was on his own, and the future was uncertain. Standing there, he thought, "Maybe I'll never see them again." But something made him mistrust the emotion he felt, and he "went back into the train and sat into a Blackjack game."

2

SCHOFIELD BARRACKS, HAWAII

CHANUTE FIELD was an Army Air Corps base one hundred miles north of Robinson. Jones arrived there wearing civilian clothes and carrying a small overnight bag. On the train he had been given coupons for his meals and had passed the time playing cards with the other recruits. They were a ragged, ill-educated group of young men who had decided, as Jones was later to write in *From Here to Eternity*, that they "could live better Inside" than they could in civilian life. They weren't "ready to starve yet."

Scared and lonely, the recruits were immediately initiated into the routine of becoming members of the Army Air Corps. Later to become the United States Air Force, the air corps was then part of the army. Jones had been posted to it because he had expressed no preference for a particular branch.

Even as he signed up in Robinson, he had regretted doing so, and his first experiences at Chanute confirmed what he had felt. Along with the others, he was assigned to barracks, took the oath of allegiance, was given physical and mental examinations, was injected and inoculated, and was handed an ill-fitting uniform, a mess kit, a knapsack, and spare clothes. Each man was issued a pair of dog tags, bearing his name, religion, blood type, and serial number. Jones's number was 6915544.

As a group, these callow soldiers attended instructive movies about military customs and venereal disease. They were told how to assemble their kits, how to make their beds so that coins could bounce on the taut blankets, and were generally kept so busy that, having to respond to reveille at five-thirty in the morning, they were not sorry to be in bed by nine-thirty. After ten days, those who, like Jones, had said they wanted to serve abroad were shipped by train to New York to be transferred to the overseas replacement depot at Fort Slocum.

Originally built to defend the outer harbor of New York, Fort Slocum occupied Davids Island in Long Island Sound, just off New Rochelle. When he arrived there, on November 24, 1939, Jones had not yet been assigned to a regiment, so he spent most of his time doing kitchen police, cleaning the barracks, picking paper off the lawns, performing guard duty, and working as a dockhand for the ferries that sailed back and forth from the island's pier. From eight to ten in the morning, the men were introduced to the rudiments of infantry training. Jones reacted angrily to the way he was treated. "This place is hell," he wrote to his brother. "They herd you around like cattle; they order you around like dogs; they work you like horses; and they feed you like hogs." But he understood why the system operated as it did. "I, who am better bred than any of these moronic sergeants, am ordered around by them as if I were a robot, constrained to do their bidding. But I can see their point of view. Nine out of every ten men in this army have no more brains than a three year old. The only way they can learn the manual and the drill commands is by constant repetition. It is pounded into their skulls until it is enveloped by the subconscious mind. The tenth man cannot be excepted. He must be treated the same as the others, even if in time he becomes like them."

Jones's social life wasn't much better. "I've been quarantined up to now," he wrote, "and the only females I've seen have been at least 100 yards off, on the other side of the parade ground, with the exception of the theater. There the officers' children, who are the only girls on the island, sit in the balcony. We common herd sit in the 'pit' as the rabble did in Shakespeare's day also. We are not allowed to associate with officers' children at all."

In order to endure all these deprivations, Jones took to gambling and reported to his brother that through playing dice he had succeeded in winning nearly $25. With his money he could enjoy himself in New York City. Also, his bunkmate, a man called Hill, from Montclair, New Jersey, who was socially well placed, invited him to spend a weekend.

Earlier in his stay at Fort Slocum, Jones had an experience that scared him badly. Discovering a discharge from his penis, he went to the base hospital and admitted having had intercourse five weeks previously, before he joined the army. He was horrified by the casual way he was examined and by the crude jokes that were made about gonorrhea. "While I was being examined," he wrote Jeff, "I didn't know whether or not I had it. I was so humiliated and ashamed at the aspect of being in that ward with those guys." Fortunately, Jones did not have a venereal disease, but he told his brother that the episode would make good material for a story or a novel.

Before the month was out, Jones was formally made a private in the air corps and received orders to sail on the United States Army Transport ship *U. S. Grant* on December 18, 1939. Along with his fellow recruits, he embarked on a ferry for the Brooklyn Army Base and there boarded the transport ship, bound for Hawaii. He wired his brother that he would be in Puerto Rico by Christmas. "Talk about sardines," he added. "Whew."

On board ship, the usual army routine continued, with the men performing KP and other housekeeping duties. They scrubbed the decks and did exercises in the open air. When the ship reached the warm climate of the Caribbean, they were shown movies on the top deck at night. The ship did not go to Puerto Rico, however, but sailed directly to Panama, arriving at Colón on the day after Christmas. The men were given shore leave while the ship made its way slowly through the canal to Balboa on the Pacific coast. Jones sent his brother a postcard showing some naked girls dancing on the beach. From Balboa, the ship sailed up the west coast of Mexico and California until it reached Fort Mason, in San Francisco Bay. There the troops were transferred to barracks at Fort McDowell on Angel Island, a place that had gained notoriety as an immigration detainment camp for Chinese workers entering the United States. Since there was little to do while the ship was made ready for departure to the Pacific, the men were given generous furloughs. Jones received a five-day pass and went to Los Angeles, where he bought a new pair of glasses and visited his Aunt Mollie.

He also saw the movie *Gone With the Wind* and went to Grauman's Chinese Theater. It was a welcome change for the lonely young man, who was especially pleased by a little adventure on the bus returning to San Francisco. "I met a swell girl," he told his brother. "She lives in Visalia, a small town in central Cal. I was invited down there to spend a couple of weeks! The visit was authentic too, because her mother was traveling with her. I'll keep in touch with her and if she isn't married by the time I get back to the States, I'll look her up."

The USAT *U. S. Grant* sailed from San Francisco on January 30,

1940, and ten days later pulled up to the dock at Fort Armstrong, beside the Aloha Tower in the center of Honolulu. On the pier was an army band and dancing Hawaiian hula girls carrying floral leis for the arriving soldiers. The men were then taken by bus to nearby Hickam Field, which was known formally as the 17th Army Air Corps Base. Recently built along the seafront, it was adjacent to the extensive naval base at Pearl Harbor.

Jones soon found that the air corps, as the youngest branch of the army, suffered from a feeling of inferiority compared to the infantry, cavalry, and artillery. At the same time, because of the technical knowledge required to handle airplanes, it drew more intelligent men than the infantry did. The most attractive opportunity in the air corps was flying, which had a special glamour unequaled in the army. Jones knew in advance that his eyesight disqualified him from flying, but he was unprepared for the distinction between those who flew and those who remained on the ground. Being a member of the support crew was made to seem unmanly and trivial.

He therefore enrolled in an introductory course given by the Technical Training Command, which he hoped would lead to his becoming a specialist, the next best thing to being in the crew. As part of the course he took an aptitude and intelligence test to see what he was best suited for. The officer in charge told him that in the verbal section he had received the "highest grade that he had seen" since he had been at Hickam Field and asked Jones if he would like to go to the much-respected mechanics school. Jones replied that he was not mechanically inclined. The officer looked at him with some astonishment but made no reply.

The next day at roll call, Jones was assigned to duty as a military policeman. His job was to guard the planes at night, walking up and down the airstrip. One evening on his rounds, he discovered a lieutenant making love to a girl in the pilot's compartment. The officer was furious at being disturbed, but Jones told him the regulations, so he and the girl left. The following morning, Jones was approached by the sergeant, who looked at him "kind of funny" and suggested that henceforth he be the guardhouse typist.

Jones was told that as long as he was on guard duty, he would not be allowed to go to school, so he tried to pull strings to be transferred; he wanted to attend radio school, for which he felt qualified. Instead, he was assigned to clerical school, an appointment considered one of the most demeaning in the air corps. "I didn't join the army to be a clerk, sure as hell," he grumbled. "So they send down clearance papers and send me to clerical school. That's the army for you."

Jones's middle-class background had ill prepared him for the reality of army life. Even with the hardships he had known at home, he assumed the luxury of choice and did not understand that the scramble for preferment in the army had little to do with merit. "I was born into the upper classes (such as they were in my small town)," he wrote, "and for personal and economic reasons of my own enlisted in the lumpen proletariat of the Regular Army." He did not fit in professionally or socially. He kept to himself, and though Hickam Field was close to the center of Honolulu, with its bars and girls, he had neither the money to enjoy them nor the courage to overcome his shyness. Sometimes he would walk four miles farther from the center to Waikiki, only to find himself impatient with what he found there. Waikiki was then a section of large private houses surrounded by gardens, with only three hotels on the beach, the Royal Hawaiian, the Moana, and the Halekulani, of which the Royal Hawaiian, with its pink walls decorated with Moorish tiles, was the most elegant.

For Jones, Waikiki offered little beyond the scenery of palm trees, and he claimed to be unimpressed. "I don't think I've ever seen a more overrated place," he said. Occasionally he would try to strike up a conversation with a tourist in the hope of getting some free drinks, but he was rarely successful. Jones also explored the downtown section of Honolulu, noting its narrow and winding streets, and observing that "about two out of every three people you see are gooks." One of these "gooks," a Chinese girl he asked for a date, he described to his Aunt Mollie as having "eyes as black as jet. I know she loves me. Her eyes shine so when I kiss her. Her hair is as black as her eyes, if possible. It has a soft fragrance that makes my heart pound in my ears like a native drum."

Later, Jones admitted this girl was an invention, a sad fantasy made up to dispel his disappointment in the reality of Honolulu. He told his brother that he wanted to buy himself out of the air corps. "I don't like being broke all the time," he said. "A war would take my mind off it, because there would be excitement, but having every nite free, and no money to do anything, and going to town with a couple of bucks in my pockets, and watching the tourists at the Royal is more than I can stand."

Actually Jones spent most of his free time at the Army and Navy

YMCA, where there was a gymnasium and a swimming pool. He would go there for weightlifting, boxing, and diving practice, and afterward would cross the street to a café called the Black Cat to buy a malted milk.

The assignment to clerical school meant that Jones was transferred to Wheeler Field, a small air corps base in the center of Oahu, right next to Schofield Barracks. With him went Everest Capra, a friend he had made at Hickam Field, who called Jones "Chinny," because of his tendency to speak his mind and get into trouble. The two men were disappointed at their transfer but made the best of their lot and took courses in bookkeeping, filing, and typing. Jones became proficient enough to type fifty-four words a minute.

The move to the country actually raised Jones's spirits. He was full of energy, involved in body building, handball, mountain climbing, and exploring the neighborhood. Sometimes he and Capra would get up at four-thirty in the morning to hike into the hills that encircle the plateau on which Schofield Barracks and Wheeler Field are laid out. Trekking through the pineapple plantations and the lush tropical greenery, they would walk toward Kolekole pass, where there was a rope bridge. It was dangerous and took courage to cross over, but Jones enjoyed the challenge. He also encouraged Capra to take up boxing. The two had visited Schofield Barracks to watch the fights, which were called smokers, between company and regimental units. Jones and Capra decided to try their luck as representatives of Wheeler Field and told the coach they wanted to volunteer. Capra was the first to climb into the ring; he was immediately knocked down. Jones followed and lasted a round and a half before he landed on the canvas. The experience taught him the difference between the infantry and the air corps, and he also learned that the army gave preferment to boxers and athletes. Pay, promotion, and privileges were based on skill in sports, and physical prowess was admired.

Jones began to visit Schofield Barracks regularly, because he believed that was where the real men were. He knew he would always be safe as a clerk in the air corps, but he didn't want to be a shirker. Admittedly, the army frightened him: "Getting my guts torn out by shrapnel, feeling the bayonet slipping into my chest." But it would be worse to avoid the challenge. "If I stay behind the lines while other guys are fighting, I'll hate my own guts," he told his brother. "Besides, if I don't get up there, I'll never find out whether I'd have turned yellow or not. I'll have to find out or I'll always be thinking about it."

Also, compared with the air corps, the infantry had a tradition and vitality that were worth writing about.

Jones talked to Capra about transferring to the infantry, claiming that the air corps was full of faggots. He quoted the old saying that if you couldn't fly, all you could do was mow the lawn. During the summer of 1940, Jones went several times to Schofield Barracks to call on company commanders in hopes of finding a place in the infantry. One day he spoke to Captain Thomas Griffin of F Company in the 27th Infantry Regiment. A burly man, Griffin was also the regimental boxing coach. He told Jones that his company was over-strength but urged him to apply again in September. Jones left the barracks believing that Griffin was "one helluva swell guy," although he was later to inspire the brutal Captain "Dynamite" Holmes in *From Here to Eternity.*

In September, Jones reapplied to the 27th Infantry Regiment and was accepted as a recruit, thus becoming a member of a famous unit. Founded in 1901 shortly after the Spanish-American War, the regiment was ordered to the Philippines to suppress an uprising caused by the Filipinos' disappointment at not obtaining independence. Following this campaign, the regiment returned to Fort Sheridan, Illinois, where it remained until 1906, when it went to Cuba on a similar mission as part of the Army of Pacification. It remained there until 1909. Next came another tour of duty at home, this time in Texas, before the regiment sailed once again to the Philippines, where it helped defend the American naval base at Cavite in Manila Harbor during World War I. Following the Armistice, the regiment traveled to Vladivostok as part of an international expeditionary force made up of British, French, Japanese, and American troops that tried to overthrow the Bolshevik régime established by Lenin. In Siberia, the 27th Regiment became so famous for its speed of movement that the Bolsheviks paid its men the compliment of calling them the Wolfhounds, a name by which they are still known. The regimental bandsmen wear the tall leather shakoes, white breeches, and crossed belts of the Russian hussars. The regimental mascot is naturally a borzoi, a Russian wolfhound. In 1921, the regiment was sent to Hawaii and stationed at Schofield Barracks as part of the newly formed Hawaiian Division.

Twenty-five miles inland from Honolulu, Schofield Barracks is reached by a road that winds up through tropical forests into barren open country bound on the east and west by two ranges of blue-green mountains jutting raggedly into the sky. Named after General John M. Schofield, it was a symbol of the creeping imperialism that reached its climax in 1898, when the United States annexed the Hawaiian Islands and declared them American territory. Schofield himself had been in Hawaii as early as 1872, sent there to explore its strategic importance to the United States at a time when many other Pacific islands were being taken over by the English, French, Dutch, and Germans. Schofield's military survey of the island of Oahu included a plan to set aside over fourteen thousand acres in the center of the island as a military post, and the first unit arrived in 1909.

The barracks soon became the largest post in the army, and an elaborate military camp was constructed, consisting of eight three-story stone quads for enlisted men and noncommissioned officers. Officers were housed in separate wooden houses laid out along palm-lined streets, and the commanding officers lived in three pillared houses at the end of a lawn called Generals Loop. Other structures included a headquarters building, shopping center, boxing ring, stables, a movie theater, library, post hospital, gymnasium, and stockade. Schofield Barracks was an immense military city arranged in rectangles with repetitive architecture, but the atmosphere was softened by palm trees and lawns and by views of the distant mountains.

Jones's transfer to the infantry meant that he had to undergo basic training all over again. Together with other new recruits, he had to learn the complete manual of arms and receive training in marching. In charge of the drill was a Corporal Bradshaw, who led the men out to a parade ground called Sills Field that had been worn down to red dust by thousands of marching feet. There the men were taught how to shoulder arms, to present arms, to stand at rest, how to march in step to cadence, how to change formations. Each recruit was required to march with his eyes fixed on the back of the head of the man in front of him, and the swing of his arms was precisely measured — six inches for the forward swing, three for the back. If he made a mistake, he was made to run three times around the track and then fall in as though he had expended no extra energy. The process was so exhausting that many men would come back with tears in their eyes. "March and cry, march and cry" was how the training was described. The recruits were formed into a company, and when finally they completed their training, they underwent a final inspection and a march-past in review.

Like the other recruits, Jones was afraid of not doing well and wondered whether he would pass muster. He was scared of Schofield Barracks, but the officers and noncommissioned officers kept him too busy for much worrying. Jones was housed with the 146 men of F Company in Quad D, which was made up of a group of four three-story buildings, painted a light beige, that enclosed the parade ground, where every morning at five forty-five the bugler played reveille. Jones lived in an open dormitory and slept on a narrow iron bed covered with a thin mattress. A footlocker was placed by the bed and another locker for clothes stood against the wall. Outside the dormitory, a lanai, or open corridor, ran the length of the building, and communal showers and latrines were placed at intervals.

After reveille, the troops gathered in the quad, fully dressed, for roll call at six o'clock. Following this ceremony, the colonel dismissed the troops for breakfast in the mess hall. In the prewar army, meals were formal, with each table presided over by a corporal. The men began their meals when the corporal ordered them to do so.

After breakfast, the men made their beds, straightened up the dormitory, neatened their lockers, and polished shoes and leatherwork for inspection. At nine, they gathered for calisthenics in the quad and afterward prepared for infantry drill. Jones had looked forward to this aspect of the work. "I love to drill with a rifle," he wrote his brother, "and for six weeks, that's about all I'll do. I'll learn the proper way to kill a man with a bayonet, and at the same time, learn how to keep him from killing me. I'll learn how to roll a pack so it will stay high on my back and not cut my shoulder blades, when I go on thirty or forty mile hikes, and I will be going on thirty or forty mile hikes, 'struth, so hep ma. I'll learn the proper way to shoot a .30 cal., 1903 type army rifle, also how to shoot the Garand M-1 rifle, which you've been reading about so much lately. Things like that are the reason I joined the army." For the first time in his life, except for his English classes at school, Jones was enthusiastic. He had always enjoyed manual labor and completing tasks, but what was more important, the army gave him a sense of purpose. He responded by working hard at becoming an exceptionally proficient soldier.

At eleven-thirty in the morning, a bugle summoned the men to mail call, and at noon they would go to the mess hall for the main meal of the day. During the afternoon, work formations were selected in turn to clean up the quad and to perform such chores as KP, but most of the afternoon was devoted to what were called quiet hours, when the men could sleep or polish their rifles or sharpen their bayonets. The final engagement of the day was retreat, at five o'clock, when the regiment, with the guard detachment and the regimental band in the lead, paraded across the quad to the Generals Loop for the lowering of the flag.

Sports activities, which had first attracted Jones to Schofield Barracks, were considered important for physical fitness and the improvement of morale. Each company fielded teams in football, baseball, basketball, track, boxing, and softball, and in Jones's time, F Company won three regimental championships in three of these sports. Boxing attracted the most attention, because the bouts were held in a ring built for spectators. As there was little entertainment available, the men liked going to the matches to cheer their company boxers. Jones tried out for the F Company team, but he was quickly eliminated. His fellow soldiers were much tougher and stronger than he had originally thought, so he had to revise his personal ambitions. He also tried out for football but injured his ankle and had to withdraw. His small size and lack of experience placed him well below army standards, and later his ankle injury would make him unfit for combat duty.

Despite these disappointments, Jones enjoyed sparring for fun with others in his company on the third floor of the barracks. He also became a friend of one man, Robert E. Stewart, who had refused to join the boxing team because he had once accidentally injured an opponent. Captain Griffin was so enraged with Stewart that he confined him to barracks and gave him extra duties of all kinds in an effort to force him to join the team.

Socially, the prewar army was rigidly stratified. Officers mixed only with officers, and enlisted men were segregated. They did not even associate with noncommissioned officers. Sometimes enlisted men who were given special duties as servants to officers, and were known as "dog robbers," would cross the social line, but it was dangerous to do so. A sergeant in F company had an affair with the company commander's wife, who was well known for driving into Quad D with her skirts drawn up to reveal her legs to the men who lined up on the balcony to look down at her.

In the evenings, the men were free to go into town, but with a salary of $21 a month, they made only infrequent trips to Honolulu. On an ordinary weekday night, a group of soldiers might stroll over to the nearby village of Waliwa, where there were bars and whorehouses, or perhaps they would go to the Chinese restaurant just outside the main gate. Every night there were movies on the post, but most of the men preferred to be sociable. Sometimes a group would gather on the steps of the main entrance to the quad, called the sally port, and sing songs or listen to the guitar players. One man might make up and sing a few lines and then another would continue. These singers were in the tradition of soldiers down through the ages, who had sung and told stories after battle. With drink fetched from the beer garden across from the quad, they would invent new lines and the songs would lengthen. "Re-enlistment Blues," the song that appears at the end of *From Here to Eternity*, was a song made up in this way, with no one person claiming authorship.

At eleven, taps was played, and everyone stopped talking as the bugler's notes sounded over the quad. Once in a while, silver taps would be played, with one bugler echoing the notes of the other. When this happened, the men were especially silent, for it meant that one of their number had died. Lights were extinguished after taps, but the men were not required to go to bed, though most of them did.

The life the soldiers led produced a communal feeling among them and gave meaning to many whose lives had seemed purposeless before they enlisted. Isolated from the mixed company of civilian life, they developed intense loyalties, for they all had the army in common. They knew the same deprivations and enjoyed the camaraderie that came with achievement. When an infantry company completed a forced march of thirty miles and returned to the gates of Schofield Barracks with bleeding feet and aching muscles, they knew they had done something. So did the army, for it always ordered a military band to meet such a company and to escort it back to the barracks with martial music. A special quality of the prewar army was that while it exacted much of its members, it provided them with a protected world in which to live.

Although Jones appreciated the community feeling at Schofield Barracks, he didn't find army life rich enough in the rewards he needed. It offered him no way to express his individual talents. He was ambitious and active, eager to learn how to do well, but he was not big enough or strong enough to excel in sports, which meant that in the eyes of the officers, particularly Captain Griffin, he was just another soldier. Moreover, he felt apart from most of the other men in his company. Many were almost entirely without education — unemployed coal miners or cotton pickers from the South with whom he had little in common. He knew that he needed more than the army to satisfy him. He had talked to his brother about being a writer, and he began to spend time in the library rather than going out to drink with the other enlisted men. He had few friends. Known as J.R. to distinguish him from another Jones in the same company, he was considered a loner.

He had had the same misgivings about the army at Hickam Field, during the uninspiring moments that he spent on guard duty and housekeeping for the few lucky men who flew the planes. There he had read Thomas Wolfe's *Look Homeward, Angel,* and one day while mowing the lawn, he was struck by the similarity between the story of the hero, Eugene Gant, and his own. He too had a drunken father and a nagging mother; he too saw the family property vanish and watched his mother take in boarders. They had the same romantic impulses; like Gant, he did not want "to escape out of life but into it." He wrote to his brother about his feelings: "I, too, like Wolfe, have felt myself different from other kids, especially while I was in high school. I never seemed to mix with other kids; I didn't think at all like they did; I never ran around with the gang of boys that were the elite of the campus, nor did I run around with the gang that envied them and disliked them. I did feel hurt about it, and I wasn't able to understand it; but I don't think I was little about it. I fell into the habit of going with myself, and expressing my 'radical' thoughts to no one."

The reading of *Look Homeward, Angel* changed his life. His unfocused feelings of failure and unhappiness found a possible outlet, and at last he had a sense of purpose. Instead of merely enduring his frustrations and disappointments, Jones discovered a positive way to act. In the unlikely moment of mowing the grass at Hickam Field, he suddenly knew, as he said, that "I had been a writer all my life without knowing it or having written." Now, at Schofield Barracks, he felt more urgently than ever the need to do something about his ambition.

It was not an easy decision, for even as a very young man, he knew the price he would have to pay. "I hate myself and my dreams and hopes," he told his brother. "I laugh at my attempts to write. And yet I cannot change. I must succeed. To be a nonentity would crack my brain and rend my heart asunder. It is all or nothing. And yet I wish that I were different, a little man with small ambitions and easily satisfied."

Appointed rifleman on completing his basic training, Jones tried to write when he could, but it was difficult. The routine was physically tiring and there were few moments when he could be alone. Occasionally there were unexpected opportunities, as when he was admitted to the base hospital to be operated on for appendicitis on December 16, 1940. The month allotted for recuperation gave him time to read and write. Shortly after he was discharged from the hospital, he was promoted to private first class and put on duty in the guardroom. There he lived in separate quarters with a small group of men and had more privacy than was possible in the barracks. Afterward, he was given special duty as a waiter at the officers' club. Such jobs were much sought after, especially by those not enthusiastic about the physical side of soldiering. Waiters and barmen lived in separate rooms on the ground floor of the club, and since he worked regular shifts, Jones had time for his writing. The experience was also useful for the insights it gave him into the mentality of the officer class, which he used later in *From Here to Eternity*.

Jones sent the sketches he wrote home to his father and brother, but otherwise he made little effort to keep in touch with his family. His mother would write him homilies, loving in tone, urging him to cooperate with his superiors so as to avoid their hostility, and his father encouraged him in his writing. "I think you have real ability, Jim," he wrote, "and will go far if you apply yourself." Referring to a story that had been rejected by *Esquire*, he added, "I think you rely too heavily on profanity and obscenity, and while I know that is the way the soldiers would think and speak, it is not primarily for them the story was written, but for prospective readers."

One day, a rather different kind of letter arrived from his father, with a message written on the envelope: "Bad news, Jim." It told him that his mother had died on March 2, 1941, at the age of fifty-two, of congestive heart failure complicated by the presence of sugar and albumin in the blood. Jones was stricken by the news. He asked for a three-day pass to Honolulu, "where I was alone, where no one knew me or bothered me," and there he stayed drunk for the three days. He was ashamed of himself afterward, but "felt a whole lot better mentally." Undoubtedly, he had feelings of guilt and remorse, even though he knew his mother was a silly and affected woman. He could probably imagine her funeral at the Presbyterian church, with the Christian Science ritual superimposed, and could picture her lying in her casket, wearing a white lace dress and holding the Minerva Club red carnation in her hand while Carrie Lee Brubaker sang:

In a land of fadeless day
Lies a City Four Square.
It shall never pass away,
For there is no night there.

The sentimental pretentiousness of such a ceremony would have sickened him, as did his memory of the "horror and revulsion" he had felt at watching her take insulin shots. "She would sit in a chair in the King Street diningroom and use the hypo on herself. Her thigh was big and ropy and flabby, covered with innumerable pock marks from former shots." She reminded him constantly of the "phantasmal presence of possible death." This nauseating memory repelled him, and in hating his memory of her, he later would blame her for his small stature, calling her "a fucking dwarf."

With such memories, Jones might have been expected to be relieved to hear of her death, but the turmoil he underwent on receiving the news suggests deeper worries, both about himself and about the nature of human existence. He was not a sentimental person and not likely to reverse his feelings about his mother, but he was probably saddened by whatever it is in life that can transform a woman who was once pretty and gay into a monster of self-pity and ugliness. How would he change with time?

As a single man, alone in Hawaii, he was always conscious of his relationships with women. Through his sister, Mary Ann, he knew their loving side, for she sent him letters addressing him as "the swellest, the grandest, the most wonderful and the bravest brother anyone in this whole world ever had or ever will have (per-i-od)." Mary Ann was only fourteen when Jones left Robinson, so her sweet letters could give him only limited comfort. He was still nervous about relationships with women his own age. His distaste for his mother did not turn him against women, however; on the contrary, it increased his desire for someone as unlike her as possible. He wanted a woman's love and her beauty, but only an extremely romantic vision would be strong enough to replace the nightmare he had known.

"Sometimes I'll lay awake at night and think of you," he wrote to Virginia Moore, the girl he had met on the bus in California before embarking for Honolulu, and with whom he corresponded a few times. "I'll hear the heavy breathing of wornout men who are asleep around me, and I will see the velvet, golden moonlight outside upon the porch. And I will dream of sitting beside you on the fragrant spice of sweet pine needles and how the moon will make the golden glints in your hair. And how I will take you in my arms and kiss your parted lips and know your eyes, your throat, and smell the fragrance of your hair. And we will know that no two people, who have ever lived, have loved as we have loved."

At the same time, he saw himself undergoing "years of agony and blackest despair, trying to be a successful writer." He could not ask anyone to share that experience, but he still needed "the love and belief and adoration of a woman," for if there was such a person, "who has faith in your ability and belief in your dreams and ambitions and has love for you shining from her eyes and encouragement for you on her lips, when your guts are black with doubt, you can conquer worlds, subdue the earth."

Jones's experience of his mother and his romantic illusions undoubtedly created problems that would affect his treatment of women for years to come. In the best of circumstances, it would have been hard for him to find someone who lived up to his standards. He was an enlisted man in Hawaii, and it was impossible for him even to have a normal relationship with a woman, let alone find someone who would fulfill his dreams. Officers had enough money to visit the Royal Hawaiian Hotel or the Moana; they could stroll along the palm-lined streets of Waikiki, stopping at a bar where they might meet attractive girls, but ordinary soldiers could not afford the prices. Moreover, apart from a few strictly controlled tea dances organized by women's groups and later by the USO, enlisted men were social pariahs. By long tradition, girls from good Chinese, Japanese, and Hawaiian families were discouraged from associating with white men, especially if they came from the mainland; and the indigenous white girls, known as *haoles*, were busy with the officers. What was left were the prostitutes, who were most easily found in the Chinese section of Honolulu, near the docks.

Here the blocks formed by King Street, Hotel Street, and other byways of the neighborhood were full of pawnshops, fish markets, and Chinese grocery shops, where whole carcasses of smoked pigs and ducks hung in rows on meathooks. They also contained bars, tattoo parlors, and photo galleries. Over such shops, on upper floors reached by long narrow staircases, were the whorehouses. They were disguised as hotels and bore names like the New Senator, the Western, and the Archer.

Usually Jones went into Honolulu alone, but sometimes a friend like Everest Capra accompanied him. After stopping at a bar they would go to Wu Fat's Chinese restaurant on the corner of Maunakea and Hotel Street. A large upstairs eatery with high ceilings and rotating fans, garish with red paint and gilded decorations, it had an exotic quality that served as an overture to the evening. After dinner, they would walk along the narrow streets by the shooting and photograph galleries. Sometimes, business at the whorehouses was so heavy that lines of soldiers would stretch into the streets outside, waiting to enter. These places made no pretense of providing night club entertainment. They simply contained rows of small rooms or cubicles that were available for a few minutes of quick intercourse. A white girl cost $3. Across the canal that runs along Front Street were native girls; they cost $2 each.

Along with his friend, Jones would wait in line outside the whorehouse, but they rarely went in. Once they reached the doorway and met the girls, they turned and ran down the stairs, tumbling over each other to get away. They were shy and nervous, but they were also afraid of catching a venereal disease. Later, with his friend John Cloninger from Schofield Barracks, Jones would go into the whorehouses to drink and dance with the girls. He liked to talk to them and find out about their lives, but if they suggested making love, he would make excuses and eventually leave. Afterward, he and his friend would go to one of the bars to have some drinks, and on the way back to the post, sharing a taxi with some other soldiers, they would boast of their conquests. In letters home to his brother, Jones also bragged about his successes with women, referring casually to "the cupcake" whose favors he received.

Already frustrated by the restrictions of army life, Jones was further sickened by these experiences. To get them out of his system, all he could do was write about them. In some of his letters he began what amounts to his first fictional treatment of this material, which reveals both his romanticism and his powers of observation. The soldier, he wrote, "lives alone with other men, who are suspicious and grasping and afraid of each other and themselves. He longs for a woman upon whose breast he may lay his head and weep, a woman who will understand, who will love, who will believe. And he cannot find one. He is lost. He becomes frantic. His entrails quake with sickness at the things around him. Uniforms! Uniforms! All he can see or smell is uniforms, a pounding, roaring sea of uniforms, and here and there he sees a barren, desert isle: a snobbish, egotistic officer with his lovely wife, and he longs to have a woman he may hold, who will love him." The tension grows, and in search of some relief, he goes to "the only place he knows: a whorehouse." And after he has gone there, he regrets it and is ashamed, "for instead of finding what he wanted, all he found was the blaring of a 'juke box,' the raucous laughter of the whores, fifteen minutes in a tiny barren room with a whore with sagging breasts and tiny bulging belly, and he is lost and disillusioned. He does the only thing he knows to erase the stench: he goes out on a drunk, and then goes back."

Jones's sensitivity to the brutal impersonality of love as he found it in Hawaii eventually made him admit to his brother that his stories of amorous conquest were false. "Did I ever tell you about the Portagee girl I had in Honolulu? shacked up with her?" he asked. "It like the others was a lie. It was an attempt to make a hero out of myself. It was a very swashbuckling picture, romantic, heart-stirring; pretty, but untrue." And as for the others, "All those women I used to write to you about sleeping with I didn't. I took care of myself instead. No very pleasant or heroic picture, is it?"

In January of 1941, Jones was appointed assistant company clerk. "About all I do," he told his brother, "is type orders and letters and run messages and that sort of thing, but it keeps me going all day long." The job also meant that he worked directly under the company commander and as his assistant was one of a small group that included the first sergeant, a communications clerk, and the company bugler, Frank Marshall, with whom he became friendly. Jones's transfer to the command post coincided with the arrival of a new company commander, Captain William Blatt, a fellow native of Illinois, a graduate of Northwestern, and a lawyer. Unlike his predecessor, Blatt was relaxed and humane and took a liking to Jones, recognizing that his intelligence would be valuable to the company. As assistant company clerk, Jones helped the first sergeant prepare the payroll and the duty roster. It was a good place to learn about the structure of the army.

Blatt found out about Jones's ambitions to be a writer and tried to help him take a summer course as a special student at the University of Hawaii. Despite his recommendation, the application came back from headquarters marked "not favorably considered." Jones was bitterly disappointed. "I don't believe I've ever hated the army as much as I did then," he wrote.

Writing was becoming increasingly important to him. In Honolulu, he visited the secondhand book shops on Nuuanu Avenue, and when not on duty he used the office typewriter for his own work. He had never made any secret of his ambition to become a writer, and he carried around a little notebook in which he would jot down his observations. Once while he was away from his desk, someone made a little sign that read GENIUS AT WORK and placed it by his typewriter. Jones accepted the joke, but he was troubled by the loneliness he was beginning to feel. "I'm working in the dark all the time," he told his brother. "Whenever I do write something, that black, forbidding doubt is in me, making me wonder if I'm just some damned egotistical fool, or if I really have that spark of genius it takes to be a really great author like Wolfe. If only I had some way of knowing. If only some authority that knew would tell me I was good and had promise, then I'd be all right." Sometimes, he added, "I get so damned low I feel like blowing my brains out."

By late 1941, these worries would become secondary, for by then it was evident that a war was coming. Nineteen forty had brought the fall of France and the Battle of Britain; the next year brought the opening of hostilities between Germany and the Soviet Union. Continued Japanese aggression in China and Indonesia caused President Roosevelt to freeze Japanese assets in the United States and to forbid the sale of oil to Japan. These tensions inevitably affected the army. When Jones enlisted, there were fewer than 300,000 soldiers on duty, but as a result of the Selective Service Acts of 1940 and 1941, nearly a million new men were inducted by the end of 1941. By December of the following year, the army numbered four million men. One consequence of this vast increase was that the Hawaiian Division, of which Jones's 27th Infantry Regiment was a part, was replaced by two new units, the 24th Infantry Division and the 25th Infantry Division, to which Jones's regiment was assigned. Both divisions preserved the old insignia of the Hawaiian taro leaf. The 25th would later superimpose on its leaf a yellow lightning bolt, and the division eventually became known as Tropic Lightning for the speed of its operations against the Japanese on Guadalcanal.

"Early that fateful morning we sighted the island of Oahu after leaving our carrier out to sea. Certain units had certain tasks to perform and if successful we would leave Oahu a mass of smoldering ruins. Over Pearl Harbor we proceeded to bomb the much overrated American Pacific Fleet. In hardly no time at all, rising columns of smoke began to emerge from many ships in the harbor including a battle-ship. Our pilots had already made short work of Wheeler Field where the American pursuit ships are stationed. They bombed ranges of air-planes on the ground, destroying them in great numbers. Hangars were completely set afire and were destroyed due to their poor con-struction. The ground troops, obviously badly frightened, displayed a poor degree of marksmanship and were merely wasting ammunition. We had nothing to worry about from them. 'Banzai,' we all shouted as we returned. The hand of Providence was with us."

A transcript of this official Japanese account of the bombing, moni-tored from Radio Tokyo, was posted at Wheeler Field on January 2, 1942, "for the information and *amusement*" of all pilots and enlisted men. But it is doubtful that many found the transcript very funny. The Japanese attack had destroyed in a few hours the greater part of America's military strength in the Pacific.

No one was prepared for the attack. "It was just another Sunday morning," Jones later wrote, "the time of rest, of eating, laziness and sleep for soldiers." He was on guard duty but as an orderly, which meant that he slept in the company barracks rather than in the guardhouse with the others. He had just gone down to breakfast, which on Sundays was special because of a bonus ration of a half-pint of milk. He had eaten two fried eggs when he heard "the explosions that began rumbling up toward us from Wheeler Field two miles away. 'They doing some blasting?' some old-timer said through a mouthful of pancakes."

Along with everyone else, Jones rushed outside to see what was going on. Huddled against a wall, he watched a Japanese fighter ap-proach, its guns firing down the street. "As he came abreast of us, he gave us a typically toothy grin and waved, and I shall never forget his face behind the goggles. A white scarf streamed out behind his neck and he wore a white ribbon around his helmet just above the goggles, with a red spot in the center of his forehead. I would later learn that this ribbon was a *hachimaki*, the headband worn by medieval samurai when going into battle."

Reporting immediately for duty at the headquarters building, Jones took up his position at the orderly's desk outside the colonel's office. He spent the morning "carrying messages for distraught officers," and he wore a special pistol that went with his job. Soon orders were is-sued that all the personnel of Schofield Barracks were to be dispersed along the beaches of the island. Following the bombing attack, the American command expected that Japanese troops would invade Oahu.

By midafternoon, Jones and his fellow soldiers were on their way; long columns of camouflaged army trucks slowly drove down from the high plateau of the barracks toward Honolulu. Machine guns were mounted on the roofs of the trucks in anticipation of new attacks. As they neared the coast, the men could see huge columns of black smoke rising high into the clear sky over Pearl Harbor. By now, Jones, like many others, had been personally affected by the war. One of the Japanese fighters, in strafing the guardhouse where Jones normally slept, had killed a number of his comrades even before they got out of bed. Among them were "three of the best friends I've had since I've been in the army," Jones wrote to his father. Inside the cover of his notebook he wrote that the book should be sent to his brother in case he was killed.

As the trucks wound their way down through the pineapple groves, Jones took stock of his own situation. "I remember thinking with a sense of the profoundest awe that none of our lives would ever be the same, that a social, even a cultural watershed had been crossed which we could never go back over, and I wondered how many of us would survive to see the end results. I wondered if I would. I had just turned twenty, the month before."

As part of the deployment of troops from Schofield Barracks, Jones's F Company was put in charge of a stretch of land on the south shore of Oahu, starting from Wailupe, ten miles east of Honolulu, to Makapuu Point around the southeastern corner of the island. It is a lovely stretch of land, with palm trees, palmettoes, and hibiscus along the sandy beaches and with hills rising abruptly from the coast, covered with low mossy plants that make them look as though they were sheathed in a velvet carpet.

The long caravan of military vehicles from Schofield had been divided into units of one or two trucks to be assigned to specific places along the shore. While the column moved along, the trucks would pull off the road to their designated positions. Campsites were chosen and the men put up their tents. Then they stretched barbed wire along the beaches and built machine gun emplacements to repel the expected enemy. All leaves were canceled, and the whole island was placed under martial law.

Jones's unit was first sent to Makapuu Point, equipped "with nothing but the machine guns and our rifles. And one canteen of water per man." But as assistant company clerk, he was soon on the move from the command post, which was moved back and forth between Wailupe and Hanauma Bay, midway along the territory F Company was responsible for. The state of war required road patrols and inspections, the distributing of food and supplies to all platoons along the coast, as well as the rotation of troops sent to difficult posts. Jones's job was to prepare the morning report and roll call and to act as chief assistant to the first sergeant as he traveled along the line.

At Wailupe, the command post was bivouacked on the beach next to the weekend house of a Honolulu physician, Dr. Harry Arnold. He and his wife befriended some of the soldiers and were especially attracted to Jones, because he was more articulate than most of the others. When they invited him to dinner, he told them of his hopes to be a writer and gave them some of his poems. "Hang on to these," he said; "I'm going to be famous one day." There was little to do on the beach position, so Jones spent a good deal of time reading and writing, and sometimes he acted as a baby sitter for the Arnolds' daughter.

Captain Blatt, who had earlier recognized Jones's promise, urged him to apply to officers' training school. Jones believed he was a natural member of the officer class, but he preferred to stay with the enlisted men, who represented the real army and had never been written about. Also, he knew he was too independent to abide by petty rules and therefore would not make a good officer. He was often late returning from town, but Blatt always supported him, and in May he was promoted to corporal.

Blatt was particularly solicitous of Jones when in March of 1942 he received a cable from Jeff telling him that his father had died. Only later did Jeff write that he had committed suicide. Even though he had fought continually with his wife, Dr. Jones went to pieces after her death. Already an alcoholic, he drank more heavily and three days after the first anniversary of his wife's death, he began drinking in his office after taking Mary Ann to school. When a patient came in to pay a bill, he found that "Dr. Jones was not in a condition to do business." After the patient left, he sat down in his dentist's chair and, with a .25-caliber Colt automatic, shot himself behind his right ear. Although the official inquest did not mention it, evidently the first shot was not effective, and he had to shoot himself twice more before he died. He was fifty-five years old.

On her way back from school at four-thirty, Mary Ann stopped at her father's office and found him lying on the floor. In fright and dismay she ran to her Uncle Charlie's office, which was nearby. He arranged for an inquest; after it was completed, Dr. Jones was buried in the new cemetery in Robinson.

When Jones opened the letter from his brother, "the last sentence in the first paragraph seemed to leap out from the paper before my eyes in letters a foot high. I didn't say anything to anybody. I folded the letter up, stuck it in my pocket, turned on my heel and walked away from the Orderly Room. I went down to my tent, sat down on my bunk, and lit a cigarette. Then I took the letter out of my pocket and opened it up and read it. Then I folded it, stuck it back in the envelope, and just sat there on my bed, smoking. Sometimes the air is awfully clear here. You can look off and see the soft, warm, raggedy roof of clouds stretching on and on. It almost seems as if you can look right on into eternity."

As he sat brooding, he remembered that the night before, he had stamped on a crab by the edge of the sea and killed it. The sea rolled in and out, and in a few moments there was no trace of the crab. Now, he thought that "life is like the sea, brutal and relentless. It can't go back. It can't stand still. Therefore it must go forward. It plays the percentage. It is governed by a law of nature. What does it matter if some little crab or human being is smashed upon the rocks?" Jones told his brother he was not surprised by the news. "Call it a premonition if you will." He and his father had discussed suicide as a possibility if life no longer seemed worth living, and his father had said, "Don't ever let anyone tell you that it takes more guts to go on living than to kill yourself, because it doesn't."

Jones knew that his father was weak and that he was a failure. He had been a poet, a sensitive man who had been destroyed by disappointment and drink. But he had a certain integrity that Jones admired. "Dad shot him *self*," he noted; "he knew what would happen." Thinking of the townspeople of Robinson he so disliked, Jones also saw the humor of the event. "I bet he got one helluva kick out of shocking the populace of Robinson like he did. The more I think of it, the more I'm glad the whole thing ended as it did."

There was no money. Dr. Jones's estate amounted to a $500 insurance policy, which was split three ways among the children. Mary Ann moved to Findlay, Ohio, where her brother Jeff lived, and continued her schooling there. A young girl of seventeen, suddenly thrust into the household of a brother fifteen years older than she was, Mary

Ann found herself out of place. Jeff and his wife had small children, and Mary Ann was too old to be another child, almost too young to be an aunt. A spirited and independent girl, she took an interest in theater at the high school. Soon, however, her restlessness led her to rebel against the restrictions her brother imposed on her, and she began to fall into bad company.

Jones knew little of what was happening to his sister; what most occupied his thoughts was the solitude his father must have lived in, which was so like his own. "The Joneses of Robinson are no more and no less than a certain number of human beings," he wrote to Jeff. They think they have "the capacity to rise above society into the rarefied air of honesty. But they don't, and that is the weakness."

As a young man of twenty, without parents, he realized how fragile life was, and he was grateful for Captain Blatt's solicitude and encouragement. But he had to rely on his own resources, and it wasn't enough just to go on living: he had to make his own mark. In a curious way, his father's death helped him decide, as he later said, "to do something with my life" and to "leave behind something that was of a semi-permanent nature."

By the late spring of 1942, the intense military activity following the bombing of Pearl Harbor had abated. It was evident that the Japanese would not invade the island, yet the United States had not yet launched a counteroffensive against the enemy. In this lull, Captain Blatt gave Jones permission to enroll in the University of Hawaii, which was in the hills above Waikiki and Diamond Head. Jones signed up for a morning course and an afternoon course, each meeting three times a week.

The University of Hawaii had been founded as the College of Agriculture and Mechanic Arts in 1907 to meet the commercial needs of the territory, but by the 1940s it was a full university, with over two thousand students. The central quad had been laid out in 1912 on rolling ground with Hawaii Hall at its head. Built in classical style with pillars, it set the pattern for later buildings, most of them named after early university presidents. Around them stood banyan trees, palms, and magnolias, as well as groves of teak and mahogany. The English department, housed in a low wooden structure built around a courtyard, fit naturally into this setting of flowers and blossoming trees.

One of Jones's courses was a class in composition taught by Laura

Schwartz, a woman of about thirty with an interest in students. The class met in a basement room, and the instructor gave assignments to the fifteen students. Jones, however, usually handed in whatever he was writing on his own. Miss Schwartz found Jones's work "strikingly different" from the rest. Even though there were errors in spelling and word choice, she recognized the energy and originality of his writing. After class, he would go to her office or visit her in her apartment to talk about his work. He told her that he wanted to become a professional writer. "The only trouble," he later wrote, "was I didn't know the first thing about how 'to write,' and I think her greatness lay in that she did not laugh. I guess I was a little in love with her too, but by this time flatter myself I was more hip about not showing such things."

The other course he attended was one in American literature taught by Carl Stroven. Jones also went round to his office after class, and Stroven immediately sensed how lonely Jones was in the army, with no one to talk to about his writing. Jones showed Stroven sketches he had written, pieces of dialogue, descriptions, and episodes. There were no completed stories, for Jones was beginning in small stages. Stroven was impressed by the strong realistic tone of Jones's work and by his compulsion to write. "There was no doubt in my mind that that boy would be able to publish," he was later to say. Laura Schwartz, who gave him an A for her course, thought "it was at once too much and too little."

Modeling his writing on that of Thomas Wolfe, the writer who had first inspired him, Jones wrote autobiographical stories. One fictional self-portrait contained this passage: "But since he had been in the army, he had come to understand his ungraspable longing and his phantasmal and belly-shrinking dissatisfaction: there were such things he wanted to be, to do, to write: He wanted to be the voice that shrieked out the agony of frustration and lostness and despair and loneliness that all men feel, yet cannot understand; the voice that rolled forth the booming, intoxicating laughter of men's joy; the voice that richly purred men's love of good hot food and spicy strong drink; men's love of thick, moist, pungent tobacco smoke on a full belly; men's love of woman: voluptuous, throaty-voiced, silken-thighed, and sensual."

Jones also used the experiences of others. One night, lying in bed with a headache that prevented him from sleeping, he remembered a sailor's telling him about the horror of drowning at sea, which he claimed was worse than death on land. "I could imagine myself in a heavy sea," Jones later wrote, "clinging to a battered piece of wood, feeling my strength ebb away, forcing numbed and weakened fingers to tighten their grip, thinking about how much fun I had had at home dancing, drinking, reading, talking, eating, diddling the girls and how sad it was that I was so young and had to die with my lungs full of salt water, when there were so many things I liked to do, until at last I couldn't make my fingers hold on any longer, and I slipped off the wood to sink down and down and down — to drown. Finally, it made me feel so blue, I got up and went into the latrine and wrote it down, at least a couple of pages of it, because my head got to hurting so bad, I had to quit."

What he wrote had feeling, but he needed instruction badly, as the first paragraph of "Of Seamen Sinking" shows: "John T. Kolinowski, Seaman, 2nd, USS Destroyer ————, spat a mouthful of bitter-tasting salt sea water back into the Pacific Ocean from whence it came and laughed aloud. He was a strong swimmer, and he had been afloat in heavy seas a bare five minutes, since he had dived overboard from the starboard rail of his erstwhile home."

Despite his lack of control over the material, Jones soon became known among the English faculty as a student of exceptional promise, and two other instructors, Gaylord LeRoy and a Mrs. Bergstrom, also took interest in his work. Between classes, Jones would study in the library. "Did you ever read Robinson Jeffers?" he asked his brother in a letter written after one such session. "He wrote the poem in free verse called 'Such Counsels as You Gave To Me.' It's damn good."

He also liked to spend time with girls he met in his classes. One of these was Tsuneko Ogure, a Japanese-American girl who later became a local journalist known as Scoops Kreger. After class, they would sit together under a tree and talk about their literary ambitions. Jones was already convinced that he would write a great novel, and the other students were impressed by the experiments he made, for example, using incomplete sentences to emphasize the starkness and directness of his sketches. He hardly spoke of himself or his family, but he was interested in his classmates, questioning them at length about their lives and ideas.

Because of anti-army feeling among the native population of Hawaii, Jones was teased by some of the students, and the dean of women told Tsuneko that she shouldn't be dating a common soldier, especially one who was white. Jones himself was proud of going out with her, because he imagined he was breaking down an artificial social barrier.

His literary confidence was virtually all he had, for in his khaki leggings and campaign hat and steel-rimmed glasses, he was an awkward figure at the university. Graceless and shy, he would nevertheless visit Tsuneko and her mother on Sundays. He tried to have an affair with her, but was unsuccessful, and later, in *From Here to Eternity*, used her as a model for Violet Ogure, the Japanese girl with whom Prewitt has a "shack job."

Another girl he knew was a buxom red-haired freshman named Peggy Carson, who worked in a clinic across the courtyard from the English department offices. They would go out on dates, and Jones met her parents. Her father liked him and gave him a hunting knife. But then Jones became aggressive and was rebuffed by Peggy. "I seem to have been born with the habit of forcing issues," he wrote her; "when I look back, I see that everywhere I've been I've done that. I suppose if I had learned to wait and let nature and the law of percentage take their course, I'd be a lot better off right now. But then I'd have missed a lot of things that I haven't missed by jumping in where angels and smart people fear to tread."

Jones later wrote to his brother that he and Peggy Carson had spoken about marriage, but that "nothing must ever come between me and my writing." According to Jones, she didn't mind the hardships he anticipated, because she believed "that if two people love each other, they can get along and be happy, which is not true, of course." Jones had been far from successful in love, and it annoyed him that "many women seem to like me, but none — or at least few — well enuf to want to sleep with me. I always end up as the friend they tell their love troubles with another guy to. That makes me mad as hell, but it happens invariably."

He tried to work out the problem for himself, and very soon after his arrival in Hawaii, he decided that the relationship between men and women was best understood as a contest. "Men go out and try to make women with as little money as necessary," he wrote, "while women try to get as much money out of the men as they can, and still keep their virginity. They figure just how far they can let a guy go. From the age they are ten they are either observing or practicing, and by the time they're eighteen, it takes a helluva line to sink them. And by the time they are old enough or bored enough to want a guy for good, the poor bastard hasn't got a chance. I like to think I'm one of the guys who can outsmart them."

But Jones had no "line" and he knew it. He really wasn't interested in a woman he would have to campaign for. As his romantic fantasies revealed, he wanted someone to fall into his arms and adore him. He could no longer complain, as he had done earlier, that all he had to choose from were the prostitutes of Hotel and King Streets, because he was now meeting attractive girls at the university. But none of them responded to him as he hoped they would, and he was not really in love with any of them. More and more, he devoted himself to his writing, which at least was something he could control. His sexual energies were increasingly channeled into his work, and he began to think of love and writing as opposed impulses. In that conflict there was no question which way he would turn. "I've always felt," he told his brother, "that my way would be the one of renouncing the woman for the writing."

Soon the problem would be unreal, and the renunciation would be in favor of neither love nor art. Jones had enrolled for the autumn term at the university, intending to continue his two courses, but he was aware of changes in the air. One evening, after dinner at the Lan Yee Chai restaurant, he went on to the nearby Waikiki Tavern and there heard from a group of drunken sailors about the Battle of the Coral Sea. They told him how the aircraft carrier *Lexington* had been sunk, and they spoke of the miraculous survival of the *Yorktown*. Jones had his first glimpse of what battle experience was like. "With their sun-blackened faces and hollow haunted eyes, they were men who had already passed on into a realm I had never seen, and didn't particularly want to see. As the petty officer said, factually, it was not the going there the one time, but the going back again and again, that finally got to you."

With the Battle of Midway in June of 1942, the tide began to turn against the Japanese. The hour for Allied military action against occupied territory was at hand. Members of Jones's unit sometimes joked that they would sit out the war guarding the island of Oahu, but few believed it or even wanted it. Then suddenly, in mid-September, the 25th Infantry Division was ordered back to Schofield Barracks for reorganization and further training. The beach positions were to be taken over by newly arrived troops from the States. There were now 135,000 soldiers in Hawaii, more than three times the prewar number. "Our training was neither intensive nor complete," Jones later wrote. "It was woefully inadequate, and we knew it. But then these were the early days of the war. And perhaps it was really impossible to train a man for combat without putting him actually in it. We jumped off some antique barges, already obsolete, and waded through shallow water and sand. We crawled on our bellies through mud under machine gun fire which was coming from MGs fixed between posts. We practiced throwing hand grenades, and practiced firing our rifles and various weapons. All this we had already done, except the barge part, innumerable times. For a week we had an hour of jiu-jitsu a day, and tried throwing each other on the ground."

Jones's reassignment to Schofield Barracks made it impossible for him to continue at the university. From time to time, he would visit Carl Stroven and Laura Schwartz, and they could see that he was upset at the prospect of being shipped out. He was overwrought, afraid that he would be killed and therefore never finish the great book he hoped to write. As the time approached for him to leave, he went to say goodbye to his two teachers. When he left the office, he heard Stroven bang his fist down on the top of his desk and say, "It's a rotten shame, a Goddamned rotten shame, that a talent like that must be lost to the world because of a stupid thing like a war." He also visited Gaylord LeRoy, whose wife had also read his work. She told him "she was certain I wouldn't die, because I had too much yet unborn inside me to be lost. That makes you feel pretty good." Jones gave LeRoy a briefcase stuffed with stories and sketches he had written during his stay in Hawaii. He asked that they be kept safely for him, and when LeRoy left the island, he passed them on to Stroven. Jones had told all his instructors that they could read the material if they wanted to, and Stroven was somewhat abashed to find that one of the sketches was an unflattering portrait of himself.

Meanwhile, Jones and his buddies got some idea of what war would be like when a B-25 bomber crashed on a mountainside above the base. Several of the soldiers went up to investigate and came back with stories of the men who had been killed, "with arms and legs burned off and bellies burst open like cooked wieners." One was described as having his lips and chin burned away, "exposing teeth and jawbones to the sky 'like a skull in a cannibal's tent.' " Jones was distressed by the ghoulish bravado of those who had gone to see the wreckage. They seemed "to get a morbid thrill out of seeing *strangers* dead and mutilated — not friends, they can't stand that, it's too horrible — but viewing strangers is adventurous and gives them a thrill."

In the barracks, Jones and his comrades continued their "more constant though less favorite pastime. Speculating on what was going to happen to us. We wondered and we waited." As the time passed, Jones brooded about the future. "I might be dead in a month," he wrote, "which would mean that I would never learn how to say and never get said those things which proved that I had once existed somewhere." He received some comfort from his brother, but now, at the last hour, he had no one in Hawaii, no woman to whom he could turn for solace. He had put all his energies into his art, and the work was hardly begun.

Then suddenly the training schedule was canceled, and Jones and his companions were loaded onto transport ships in Pearl Harbor. It was almost a year to the day since the Japanese had bombed the American fleet, and the hulks of sunken ships still protruded from the water, a cheerless sight for those about to embark on what Jones called "the wastes of the trackless Pacific." For the soldiers on board, there was little to do but wait — and do "what we had done at Schofield, in our few spare moments, the same as we had done all during the six months before. The rumor was still Australia."

3

❦

GUADALCANAL

BUT THE RUMOR was wrong. They were sent instead to Guadalcanal, an island virtually unknown before the long campaign that made it famous as the site of the first successful American offensive after Pearl Harbor. The United States Marines had landed there on August 8, 1942, but bogged down without displacing the enemy. Although the Japanese originally had only a small garrison on the island, they appeared to have successfully built up their troops, by an airlift known as the Tokyo Express, despite the presence of a large number of American warships. In fact, the battle for Guadalcanal was mainly a naval war, and the body of water separating it from its neighboring islands, Florida and Savo, became known as Ironbottom Sound because of the many ships that were sunk there. By the end of the year, the conflict had become a stalemate and the 1st Division of the marines, which had taken on most of the fighting, was badly in need of replacement.

The high command in Washington was preoccupied with the war in Europe, and especially with the conquest of North Africa and the defeat of Field Marshal Erwin Rommel. But when they realized how precarious the American position was in Guadalcanal, they ordered new forces. They first sent units of the Americal Division, and these were soon followed by the 161st and 182nd Divisions of the United States Army as well as by units of the 2nd Marine Division. The newly formed 25th Division, under the command of Brigadier General J. Lawton Collins, completed the replacement, and the whole group was united as the XIV Corps.

The 25th Division left Hawaii in three convoys, of which the second, carrying Jones's F Company and the larger part of the 27th Infantry Regiment, left on December 6, 1942, crossing the equator on December 11 and arriving at Suva in the Fiji Islands on December 18. There they took on fresh supplies before sailing for the Solomon Islands, and arrived at Lunga Point on Guadalcanal on December 30.

Life on board the troopship *Hunter Liggett* was at once tedious and anxious. Four thousand men were on board what had once been a Matson liner designed to carry one thousand passengers. The troops were bedded down in tiered bunks below deck. There was little fresh air, and the temperature soared when the ship reached the tropics. Because of the crowding, the men were allowed on deck for fresh air and exercise only for brief periods. While waiting for meals, they killed time by playing cards and reading. Underlying the discomfort and boredom was fear. On the last night before landing at Guadalcanal, Jones went up on deck to talk to his friend John Cloninger. Wearing only an undershirt, he began to talk about what was in store for them. He leaned against the rail of the blacked-out ship and spoke of his writing and his hopes, but mainly he just stood there and looked down at the sea. Before going back down to sleep, he showed Cloninger the four extra identification tags he had taped to his body. Normally a soldier wears only two on a chain around his neck, but Jones had two on his wrists and two on his ankles as well, to make sure his body was identified should he be killed the next morning.

When the ship pulled into the bay next to Lunga Point, Jones was astonished by what he saw. "I remember exactly how it looked the day we came up on deck to go ashore: the delicious sparkling tropic sea, the long beautiful beach, the minute palms of the copra plantation waving in the sea breeze, the dark green band of jungle, and the dun mass and power of the mountains rising behind it to rocky peaks. The jungle stillness and slimes in the gloom inside the rain forest could make you catch your breath with awe. From the mountain slopes in midafternoon with the sun at your back you could look back down the beach and off across the straits to Florida Island and one of the most beautiful views of tropic scenery on the planet."

This gorgeous place, which many who fought there described as a "bloody stinking hole," was inhabited by Melanesians, a people with little of the openness and gentleness of the Polynesians. The island was discovered for the first time by Westerners when Don Alvaro Mendaña stopped there while sailing from Peru in 1568 in search of Ophir, the legendary place from which King Solomon was reputed to have brought gold, silver, and sandalwood for his temple at Jerusalem. Although he found no gold, Mendaña named the long archipelago the Solomon Islands, after the biblical king.

The Spaniards soon abandoned Guadalcanal and its neighbors, and for two centuries the Solomons were forgotten by explorers, even disappearing from nautical charts. In 1767, they were rediscovered by the French explorer the Sieur de Bougainville, after whom the northern island of the archipelago was named. Once again the steamy climate and native hostility prevented serious settlement, and not until the nineteenth century were Guadalcanal and the other islands colonized. The Germans claimed Bougainville, and the English took over the rest of the archipelago. They established their capital in a small, relatively healthful island called Tulagi, and soon missionaries arrived, along with British and Australian pioneers, who laid out coconut plantations in response to a worldwide demand for copra and coconut oil.

When the Japanese arrived in May of 1942, the local garrison consisted of only twenty riflemen, and the Australian government, which maintained a small air base near Tulagi, ordered an evacuation. The Japanese had welcomed the Melanesians into their Co-Prosperity Sphere, but they were so cruel and brutal to the local population that when the Americans arrived, three months later, the Melanesians set up warning systems to alert them to Japanese attacks and rescued American airmen who crashed in the interior of the island.

The American decision to attack Guadalcanal came about almost accidentally. The original plan, drawn up by General Douglas MacArthur and Admiral E. J. King, was for American forces to pass by the Solomon Islands in the long campaign that would lead up through the Pacific toward the Philippines and the eventual invasion of Japan. But when an Allied reconnaissance plane reported that the Japanese were building a large air base on Guadalcanal, the Americans realized they could not ignore it.

By the time the 25th Division landed on the island, the major part of the battle for Guadalcanal had already taken place, but the men did not know it at the time. Indeed, the Japanese tried to bomb the troopships on the day they arrived, and Jones watched the raid. "Those of us already ashore could stand in perfect safety in the edge of the trees and watch as if watching a football game or a movie. Around us marines and army oldtimers would cheer whenever a Jap plane went smoke-trailing down the sky, or groan when one got through and water spouts geysered up around the transports. Neither transport took a hit, but one took a near-miss so close alongside it sprang some plates, and had to leave without finishing unloading. Almost immediately after, a loaded barge coming in took a hit and seemed simply to disappear. A little rescue boat set out from shore at once, to pick up the survivors. It seemed strange and curiously callous, then, to be watching and cheering this game in which men were dying."

Jones's F Company was immediately ordered to Henderson Field, built first by the Japanese and later much expanded by the 1st Marines. Along with other army units, F Company bivouacked on a hill overlooking the airfield while General Collins conferred with the various regimental commanders and with General A. M. Patch, who was commander-in-chief of XIV Corps. The corps's job was to prepare a campaign against the Japanese who occupied inland positions from which they could be dislodged only with the greatest difficulty.

The route leading up to these strongholds was steep and wearing. By eight o'clock in the morning, the sun was so hot that sweat poured off the men. The dense tropical forests through which they had to go were filled with animals and other wild life, including cockatoos and mynah birds, but underfoot the black mud was so heavy and viscous that it clung to the soldiers' boots and made walking nearly impossible. The humidity brought vicious flies and mosquitoes, and virtually all of the troops soon came down with malaria.

The men pressed on, hoping that higher ground would be better, but the wide treeless fields were filled with kunia grass, which grew to seven feet and was ridged like a saw so that it tore at the men as they tried to make their way through it. No roads led inland, and a track first had to be cut that would allow for the passage of jeeps with machine guns, mortars, and howitzers.

While these preparations were being made, the general staff of XIV Corps decided to attack the enemy in four columns. On military maps, the terrain was identified by numbered hills and promontories, but some were also given names, like Galloping Horse, Gifu and Sea Horse, for the way they looked in aerial photographs. American strategy was to drive the Japanese from the high land they occupied and force them northward to Cape Esperance, where they would have to embark on ships or surrender.

The battle began on January 10, 1943, with an attack on the heavily fortified position of Gifu. This proved to be one of the bloodiest engagements of the war, and the fanatical officer in command of the

Japanese sacrificed all of his men in a suicide attack against advancing units of the 35th Infantry Regiment. During this encounter, Jones's company, as part of the Second Battalion of the 27th Infantry Regiment, was held in reserve while the other two battalions moved toward high ground. Proceeding through difficult terrain in the face of Japanese mortars and machine guns, they captured much of Galloping Horse and on the second day consolidated their gains.

Jones worked both as infantryman and assistant company clerk. He ran messages, prepared lists, and handled all the clerical work that even in combat had to be maintained. Like the rest, he had to carry everything he needed, from his rifle and pack to his food and water canteen. Captain Blatt soon became notorious for exposing himself to danger, so assignment to the command post was no guarantee of safety. "I went where I was told to go," Jones later wrote, "and did what I was supposed to do, but no more. I was scared shitless just about all of the time."

The tactical objective of each day's encounter was to occupy land previously held by the enemy so as to proceed to the next stage of the battle. "High ground before nightfall" was General Collins' dictum. On the third day of the campaign, F Company, already ensconced on Hill 52, was given the task of attacking along an outcrop, later known as Sims Ridge, in the hope of reaching Hill 53, the objective of the battle. When the assault began, at six-thirty in the morning, Jones was part of it. After initial progress, the Americans ran into fierce opposition from enemy machine gun posts covering all approaches. Directly ahead lay a precipice the men found virtually impossible to climb, especially in the face of enemy fire.

At ten-thirty, with conditions far from promising, Jones was hit, "wounded in the head by a random mortar shell," as he later recalled. "I think I screamed, myself, when I was hit. I thought I could vaguely remember somebody yelling. I blacked out for several seconds, and had a dim impression of someone stumbling to his feet with his hands to his face. It wasn't me. Then I came to myself several yards down the slope, bleeding like a stuck pig and blood running all over my face. It must have been a dramatic scene. As soon as I found I wasn't dead or dying, I was pleased to get out of there as fast as I could."

Wiping the blood from his eyes, he stumbled up a hill that was being swept by sniper fire. Somehow he wasn't hit again as he made his way into the protection of a clump of trees. There he found a nineteen-year-old boy who was lying dead in a stretcher. He had been hit a second time and left by the stretcher bearers. He had been wounded so badly that blood filled the depression made by his hips in the stretcher. "And that has always stayed with me," Jones wrote. "It didn't seem a body could hold enough blood to do that. His hips were awash in it and it almost covered his belt and belt buckle. And somehow, although he was lying on his back, head uphill, blood had run or splashed from his head so that there were pools of it filling both his eye sockets. All the blood had thickened and almost dried, so he must have been there since early morning." Nothing could be done for him, but he looked so pathetic that Jones "wanted to cry for him. But I was gasping too hard for breath, and was too angry to cry for anybody. I don't even know what I was angry at. I certainly wasn't angry at the Japanese for sniping wounded, we expected that. I was just angry. And that was all. I went on up the hill and left him." Wounds in the head usually bleed excessively even when not dangerous, and fortunately the cut Jones had received, just at the hairline, did not prove serious. He was given morphine and taken down in a jeep to the divisional hospital, where he was admitted and given a sulfa powder dressing. He was later awarded the Purple Heart, the medal given to those wounded in action.

After ten days, Jones returned to his unit with a bandage around his head, covering one eye, and was assigned to the command post as company clerk. His job was to supervise the arrival of supplies, food, and ammunition for the men in the field and to assist the first sergeant. By this time, the campaign had moved rapidly, but the main reason for success was that the fifty thousand American soldiers involved greatly outnumbered the Japanese. When American naval and air corps planes noticed the large number of Japanese troopships arriving off Cape Esperance, they assumed they were bringing replacements. But in fact the Japanese were secretly evacuating troops. They had decided on this course even before the United States sent in XIV Corps in January.

The imbalance of power in no way diminished the violence of warfare. In taking Hills 88 and 89, the 27th Regiment had to pay dearly for their success. In another engagement, Captain Blatt received orders that he knew would cause the needless slaughter of many under his command. He therefore chose an alternate route that achieved the same results with less loss of life. Because he had disobeyed orders, however, he was relieved of his command.

Jones was lucky in surviving with a minor wound. And with the loss of his glasses, he discovered that he really didn't need them. But the experiences of this time fundamentally changed his life. After his return to duty from the hospital, he was sent with a group of other men, armed with shovels, to dig up the corpses of soldiers who had been left in temporary graves so that they could later be identified by their metal dog tags. "When we began to dig," Jones later wrote, "each time we opened a hole a little explosion of smell would burst up out of it, until finally the whole saddle where we were working was covered with it up to about knee deep. Above the knees it wasn't so bad, but when you had to bend down to search for the dogtag (we took turns doing this job) it was like diving down into another element, like water, or glue. We found about four bodies without dogtags that day." Jones asked the lieutenant what would happen to the unmarked corpses, and he was told, "They will remain anonymous." And the others? "Well, they will be recorded" was the laconic reply.

On another day, while on duty at the command post, Jones stepped into the jungle to defecate. Squatting down, with his trousers around his feet, he suddenly heard a high keening sound. Whirling around, he saw a Japanese soldier running at him with a bayoneted rifle. Jones got up as quickly as he could and the two men began a bloody and gruesome duel, which Jones later described in *The Thin Red Line*. Although the man was badly wounded, he refused to die, and only with the greatest difficulty did Jones finally succeed in killing him. Covered with blood, nauseated, filthy, and exhausted, Jones went through the man's pockets and found a wallet containing two snapshots of the soldier standing with his wife and child. He staggered back to the command post, told the captain what had happened, and said that he would never fight again.

Exposure to ghastly experiences gradually changed the values and attitudes of all the men. When a friend of Jones's lost a hand, the man wasn't so much horrified by the wound as angry. Gesturing toward the severed part, he cried out, "Get that hand out of here. I'm a farmer!" He knew that after the war he would never be able to take up his work again.

The unending strain of malaria, exhaustion, and fear imposed a terrible burden, so those who survived began to have a distaste for those who were dead or wounded. "They had been initiated into a strange, insane, twilight fraternity where explanation would be forever impossible. Everybody understood this. But there was nothing to be done about it." They were fearful of the dead; there was "a sort of in-stinctual dislike of touching them, as though what had happened to them has contaminated them and might contaminate the toucher." They treated the wounded as gently as possible, but they also looked at them with a "commingled distaste, guilt and irritation."

The emotional strain created by these experiences placed a terrible burden on the men, most of whom desperately wanted to escape the horror of their daily life. They were often sleepless, having had to spend the night in a dugout to survive enemy bombing while also keeping the rats at bay. Frequently, they were soaked to the skin by heavy tropical downpours. The powdered eggs and milk, the dehy-drated potatoes and preserved canned meat, did little to raise their spirits. Sometimes, the soldiers would toss a grenade into a river to get some fresh fish and even try to get some relief from a swim. But as often as not, their pleasure would be spoiled by finding the bloated corpse of a dead Japanese caught in a snag by the river's edge.

To survive the constant pressure of such horrors, the men often drank themselves into oblivion, especially during lulls between en-gagements. The only source of Scotch was the corps of Seabees build-ing the airfields; they would sometimes sell a quart flown in from Australia or New Zealand for $50 or exchange it for Japanese swords or pistols. More commonly, the men made their own booze. One fa-vorite was called Pineapple Swipe. They would steal a five-gallon can of peaches or pineapple from a food supply depot, add sugar or Coca-Cola or lemon extract, and put the mixture in the sun to fer-ment. A piece of cheesecloth kept the bugs out. "It was the most godawful stuff to drink," Jones recalled, "sickly sweet and smelling very raunchy, but if you could get enough of it down and keep it down, it carried a wonderful wallop. The worst, most terribly awful bar-none hangover I ever had in my life before or after, I got from one of these late night 'swipe' parties where I passed out, to wake up lying in the mud in full tropical sunlight in the coconut groves not far from our tents." Mennen's aftershave lotion was also used for drinks; after drinking it one night, some friends of Jones woke up the next morning to discover that it had eroded the aluminum cups they had drunk it from. Even so, it seemed preferable to facing the realities of war while sober.

Although Jones was not incapacitated by his head wound, he suf-fered from malaria, jaundice, and dengue, which the men called dingy fever. This tropical disease causes fever, a rash, and swollen joints. Jones also had difficulty in walking long distances. His injury from playing football at Schofield Barracks worsened, and he frequently dislocated his ankle and fell to the ground. It would return to its normal position, but he would go white with pain. Jones was aware of the difference between a combat wound and an injury so seemingly trivial as a sprained ankle; he therefore wore an elastic bandage and tried to strengthen the ankle by exercise. Then one day he fell in the presence of the first sergeant, who told him to report his injury to the doctor. "If it's as bad as what I just saw," the sergeant said, "it would get you out of here. If it's as bad as what I saw, you got no business in the infantry." Jones did not want to be accused of malingering or cowardice, so he consulted his buddies, who all urged that he go to the hospital. "What about the company?" Jones asked. "Are you kidding?" one sergeant replied. "I'd be out of here like a shot."

Realizing that his presence would make no appreciable difference to the war effort, especially since the Guadalcanal campaign was now successfully completed, Jones reported on March 15, 1943, to the divisional hospital for treatment of his ankle and for skin infection. The surgeon told him he should not be in the infantry. "He looked at me and grinned," Jones later recalled. "I grinned back. If he could only have known how I was hanging on his every word and expression. But perhaps he did."

His admission to the hospital broke the psychological tension Jones had been living under during the two months since he had received his head wound. He had survived for a while by living "in the present from one day to the next without hoping for anything." But gradually he became oppressed by the fear of being killed. He was used to feeling sorry for the fate of soldiers in general, but now he felt personally sad. "I probably won't get to write about people or anything else," he told his brother, "and so it hurts like hell, this new sadness; that's why I want to avoid it. It's hard to talk about that; it's too personal for anybody who doesn't know what I'm like inside to understand. Maybe that's why I'm telling you; I have no real friends here — or anywhere, for that matter, except you and the Eng. profs at the University."

When Jones's skin infection subsided, he was shipped to Efate, one of a small group of islands in the New Hebrides, a thousand miles southeast of Guadalcanal. After it was liberated from the Japanese, Efate had become the site of Naval Base Hospital Number 3 for wounded American servicemen. The surgeon who operated on Jones's ankle performed what is called an open reduction and fixation, in which silver wires are used to hold the bones in place. The operation took nearly three hours, and during the last twenty minutes, when the anaesthetic wore off, Jones pushed his face "into the belly of the nurse who stood on my left and kept running her fingers thru my hair and wiping the sweat off me." Since the operation required a lengthy convalescence, Jones was sent on another hospital ship to New Zealand, where, on April 27, he was admitted to the 39th General Hospital in Auckland. There he met a number of men from his regiment and noted in his diary that "everybody that can is getting out." Even with people he didn't know well there was now "an unspoken feeling of comradeship that one feels between strangers who are bums that meet, a feeling that comes from being kicked around by the same boot. We have the same feeling now that we had under fire."

Jones remained in New Zealand for only about ten days, but he was mobile enough to go into Auckland on a pass with some friends to spend a few hours in the local pubs and to meet the girls, who liked the Americans because they had more money to spend on them than the New Zealanders had. Rivalry between different groups of soldiers was common and helped cause the Battle of Queen Street, a brawl that broke out between a newly arrived regiment of United States Marines, whose youth and cockiness annoyed the wounded and battle-weary veterans of Guadalcanal. The new troops strutted through the streets in freshly tailored uniforms, whereas the veterans had to hobble along in the baggy clothes that were issued by the hospital. The girls were naturally attracted to the new marines, some of whom began to wear Purple Heart ribbons to which they were not entitled. This was too much for the veterans, and Queen Street was soon enveloped by fighting American servicemen. With his bandaged foot, Jones could do little but stand in a recessed doorway. "When anybody wearing ribbons or a well-cut uniform stuck his head in, I would use one of my crutches like a bayoneted rifle, and jab him with the rubber foot or buttstroke him with the handle." The MPs were called in to quell the riot, as were some British soldiers from the docks, but it took a battalion of Maori troops with fixed bayonets to suppress the violence. Thinking back on this senseless episode, Jones commented, "The truth is I think we were very nearly a little crazy. We didn't give a shit about anything during that time."

In early May, less than three weeks after arriving in New Zealand, Jones shipped out on a white hospital ship, the former liner *Matsonia*.

It was painted on both sides with a large red cross and was bound for San Francisco. Although it was a relief to escape from the heat, disease, and danger of the Pacific, the horrors of war were everywhere present. Jones shared a cabin with a young marine who was paralyzed from the waist down. "He can't hold his water or control the muscles of his rectum," Jones noted in his journal. "They were cleaning him off when I was there. They had a rubber ring under his hips to catch the feces. They had a tube taped to his prick that runs to a duct in the floor. They turned him on his side to clean him and the shit was soft and mushy and stuck to the cheeks of his ass. Every time they moved him he would moan in a whiney voice that reminded me of a child."

Jones was willing to look at and record what most writers would ignore. With his own comparatively light injury, he was able to move about the ship and observe the wounded men. He soon understood that most written accounts of heroic behavior by wounded soldiers were false, invented to please a public that does not want to know the truth but prefers to think of soldiers as "suffering immense pain stoically and silently." Jones discovered there was nothing at all heroic about the wounded marines. In general, he found that the wounded reacted to their condition with bitterness and self-concern. He heard one wounded man, who had lost both legs and one arm, ask the doctor, "Why in hell don't you just kill me?" Another had long since lost interest in what others thought of him, especially if they had never been wounded. "If groaning or crying makes him feel better, he does it," Jones noted.

On May 19, 1943, the white hospital ship passed under the great span of the Golden Gate Bridge. Like most of those who could move about, Jones was on deck for the occasion. "I stood on the upper deck on my crutches and watched grizzled and tough old sergeants and petty officers break down and cry. I had been away three and a half years."

On arrival, Jones was taken to Letterman General Hospital in the Presidio of San Francisco, overlooking the bay. There the men were immediately confined to their wards, and even those who could move about were denied passes to go into town. Jones managed to telephone his brother to tell him of his safe arrival, but at the hospital he felt more like a prisoner than a returning hero. Finally, after a confrontation with the authorities, Jones and the other mobile patients were allowed to go into the city. But again he was frustrated. If there were any whorehouses, he didn't know where to find them, and without any friends in San Francisco, he could hardly pick up a girl in one night. In the end, he just got drunk. On another day, he went on a Red Cross tour. "Everywhere you looked you saw girls, unescorted," Jones noted, but he didn't know any of them and was too shy to approach them. After a few days, he was put on a train to be shipped across country. In accordance with an army policy that placed veterans in hospitals as near as possible to their relatives, he was assigned to Kennedy General Hospital in Memphis, Tennessee.

Three quarters of an hour's bus ride from the center of the city, the hospital was a cluster of single-story barracks made of red bricks and white trim. They were laid out informally in a park filled with shady trees and walkways. Jones was assigned to Ward 4-A, where the doctors examined his ankle. On June 3, his cast was removed, and the next day X-rays were taken. They showed no evidence of fracture or dislocation, although the bones had become somewhat porous. Jones was given physical therapy and by June 17 was able to get about with a cane. Three weeks later, he no longer required the cane, but because he complained about continued pain and weakness in the ankle, he was sent to a convalescent barracks for an additional month.

Jones's unit was one of the first group of wounded veterans to reach the hospital, so he expected that they would be treated well, but during the three months of his stay at Kennedy, he encountered a full range of horrors. Generally, soldiers with similar wounds were housed in the same ward because they could deal better with their fate together than if they were scattered about. The blind, for example, could laugh or cry or curse their common condition, and it eased their misery to be together where they could help one another. On the way to the mess, they would line up in the hall and, taking hold of the shirttail of the man in front of them, would be led in a group along the corridors to their meals.

Able to move about more than others, Jones was conscious of the grim hospital atmosphere. He noted that the men "did not laugh and smile about their wounds as they always seemed to in *Yank* and the civilian magazines." Two wards were full of "foot and lower-leg amputations from frozen feet in the invasion of Attu in the Aleutians, where some forgetful planner had sent the troops in in leather boots." The survivors were clannish and withdrawn, absorbed by their own dreadful condition. They kept to themselves in a grim brotherhood of marked men. Jones noted that "almost without exception, they were uncheerful about their wounds."

Many were permanently disfigured. Facial burns pulled the skin back taut from the teeth and flattened noses. Some of the wounded failed to respond to treatment and died. Others, convalescing, would be sent to their families, only to return, unable to stand the pitying stares and weeping their presence provoked at home. For yet others, the process of rehabilitation was maddeningly slow, and no amount of comfort from a nurse or chaplain made an impression. In military hospitals, people face reality as nowhere else, and it often drove men mad, creating states of deep depression or manic hilarity.

The prevailing horror made those who survived wonder how they had escaped. What meaning had life when some were terribly maimed and others were not? What chance led a bullet to one man and not another? These questions drove many to despair and nihilism.

For some, there was no life other than the hospital, but those on the mend like Jones could get passes and take the bus to town. The first group of wounded to reach Memphis, they were treated as heroes when they came into the center. Many of them had received back pay for the long periods they served overseas, and with this money, often amounting to thousands of dollars, they took rooms at the Peabody Hotel, the Gayoso, or at the Claridge next door. Of these, the Peabody was the most popular, with its high Turkish lobby and water fountain where ducks paddled about. There were overstuffed chairs and brass reading lamps, and at one end of the lobby was an elegant dining room presided over by Alonzo, the head waiter, who was famous for never forgetting names. At the other end was the Creel Room, where beer was served. Here the soldiers would meet young women, later perhaps taking them to the night club on the hotel roof, where there was open-air dancing. The anonymity of the army created a democratic feeling, and the girls, who often had men overseas and were lonely, were unusually spontaneous and open. "It was a wild time then," Jones later recalled. "I had a two-room suite at the Peabody six weeks straight and loaned the key to anybody who wanted it when I couldn't get into town." There Jones would go with one of the women he had met in the lounge. Days and nights at the Peabody became an extended house party, for neither the men nor the women had made love for a long time. The girls were not prostitutes; many of them worked in defense industries while their men were in the army. The return of the wounded veterans provided a wonderful release, but the hilarity was mixed with a sadness that came from seeing how physically and psychologically damaged many of the men were. Jones had hoped that at last he would get the reward he felt he deserved for his long time away from home and, more important, the romantic connection he yearned for. But he soon became aware of the false note that underlay these encounters. "Inside I was bored with the whole mess: people trying to have a good time and failing. I've found the fun comes from inside." Soon his sexual enthusiasm waned, and of one of the girls he wrote, "I can't get pleasure from laying her unless I'm drunk."

One offshoot of the lovemaking was violence, much of it encouraged by hard drinking. One night in a Memphis bar, Jones picked a fight with a man and knocked him down with one punch. It pleased him so much, watching the man coil around himself and slowly slip to the floor, that he began to pick more fights, enjoying the danger and irresponsibility of obeying an impulse after more than three years of army discipline. It was a throwback to the violence of Robinson, only the immediate causes of his anger and frustration were different. Returning to the civilian world, he was angry with the profiteers and all those who ignored the sacrifices of the wounded veterans; hating the army, he also knew what the army had done to save America.

Personally, he was glad he was not badly wounded, like so many of his comrades at Kennedy General, but he also felt pangs of guilt for having escaped, especially because he had done so through an accident rather than a wound. The comradeship he had felt with other soldiers in battle, which had come from shared experience, was now beginning to dissipate with the return to America, and he was unable to find a woman he could really love and who would give more meaning to his life. Because he was still in the army, with an uncertain future before him, he could not settle down to write. His life was in knots, and he was driven by contrary impulses. He therefore struck out at whatever target was handy, rebelling vehemently against everything that had combined to bring him so much unhappiness.

Although he was now involved in the civilian world, he was still living in the nightmare world of the South Pacific. The contrast between the two was especially vivid in August, when he was granted a three-week furlough and went to Miami Beach to visit Jeff, who was working there for the Red Cross. After they met, they went straight to a bar, and Jones began to drink hard. "He was never really drunk,"

Jeff recalled, "but he was never exactly what you would call sober either." The two brothers would meet at the end of the day at the Spanish Village Bar on Washington Street and would drink ale, talk, and play the slot machine. It was a cozy quiet place and they got along well with the owner. One night, another customer, mistaking the banter, suggested that Jones leave the place. "Were you talking to me?" Jones asked. The man got down from his stool, but before he could make another move, Jones hit him, and he went down without a sound. Jeff was startled and asked why Jones was looking for trouble. "Why that's not trouble," Jones answered. "That's fun. And besides he didn't have any business sticking his nose into what I say."

A few days later, while walking down Collins Avenue, Jones was startled by the sound of someone raising a venetian blind, which made a *rat-tat-tat* sound. Jones dropped to the ground and rolled hard against a fence for protection. Looking up at his brother, he realized what had happened and said, "What the hell are you gawking at?" When he calmed down, he told Jeff about a Japanese machine gun. "That damned thing sounded more like a Nambu-gun than a Nambu-gun," he said.

At night, he would have terrible dreams, and Jeff and his wife, Sally, would hear him moaning and tossing in his bed. During one nightmare he jumped out of bed and ran into a doorjamb. When Jeff and Sally reached his room, they found him bleeding heavily from a cut over his eye. As they bandaged him, he told them about the dream. He was trapped in the middle of a bombing raid. He could see the grenades coming at him and had tried to run away.

Such dreams also made him conscious of what he was missing by no longer being with his old unit. During the time of his furlough, the 25th Division was engaged in a fierce battle to liberate Bougainville. Jones followed the struggle in the daily newspaper reports from the front. Earlier, he had heard that at one point the men in his own company had been so frightened that they couldn't stand the tension and something snapped. "They went kill crazy. They bayoneted sick and wounded Japs. They shot them when they came out naked. They spit in the faces of dying Japs."

Back safely in the United States, Jones felt the inadequacy of his own injury, and he told people that he had been wounded in the leg. He later admitted to Jeff that he was "glossing over" the facts in order to present a romantic picture of himself.

Apart from these moments of bravado, Jones spent time at the hospital trying to write. He showed some of the girls he knew the stories and sketches he had written. One of them told him he needed to learn the fundamentals of his craft, "meaning vocab, grammar, etc." They talked about the postwar world of America, and of how returning veterans felt lost when they returned to civilian life. Jones believed that conventions of social behavior were "belied by falseness underneath."

One of the stories he wrote at the time deals with a hospital nurse who attracted him. It is about a young soldier, David Michael Robertson, who is sent to the Weinerbaum General Hospital in Leripidis, Tennessee. He meets a Red Cross volunteer, but she is disconcerted by his intensity and says, "I pity the woman who ever falls in love with you." In a later version, the protagonist is revealed as a writer who aches "for someone to whom he might show the new poems and stories he has created, someone who would read them and like them and would tell him that he had talent, assure him that someday he would be a writer." But he is too shy to show her his work and pretends to be a roughneck, interested only in drink or women. "When he saw a person with whom he could have talked, he withdrew into a shell of expressionless eyes, wry mouth and eyebrow raised in sarcastic irony — because he wanted the opposite so badly."

The tortured syntax seems intended to reproduce the complexity of feelings Jones wished to express, especially in his poems about women:

Love Without Love

I wandered down a thousand weirdly lighted streets
I see a million women
I stop each one and speak
I smile a tremulous fearful smile

My Epitaph

Posterity shall ne'er survey
An emptier grave than this.
Here lie the bones
Of James R. Jones
Stop, traveler, and piss.

Another poem, called "Bloody Claws," is set in a night club in which a soldier, sitting at the bar, has a vision of a black panther clutching a white beast and ripping its back with its claws. To the music of the juke box, the soldier's eyes clear, and he see that what he thought was blood is just the nail polish and lipstick of a whore, and the white animal is a sailor.

Many of the poems are nightmarish and violent, as these lines suggest:

> I am in a hospital and it is the middle of the night
> I cannot sleep
>
> . . .
>
> My brain is slavering and drooling spittle
> Like a great hound straining at its leash
> My brain has broken loose and left me
>
> . . .
>
> Crumbling holes half-filled with stagnant rain
> A twisted bit of steel that might have been a helmet
>
> . . .
>
> I would run: my legs laugh in my face
> For across the crest they come
> And the mad, laughing gods with sperm-smeared lips
> Looked down and chortled with their tongueless mouths
> As they filled their cups with killers blood

At the end of August, Jones was examined again and released from Kennedy General as fit for duty. Hoping to be discharged from the army altogether, he was so cast down by this news that he went on a drunk. He also knew that his ankle was weak, and he therefore appealed for another examination and was recommended for noncombat service. When his orders came, however, in November of 1943, he found that he was to go to Camp Campbell in Kentucky, to be assigned to Company K of the 101st Infantry Regiment, part of the 26th Division.

Jones was so embittered that instead of going directly to Kentucky, he decided to go absent without leave to visit Robinson, and traveled there by overnight bus. Exactly four years had passed since he had left, and returning now, with his parents dead and no home of his own, he was upset and once more turned to alcohol. Through his Aunt Sadie, he nevertheless managed to meet an older woman, Lowney Handy, who was eventually to change his life. When he first swaggered into her house, wearing dark glasses and acting tough, she showed him her books and he immediately sat down on the floor and started to read. "I just stood there and looked at him," Lowney later recalled. "The chip on his shoulder was gone. The poor guy. The poor lost guy."

Jones was not court-martialed on reaching Camp Campbell, because a sympathetic warrant officer adjusted his orders, but he was depressed by having to leave Lowney and the civilian world. "I am afraid the Army is killing what artist there is in me," he wrote in his notebook. "That's good for now but what about later? Today have already begun to feel old monotony and boredom, old exasperation at total inefficiency. But have more acceptant attitude toward it. That worries me: I want to like the army and understand — but never to be satisfied with it."

Camp Campbell occupies a stretch of land that straddles the border between the western parts of Kentucky and Tennessee. The countryside is hilly, with a few scattered villages, and the closest town is Clarksburg, Kentucky. Soon after he arrived, Jones had to take part in month-long maneuvers, preparatory to going overseas again, but his ankle was never right and plagued him with pain. Angered at not having his disability recognized and sure he would be killed when his new unit was sent to Europe, Jones went AWOL again on a three-day drunk over Thanksgiving. When he returned, he was reduced to private. After the inquiry into his behavior, he was released from the infantry and transferred, just before Christmas, to the 842nd Quarter Master Gas and Supply Company, which was also stationed at Camp Campbell.

At the time he joined it, this company had no more than a cadre of seven men who were chosen to set it up. Its function was to supply gasoline for bombers and fighters in the forthcoming invasion of France. Most of the new men assigned to it were misfits or recent draftees, and Jones was appointed company clerk. As one of the few veterans in the group, Jones made a point of wearing his battle ribbons and Purple Heart. Since their work was mainly learning how to handle five-gallon drums of gasoline, the men were bored and discontented and felt they were living in the middle of nowhere. On Saturdays, Jones and a buddy, Hugh Milanese, would go to the nearby village of McDougal, where they would find a bar and get drunk.

On March 1, 1944, Jones was promoted to the rank of sergeant. He

was soon irritated, however, by the way in which the army treated a
Jewish officer he liked and replaced him with a martinet who seemed
to enjoy giving Jones humiliating orders. Again he went AWOL without consequence, but in May he decided he had had enough. He got
drunk on beer at the PX and then packed his clothes. "I caught the
bus at midnight," he later wrote, "aware I was leaving for good
though I didn't know where or how or what would come of it, and
didnt much care, and left the Post, and looked back from the bus and
watched the lights fade away. At the risk of sounding sentimental, I
will say I loved the post I was leaving, all of it. I also hated it."

Jones had been working hard on a novel about returning veterans
that was to be called *They Shall Inherit the Laughter*. All during the
day, "ideas, sentences, whole paragraphs" would pop into his head,
but since he was working as company clerk, he had no opportunity to
jot them down. He would therefore write at night, even though the
atmosphere wasn't conducive to good work. "I'd write page after
page and tear it up and throw it away," he told his brother. Finally,
when he was AWOL, he could work as he liked. Staying with a friend
in Indianapolis, he spent his time working and produced about
twenty thousand words. He was nervous about being caught and getting his friend into trouble for harboring him. Eventually, Lowney
Handy received an inquiry from his commanding officer. She phoned
around, and when she discovered where he was, she went to Indianapolis and talked him into going back.

When he returned to Camp Campbell, he was charged with being
absent for two weeks and was placed in the stockade. His stay there
was brief, but he had glimpses of the sort of violence he later described in *From Here to Eternity*. The worst outrage he witnessed was
seeing a man have his ears torn from his head.

He was transferred to the prison ward of the station hospital at
Camp Campbell, where he was interviewed by a psychiatrist. "I told
them everything I could," Jones wrote his brother, "that I am genius
(altho they probably won't believe that); that if they attempt to send
me overseas again, I'll commit suicide; that if I don't get out of the
army I'll either go mad or turn into a criminal — which is just next
door to a writer anyway; that all I want to do is write, and that nobody and no thing means anything to me except writing." He said
that he hoped he could live with his brother and that he thought he
deserved being discharged. "If I hadn't been overseas, if I hadn't done
all a man could be expected to do, it might be different. If my ankle

were a wound instead of an operation as it is, I would have requested
a discharge. More than once I've seriously considered sticking my leg
under a train here. It'd be worth the loss of a foot to get out so I could
have some peace and write. I just can't take it any more."

On June 1, Jones was given a full physical examination and sent to
the neuropsychiatric ward for observation. Captain Howard E. Roberts of the Medical Corps kept notes of his conversation with Jones:
"Feels he has done his share and wants out to write because of intense
desire to express himself. Says if he gets ordered overseas again he will
commit suicide but the world will be the loser by missing his writing.
Patient feels depressed mostly but has brief spells of elation. Sometimes feels he stands outside of his body and sees himself as an actor in
a play. He has disturbed dreams and is bothered by memories of combat, blood, stench of dead and hardships. Feels it was valuable to him
tho as background for his writing."

Jones's ailment had first been described generally as an "acute depression," but after observing his "mood swings, compulsive behavior
and some schizoid characteristics," Dr. Roberts modified the diagnosis as "psychoneurosis, mixed anxiety and compulsive types with
schizoid trends." The doctor noted that Jones talked in his sleep and
stammered when he was angry. On June 2, Roberts and Jones had another conversation, and Jones told the doctor about a dream he had
had in which he was with a couple of officers of a type he didn't like.
They were condescending and made enlisted men feel small and infe-
rior. Jones felt "trapped and depressed" being with these officers, as if
he were under arrest.

In the ward, Jones was withdrawn at first and would not mix with
the other patients, but by the end of the week he had become cooperative. An orthopedic surgeon examined his ankle and noted in his report that Jones seemed to be exaggerating his complaint. As the days
went by, Jones's disposition improved and he spent much of his time
reading. One Sunday, however, he became agitated about a religious
service that was held in the ward, and the nurse made note of his
anger. On June 21, he was judged well enough to be transferred to an
open ward.

Meanwhile, outside the hospital, the authorities continued to investigate Jones's case. His commanding officer, Captain Eugene
Mailloux, wrote to his brother, who later agreed to be interviewed by
a social worker employed by the army in Miami. She concluded that
Jones was a person of high principle and honor who was nevertheless

such an individualist that he would never fit into the army. Lowney Handy was also active on his behalf. She had visited him at Camp Campbell, and through political connections with the Democratic Party in Illinois, she undoubtedly reported her concerns to her congressman. Jones's superior officers were asked their opinion of his future prospects as a soldier, and they reported that they were not good. On June 19, assessing the accumulation of such consistent evidence, the provost marshal's office decided to drop charges against Jones for absenteeism. Instead, he was ordered to be given a certificate of disability for discharge. This document stated that because his psychoneurosis did not exist before his enlistment and was no fault of his own, he should be discharged "for disability in line of duty and not due to his own misconduct." Jones's case was finally disposed of on July 6, 1944, when he was issued an honorable discharge from the army.

Lowney Handy later wrote of Jones that she had "managed to get him out of the Army" in the face of his commanding officer's desire to make an example of him by sending him overseas. Perhaps her influence was important, for many years later Jones alluded to his own insignificance at the time. "I was unknown, and being unknown you get the shortest possible shrift."

⋙ TWO ⋘

4

THE SHINING
DREAM

"OF COURSE, he knew the town when the bus slowed up coming into it. A man's home town, the one where he was born and raised, was always special. It was as if secretly all those years your senses themselves had banded together on their own and memorized everything about it so thoroughly that they remembered them even if you didnt. Even with the things you did remember, your senses kept remembering them first a split second sooner without asking permission and startling you. And it didnt matter whether you loved the thing or hated it. He shifted a little in his seat, suddenly selfconscious of the person, a man, beside him. Your senses didnt feel. They just remembered. He looked out again."

These opening lines from *Some Came Running*, Jones's second published novel, written with experimental spelling, were based on his return to Robinson for the first time when, in November 1943, he went AWOL instead of going directly to Camp Campbell. On that trip, he had taken his bag and stepped out of the bus into the courthouse square. Near the corner was Si Seligman's newspaper agency, where he used to work. His only relative in town was Uncle Charlie, who now lived in Jones's grandfather's house with his wife, Sadie, so Jones picked up his bag and walked down Main Street toward the big Southern-style mansion. Suddenly, he couldn't go in; he kept walking down the street until he saw his high school classmate Annis Skaggs coming toward him. They looked at each other from a distance without saying anything. When they met, Annis told him to go to his uncle's house and promised to have dinner with him that evening.

Jones had hesitated to stay with his uncle because he resented his living in splendor in George Jones's house while Jones and his sister and brother received little or nothing of what remained of their grandfather's inheritance. Charles Jones, a lawyer in Robinson, was in charge of distributing the assets, and his suddenly improved standard of living made members of the family wonder whether he had taken advantage of his position. Despite his reluctance, Jones nevertheless stayed with his Uncle Charlie and Aunt Sadie and spent his first afternoon at home visiting his childhood companions. He noted in his diary that he was greeted as "a hero returned from the wars." That evening, he took Annis to a football game at the high school and realized that the last time he had seen the players, they were little children.

He had been drinking much of the day. After the game he took Annis home, and they sat outside in the car until six o'clock in the morning because he didn't want to leave her and go back to his uncle's house. There had already been a good deal of talk about what he was going to do after the war. Uncle Charlie was skeptical about his literary ambitions and thought he should get a job. The next day was his twenty-second birthday, so his uncle gave him a party at the Elks Club. There he became very drunk; he smashed glasses and broke a mirror. Before leaving, he made a speech in which he denounced the "sons of bitches" who were present in the room and promised to write a book in which he would expose their "conniving souls and sneaky love affairs."

Annis took him away from the Elks and drove him around to cool off. As they rode along the highway, Jones leaned his head on the window frame for fresh air. When they returned to his uncle's house, Annis woke Uncle Charlie to help take Jones up to bed, but suddenly Jones was completely sober. Annis had the feeling that Jones had put on a drunken act just to annoy his uncle and shock the people at the Elks.

The next day he was still drinking, and when in the evening he went to a local restaurant named the Mission Tea Room, he passed out. The night policeman took him to his uncle's mansion on Main Street, but the next morning he woke up in jail. When he later found out that his uncle had refused to take him into the house and had actually arranged to have him jailed, he was astounded. He knew about the hypocrisy of small towns; in the diary he kept of his trip, he noted that "everybody lies about his life." But his uncle's action outraged him, and Jones denounced him furiously for "trying to break me thru fear and humiliation."

Shortly afterward, he learned of another sickening betrayal by his

Uncle Charlie. Jones had tried to get a transfer from Camp Campbell to George Field in Vincennes, Illinois, so as to be closer to his family and to Lowney Handy. As company clerk, he saw much of the correspondence that came into the office, and one day he saw a letter that Charles Jones had written to the commanding officer, discouraging this transfer. Appalled that his uncle would go behind his back to harm him, Jones wrote him a letter in which he told him to "disregard the fact that I am a Jones and your nephew." He added that when he came to Robinson, he would "not stop in to see you nor will I stay in your house. Just forget that I am a part of the Jones clan; just teach yourself that you have no nephew named Jim."

After his discharge from the army, in the summer of 1944, Jones decided to make a pilgrimage to Asheville, North Carolina, before returning to Robinson. He wanted to see the house where Thomas Wolfe was born and which was the setting of *Look Homeward, Angel* and the other autobiographical novels that had so inspired Jones in Hawaii. He felt a kinship with Wolfe both in subject matter and in literary style, and he needed the strength of his example before facing the difficult task of returning to Robinson.

What he needed most was quiet and support, and he therefore went straight to Lowney's house. He had first met her when Aunt Sadie had introduced them in the hope that Lowney could make him see how unrealistic his literary ambitions were. Instead, after reading some of his work, she was forthright enough to tell him that she was jealous that anyone so young as Jones "could write so magnificently."

At that time, Lowney was forty, seventeen years older than Jones. Born in Marshall, a town thirty miles north of Robinson, she was the eldest of nine children. Her father, an active Democrat, was sheriff of Marshall and later its chief of police. As a child, Lowney hung around the jail, where she showed concern for the welfare of the prisoners. She was vivacious and liberated, in many ways ahead of her time, interested in feminism and Zen Buddhism. She had a good figure, wore her hair in braids, and was frank and outspoken. She also had a lively sense of humor; as one of her friends said, "She could make a monkey laugh." She liked young people, and during the war she would meet servicemen when they returned to town on leave, and give them food, lodging, and money, and sometimes even sleep with them.

Lowney's independence earned her a bad reputation in the small town where she lived, partly because she was indiscreet. Most of her eccentricities stemmed from the nature of her marriage to Harry Handy. The Turner family, to which Lowney belonged, and the Handys were among the leading citizens of Marshall, and the children had grown up and played games together. Lowney was aware of Harry Handy's abilities and believed that through a marriage to him she would maintain her social position. His father was a state representative, and Harry was bright and personable. Trained as an engineer, he was employed by the Ohio Oil Company and soon rose to the top as manager of the large refinery in Robinson.

The marriage seemed ideal, but it was soon blighted by an episode that affected Lowney's behavior and colored her attitude toward society in general. Not long after her marriage, Lowney contracted gonorrhea from her husband. It infected her fallopian tubes, and the operation she underwent made it impossible for her to have children. The relationship between the two was never the same after that, and for most of his adult life Harry was an alcoholic. Jones later used their story as the basis for the marriage of Karen and Dana Holmes in *From Here to Eternity*. Lowney's hysterectomy made her suspicious of sex from then on and opposed in principle to marriage. She liked men but was reluctant to have much to do with them sexually, except as an act of charity. Nevertheless, her friendships with young people gave her the reputation of being promiscuous.

When Jones returned to Robinson in August of 1944, Lowney immediately installed him in the upstairs bedroom of the Handys' house. A white Cape Cod house, it was located across the tracks at 202 Mulberry Street, in a quiet, tree-shaded, middle-class section of Robinson. Since it was summer, Jones and Lowney spent a good deal of time outside, lying on the grass on the front lawn behind the white picket fence. They enjoyed sunbathing, and both wore shorts, which people rarely did at the time, so inevitably there was gossip. Lowney didn't mind: she loved having young people to her house and would invite eight or ten in at night to talk about art and literature. She was enthusiastic and liked to stir up the young. Anyone with talent she encouraged to write and already had two other protégés, Willard Lindsay and Don Sackrider.

Although Lowney and Harry Handy were later to "adopt" Jones and consider themselves his foster parents, Jones and Lowney had a close relationship from the start. It began two days after they met in 1943, and Jones wrote in his diary for November 8 that he "spent all day in bed with Lowney," adding that because she admired his writing, "she subjected herself to me; she made herself my disciple in everything from writing to love." As for Harry, Jones noted that he was "a wonderful guy: he knew Lowney and I made love all day but he didn't mind — rather he understood — and was glad." He even covered up for the lovers so that Aunt Sadie wouldn't know what was going on.

Jones's relationship with Lowney did not remain primarily sexual, however, because she was mainly interested in trying to develop his talent. Her support raised his spirits enormously. "Lowney is an artist," he told his brother, "not in the hackneyed sense — perhaps it would be better to call her a screwball, in the same sense I am. She loves Tom Wolfe, hates the falseness of our doctrine of 'civilization' as much as I do, wants to write, has written quite a bit but it isn't great stuff and she knows that." She told him that perhaps her destiny was "to furnish a haven" for him, and certainly her presence inspired him. "I am a natural: egotistical, brilliant, comically optimistic of my talent, a genius really, more or less. I am at ease, in my element."

Jones had brought with him the sketches he had been working on in the army, including the manuscript of the novel he had started in Indianapolis. He also sent for the material that was left in Carl Stroven's hands in Hawaii. With Lowney's encouragement, he devoted the rest of the year to finishing this novel. Yet despite his optimism, he knew that he needed more education; he had to read more and he needed instruction in writing. He had a disability pension from the army, but $46 a month was not enough to live on. He was eligible for a Vocational Rehabilitation Award, however, as long as he was a student. Accordingly, he decided to go to New York, the center of the literary world in the United States, and to apply for admission to New York University, where Thomas Wolfe had once taught, and to Columbia, for the spring term starting in February 1945.

Admitted to New York University, he left Robinson with an introduction from a local friend to Ruth and Maxwell Aley, who were prominent literary agents in New York. Jones sent some of his stories on ahead, and when he reached the city, he went straight to the Aleys' house. He was carrying a large suitcase and, in his store-bought suit, he looked every inch the country bumpkin. The Aleys took him in for a week while he registered at NYU and looked for a place to live.

Maxwell Aley was extremely interested in Jones's completed novel, *They Shall Inherit the Laughter*, which he had brought with him, but he knew that it wasn't publishable and urged extensive revisions. Having received much praise from Lowney, Jones was furious at the suggestion and decided to take the manuscript to Maxwell Perkins at Charles Scribner's Sons. Aley had already spoken of Perkins as an editor famous throughout the literary world for his skill with such novelists as Thomas Wolfe, Ernest Hemingway, and F. Scott Fitzgerald, and Jones wanted to work with him.

On his own, he therefore went to Scribner's at 597 Fifth Avenue and took the elevator to the editorial offices on the fifth floor. His manuscript was in a typewriter-paper box and was tied with string. When he asked for Perkins, the receptionist told him that Perkins was not in the office but that he could leave the manuscript with her. "No," answered Jones, "if I can't see Perkins then I won't leave it." The receptionist left the room and came back to say that Perkins had just returned to his office through the back door and would see Jones. They talked together for about an hour, and Jones told him of his war experiences and hopes as a writer. He left the manuscript. Only years later did he learn that there was no back door to Perkins' office.

Jones hoped to take only fiction-writing courses at NYU, but the person supervising his scholarship told him that would be impossible under the terms of his vocational grant, since writing was not a lucrative profession. He therefore signed up as a journalism student in the Washington Square College of Arts and Science and was entered as a beginning freshman studying for a B.A. He had a busy and demanding schedule; most of his classes met four times a week. He had French, history, and mathematics in the mornings; after lunch, he had English and philosophy. He was originally enrolled in a freshman composition course, but was moved to an advanced course by Frank McClosky, an associate dean of the college and the author of *How to Write Clearly and Effectively.* There Jones was able to write what he wanted and read such books as Thomas Uzzell's *The Techniques of the Novel,* which had been recommended to him by Lowney.

By the time the term began in February, Jones found rooms at 25 West Eighty-fourth Street in a five-story brownstone walk-up, not far from Central Park. Lowney came to visit but could not stay long. At NYU, Jones seems to have been treated with some deference, because word of his precocious talent had been spread by Maxwell Aley. He was a striking figure, with his Western boots and open shirt and his newly grown pencil-line mustache. He soon met another student, Arthur Pearlroth, who also had literary ambitions.

After class, they would often lead a group of students, including a couple of girls, to a bar on University Place. Jones and Pearlroth did most of the talking, joking and quoting writers to each other. Most of the others were younger than Jones, and they would listen, impressed by the intense look and set jaw of this veteran in tweeds.

In part, their talk was designed to impress the girls, and Jones and Pearlroth would take a couple of them for a steak at Nick's, hoping to lure them afterward to Pearlroth's nearby apartment. Jones was quite frank in admitting that being a writer made it easier for him to get a girl. He made no lasting friendships at NYU, however, because he was consumed by his own writing and was occasionally visited by Lowney. If any young woman he knew tried to be possessive, he would be offhand or tough and tell her to "beat it."

Sometimes Jones and Pearlroth visited Warren Espy Bower, the instructor of their English course, who had a house in Greenwich Village where he frequently entertained students and faculty members. In the immediate postwar era, universities were full of veterans who were both hungry for literature and impatient of pretense. Jones was one of these, for he believed that there should be no artificial barrier between life and art and liked to tell stories about his family and about life in the army. Finding the conversation at literary parties highly artificial and precious, as well as beyond his experience, he began to think that literary critics were like the officer class in the army. Both were remote from the action, but they were full of opinions about it. Although Jones loved his classes for what they did to help him as a writer, he did not feel at home in the academic atmosphere of the university. It made him cynical about something he truly loved, and he disliked it for spoiling his innocent enthusiasm.

Not long after Jones submitted *They Shall Inherit the Laughter* to Scribner's, Maxwell Perkins returned it, confirming Maxwell Aley's view that it needed extensive revision. Now Jones began to spend the major part of his free time in New York working on this manuscript. A novel about four returning veterans, it was originally called *Homecoming* and dealt with the alienation soldiers feel when they return to civilian life. Jones placed the novel in Greenfield, a town modeled on Robinson, and his principal character is Peter Pringle, whose family were once prominent in the town. The parents are now dead, and Pringle meets an older woman, Corny Marion, who encourages him. The novel was intended to be written in a comic vein, with the intense mad humor of a veteran whose experiences have made him see

the world as insane. The characters spend most of their time unpro-
ductively, questioning their condition. In the words of a short story on
the same theme called "Backlash," they ask, "Why is it that this is our
only outlet? Is this to be the only purpose of our lives? Are drinking,
whoring, laughing the only reasons we can find for living?"

The veterans have returned to the cultural vacuity of an America
untouched by the war, materialistic, empty, meaningless. "All fight
for the same choice of heritage," Jones explained in a letter to Upton
Sinclair, "utter disillusionment, or the alternative, the Businessman's
Code of Success." Three of the characters fail, but the fourth, based
on himself, becomes an artist. As a creative person, he finds that the
real issue is not so much the goodness of man but the irrelevance of
that question, since "his time is so short."

Jones also wrote stories while at NYU and in May of 1945 published
one of them in *The Apprentice*, the university's literary magazine.
Called "Father, Dear Father, Come to Me," it is a story about two
veterans in a bar, one of whom reflects what Jones thought of himself.
"No matter how much he drank or how many soldiers and sailors he
talked to, he was still an outsider. The old urge and bitterness and hatred wasn't there any more. He was only very lonely and unhappy."
He is offered an introduction to a girl but rejects it, saying, "It isn't
worth the trouble." Then he explains why. "I'm a writer. I'm writing
a book about this war, and I'm really going to blow the lid off."

Life and art were easily confused in Jones's early writings. Although
he pretended to dismiss women, he often wrote poems about them.
These poems were less violent than what he had written in Memphis,
but they reflected his solitude. One was called "Dirge to a Reluctant
Virgin," in which he described various bizarre and romantic settings
for lovemaking, implying what the girl would miss if she continued to
be so hesitant. He took care of some of his excess physical energy by
going to Stillman's Gym, where he could box. It was the one sport he
loved and remained interested in. Alone on a Sunday, he would often
go to jam sessions at Jimmy Ryan's on Fifty-second Street. There he
would nurse one beer all afternoon and listen to the music. He had
collected records from childhood and was delighted to have a chance
to hear Sidney Bechet, Wild Bill Davidson, and Eddie Condon.
Nourished by the warm glow of Dixieland jazz, Jones made a point of
meeting the musicians. "Almost without exception they were men
who had lived on the wrong side of the tracks, as I had after 1929,"

Jones later wrote, "essentially anti-social beings who had had to learn to live with the American Puritan hypocrisy and snobbism as I was having to, sustained only by their talent and their art and artistry to rise up out of this welter of crap as I hoped I would be able to do. They could spot a phony in less time than it took him to smile his smile. A pungent, flagrant sense of humor helped such men enormously, I was learning. They were enormously helpful people to be around on occasion, there at Ryan's."

If Jones's life seemed lonely, it was full enough to make him want to continue at NYU. He had received honors grades in all his first-term courses and was on the dean's list. With the help of Max Aley, he applied for a Twentieth Century–Fox fellowship that would give him enough money to live on, since the government grant covered only tuition. But in the end, he decided not to stay at NYU. He was twenty-four and he felt too old to be starting on an undergraduate degree. More important, he was confused; he "didn't know who he was, or where he was, or where he was going, or how he was going to get there." A friend of his at the university later wrote to him, recalling how he had been at the time. "I remember how black discouraged you were, the kind of help you needed and didn't get at school, and the stuff you did get, lectures on being restrained and disciplined. You stood out because you had a kind of suicidal devotion air about you and when you left school I just felt mad, this talent going down the drain because of betrayal by ABCD and country, home and God."

Jones remained in New York for only a short time after the end of the term. Lowney was coming, and for a brief period he moved to another address, 134 West Sixty-sixth Street. Lowney's presence would help him deal with "the intolerable loneliness of New York City," but he was still tense and unhappy. He did not want to return to Robinson, where there were bitter memories and where he had sometimes become so overwrought in conversations that he would burst into tears. Toward the end of the summer, Jones had another examination at a Veterans Administration Hospital; it showed that he had not yet adjusted to civilian life. "The patient dislikes society, he has always been a nervous high strung individual who has no interest in anything other than being a writer, is resentful of regimentation, loses his temper, and as he says, if he has a plan in mind he will carry it out regardless of consequences involved."

. . .

In May, Jones drove down to Florida with Lowney. They took a room at the Archway Ocean Villas on Collins Avenue, facing the ocean at Miami Beach, and Jones settled down to complete the revisions of *They Shall Inherit the Laughter.* The work did not go easily. Max Aley had tried to help him, pointing out examples of "careless writing" and "places that are sloppy and inept." He told Jones that he was "like a good pianist playing Beethoven badly." Jones himself was aware of his weaknesses. "My transitions are too heavy and awkward and long winded," he admitted to his brother, "taking up too much space." He even thought of paying an editor for a professional critique of the novel.

In January of 1946, he sent the completed manuscript to Perkins, but before receiving a reply he wrote again, mentioning several other projects he had in mind. "I have always wanted to do a novel on the peacetime army," he said, "something I don't remember having seen." He then quoted from his notes to give some idea of the material. Of the character who would eventually become Prewitt, he spoke of his "intense personal pride, his six months on stockade rockpile rather than admit he was wrong and accept company punishment when he felt he was right in his actions. The small man standing on the edge of the ocean shaking his fist, the magnificent gesture."

Jones had written this letter from Florida, where he had spent six months writing in Miami and Tallahassee and working on a fishing boat in Marathon, before returning to Robinson for the spring. When he did get to Robinson, he found a telegram from Perkins asking for more revisions on *They Shall Inherit the Laughter,* but also offering a $500 option for the second novel. Jones was both disappointed and pleased and wired his acceptance immediately. In a letter that followed, he wrote Perkins, "I'm putting myself in your hands, not Scribner's exactly, but you personally, because I have more faith in your ability to see further and clearer than anybody I've met or heard of in the writing game." He was very unsure of himself, however, and within the month he wrote again: "I'm stumbling along in the dark, and there seems to be nobody to teach me what I must learn in the manner in which history is taught to a history student."

Perkins responded by passing on hints and suggestions he had gathered over the years. He told Jones how a person could tell whether he really was a writer. When he began to write about a particular day, a true writer would find "that he could recall exactly how the light fell and how the temperature felt, and all the quality of it." Perkins also suggested that Jones keep a notebook or a set of file cards on which to record ideas and feelings that interested him. He should group them under key words, such as *fear*. "Then," advised Perkins, "just let the cards accumulate for quite a period, and then group them together under the key words. I think if a writer did that for ten years, all those memories would come back to him, and he would have an immense sum to draw upon."

By April of 1946, Jones was settled at the Handys' in Robinson and had completed eighty pages of the new novel. He conceived of it in three parts, the first and second at Schofield Barracks, the third ending with the death of Prewitt in New Georgia. Jones first prepared a synopsis of thirty-eight pages in which he fixed the central axis of the book as a contrast between two characters, Prewitt and Sergeant Milt Warden, who were drawn from men he knew in F Company; in June, he sent off the first fourteen chapters to Perkins. He knew that he had to realize more clearly the major themes that lay behind his characters. "Having known a number of these men, I am convinced that the great majority of criminals — not petty thieves but criminals — are what they are because of a high personal integrity and a high personal pride. The same thing that sets an artist out to correct the baseness of his society makes a criminal repudiate his society. This is one of the things I want to show in the character Prewitt."

Perkins responded to the fourteen chapters with encouragement. "I do not know whether this book will sell," he wrote, "and I think there will be a very hard struggle in cutting it and shaping it, but I think it exceedingly interesting and valid. The Army is *something*, and I don't think that anyone even approached presenting it in its reality as you have done." Nevertheless, Perkins thought there was too much explanatory material. "When you come to revise," he said, "you must try to make the action, and the talk (which is a form of action) tell it all, or almost all." As proof that he was "deeply interested" in the book Perkins sent an additional $500 as a continuation of the option.

During the summer, on his way to visit his brother in Tallahassee, Jones hitchhiked to Georgia for a Red Cross lifesaving course that would prepare him for a job as a lifeguard, which he had been offered in Robinson. Word had got out about his connection with Scribner's, and the townspeople were now disposed to help him. Many of them had previously assumed, said Jones, that the Handys were harboring "a social criminal who was liable to murder them in their beds," but now they were impressed and kept asking him when the novel would be finished. Jones began to be afraid that because of their constant prying, "the shining dream" of his book would "vanish into nothingness."

When he returned from Florida, Jones found that Lowney and Harry wanted to extend a room in the back of the house and turn it into a bed-sitting room where he could work and sleep. Plans were drawn to install a separate bathroom and to build an outside wall of glass that would let in light. Jones helped panel the room and put in bookcases and bought a Navaho rug for the floor. There was now room for the beer steins and records he had begun to collect, and his brother sent him a sword, which Jones accepted, saying that he could always have it back and show it off as "the little sword of your kid brother who fit bled and died and is now a genius, thank God. Due to the dying, probably." The new room was the first real home he had had since 1939, and it gave him "a sense of stability and security."

Jones wrote frequently to Perkins and to his brother about his work and states of mind. "I am learning gradually what to leave out," he told Perkins. "To me it seems largely a matter of emotion projected, even the thought must be basically emotion in fiction or else it becomes essay." At the same time, brevity had its own perils. "It is a constant battle between a conservation of space and a desire to get things right." He had read the work of Erich Maria Remarque, who was able to write short scenes that were effective. Jones felt, however, that in being brief, Remarque "leaves out much, too much I think, to be left to the reader's imagination. Consequently, his books are thin and do not stand rereading."

Because he planned to write on all phases of war, he read many books that dealt with combat, among them Remarque's *All Quiet on the Western Front* and the play *What Price Glory?* by Maxwell Anderson and Laurence Stallings. He was undoubtedly attracted by the play's vehement lack of romanticism and its honest portrayal of the relationship between enlisted men and officers. At the same time, he thought that the play was exaggerated and that the characters were archetypes "rather than real living persons, so that a reader had no way to understand or associate them with his own personal life. I want to avoid that mistake."

In thinking about writing, Jones often made analogies with other arts and then tried out his ideas on Perkins. "Just as in music," he wrote, "Stravinsky and neoclassicism were forced into using the discord to express something entirely new in the world they lived in, because there was no way in the old harmonic laws to do it. I think that writing is going to have to discover some way of doing the same thing, eventually if not soon, in the novel."

Jones had tremendous ambitions for his book. He wanted it to be on the very highest level of literature, regardless of time. Steeping himself in such famous war novels as Tolstoi's *War and Peace* and Stendhal's *The Charterhouse of Parma,* he was eager to render the modern army as they had rendered the armies of the preceding century. He knew that in the modern age, military conflict had to be presented in modern terms, but he wanted to preserve the scale of the great nineteenth-century novels to which he hoped it would be compared.

Jones's interest in technique and in rendering modern life led him to make some experiments of his own, similar to those he had admired in music. One of the most noticeable was his habit of leaving out apostrophes, so that "can't" became "cant" and "I've" became "Ive." Made in an attempt to get closer to the spoken language, where punctuation marks don't exist, these changes in spelling were often confusing and more an annoyance than a help. They looked like mistakes and called attention to themselves. Nevertheless, Jones adopted these mannerisms in both his correspondence and his fiction for about ten years.

Jones's restlessness and love of warm weather brought him back to Florida for the winter of 1946–1947. Mainly he stayed with his brother, but he also worked again as a fisherman. His writing was going so slowly that he decided he needed a change of pace from the novel and began to write short stories in hope of earning some money. Using material from *They Shall Inherit the Laughter,* he wrote five in about six weeks, of which "The Way It Is" was based on his experiences at Makapuu Point in Hawaii, where he had been stationed after Pearl Harbor. A story about a leading Hawaiian businessman who breaks the curfew and is so furious at being arrested that he forces the army to change its procedures, it shows how commerce can corrupt even the army and endanger the safety of the country. "Emotionally, this story was written," Jones later remarked, "because I hate, not dislike but actively hate, the present system by which the Army of the United States is run. It is as Gibbon said of the British Army in comparing it to the Roman Legions, they aint changed it any."

"Just Like the Girl" is a story based on Jones's childhood experience of being forced by his mother to spy on his father because she thought he was having an affair. The story is written under the specter of divorce, and Jones said he wrote it "because I like children and hate to see them so perpetually abused by adults simply because the adults can whip them." He showed the manuscript to a newspaper editor in Robinson, who was shocked by his writing so directly about his parents. "Even if it's true, why do it?" This remark, Jones said, "was worth to me all the effort I put into writing it."

In both of these stories, Jones tried to eliminate explanation. He wanted "to present life moving pictorially like a movie, but tied closely to the mental life which moves right with it." The technique involved "the weaving of the physical and mental passages together, in and out, in the same paragraph," a method he elaborated on in *From Here to Eternity.*

"The Temper of Steel" and "Two Legs for the Two of Us" were also extracted from *They Shall Inherit the Laughter* and were based on the return of servicemen to America. "Secondhand Man" deals with despair and defeat among men who allow themselves to become self-indulgent. About an alcoholic journalist who is advised to go to the mountains to dry out, and who succumbs at the first temptation, it is a study of weakness. "Most every intelligent man," Jones later generalized, "in his youth, must choose between Art with a capital A and Society with a capital S. It's not so much that they compromise, but they lie to themselves saying I had no choice, and then grow old trying to force the new generation into the same groove of Lie, and even becoming, in the last extremes of avoiding reality, suicides, which my father was."

While work on the stories and correspondence with Maxwell Perkins kept Jones in touch with the world of literature, at Robinson he was undergoing a course of training that would have an impact on his development as a writer. Lowney had not taken Jones in simply as a guest nor as a lover; she wanted to develop him as a person so that he would be capable of writing the novel she sensed was in him, struggling to get out. She herself was self-taught, and her personality had been formed by reading the American transcendentalists. Aware of the hypocrisy of her fellow townspeople, she was attracted to the individualism of Emerson and Thoreau. But she also went to their sources and made a study of Asian philosophy. Having achieved a strong identity of her own, she believed that creative activity of any kind required a philosophic and religious basis, and that is what she wanted to impart to Jones. "I told you I would help you," she wrote him at the beginning of their relationship. "I will help the inner you but from now on I will not help the outer you. A man has to stand on his own two feet. You've had a raw deal, but everything that happens to us is part of our making."

By the time he began *From Here to Eternity,* Jones had read a good deal beyond the nineteenth- and twentieth-century English and American novelists who first nourished him. He had read William James and Alfred North Whitehead, and, overcoming his antipathy to religion, he had also read widely again in the Bible. Lowney introduced him to *The Source of Human Good,* by the Chicago philosopher Henry N. Wieman, who proposed a theory of "creative good" as a means of attaining the highest values from life. Citing the twelve apostles of Jesus, Wieman points to the group's creative energy, which went far beyond any selfish individual ambition. In subjecting ourselves to a higher force, he said, we unleash "a power which works in our lives to achieve a good we cannot encompass and cannot discern until some later time in retrospect."

To aid the release of his artistic energy, Lowney introduced Jones to her considerable library of Eastern philosophy, especially books from India and Japan and including Madame Blavatsky's theosophical works. Jones well knew the saying of Jesus, that "whosoever will save his life will lose it: and whosoever will lose his life for my sake will find it." But another contemporary philosopher on the East, Paul Brunton, to whom he was introduced by Lowney, dramatized the process in a way that Jones could apply to his own development as a man and an artist. "Death is the secret of life," wrote Brunton. "We must empty ourselves if we would be filled. When the mind has poured out all its thoughts, a vacuum is created. But this can last only a few seconds. Then a mysterious influx of divine life will enter. In this strange moment the intellect temporarily cremates itself, and out of its ashes rises the phoenix of the true self, the imperishable Overself of man."

Undergoing a process similar to a religious conversion, and perhaps unconsciously nourished by the American Protestant fundamentalism with which the Middle West was permeated, Jones learned from Lowney's philosophical training how to overcome personal bitterness. Private anger had given the original impetus to his work but had also hindered its best expression. Jeff had written that he was afraid that Jones had *"actually* become as hard inside as you'd like people to believe you are," but he hoped that Jones would want to become a fine writer "not to Show those Bastards, but for the satisfaction and beauty of accomplishment." Jones knew that his feuds with people like his Uncle Charlie robbed him of the tranquillity needed to create work that would be more than a personal complaint against the world. In order to transform his experience into something universal, he would have to get rid of petty egotism and of any illusions about himself as being someone special or heroic. "Before I could learn," he later explained, "I had to be *broken*. And boy, I mean broken. Lowney cut the ground out from under me until I had absolutely no place to stand. I was completely lost. Every way I turned for aid or escape, Lowney was there and cut me off. Until in the end I had to either face myself or die. And I mean that. I have no family to raise, and if my writing is not at least in some sense bound to creativity, then my life is completely useless. Ive put all my eggs in one basket, sort of. And if I dont succeed in aiding the creativity of the world, at least a tiny bit, then my whole life is useless. I went down to 138 lbs because of it. I was constantly reminded of Wheelock's poem — 'There is a panther caged within my breast.'"

It was not an easy process and in some ways went against the habits of a lifetime. "Several times I actually thought I would boil myself to death inside," he wrote. "Finally I ran off. I was going on the bum and be romantic. But in the end I came back, because the me that used to exist is no longer alive at all. For one thing Im too sensitive to face the bum — unless circumstances actually forced me to it. All Ive lived and worked for was here. I had to swallow my pride and come back."

In addition to reading the oracular and philosophical books that Lowney gave him, Jones studied yoga and began to practice meditation in accordance with instructions outlined in Brunton's *The Secret Path*. Lowney would wake him up at five o'clock in the morning, and after reading some Brunton, he would sit cross-legged on the floor and meditate. He also practiced breathing exercises. He wasn't very good at it, but once, he told his brother, "for about three or four seconds I achieved a state of complete mental quiet." Sometimes, before meditation, he would say the Lord's Prayer, "silently, mentally, concentrating hard on the words and also upon their deeper meanings — this helps to put the mind in the right frame for meditation. After I say the prayer, I repeat several times 'Thy will be done.' And concentrate on it hard. It helps to relax me somehow to meditate. I also say this same sequence over every night after Im in bed and before I drop off to sleep."

Jones also followed a routine that involved physical exercise and at least one bath a day. He did twenty push-ups, twenty deep knee-bends, and twenty sit-ups, touching his toes. He had his hair cut short, because he thought that long hair induced depression. He obeyed dietary instructions provided by an Indian doctor, taking only liquids for breakfast, a solid meal at lunch followed by a three-hour siesta, and then milk or coffee in the evening. In time, he worked up to more drastic diets, drinking nothing but water for a week and giving himself warm water enemas to cleanse and purify himself.

This regimen inevitably affected Jones's sex life, and again he was influenced by Lowney. Jones frankly admitted his need for sex. "I like sex," he wrote. "In fact, I love it. Ive always been oversexed. I am constantly fighting for control of myself not to think about it all the time." Lowney had taught him, after the meaningless orgies of Memphis, that sex with love was "the Solution," and he looked back fondly to "the early days of love," when they had gone to the Bellevue-Stratford in Philadelphia for a week, and where they had "breakfast served in bed, dinner in the dining room among the rich fools, alternating between bouts of love and reading in the room on the bed while the world is stopped and held at bay by the revolving doors downstairs."

But experiences like that, Lowney had taught him, were not reality. "Love is the prime escape *from* reality. Its very *purpose* is a denial of reality." Moreover, "when it ceases to escape reality it ceases to be love. It becomes, instead, marriage." Jones jotted down Lowney's words: "You'll get over this, she tells me (painfully). In ten years you probably won't be able to remember it. You'll be going on, to new things, to others. This will fade, she tells me."

Lowney was trying to reduce his sexual life not only for the future but because she thought that too much sex would be bad for him. Apparently she succeeded. "I might very easily have killed myself by fucking," he told his brother, "if I hadn't been *forced* to see that it was not an answer." The rationale for moderation was this: "Every sexual bout I have consumes so much energy. Every bit of energy consumed thru sex is energy that cannot be placed elsewhere. Then if I wish to write 6 hours a day, I can only take so much sex without taking energy from my work."

In the increasingly monastic Handy household, Jones was aware that he had "renounced society." Yet the regimen of yoga and philosophy was beginning to have useful literary consequences. He now saw how far he had gone astray in early drafts. He had been "trying to associate Prewitt with myself, and *was trying to make him a Hero. Every line I wrote was forcing me further back, because I wanted thru Prewitt to be accepted as a Hero.*" Now he had a new perspective. Once he recognized that with Prewitt and Warden he had been "trying to make them both Jim Jones," he knew that he would have to give them their independence. He would have to see them as he now saw himself, without illusions or pretensions. Conceiving them as real people, he could "just put them together" and "they will make their own plot and it will be life and not formula."

The routine of life and work in the Handys' house suited Jones. "I have a fine place to work, and comforts here that I could never have in New York by myself," he informed Maxwell Perkins. But the work itself worried him. "I sometimes despair of ever learning technique," he wrote, "so I can just sit down and write. I have trouble with transitions in the middle of chapters." Perkins responded with gentle praise, urging flexibility. "A deft man may toss his hat across the office and hang it on a hook if he just naturally does it, but he will always miss if he does it consciously."

Jones quickly got the point and told his brother that learning how to write seemed to be "the development of a particular set of muscles, and thats all it is; just like with an auto mechanic or high jumper. When you can admit that to yourself, you will be there, all the way." He was also beginning to see that with writing, "no one can help you. A writer is alone with it, by the nature of it."

Perkins was useful, however, when Jones began to think of a title for the book. He had been considering *Old Soldiers Never Die, If Wishes Were Horses,* and *They Merely Fade Away.* But he settled on *From Here to Eternity* when he heard the refrain of the famous song sung by the Yale Whiffenpoofs. Perkins pointed out that the words came originally from Rudyard Kipling's "Gentlemen Rankers" in the *Barrack-Room Ballads,* and Jones was somewhat chagrined by his ignorance.

Perkins' faith in Jones was a basic element in his development as an artist. At night, alone, he would sometimes take out Perkins' letters and read them over. On one occasion, he noted, "I experienced such a feeling of joy as is hard to describe without exaggeration. I felt an actual impulse to shout with glee and belief in my own powers. Actually, I mean; not figuratively." Reading Thomas Wolfe's *Story of a Novel*, he saw that at the age of twenty-four, he "had learned things that Wolfe did not until he was past 35." It astonished him that he, "Jim Jones of Robinson, Ill.," should be writing to the editor of Wolfe, Hemingway, Fitzgerald, Nancy Hale, and Marcia Davenport. Yet, he wrote, "I have at the same time known that I would someday be writing to him, on equal grounds. I have always known it, as if it were foreordained, and it seems to me the most natural thing in the world. In the midst of my surprise."

Jones's last letter to Perkins never reached him. Overworked, recovering from a car accident, and weakened by drink, Perkins died in June of 1947, at the age of sixty-two. When Perkins' colleague at Scribner's, the poet John Hall Wheelock, wrote to tell Jones what had happened, Jones went about repeating a phrase of Thomas Wolfe's that had led him to writing in the first place: "O lost, and by the wind grieved, ghost." He had openly acknowledged Perkins as a father figure, but knew that the time of Perkins' best work "was with Thomas Wolfe and not with me."

Jones had been introduced to several of the other editors at Scribner's, among them Wheelock and Burroughs Mitchell, but when they divided up Perkins' authors among them, they somehow overlooked Jones. Once they were aware of their error, Mitchell wrote to Jones, suggesting that he could work with a group of editors or choose one for himself. Jones's reply was characteristic. "I would prefer to work with one man, as individual to individual," he said, adding that he would like to work with Mitchell, "if it is all okay there."

By November, he had finished the first eleven chapters of *From Here to Eternity* and sent them to Mitchell. He was now twenty-six and, having settled into his routine in the new room at the Handys', had begun to change his values. The old loneliness and sense of insecurity that had plagued his youth were gone, and following Lowney's precepts, he had made writing the most important part of his life. He became more self-reliant and confident. "I am learning things now that I have never dreamed of before," he told Peggy Carson, the friend from the University of Hawaii to whom he had once written romantic letters. "I am learning in weeks what most men never learn, or else spend painful years acquiring."

He did little at home but work, for his sexual relationship with Lowney had begun to change. When he felt "the need of a good big drunk to relax on and a woman to relieve the pressure of sex," he would go to Terre Haute or Indianapolis for a few days. "Then it's back to lovely work for a couple of months." Under Lowney's tutelage, he had lost his former yearning for a woman to love, and now looked upon sex simply as a biological urge that needed occasional tending. A prostitute was perfectly adequate for filling that need, and he lost his old distaste for whorehouses.

The despair he had known in Memphis when, surrounded by dozens of available women at the Peabody Hotel, he could find none to supply him with the love and attention he yearned for was now replaced by his confidence in himself as a writer. Work overcame his loneliness. "I will never sacrifice my personal Self to any woman," he wrote in the same letter to Peggy Carson, "any more than I would demand hers — even if she wanted to give it. The only path toward alleviating loneliness is inside, never outside. If you will think seriously and *honestly* about it, you will admit to yourself that the happiest youve been has been when you were alone — not with me (or any lover) but when alone with yourself you either dreamed, hoped, or planned with an imaginary lover."

But the imagination has its limits, and in early November 1947, Jones wrote to Burroughs Mitchell about visiting New York to discuss the chapters he had sent in. "I want to go through the Met and the Modern Museum," he added, "see some plays too, all the things I've starved for so long and cant get out here."

The meeting with Mitchell was important, for he was the man Jones would have to work closely with when the time came for final revisions. Fortunately, Mitchell had a good deal of the same skill and tact that Perkins had possessed, and the two men hit it off from the start. A mild man, he was impressed by Jones's gregariousness and his "ability very quickly to establish a relationship with a stranger. Once interested (and he was easily interested), he went straight at the person, asking, probing, carefully examining everything said. And people were drawn by his sometimes ferocious forthrightness and by the country humor he employed so cannily." Mitchell also found that Jones could be difficult, especially after drinking. "He could become harsh, even savage, lashing out when something outraged or disgusted him."

In New York, Jones also saw a good deal of John Hall Wheelock, of whom he became especially fond. A distinguished poet, Wheelock was a kindly figure in the literary world of New York, and he took a fatherly attitude toward Jones, inviting him for dinner and giving him inscribed copies of his books. Wheelock was the first real writer Jones had ever met, and he welcomed Jones to an intimacy he did not grant to many people.

After a week in New York, Jones returned to Robinson, but soon became restless and, with the coming of winter, decided to go to Florida. He had now made a habit of going south and had spent the past three winters there, moving back and forth from Tarpon Springs to Naples and Venice, small towns on the Gulf of Mexico. "I'm not looking forward to the trip," he told Wheelock, "and I think that's good. They always turn out better that way." At least the anonymity he found in Florida was better than the curiosity of his neighbors in Robinson, whose unreliable friendship "drifts like dandelion seed before the winds and never does have roots." Their prying made him nervous and forced him to leave. Also, he enjoyed meeting new people, boat owners in Marathon, fishermen, waitresses he encountered at restaurants. Always attracted to simple people who had ordinary jobs, he was curious about their lives and liked to relax over drinks with those willing to talk to him. "Everybody drinks a lot down here, but the fishers are the hardest working hardest drinking crowd."

Because he moved away from Robinson so often, he decided that buying a trailer would be cheaper than staying at hotels and would also give him flexibility. In February of 1949, Harry Handy bought him a twenty-six-foot trailer against a note, and Jones was delighted with the freedom it gave him to move about the country and have his home with him wherever he went. He would simply drive into a trailer park and find himself in a familiar place. "The same identical home you closed, locked and left this morning. You take your radio and books off the couch (where you have kept them, traveling) and set them back up on the shelves. You're ready to cook your own supper with your own food on your own stove."

With his typewriter and manuscripts at hand, he could work, and it was cheap. Twenty-five dollars would pay for a five-week stay. Also, he could make extra money hauling trailers from one location to another. With their communal wash houses and ramadas where there were Ping-Pong tables and places to talk, trailer parks were sociable. Jones was attracted to the "closeness and intimacy," which he found was "the antithesis of a New York apartment house." He made friends with the owners, "listening avidly to their tales," and he thought that the parks represented a miniature of America. He was attracted especially to workingmen, whom he'd meet by going to the bar nearest the park. "They are a stiff, proud, independent bunch, used to traveling, and inclined to be captious if you're wearing a white collar; otherwise they're friendly. If you're dressed in a T-shirt and Levi's, they like you — even if they know you're a writer. And if you admire crafts and skills you can't help but like them."

Sometimes traveling with Lowney or with her protégé Willard Lindsay, Jones liked the privacy of trailer life and was touched by the "curious sense of poignancy which is lent to trailer-camp life by the awareness that before long you'll be leaving." He was like Mark Twain discovering America and was moved by the details of ordinary life. "Even a simple thing," he wrote, "like going to the community wash house for a shower can become an intensely emotional act in a trailer park you like."

Despite help from the Handys and money earned from occasional odd jobs, Jones was chronically short of money. His disability pension was so small, he decided to ask for yet another examination at a Veterans Administration hospital in the hope of having it raised. Jones always became exceptionally nervous at the prospect of an examination. "I dread them as much as a case of typhus," he said. Nevertheless, the neuropsychiatric report given him in 1949 showed that he had improved a good deal since his previous test in 1945. "I am absolutely contented and happy," he was reported as saying; "I am living the life I like." But he admitted to being "a little lonely-like." Since he was sharing his trailer with Willard Lindsay, he was asked about homosexuality. Jones answered that, although he knew about it, he had never engaged in it. Jones's examination produced so favorable a report that, to his dismay, his disability pension was reduced to $30 per month.

The urgent need for money was an incentive to try to sell some of the stories he had written earlier in Florida. He first tried *Esquire* and *The Saturday Evening Post* but was rejected. Diarmuid Russell, an agent he had consulted after leaving Max Aley, told Jones he was up against the prejudices of "family magazines," which for fear of losing their subscribers rarely accepted stories about children or old people, sex or disease.

Jones then approached Edward Weeks at *The Atlantic Monthly* with the bravado that typified his dealings with magazine editors. "There are five stories here," he began his letter, "all of them good, at least two of them excellent." In a chatty fashion, letting Weeks know about his novel and his friendship with Maxwell Perkins, Jones suggested that he was a good candidate for an "Atlantic First," the award given by the magazine to a story by a hitherto unpublished writer. "I've never published a word up to now and you've got a Sunday shot at a discovery. Because unless I get drafted into the next war or hit by a truck I'm going to be one of the best to come out of the New Post War Generation, or whatever they will call it."

Weeks accepted "The Temper of Steel," a story about a veteran at a cocktail party to whom a knife enthusiast talks breezily about knives, without knowing that the veteran once had to knife a Japanese soldier to death. Autobiographical, the story was also an attempt to rewrite a famous scene in Remarque's *All Quiet on the Western Front.*

Jones was naturally pleased with the acceptance of the story and the $200 that came with it. When the galleys arrived, he saw his work for the first time in print. "I'd read about it, of course," he said, "but I didnt realize how for some reason how much clearer it made you see it." He also learned that "after the first flush of joyful disbelief," the publication of the story "changed my life almost not at all."

Jones also succeeded in selling two stories to *Harper's Magazine,* "Just Like the Girl" and "The Way It Is." The stories were copyedited at *Harper's* and returned to Jones with many corrections and emendations. The changes so enraged Jones that he wrote a twelve-page letter of complaint to Merle Miller, one of the magazine's senior editors. Assuming that the copy editor was a woman, he attacked the "literary-cocktail-party stenographer" for trying to rewrite his stories. "The things I write are the only damned things I've got to show for my life, and I hate like hell for some self-styled intellectual who works as a third-rate editor in your office to attempt to teach me how to write."

He was upset by the editor's insistence on uniformity in spelling and punctuation. "When I write 'it is' as 'its' without an apostrophe, I know what the hell I'm doing," he wrote. "I'm doing it for a reason, neither from ignorance, nor from carelessness." Jones also had to defend his right to free expression. In "Just Like the Girl" the editor had changed a phrase about lovemaking from "he would get to see them doing it" to "he would get to see what they did." Jones was outraged by the prudery that dictated this change and claimed that it made the story meaningless. "Am I writing this for the *Ladies Home Journal?*"

he asked. "How the hell can you write a story about sex if you do not mention sex?"

The person responsible for the changes turned out to be Frederick Lewis Allen, the editor-in-chief of *Harper's*. "I have been puzzled by your letter," he replied, "because in a great many years of editorial experience I have never got one quite like it." Allen said he could not see what difference Jones's spelling changes made, but he apologized for poor communication between the magazine and the author. "The Way It Is" was published for the most part as originally written, but Allen did not print "Just Like the Girl," because, he said, he wasn't up to further argument.

The publication of Jones's stories in national magazines was good for his morale in the drawn-out period in which he was writing *From Here to Eternity*. During the four years it took to write, he often doubted his ability to finish it. "I work very slowly, and painfully," he reported to Burroughs Mitchell. "Now and then I'll write like mad for a week or two and knock myself out and then it's a page or two a day until another spasm seizes me." He tore up three quarters of everything he wrote. "It is not pleasant to be your own worst critic," he said. The size of the book, the large number of characters, and the complexity of their relationships made him question everything. He worried about plots. "Life is plotless," he wrote, "except in rare cases. Therefore I not only must make a plot but must also make it a *plotless* plot, which not only sounds natural to life but also has a spiritual meaning, at least for me." He was also perplexed by language. "I dont know and cant discover what it is that gives one line a ring and feel of life," he told Burroughs Mitchell, "a sort of grasping of all life in one line. I can feel it but I cant define it. I have to sweat like hell to get that feel in it, to get one living line, one pulsating word that implies tenfold what it says." Yet another problem was that he had to invent so much. The characters were drawn from the soldiers he had known at Schofield Barracks, but Jones had to make up everything they did. The strain on his imagination was so great that he told Mitchell that in his next book he wanted to "write about something that happened for a change."

Having to do so much by himself made him feel lonely, but he was proud of his calling and knew he was in good company. "It's always the lonely ones, Tolstoi, Wolfe, Dostoievsky," he wrote, who survive. "I think they live because they have come up against the last veil between themselves and reality: Themselves." But now the pressure to finish was on. He could delay no longer. The announcement of Norman Mailer's *The Naked and the Dead* meant that his subject might be pre-empted and make another war novel uninteresting. "Nobody believes I'll ever finish it," he lamented, "and I'm damn near the same opinion myself. I just go on writing and writing and writing, on into eternity, a long line of typed pages stretching off like railroad tracks coming together, right on the Millennium, and beyond, on one book, the same book, the eternal book, the forever book, the book that never has an end, only a beginning, the eternal serial." But then Jones caught himself and added an afterthought: "I feel better now. I see I've slipped off into rhetoric, so I must be feeling better."

As he sent in completed chapters to New York, he was encouraged by the response he received. John Hall Wheelock praised him highly when he commented that "without romanticizing anything, there are moments when from reality itself, presented with fidelity, an exalted kind of poetry is wrung." Then on October 30, 1949, he sent in the chapter, from the end of the novel, that describes the Japanese attack on Pearl Harbor. "Here is the *pièce de résistance*, the *tour de force*," he announced. It was written under pressure, in Albuquerque, where he had taken his trailer, gradually making his way west by Colorado Springs. "I, personally, believe it will stack up with Stendhal's Waterloo or Tolstoi's Austerlitz. That was what I was aiming at, and wanted it to do, and I think it does it. If you don't think it does, send it back and I'll rewrite it. Good isn't enough; not for me, anyway; good is only middling fair. We must remember people will be reading this book a couple of hundred years after I'm dead, and that Scribner's first edition will be worth its weight in gold by then. We mustnt ever forget that."

As Jones neared the end of the novel, he and Willard Lindsay were joined in Tucson at the Princeton Trailer Park by Lowney, who also wanted to get away from the cold weather in the north. Another letter of congratulations came from Wheelock, who had now read all but the final chapters. "I can't resist telling you how deeply moved, and excited, I have been by this splendid, often beautiful, often terrible book. It is an achievement of the first water and one that I believe will be so recognized. I know of no novel in which the comradeship of men has been so sensitively portrayed — a masculine book, sometimes harsh but always charged with a tremendous compassion."

Lowney was also caught up in the excitement and enthusiasm. It had cost her a good deal, for she had given up her own literary ambitions to help Jones. She told Burroughs Mitchell she thought *From Here to Eternity* would prove to be the best book ever produced by an American. "I am not over-enthusiastic," she wrote. "I have given seven years of my life, one track mind, fight, praise, my family and my friends, my own writing included, in order to have a hand in the creating of a *great* book."

Soon, Harry Handy also came to Tucson, and the entire group started south to Mexico, where Jones had heard you could buy six filets of steak for thirty-five cents and the best American cigarettes for eleven cents a pack. Jones had chosen Guaymas, a small town on the west coast of Mexico, with the intention of staying there until he finished the book. But "it turned out to be a veritable dump," Jones wrote Mitchell. "Electricity not strong enough to turn on the refrigerator starter motor, water pressure going clear off several times a day, almost no American food such as clean milk available." After a week or so, they returned to the United States and drove up the coast of California to Los Angeles, where Jones put the trailer in Valley Park on Lankershim Boulevard in North Hollywood, just over the ridge from Universal City. Harry went home, and Willard and Lowney took separate places in Hollywood while Jones finished the book. He was afraid that the chapter describing Prewitt's death might be sentimental and wrote Mitchell for reassurance. While writing, he was rereading Machiavelli's *The Prince* and *The Discourses*. When he had first read them in the hospital in Memphis, he thought they were bitter, and that is why he liked them. But now he found a new quality in them. "They are not bitter at all," he wrote. "They are a statement." It was what he was aiming for in his own fiction.

On February 27, 1950, he finally completed the book and celebrated by drinking three dry martinis. Then he wrote a letter to Mitchell. "I really feel very peculiar. Not elated. Not depressed. But peculiar. Maybe humble." He felt that much of what he had accomplished was due to others and told Mitchell that he intended to add a note of acknowledgment to the end of the book.

Lowney moved to the trailer to be with Jones. There was something strangely anticlimactic about finishing the book in a trailer park in an anonymous tract of America. Yet the ordinariness of the setting was also appropriate. To distract himself, Jones began thinking about Lowney's book, which had been so long neglected. He didn't feel like embarking on the drunk he had so long planned to celebrate the end of his novel. Rather lamely, he concluded his letter to Mitchell: "Anyway, since this is such a great day, Lowney and I are going out and eat at a Chinese restaurant we've discovered in North Hollywood to celebrate. Pork chow mein, egg foo yong, green vegetable chop suey, egg flower soup, almond cookies et al. Then we'll probably go to a show."

5

FROM HERE
TO ETERNITY

THE ARRIVAL of the final pages of *From Here to Eternity* at the Scribner's offices on Fifth Avenue produced an outburst of enthusiasm. John Hall Wheelock wrote Jones to tell him of his "excitement and delight" in reading the ending. "You have done it," he said, "and I hope you are as happy about it as we are." Burroughs Mitchell told Jones that the head of the sales department had never before been so enthusiastic about a novel, and as for himself, Mitchell added, "I am going to take the risk of using a word that I am very chary of, very chary indeed. I think this is a great book." As an agreeable dividend, Jones received a copy of *Editor to Author: The Letters of Maxwell E. Perkins* from Wheelock, who edited the book, and Jones found that it included three letters to himself.

Reading the now-completed novel, Mitchell decided to send back a few chapters at a time so that Jones could consider the suggestions he was making for alterations. Some cuts were simply to reduce wordiness; the more difficult ones related to propriety. Mitchell explained that the use of certain expressions "would lay the book open to legal action in many states. The bookstores would not carry it, for fear of action against them."

Privately, Jones was not bothered by the suggested excisions, and he told Lowney he "could make every cut they suggest and not change the effect appreciably." Nevertheless, he resisted a number of Mitchell's suggestions. Jones's use of the word *fuck* — which in their correspondence came to be referred to as "the Word" — was causing problems. Mitchell was not opposed to its use and had no intention of substituting *fug*, as Mailer had done in *The Naked and the Dead*. That strategy had been discredited by Tallulah Bankhead's remark that, although she liked his book, she was surprised that Mr. Mailer didn't know how to spell *fuck.* Mitchell wanted to introduce the word gradually so that readers would get used to it and not be shocked.

Jones objected to Mitchell's cutting of the word *cunt,* however, which had already been used by Faulkner. He didn't use it to shock, he explained, but to be realistic. "Officers are inclined to be a bit more polite about these things," he wrote. "But the thing is, it is, to be crude, 'cunt' that us men of the lower classes, especially in the Army, are interested in. It isn't love; the love only comes later, if at all."

Mitchell had also suggested the omission of a scene in which one of the characters has a wet dream. "I saw that, with my own eyes, I saw it a great many times," Jones wrote. "Christ, Mitch," he added, "the people of this country dont know what the hell goes on in it."

In an attempt to put *From Here to Eternity* in context, Mitchell told Jones that Hemingway had said he didn't want to be known as a "dirty" writer. Jones rejected this bait and said he thought Hemingway's ambition was fatuous. "That is one worry *I* do *not* have. I dont care if anybody thinks I'm a dirty writer. Maybe I am. After all, I've only my American background to pattern after."

At first, Jones had not minded remaining in Los Angeles after sending in the final pages of the book. He liked the warm weather, and in the afternoons he would go down into Hollywood and then "hike bare-chested through the hill trails of Griffith Park. Getting browned up. Lazy, slow-moving, loafing, yawning. Luxurious like a stretching cat. I live in a perpetual — I dont know what to call it — pure ecstasy of loving the spring air and the sun and the whole goddam fucking earth. A curious feeling as if all the sperm in my balls is roiling through me slowly with a sunglow of radioactivity that must extend its aura outward at least by several feet."

But after a while, he began to feel jittery. Although the mechanics of editing *From Here to Eternity* occupied his time, Jones had not yet felt the satisfaction he had hoped for when he finished the book. That piece of work, which took five years of his life, was proof of his seriousness and dedication as an artist and certified his human and literary growth. The bitter young veteran who had come home without money or position was now *someone.* Lowney's support and regimen had helped him achieve that identity, but the real work was his; he had taken his gifts and made something of them. He had also paid a price, leading a solitary life and controlling his sexual drives and feelings, dedicating himself with puritanical single-mindedness to his work. Now he wanted some of the rewards of achievement. He was already planning his next novel, but Jim Jones of Robinson, Ill., was about to become James Jones, the author of *From Here to Eternity*, and a number of changes were in the offing.

Feeling confined in the trailer, and short of money, he had little to distract him. "I'm just sweating the manuscript," he wrote Mitchell, "and with nothing to take my mind off it." He began to think of Los Angeles as a "modern Pompeii" and found no one to share his thoughts with. Willard Lindsay and Lowney had left, and he felt isolated. "All the people I can talk to are home, in Robinson, a long ways away." He had planned to drive back to Illinois by way of the Grand Canyon and Bryce Canyon but had to change his plans when Lowney returned to California for three weeks. Jones continued to work on the manuscript, but his heart was elsewhere. "I am hungry for the Middlewest," he told Wheelock, "and am going back home to Illinois."

Jones did not intend to use his successful completion of *From Here to Eternity* to celebrate his importance as a returned native or to score off old enemies. What mattered was the new confidence he felt inside. Instead of returning to the Handy house on Mulberry Street in Robinson, Jones decided to park his trailer in Marshall, twenty-eight miles to the north, where Harry Handy had a four-acre farm. This was to be the site of the future Handy Colony, which, after much discussion and planning, Lowney and Harry had decided to build as a center for young writers. Jones's success in completing *From Here to Eternity* encouraged them to begin work on the camp. As manager of the Ohio Oil Company's refinery in Robinson, Harry was able to move a construction company's "field office" to Marshall, where it was converted into a cabin containing a living room, bedroom, kitchen, and bathroom. No outside carpenters or plumbers were employed, for all the work was to be done by the future colonists. Jones was eager to be involved; he had written from California that "right now the greatest thing in the world to me would be to lose myself in plain old physical labor. Manual labor."

He got plenty of it as he and the Handys, together with Willard Lindsay and Don Sackrider, dug ditches for pipes and poured concrete for the cabin and for the sites on which tents would be raised. A bathhouse was built and tiled, and they laid out paths, using old bricks Harry had procured from houses razed in the neighborhood.

Then suddenly, in August, Jones was summoned to New York to go over the proofs of *From Here to Eternity*. The galleys had been shown to the Scribner's lawyer, Horace Manges, who was worried about possible charges of obscenity. Jones was both "elated and depressed" at having to go to New York. He was looking forward to seeing Wheelock and Mitchell and to staying for the Labor Day weekend at Mitchell's house in Piermont, a village on the Hudson River. At the same time, he thought the obscenity problem had been solved. "Surely, there is not anything in 'Eternity' that is more obscene than Molly Bloom's soliloquy," he said.

In New York, he stayed at Mitchell's apartment on Eleventh Street in the Village and spent his days at Scribner's with Mitchell and Horace Manges. Fifty galleys containing material Manges thought troublesome had been set aside for discussion. They went through potentially difficult scenes one by one. Jones was asked to cut a large part of a love scene between Prewitt and Lorene, as well as any mention of "one-way, two-way or three-way girls" working in whorehouses. He was cooperative and sometimes was able to turn a cutting to his advantage so that the scene would have a twist it did not have before. "I think they were pleased with my reaction," Jones wrote to his brother. "I think they were scared I would blow up and go temperamental, but I didn't"

One of the meetings took place in Manges' office in the Lincoln Building, across from Grand Central, and there Jones rewrote several scenes and did some horse trading wth Manges, agreeing to cut one thing if he could keep another. Their meetings were good-humored and without rancor, for they had a common goal. Most of their trouble arose over individual words. Manges had kept a score sheet while reading and, as Jones later reported, "there were 259 fucks, 92 shits and 5 pricks. He did not count the pisses for some reason. Well, Mitch and I went through it later, working in the Scribner office, and cut the fucks to 146, the shits to 45. This was all subject to Manges' approval." Jones then withdrew from the discussion, and Mitchell cut some more, even though he "got tired of counting small words." Eventually, the procedure became so absurd that Mitchell went to Charles Scribner, the head of the firm, and asked his permission to print the book as it was, and Scribner agreed.

Apart from the work, Jones enjoyed himself in New York, meeting all of the Scribner's editors and having all his expenses paid. He was not yet a celebrity, but he was beginning to get the attention that a successful author receives and to savor the good life in New York. He was fascinated by the ritual of the publisher's lunch, for he was taken every day by one of the editors to the Chanticleer or another midtown restaurant. "They all knock off at about a quarter to twelve and go out and have two or three martinis, then eat a lot and drink coffee to make them sober enough to go back to work, and usually get back to the office between two and two-thirty. I really had a wonderful time, fine drinks, fine food, all on Mr. Scribner." Although Jones admitted drinking a good deal himself, he denied that it affected him, but Charles Scribner, Jr., was astonished to see him consume five martinis one day at the Barclay.

Jones was also attracted to the small restaurants that line the side streets in the Fifties off Fifth Avenue. With their canopies and with menu cards stuck in the window, they were intimate and clublike, quite different from restaurants he had known before. He was struck by the "curious combination of Italian and French cuisines" that typified many of them. He was beginning to shed his Midwestern provincialism and to enjoy cosmopolitan living. "I can safely say that this is the first time I ever spent any time in NY that I did not begrudge every minute of it. For the first time in my life I can say I like NY. Of course, without the money and the connections and all, it would be quite different."

On December 16, 1950, Scribner's took the cover of *Publishers' Weekly*, the industry's trade journal, with a full-page advertisement for *From Here to Eternity*. Along with a photograph of Jones were the words "A prediction! A great new career in American fiction will begin with . . ." and on the following two pages, *From Here to Eternity* was compared with such other famous Scribner's first novels as *This Side of Paradise, The Sun Also Rises, Cry, the Beloved Country,* and *Look Homeward, Angel.* The publishers announced an initial advertising budget of $10,000 and priced the book at $4.50. Mitchell sent Jones a copy of the magazine, and Jones was startled when he slipped it out of the envelope "and discovered me staring at me belligerently." The announcement gave him "a tremendous kick of ego-gratification," but the next day, he realized that the act of publication had brought about a profound change. "I discovered that in the process I had lost 'Eternity.' It wasnt mine any more. All the work and fear and sweat and blood, and you know I am not romanticizing, it all went for nothing now. Because now it was bound, and irrevocable, and ready to be sold to people who could never possibly feel as close and loving to the whole thing as I have. And now it is just another book, to be laid on shelves and handled by prospective customers and maybe bought."

Scribner's had sent out galleys to prominent authors for comment, and as the replies came in, they were prepared for future advertising. John Dos Passos wrote that Jones's characters "reach something of the greatness of figures of tragedy because their hopeless dilemma expresses so glaringly the basic human dilemma of our time." Norman Mailer, whose *The Naked and the Dead* had been published in 1948, told Mitchell that he thought the book had an "awful title," but he praised the novel in his official statement as "one of the best of the 'war novels' and in certain facets perhaps the best."

In advertisements, these statements were added to one issued by the editorial board of the Book-of-the-Month Club, which had accepted the novel as an alternate selection. The board ranked Jones's novel "with the best of such American realists as Dreiser, Wolfe, Hemingway, Faulkner" and stated that *From Here to Eternity* "marks the advent in American letters of a young writer who, thoughtfully and with a born talent, is following in the great tradition of the novel."

Meanwhile, acting as Jones's agent for foreign rights, Scribner's sold the book in England to William Collins and Sons. There the threat of prosecution for obscenity was greater than in the United States, and the book had to be printed in Holland for fear that the British printers' union would refuse to set it. In France, it was translated as *Tant qu'il y aura des hommes* and published by Presses de la Cité.

For the possible sale of movie rights, Scribner's put Jones in touch with Ned Brown, an agent who handled films for MCA, the Music Corporation of America. Jones said he would be willing to go to California, because he wanted to write a Hollywood novel, but he professed to show no interest in a movie version of *From Here to Eternity*, except for earning as much money as possible from the sale of rights. "I don't give a damn what they do to the movie," he said; "the book will stand by itself long after the movie is forgotten."

With so much activity before the book was brought out, actual publication threatened to be anticlimactic for Jones. But Scribner's produced as much fanfare as they could when *From Here to Eternity* was published on February 26, 1951. The book was immediately noticed, favorably and at length, all over the country. *The Saturday Re-*

view of Literature, with a cover story, the daily *New York Times*, the *New York Herald Tribune*, *The Atlantic Monthly*, *Harper's*, as well as papers throughout the Middle and Far West, gave it extended space. The most important review of all, David Dempsey's in the *New York Times Book Review*, typified the praise Jones received. " 'From Here to Eternity' is the work of a major new American novelist," he wrote. "To anyone who reads this immensely long and deeply convincing story of life in the peacetime army, it will be apparent that in James Jones an original and utterly honest talent has restored American realism to a pre-eminent place in world literature." Dempsey concluded his review by saying, "Make no mistake about it, 'From Here to Eternity' is a major contribution to our literature, written with contempt for the forces that waste human life, and out of compassion for men who find love and honor and courage in the lower depths."

The reception was extraordinary, especially for a first book by an unknown novelist. Critics are always eager to discover talented new writers, but book review editors have to give most of their space to established authors. Jones, however, was celebrated immediately and prominently, almost everywhere. Naturally, he was pleased. "It's a damn good book, I guess," he wrote to his brother, "yet I am becoming increasingly aware of how many faults — technical faults — there are in it. Which is good, of course."

Instinctively, Jones had decided to stay as far away as possible from the centers of publicity during the period of the book's publication. He and Lowney were already in Florida, and they decided to stay there. Along with three new members of the incipient writers' colony from Marshall, they had taken rooms at a tourist court called King's Cottage in Fort Myers Beach, on the west coast of Florida. Jones worked on some new projects, but was generally relaxed; he even took a fishing trip to the Dry Tortugas. Burroughs Mitchell told him that New York was "sizzling" with excitement over *From Here to Eternity*, but in Florida he lived quietly, "playing football on the beach, getting tanned, working every morning. It's an odd effect."

The success of the book brought letters from friends and other writers, one of them John P. Marquand, who had written about it for the Book-of-the-Month Club. Marquand criticized the *New York Times Book Review* for not giving front-page coverage to its review of *From Here to Eternity*, "since it was a piece of news in the literary world that will not repeat itself for a considerable period of time." He also sympathized with Jones's involvement with his characters, under-standing that they meant "a lot more to you than the people around you."

The sales of the novel kept pace with its good notices, and by March, Scribner's doubled its advertising budget. By April, the book had become the country's number one best-seller, according to both the *Times* and the *Herald Tribune,* and by May, 163,000 copies had been sold, with sales continuing at the rate of more than four thou-sand a week.

In the midst of this success, Jones traveled to New York to consult Mitchell and to deal with business matters that had come up as a re-sult of his success. He had previously flirted with the idea of engaging a literary agent after leaving Maxwell Aley and had talked to Diar-muid Russell and Howard Moorepack. What kept him from signing up with an agent was his fear of jeopardizing his relationship with Scribner's. As he told Marian Ives, another agent, "I have a horror of anything that might even remotely possibly come between me and my publishers." He resolved the dilemma by asking Horace Manges to act as his lawyer in all literary matters, except his stories, which he would handle himself.

The trip to New York was less buoyant than he expected, partly because it came after rather than before publication. Jones felt oddly remote from the book, even when he saw a window at Scribner's Book Store filled entirely by a pyramid made up of over a hundred copies of *From Here to Eternity* and displaying enlarged copies of the reviews and a photograph of himself. Jones had noticed that the other window of the shop contained copies of novels by F. Scott Fitzgerald, whose work had been out of print for many years, and he was re-minded of how fickle popularity could be.

New York's literary journalists were eager to meet Jones. Like Theodore Dreiser, Sinclair Lewis, Ernest Hemingway, and Sherwood Anderson, he was in the great Midwestern tradition of American fic-tion, but somehow Jones seemed even more original and legendary. Wearing only a striped T-shirt in the Scribner's publicity photo-graphs, he looked like a modern-day Natty Bumppo or Huckleberry Finn brought to life, and everyone wanted to meet him. Interviewing him for the *New York Times Book Review,* Harvey Breit found him "youthful, earnest, spontaneous, honest, unembellished and spare," and to the reporter of the *New York Post,* "he was like a lonely rock; he is stubby, tough, with a craggy jaw, jutting eyebrows, and there's something rocklike too in the hard fix of his narrow eyes." Jones came through as blunt and unpretentious; he defended what he wrote about the army by saying, "If you're not free to call the turn on the way you see it, there's no freedom worth fighting for." He also disarmed interviewers by showing them how he had spent the money he earned. In his hotel cupboard, he had two new suits and a topcoat, bought at $75 each, and he had an Italian stiletto, fencing equipment, and a skeet gun. He also went to Dunhill's, where he bought a velvet box of seven pipes, one for each day of the week. He had long starved for things he wanted, but he made one journalist who interviewed him promise not to write about the pipes, because he didn't want to be thought of as a pipe-smoking author.

On March 6, a month before he came to New York, the *Times* announced that Columbia Pictures had bought the movie rights for *From Here to Eternity* for $82,000, which was described as "an exceptionally high price by current standards." The sale pleased Jones, despite his alleged indifference to the film version of his book, and he and his film agent, Ned Brown, discussed the possibility of his going to Hollywood to do the screenplay himself.

These business matters took up much of Jones's time in New York, but more important to him as a writer was meeting John P. Marquand and other members of the Book-of-the-Month Club board, Henry Seidel Canby, Christopher Morley, and Clifton Fadiman. Although they had not chosen *From Here to Eternity* as a main selection, perhaps fearing it was too outspoken for their membership, they were eager to meet Jones, imagining him to be a wild sort of primitive. Jones quickly caught on to what was expected and charmed them with his country manners. He was interested in the men of power and influence he was meeting in New York, for they represented a world he was ignorant of. His common sense and army experience made him sensitive to power, and he wanted to control his own destiny as much as possible. Jones also made a point of knowing the publicity men at Scribner's; he would join them and publicists from other publishing houses at the bars along Madison and Lexington Avenues where they met after work.

At Marquand's house in the East Fifties, Jones also met Marquand's son, John, a young writer who was later to publish a successful novel, *The Second Happiest Day*, under the name of John Phillips. Marquand made a point of introducing Jones to other of his contemporaries, all of them impressed by his success, and took him downtown to see William Styron. *Lie Down in Darkness*, Styron's first novel, was due to be published later in the year, and the two writers formed a lasting friendship. Burroughs Mitchell helped extend Jones's acquaintanceship with writers of his own age by introducing him to Vance Bourjaily, who was then living in New York. Bourjaily found Jones charming and reticent but was surprised by his desire to meet prostitutes.

The attention Jones received in New York was only a small sign of the extent to which *From Here to Eternity* attracted the interest of the American people. The link with the recently ended World War II might explain some of its success, but it affected readers far more deeply than did *The Naked and the Dead* by Norman Mailer, or James Gould Cozzens' *Guard of Honor*, John Horne Burns's *The Gallery*, or Irwin Shaw's *The Young Lions*. Readers found it so universal and authentic in language and situation that it was immediately placed in a category apart.

By limiting his setting to Hawaii, Jones had made Schofield Barracks stand for the world as a whole. It is a world seen from the inside, for unlike most other military novels of the time, it does not present the army from the drafted soldier's point of view but from that of the enlisted professional, for whom the army is society in miniature. For this reason, *From Here to Eternity* is a better study of individual soldiers than is found in most combat novels. The book's tight structure and psychological honesty account for much of its power.

Private Robert E. Lee Prewitt and Sergeant Milton Warden represent two opposed forces that together produce deadly results. Prewitt, the bugler and one-time pugilist who refuses to box for his company, is a man of principle and honor. An extreme individualist, he stands up against the army and the world; and in obeying his individual vision of the truth, he destroys himself.

His counterpart, the company sergeant, is a cynic. Warden understands Prewitt's idealism, but he has to live in the "real" world, where there are no ideals — only compromise and the daily routine, with its share of efficiency and dishonesty. Warden knows the rules and lives by them; he gets things done and limits his responsibility. He is no dreamer like Prewitt. If Prewitt stands for the individual, Warden stands for society. He survives, battered and embittered, but alive.

The contrast is extended in the relationship each man has with his girl. Prewitt falls in love with Lorene, a prostitute; he learns that her real name is Alma and wants to marry her. But she is like Warden; she

knows the real world and wants more money and status than an enlisted man will ever be able to provide. Warden has a dangerous affair
with Karen, the lonely wife of his company commander. They are in
love but are permanently separated by the habits of mind their different societies have created. They cannot go on together.

Women naturally played a minor role in the prewar military
world, especially for private soldiers. As in the Honolulu whorehouses, women existed mainly for sex. For American soldiers in the
1940s, brought up in the puritanical atmosphere of the United States,
prostitutes were at once exciting and frightening. They would do
things that the girl down the block wouldn't do, but they were also
beyond the social pale. In *From Here to Eternity,* Jones shows the
consequence of this status, how their sexual activities determine the
inner ambitions of his two female characters, Lorene the prostitute,
and Karen, the wife of Captain Holmes.

Whereas in ordinary life sexual relations usually develop after social connections have been made, in the army they begin with sex.
Prewitt and Warden are pleased with their conquests and then want
to bring deeper feelings of love into the relationships so that they can
become permanent. At this point, the conflict arises, for the women
put practical considerations before feelings. Lorene wants to marry
into a respectable middle-class family; Karen will marry Warden only
if he agrees to become an officer. The two men interpret these ambitions as an attack on their own identity; they feel they are being
manipulated, that the women have used their bodies in order to possess the souls of the men.

From Here to Eternity accurately portrays the reactions of Prewitt
and Warden to their women, but Lorene and Karen are not convincing. Jones was undoubtedly influenced by Lowney Handy in presenting his interpretation of female behavior. Lowney's cynicism about
marriage nurtured Jones's own bitterness and loneliness. He therefore
saw the relationship of men and women as one of mutual blackmail.
Nevertheless, *From Here to Eternity* is an accurate mirror of the feelings of most of the men Jones knew and portrayed at Schofield Barracks. It shows how, instead of easing the predicament in which men
find themselves, sex adds to their burden because of the romantic and
cynical attitudes with which they view it.

In general, Jones's novel is about the conflict between human aspirations and the demands of society, but it is not didactic. There

are no solutions, because the novel does not answer questions but asks them. Nevertheless, *From Here to Eternity* has a theme. What Jones wanted to show, he wrote, "was that the Army had an infallible way of destroying its own best advocates and adherents. The type of which Prewitt was one are almost always the best examples of real combat soldiers. I have seen such men do absolutely unbelievable things in combat. And yet — what amazed me — was that these very characteristics and ideas which made them the best possible soldiers in combat are the very same things which always threw them into conflict with authority out of combat, or even in combat, for that matter. There seemed to me here a very ironic paradox which the smugness of the Army (i.e., society) does not allow itself to see. I wanted to present it so that it had to be seen. I think that had Prewitt lived, and continued to live, he would have eventually become a Warden. That would mean compromising on his part, and the only alternative was death.

"Now I can look back and see that the Army did not really kill Prewitt. Prewitt killed Prewitt. Else why did not the Army also kill Warden? Warden knew the Army would kill Prewitt, if he could not in some way teach him something — something perhaps distasteful to learn — that he himself had had to learn in order to stay alive and retain a modicum of self respect, and personal integrity. I suppose that subconsciously this came over me as the book progressed and caused it to take the course it did. But the tragic essence of Prewitt was from the beginning the sense of foredoomed knowledge that he must die. That inevitability of avoidable disaster is the essence of all tragedy, from the Greeks on down."

The strength of *From Here to Eternity* lies in its emotions and poetic vision. Jones shows the contradictory truths of life and the irreconcilable impulses of his characters. Prewitt wanted to be the best bugler in the army and to marry Lorene, but it wasn't to be. Warden wanted to have Karen and to remain comfortable with himself as the company sergeant. But these ambitions were frustrated by other desires and needs. So Jones sees the reality of Schofield Barracks. It is simply life that Jones presents, and it is revealed truthfully, as it is in all high art, whether in the mismatched yearnings of Charles and Emma Bovary or in the conflicting desires of Othello and Iago.

Jones expresses his view of human possibility through Prewitt, the central character of his novel. Here he gives strength to his book by providing a psychological structure to Prewitt's behavior that parallels the traditional themes of the literature of quest, which goes at least as far back as the Greek tragedians. Prewitt's ambition, which is to live by only the highest standards of human integrity, is honorable and worthy of praise. But it is also an indirect affront to the gods. It suggests a prideful belief that a man can be in charge of his own destiny. Such a theme was very close to Jones, who as a young man often had to face the opposition of society to individual will. Jones's personal experience, coupled with the rich literary heritage from which he drew his story, gives it a universality that takes it beyond the barracks quadrangle.

Jones is able to express the conflicts he sees in Prewitt and the other men because of the beauty he finds in the spectacle of human confusion. The soldiers at Schofield Barracks both love and hate the army; they are at once proud of it and afraid of it; it supports them and emasculates them; they are both individuals and part of a company of men. One scene in particular that Jones uses to bring these forces together is one in which Prewitt, no longer the regimental bugler, plays taps.

"The first note was clear and absolutely certain. There was no question or stumbling in this bugle. It swept across the quadrangle positively, held a fraction of a second longer than most buglers hold it. Held long like the length of time, stretching away from weary day to weary day. Held long like thirty years. The second note was short, almost too short, abrupt. Cut short and too soon gone, like the minutes with a whore. Short like a ten minute break is short. And then the last note of the first phrase rose triumphantly from the slightly broken rhythm, triumphantly high on an untouchable level of pride above the humiliations, the degradations.

"He played it all that way, with a paused then hurried rhythm that no metronome could follow. There was no placid regimented tempo to the Taps. The notes rose high in the air and hung above the quadrangle. They vibrated there, caressingly, filled with infinite sadness, an endless patience, a pointless pride, the requiem and epitaph of the common soldier, who smelled like a common soldier, as a woman once had told him. They hovered like halos over the heads of the sleeping men in the darkened barracks, turning all grossness to the beauty that is the beauty of sympathy and understanding. Here we are, they said, you made us, now see us, dont close your eyes and shudder at it; this beauty and this sorrow, of things as they are.

"This is the song of the men who have no place, played by a man who has never had a place, and can therefore play it. Listen to it. You know this song, remember? This is the song you close your ears to every night, so you can sleep. This is the song you drink five martinis every night not to hear. This is the song of the Great Loneliness, that creeps in like the desert wind and dehydrates the soul. This is the song you'll listen to on the day you'll die. When you lay there in the bed and sweat it out, and know that all the doctors and nurses and weeping friends dont mean a thing and cant help you any, cant save you one bitter taste of it, because you are the one thats dying and not them; when you wait for it to come and know that sleep will not evade it and martinis will not put it off and conversation will not circumvent it and hobbies will not help you to escape it; then you will hear this song and, remembering, recognize it. This song is Reality. Remember? Surely you remember?"

As *From Here to Eternity* remained for month after month at the top of the best-seller list, it began to receive fresh assessments. In an article in the *New York Times Book Review* that constituted a second review, J. Donald Adams pointed out as a weakness that whereas Jones's descriptions of men were convincing, in his writing about men with women, "his realism turns to fantasy so inept that the effect is painful." The nonmilitary aspect of the book was noted somewhat differently by John W. Aldridge, the author of *After the Lost Generation,* who wrote, also in the *Times Book Review,* that the army provided "an immense moral scaffolding on which" Jones was able to display his talent as a writer, and that this is what "charges the novel with meaning and life." Aldridge claimed that *From Here to Eternity* was in fact "a novel of morality and manners in the same sense and to no less degree than the novels of Jane Austen and John Galsworthy."

Readers found in the novel what most interested them, and it is a sign of its complexity and depth that it could feed so many mouths. In its critique of the officer class, which is shown as physically and psychologically ineffective, the novel was welcomed by some for its apparent leftist sympathies. The enlisted men, by contrast, are shown as having to face life every day and forming a fellowship from their experiences. They fight, go to whorehouses, get drunk together, look after one another, and care for their fellow men. Yet despite his sympathies for enlisted men, Jones had no political purpose in *From Here to Eternity* that was comparable to Norman Mailer's in *The Naked and the Dead.* He was always profoundly skeptical of political theory and preferred to deal with observable facts.

The intensity of feeling that *From Here to Eternity* generated when it was first published was undoubtedly affected by readers' experience of World War II. For those who fought in that war, it was the great experience of their lives; for those who remained at home, fearing that the names of their relatives would appear on casualty lists, it was a nightmare. France and England had gone through a similar experience during the First World War, and such writers as Ford Madox Ford, Erich Maria Remarque, and Robert Graves wrote vividly of their experiences of trench warfare. World War II did not produce another literary response in Europe; it was to be the great traumatic experience for Americans. The great number of American war novels is evidence of its importance and emotional power. Of them all, *From Here to Eternity* has been almost universally acknowledged to be the most successful for the authenticity of its reporting, its emphasis on the life of the enlisted man, and its emotional power as a piece of fiction. Jones was able to catch the language of the ordinary soldier at Schofield Barracks in a way that rang true. Readers recognized that immediately and trusted him for it. But Jones was not merely reporting, for, as we have seen, he intended *From Here to Eternity* to be on the same scale as *War and Peace* and *The Charterhouse of Parma*.

The second summer in the life of the Handy Colony was devoted mainly to further building. Harry Handy arranged to have a former garage brought down from Robinson by his oil refinery workers and converted into a two-room cottage for Lowney. The original cottage was turned into a common room, and a screened-in ramada, inspired by similar structures at trailer parks, was added as a gathering place, with a fireplace, bookshelves, a Ping-Pong table, and slot machines. Two barracklike structures were later added, with small dormitory rooms, each containing only a bed, a desk, and a typewriter. The following summer Harry arranged to have refinery bulldozers dig out some of the land near the dormitories for a natural swimming pond for the use of the colonists.

To help pay for these additions and as a sign of his gratitude to Lowney, Jones contributed $65,000 from his royalties to the colony. It was soon legally incorported, and Lowney was appointed president, with Jones vice president and Harry secretary-treasurer. The success of *From Here to Eternity* helped make the colony attractive to beginning writers, especially when *Life* magazine ran a nine-page article, with photographs of Jones and the colony, called "James Jones and

His Angel." After that, applications for admission began to arrive in great numbers. Confident that her methods could be applied with equal success to other writers, Lowney devoted all her energies to the colony without remuneration of any kind.

As a joke, Jones put up a sign reading THE LAST RETREAT on the white board fence that enclosed the colony grounds, but from the first, the place was run on Spartan principles. The colonists all had to rise at six-thirty and were allowed to have only a cup of coffee or tea. Lowney did not believe in full breakfasts; from her study of yoga, she learned that it was better to write on an empty stomach. Lunch was served at noon, and a typical meal consisted of unpeeled boiled potatoes, corn on the cob, and a meat dish with pimientos. Plentiful supplies of cottage cheese were placed on the table in plastic containers. There was no butter or milk, which were disapproved of by Lowney, and the colonists were not allowed to drink water with their meals.

The afternoons were devoted to physical work, with everyone planting trees or bushes, laying bricks, or otherwise improving the appearance of the grounds. Supper was served at five-thirty, and afterward the colonists returned to their rooms, where they could read until lights were put out at eight. No one was allowed to have alcohol at this literary boot camp, except for Jones, who drank martinis after his morning work; nor were newspapers or radios permitted: Lowney believed they were full of lies and represented only the vested interests of their owners. Once a week, the colonists walked into Marshall, a quiet tree-shaded town with a main street and houses set back from wide streets. There they might go to Tom's restaurant, which was owned by a Greek, or stop in for drinks at Lee's Delight Bar. Lowney did not permit any outsiders except members of her own family, the Turners, to enter the grounds of the colony, so the colonists' social activities were limited to these people. Lowney's refusal to admit women writers to the colony did not blind her to the physical needs of her young men, however. Once a month she doled out $50 to each of them to spend in Terre Haute. Usually, they went together in Jones's new Chrysler, stopping first at a bar like the Idaho Club or the New Congress Club, where prostitutes were found. Otherwise, they would walk along Wabash Avenue or go to Second and Mulberry, the red light district, where girls in flimsy clothes sat in the windows of houses, rapping on the glass to attract passing men.

The austerity of life at the colony was in keeping with Lowney's definite ideas about writing, drawn from manuals and based on what she had read in philosophy and psychology. She had seen her theories of behavior work successfully when Jones developed the discipline and self-knowledge necessary to write *From Here to Eternity*. Now, outspoken, even crude, she talked to the young colonists who came to her, free of charge, hoping to become writers. She told them that in order to write they would first have to change themselves spiritually. They would have to rid themselves of all external relationships and ambition. "Lose that ego," she would say. That meant giving up all accepted literary notions, family, friends, and even girl friends. "A man who gets married and becomes a Householder will never be an Artist" Lowney told the colonists. "An Artist must carry the Yellow Begging Bowl, as the Masters of the Far East say, and go from house to house." Lowney turned her charges against their parents and tried to make them break all links with their past. She inveighed especially against women. "You think a woman spends her time listening to Chopin and reading Shelley and being wooed with roses?" she asked. "You think she's *romantic?* Bullshit. A woman is the most cold-blooded creature on earth when it comes to selecting a man. She spends every hour of the day in the process. She wants to know how much money that man is going to bring in in his lifetime, how strong he will be in protecting that nest, how a baby by him will fare. You poor sons-a-bitches. You think women are delicate and need protection, but that's a myth created by a matriarchal society."

In place of the books they had been taught to admire in college, Lowney urged them to read tough, feeling, manly books. She dismissed such writers as T. S. Eliot and Wallace Stevens as effete and academic. She urged a similar forthrightness in language and behavior. Her generosity was mixed with tyranny, and the young colonists soon got the message. "We said fuck, shit and piss, and were allowed delicately to delineate how our mothers had ruined our lives," John Bowers recalled of his experience there.

Wearing a lumberjack's shirt, blue jeans, and Indian moccasins, Jones was a natural exponent of the régime. "When he ate," Bowers recalled, "his whole hand gripped his fork, palm down, and he leaned over to within inches of his food. Frequently he removed his bridge-work and sucked out hidden slivers of meat there. Burps rolled at the table, fingers were licked of grease, and once in a great while came the report of a fart fired backwards toward the screen. We were taught to have no hang-ups about the bathroom. 'The fucking moth-

Elsie White Blessing and William Henry Blessing, Jones's maternal grandparents. Elsie White's forebears settled in Massachusetts in 1636; she and her husband moved to Vinton, Iowa, by covered wagon.

The mansion on Main Street, owned by Jones's paternal grandfather, George W. Jones, a prominent lawyer in Robinson, Illinois

Jones's mother, Ada Blessing Jones, who was later a diabetic. Her husband, Ramon Jones, shown in his uniform as captain of Northwestern University's football team, became a dentist in Robinson.

Earliest photograph of James Jones, age three, 1924, on the living room couch in Robinson, already interested in books

Jones with his sister, Mary Ann, who was born in 1925; at home in Robinson, 1927–1928.

Jones on his tricycle in Robinson. He was described by his father as looking like a car coming down the street with both doors wide open.

Jones's elder brother, George William, known as Jeff, born 1910. Interested in becoming a writer, he worked for the Ohio Oil Company and the Red Cross.

Jones at the age of fifteen. He wore glasses because of weak eye muscles.

The three Jones children together in Robinson, circa 1935. Mary Ann, who also wanted to become a writer, died suddenly at the age of twenty-seven.

The Robinson Township High School band, 1939, in which Jones played trombone

Annis E. Skaggs Fleming

The 27th Infantry Regiment, known as the Wolf-hounds, at Schofield Barracks, Hawaii, February 1940. Jones transferred to this unit from the Army Air Corps to prove his courage. "If I stay behind the lines while other guys are fighting, I'll hate my guts." Jones is shown at left in his air corps uniform, Hickam Field, Hawaii, 1940.

Jones with Lowney Handy, who in 1943 became his mistress and foster mother and supported him for the first fifteen years of his literary life

Lowney and her husband, Harry Handy, built an addition to their house in Robinson, where Jones could live comfortably and work on *From Here to Eternity.*

During the years it took to write the novel, Jones often traveled to Florida to work and fish.

626 526

He also lived in a trailer in Arizona, where Lowney visited him.

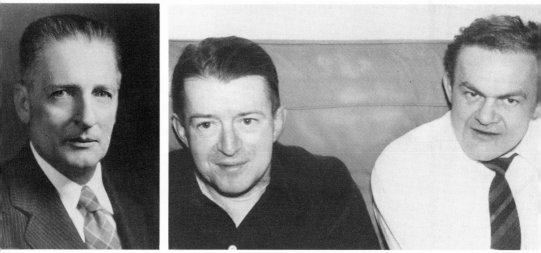

Maxwell Perkins *(far left)*, of Charles Scribner's Sons, was famous for working with F. Scott Fitzgerald, Ernest Hemingway, and Thomas Wolfe. He became Jones's editor in 1946. After Perkins' death in 1947, Burroughs Mitchell *(center)* became Jones's editor.

Advance sales and reviews indicated the coming success of *From Here to Eternity*. Scribner's devoted an entire window of its Fifth Avenue bookstore to the novel, with enlargements of photographs, testimonials, and newspaper articles.

Scribner's publicity photographs of the unknown author introduced Jones dramatically as a new kind of writer, quite different from the usual, tweed-clad novelist.

Jones's appearance in New York attracted public attention. He is shown with Sidney Bechet, the jazz musician, and with Burroughs and Helen Mitchell, celebrating the success of his novel.

Pat Meara

Unable to work in New York, Jones returned to Marshall, Illinois, where he and Lowney, shown eating spaghetti with friends, established the Handy Colony for young writers.

Jones in Fort Myers Beach, Florida, receiving mail after the success of *From Here to Eternity*

With the money he earned from the book, Jones built a large house on the grounds of the Handy Colony. There he wrote his second novel, *Some Came Running*.

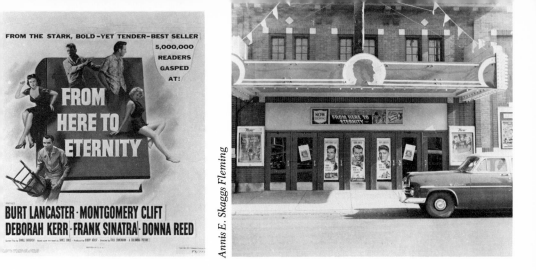

The success of the movie version of *From Here to Eternity* greatly increased Jones's fame. A Columbia Pictures poster (*above, left*) emphasizes its origins as a novel. In Robinson, Illinois, the Lincoln Theater was bedecked for the first local showing of Jones's film.

The KP scene with Burt Lancaster as Sergeant Warden humiliating Montgomery Clift as Prewitt

After the film was made, Clift occasionally visited Jones in Marshall.

Gloria Mosolino from Pottsville, Pennsylvania, married Jones in 1957. She had been an actress in New York and appeared briefly in several films, including *(above)* Elia Kazan's *A Face in the Crowd*, 1957.

Right: A strip from a New York subway photo booth, taken during their courtship in New York

Jones and Gloria spent their honeymoon in Haiti at Oloffson's Hotel, where they were visited by friends, including Tom Chamales *(below)*, a former member of the Handy Colony.

nes at Oloffson's Hotel, 1957

Tom Hollyman

nes and Gloria in the John
ielgud Suite of Oloffson's Hotel

turning to New York, they saw
any old friends, including
orman and Adele Mailer and
rroughs Mitchell, Jones's editor,
own dancing with Gloria.

The Joneses moved to Europe in 1958 and traveled widely. They spent the summer of 1959 in Portofino and in 1961 went to Yugoslavia, where Jones resumed his interest in scuba diving and brought up a number of Greek amphorae from the bottom of the sea.

In the winter, they went to Switzerland for skiing at Klosters.

ers of this country have made us all ashamed of our bodies' functions,' Jones would say. 'Everybody is terrified of being human.' "

Jones enjoyed being cock of the walk in the Handy Colony. The rules imposed on the younger colonists did not apply to him, and he lived a relatively normal life in his Silver Streak trailer. Among all the privates in the colony, he was like a top sergeant, and he adopted the exaggerated gestures and swagger he had first observed among noncommissioned officers in the army. Wearing bracelets of heavy copper and turquoise, he began to initiate sports, making the colonists box with him or race on motorcycles. When he rode his tan Harley-Davidson, he dressed up in a black leather jacket with silver studs and a black cap with dark glasses. He loved this Hell's Angel costume because it was the symbol of the outlaw, the individualist.

Sometimes he would go to Robinson and stop at the country club, wearing his motorcycle costume or just a ten-gallon hat with blue jeans cut off at the knees. He knew that because he was James Jones, he would have to be served, and it amused him to be outrageous. He enjoyed being the tough guy, gnawing a turkey leg at the country club buffet; it was his way of thumbing his nose at the upper class of his town.

Such behavior didn't suit him, but it was part of a public personality he had developed. From early childhood, Jones had adopted certain protective mannerisms to help him cope with his surroundings. When he thought it necessary, he would be tough and aggressive; in the army, where he was surrounded by people tougher than he was, he would keep to himself and try to avoid trouble. He was aware that in putting on an act, he was not being entirely honest with himself, but he realized that his role playing was effective. Once he became famous, he knew that he would often have to deal with strangers. Since he refused to pretend that he was polished or urbane, he reverted to his roughneck manner, even though those who knew him understood that it was an act designed to cover his sensitive inner nature.

Warmhearted and intense, energetic and liberated, Lowney devoted herself passionately to her charges. But if any of them came to Marshall imagining they would participate in workshops or exchange ideas about writing with the other colonists, they were greatly mistaken. Talking about writing was forbidden, and Lowney, generally after consulting Jones, alone would comment on their work. But even before the colonists did work of their own, they were required to sit

down at their typewriters and copy out lengthy passages from published novels or complete short stories. The stories that had to be copied word for word included "A Rose for Emily" by William Faulkner,
"The Snows of Kilimanjaro" by Ernest Hemingway, and "The Downward Path to Wisdom" by Katherine Anne Porter. The novelists
whose work was chosen were selected according to the individual's
needs. If a colonist seemed unable to express feeling, he was told to
copy Thomas Wolfe; for dialogue, he would be told to copy passages
from *The Sun Also Rises;* for style, *The Great Gatsby.* The act of
copying was also intended to make young writers find out what it is
like to finish an extended piece of work. Jones himself said that one
could read until his eyes are red, but only by copying word for word
could one see how a writer builds up his effects. The copying was also
intended to help young writers learn how to handle transitions from
one scene to another. They were to learn economy of expression and
become less prolix.

Lowney did not want her writers to imitate the writers they copied; on the contrary, she chose passages for copying that were unlike
the young writer's own style in order to force him to develop other
ways of expression. She would have the colonists type out sections
from Dashiell Hammett and Raymond Chandler, not because she
wanted them to write detective fiction but because she admired the
writers' dialogue. What she hoped for was a process of osmosis from
the published writer to the unpublished.

The writers to be copied were limited to American contemporaries
like Dos Passos, Conrad Aiken, and Hemingway. Lowney was scornful of foreign writers like Proust, whom she considered effete, and she
disliked Henry James. The niceties of their styles were not appreciated in Marshall; indeed, colony neophytes were encouraged to use
double negatives and coarse language — "I ain't got nothin' here" —
in an effort to be truthful to their inner natures.

Jones was aware of the limitations of the Handy Colony and of
Lowney's provincial attitudes toward art and literature. When Robert Cantwell visited Marshall to do a piece on Jones for *The Saturday
Review,* he complained that the atmosphere of the place was insensi-
tive. Jones admitted that Cantwell was right but explained that it was
"a direct reaction against the hyper-sensitive esthete attitude of the
Bowles-McCullers, Vidal, etc. axis which, at least I feel, is destroying
itself and its ability to communicate." As a member of the colony,

Jones was naturally loyal to it in an automatic way, but he was also glad of opportunities to get away.

In the summer of 1951, he accepted an invitation to Chicago to be interviewed when one of his stories appeared in *Esquire* magazine. He stayed with Herbert Kogan, the book critic of the *Chicago Sun-Times,* and was happy to sleep on the living room couch and play on the floor with the Kogans' one-year-old child. Twice during the visit he met Nelson Algren, who, jealous of his success, snubbed him the first time. They met at a bar the second time and became such warm friends that they cut each other's wrists with a glass and swore to be blood brothers forever.

On display as a celebrity, Jones sometimes played the country hick. He knew there was a thin line between what was intentional in his behavior and what was not. He was ignorant of many things and kept lists of words he did not know in a conscientious effort to increase his vocabulary. He also knew what people thought of him, aware that to a certain degree they were right, so he often played their game and adopted an expected role, saying "yup" and dropping his g's. At the house of a pretentious Chicago matron, he once described how he was going to "architect" his house in Marshall, sure that she would wonder how he could ever write a book.

With the coming of cold weather in November, Jones and Lowney drove down to Fort Myers Beach, where they had stayed when *From Here to Eternity* was published. This time, they took separate rooms at King's Cottage, for both were working and their relationship was showing signs of strain. "We see each other for meals — sometimes," Jones told Burroughs Mitchell. He was trying to get back into the routine of the time when he was writing *From Here to Eternity,* but it wasn't easy. "It is hard, painful, unpleasant, and thoroughly horrible. I hate it," he said. He got up at seven, had coffee and toast at eleven, "enough food to keep my gut from grumbling but not enough to make me sleepy," and would then continue his work until three in the afternoon. He would then have his one big meal of the day and read until bedtime. "Doing lots of reading," he commented, "and need it." The routine left little room for pleasure. "It's a monotonous, grueling existence, with absolutely no compensations. I wonder why I do it. I suppose its because I want to be a great writer." He felt terribly remote. "Is New York still there?" he asked Mitchell plaintively.

Jones was soon to learn what was going on in New York when it was announced in January that he had won the National Book Award for fiction for *From Here to Eternity*. Only in its second year, the award was given by the Book Publishers Council as a response to the somewhat bland awards that had been made by the Pulitzer Prize committee in recent years. The principal difference in the selection procedure was that instead of having anonymous critics choose the winners, the decision was made by a committee of professional writers. The fiction jury for 1951 comprised Robert Gorham Davis, Brendan Gill, Lloyd Morris, Budd Schulberg, and Jean Stafford.

The leading candidates for the fiction prize were Herman Wouk's *The Caine Mutiny*, J. D. Salinger's *The Catcher in the Rye*, and Jones's *From Here to Eternity*. The jury met and was deeply divided. The main supporters of Jones's novel were Jean Stafford and Brendan Gill, who believed that it was a far more literary work than its principal rival, *The Caine Mutiny*. Their views carried the day, but the award was not unanimous.

The awards ceremony was held at the Commodore Hotel on January 29, 1952. Jones was summoned from Florida by Burroughs Mitchell and appeared in a wide-lapeled tweed suit, a bright red tie, and a pencil-line mustache. The nonfiction winner was Rachel Carson for *The Sea Around Us*, and Marianne Moore was cited for her *Collected Poems*. Six hundred people were in the main ballroom when John Mason Brown, the theater critic, handed out gold medals to the winners. The fiction jury's citation stated that *From Here to Eternity* was "a novel of scope and dimension which develops a major theme with passionate honesty and profound feeling. Mr. Jones has given us a directly experienced and yet imaginative re-creation of social circumstances that transcends the merely documentary."

Each of the recipients responded to the award, and Jones's comments produced a good deal of controversy and amusement. Few in the audience knew what to expect of this unknown phenomenon out of the Middle West, and Jones's initial modesty charmed the audience. But when he reached his text, taken from correspondence with Maxwell Perkins, he puzzled his listeners and made them think he was naïve. Writers, he said, "seem to have a phobia about not being rascals — or at least for concealing that they are rascals. No one but a rascal would expose to the world all of his friends' intimate secrets along with his own. No one but a rascal would allow his wife to go hungry, his dog unwashed, his child undiapered, while he sat picking obliviously at a typewriter as if he hadn't a care in the world.

"It is my contention that if we can inject a little rascality into our writers, make them once again be capable of malice, envy and hate, this hopelessness automatically will clear up of itself. It seems to me that the weary futility and deep depression we all hate to see in our literature today are caused by this fear of rascality in our writers which is turning them unwittingly into moralists."

According to newspaper reports, the audience was united in its appreciation of Rachel Carson and Marianne Moore and enjoyed the address given afterward by Whitney Griswold, the president of Yale University. But many thought that Jones was on a perceptibly lower level of accomplishment and probably would never write another book. Jones himself was nervous, sweating profusely; he gave the impression of being in a panic. At the press conference that preceded the ceremony, he had been bluntly asked, "Are you Prewitt?"

Sitting at a table between the other award winners, his hands pressed together so forcefully that his knuckles turned white, he replied, "Of course I'm Prewitt. I'm every one of the characters in that book. I wrote it." Jones was also asked many questions about the four-letter words in his novel. His response, later published in *Life*, was "You can't have a tough master sergeant go around saying 'gee whiz.' "

Jones was aware that his book's popularity contributed to the animosity of many in the audience who equated literary quality with modest sales. "To see the Award added to the already great commercial success of my novel must have been very trying to the souls of some of the more powerful book reviewers," he later wrote. At the same time, he considered that it was "an award to a professional by professionals," and that made him value the prize.

The trip gave Jones an opportunity to see some of his fellow writers, many of whom had been encouraged by their publishers to attend the ceremony. Vance Bourjaily introduced Jones to Norman Mailer and invited them both to dinner at his apartment in Greenwich Village. Mailer had expected a swaggering masculine encounter, but Jones "was completely without front, very plain mid-western with good manners. With his blond hair, blue eyes and good coloring, he looked like a farm hand. I had known such people in the army, but here was one who could write." Subsequently, Jones and Mailer had many long talks, and Mailer found him a "sensationally great guy." At the same time, acknowledging that *From Here to Eternity* was better than *The Naked and the Dead*, he recognized that Jones was the new star, and he was both curious and apprehensive about what he might do next.

During his stay in New York, Jones and Mailer went to many of the same parties and visited bars along Eighth Avenue. Mailer also gave parties at his apartment at 41 First Avenue that were attended by such writers as Hortense Calisher, Louis Auchincloss, William Styron, and Calder Willingham. When Jones was in attendance, he was open and fun, obviously having a good time as a celebrity. Whenever he came into a room, people were drawn to him and gathered round.

Many of the parties were noisy and drunken, and at more than one, women took off their clothes late at night. Jones had little experience of this sort of thing, but he was enthusiastic. "Let's go and knock over some garbage cans," he would say, in prelude to a night out; and he would often importune his friends for women, offering to pay for a girl to keep him company. He was like a soldier on a weekend pass, wanting to make the best of his opportunities. Among strangers, he would sometimes revert to his tough-guy army pose or pretend to be a country hick, blowing his nose with his finger and claiming it was unhealthful to put a used handkerchief back into his pocket. But with writers, he was so caught up in a feeling of camaraderie that he behaved naturally. After so many years of loneliness and solitude, so many nights alone in the trailer, he was not only accepted as a writer; he was admired and praised and sought after. Moreover, he was liked as a person and he knew it.

This feeling was confirmed one night in Greenwich Village when Styron, Jones, and Mailer went out together. They had to pause for a stoplight before crossing the street. Styron, the tallest of the three, threw his arms over the shoulders of his two companions and said, "Here we are, the three best writers of our generation, and we're all together!"

6

❦

THE COLONY

THE PRICE for writing a successful first book in America is usually paid by the second. Many writers attempt to avoid the challenge by following up with an intentionally minor work that will evade damaging comparisons with the first. This is the safe way to get over the hurdle of the second book, designed to protect a literary reputation from critical attack. But James Jones was never one to avoid risks: he wanted his second book to be even better than *From Here to Eternity*. He therefore set out to write a vast panoramic novel that would deal with both social issues and human relationships. In the period immediately following the publication of *From Here to Eternity*, Jones wrote some short stories, partly to warm up to his theme, but soon he was hard at work on a new novel that would eventually be published as *Some Came Running*.

He had thought of the book as early as 1946, when he told Maxwell Perkins that he wanted to write a novel about "the perfect citizen, as our society wants and expects a man to be, a man who has fulfilled all the obligations asked him by society, but who has not received the awards society promises to such a man, as no honest person ever has, I think." Jones modified this idea by combining it with the central theme of his abandoned novel, *They Shall Inherit the Laughter*, which dealt with the return of war veterans to civilian life. Basing the story on his own experience, he decided to choose as a central character a young writer, Dave Hirsh, whose return to a small town in Illinois will have an "explosive effect" and "change damn near everybody's life in the town one way or another."

The town, called Parkman in the novel, was closely based on Robinson, but Jones did not intend to ridicule it. Living at the colony in

Marshall, he was more inclined toward a balanced assessment of the Middle West. What interested Jones about Marshall, and by extension Robinson, was "a curious combination of Eastern frugality and taciturnity, and Southern laziness and easy-going living. You can feel this strange mixture of national character types as you walk along the streets up town. The architecture of the courthouse, set in its square of big trees with the bandstand still sitting in the corner, is equal parts Eastern plainness and Southern rococo."

The character who best stands for the relaxed Southern aspect of the town is 'Bama Dillard. He represents working-class virtues, pleasure taken immediately and for its own sake, and a casual attitude toward sex. Opposed to these values are those of Frank Hirsh, the successful elder brother of the protagonist who is based mainly on Jones's Uncle Charlie. He represents middle-class ambition and propriety.

Even more important to the social and financial relationships of the town were the sexual, and Jones wanted to use his own experience in his novel — "my love for Lowney, my living in her house as her lover, and the impact of this act upon the town; and what follows in their abrupt aboutface when I became successful as a writer."

In attempting to combine social, sexual, economic, and artistic themes, Jones was undertaking an exceptionally ambitious novel. Moreover, Parkman, Illinois, would not provide the neat social structure that made Schofield Barracks so separate and easily definable in *From Here to Eternity*. The autobiographical elements would be modified as the characters took on their own lives, but what mainly concerned Jones in the early stages of his work was to understand and sympathize with his characters so as to re-create them convincingly.

Upset by the middle-class values he encountered on his return to Robinson from the army, Jones had taken solace in the company of the working-class people he met at bars and at the American Legion post. They seemed more honest and open than the people who belonged to Uncle Charlie's world. He had put two of them in a story, "None Sing So Wildly," but soon he found himself having doubts about them: the better he got to know them, the weaker they appeared, and he was reminded of the troubles he had had in characterizing most of the enlisted men he knew while writing *From Here to Eternity*. "I think one of the main problems with this book," he wrote Burroughs Mitchell, "with me anyway, is that I have really to believe these people are capable of integrity. Of sacrifices, of Love, of Hate. I think I really dont believe they are. Like Prewitt and Warden — if I had written them as they really were in real life (which is what I'd really *like* to do) I wouldnt have had any story. It is really only *my* vision, *my* picture of them that makes them so. I was intrigued by these two guys in Robinson. But actually they were just a couple of bums, who posed as being — well, whatever it was: with integrity. I obviously romanticized them."

The problem was complicated by his own changing attitudes. "I find, Mitch," he wrote in another letter, "that I'm getting more and more cynical about the human race. Logically, the danger in this is that in becoming so detached and objective, I am in danger of not being able to get inside my characters any longer. Now, it seems, instead of having to rewrite to excise sentimentality, I have to rewrite to inject a little sentiment. I do not want to become a Dreiser, or Norris or Farrell — despite reviewers. I want to love people — including myself; but they are all such fucking damn fools — including myself." In an effort to get back on an even keel, he reread Flaubert's *Madame Bovary*, and Mitchell sent him Ford Madox Ford's *The Good Soldier*.

Jones continued to work hard, writing every day from six to eleven in the morning, but he was filled with dark forebodings and haunted by the fear of being a one-book novelist. "I've been depressed for quite a while," he wrote Mitchell. "I fear I've lost my drive to write because of being successful. I fear I've lost my ability to really like people." He had meantime begun to fear that his ideas about society and sex might prevent him from writing convincing fiction. He told Robert Cantwell that he was trying a new system to make sure that his writing was still spontaneous. "I'm working totally consciously and I know it. But I've taught myself a trick which is to do all my *thinking* when I am not *working*. Thus, in effect, I really employ two levels of creativity: the thinking level, and the working level. I think up what I want to say when Im *not* working, and deliberately forget it when I *am* working. Thus I think of meaning, and organization and direction and often even individual episodes (which are the only things I make notes on), but when I sit down to work I close this part off and write only to make it real, and often in so doing find Ive changed course completely — while still hanging on to the original skeleton."

Deeply interested in philosophical questions, Jones was nevertheless afraid of the negative influence they can have on fiction. "The intelligent writer," he told Cantwell, "must always keep in mind what is moral (philosophical) today will not be so tomorrow." What endures is the depiction of actual life, for it alone can encompass contradictions and reconcile opposites, which by definition a strict philosophy cannot do. In fiction, truth can have many faces, and does; in philosophy, a coherent system is required. "No philosophy will ever even begin to approach reality," said Jones, "until it accounts for Paradox, you know. As long as paradox exists, there isn't any such thing as philosophy. At least not for me."

Jones wanted to go deeper than philosophy; he wanted, as he informed Cantwell, "to get *beneath* the soul, some way, and find out whats really there. Everybody has a soul, you know; which he cultivates and waters and nurtures like a small garden and with which he competes for a prize in the annual Garden Show. Its like owning a car, having a soul is. You may live in a disintegrating tumbledown shack, but you own a car. You just need it. Its so hard to get around and do your shopping without one." He wanted to know what we really are underneath: "Underneath the body is the personality, and underneath the personality is the soul, but underneath the *soul* . . . what?"

In correspondence with friends, Jones was always raising theoretical questions about the mystery of art. There were no simple answers to any of the points he raised, but the letters were useful in making him reflect on what he was doing and consider its relationship to daily life. He came closest to defining his artistic method in a letter to Shelby Foote: "If a man can *become* every character he writes about in a given book, no matter how contradictory, he can have the same passion for explaining *himself* (which is then every character) that he would have for the main character in an autobiographical novel. Thats the only way I can describe what I feel. Tolstoi was very good at that, when he wasnt preaching. That old quote of Stendhal: 'I never heard of a crime I too could not have committed.' "

Despite his preoccupation with the new novel, Jones was involved not only with the life of the Handy Colony but also with his brother, Jeff, and his sister, Mary Ann. Jeff had written poetry and fiction, and Jones passed on his manuscripts to Maxwell Perkins at Scribner's. Unfortunately, Jeff never succeeded in finding a publisher, but he married and brought up a family of three boys. The Jones brothers corresponded frequently and once took a joint camping trip in Michigan in search of Hemingway's Big Two-Hearted River. For a time they were very close, but eventually they drifted apart. Jones later criticized Jeff's domesticity by saying that "in reality he didn't want to write. He wanted to have written."

Jones also kept in touch with Mary Ann, who had developed literary aspirations of her own. Rebelling against Jeff, with whom she had been living since her father's suicide, she left his house and obtained a false birth certificate so that she would seem older than she was and could work as a waitress in a bar. Jeff and his family were then living in Miami, and there Mary Ann began her independent and marginal life. She was soon involved with drugs, and in 1944, only nineteen, she married a black man who treated her so badly that she tried to commit suicide by cutting her wrists.

With a friend, she embarked on a peripatetic life, wandering across the country. To procure lodgings for the night, the two girls would pose as prostitutes and take men to a motel, where, after registering, they would occupy one room and lock out their would-be clients. Eventually they reached Hollywood, where Mary Ann, now calling herself Marianne, hoped to become an actress. She lived with her aunt, Mollie Haish, but like so many young women who dreamed of stardom, she failed to get a part and gradually lost her figure. Meanwhile, she sent Jones some of her writing, and he was impressed by her literary gifts. He had always tried to support her, but time and distance kept them apart. As he later admitted, he had been attracted to her physically but, frightened of the possibility of incest, had kept his distance. As time went on, Mary Ann's life became increasingly unstable, until Lowney eventually offered to take her into the Handy Colony, where she lived in a trailer.

As the only female colonist, she was somewhat disruptive and had trouble concentrating on her work. Nevertheless, she completed a substantial part of an autobiographical novel called *The Third Time You Killed Me*, which is about a girl who runs away from home because her prudish aunt disapproves of her. She ends up in Miami, where she falls in love with a soldier who is obviously modeled on Jones.

One morning in June 1952, Mary Ann was found dead on the floor of her trailer. At first, it looked as though she might have died falling from an upper bunk, but evidently she had had a seizure, caused by a brain tumor, during which she swallowed her tongue. Mary Ann's sudden death at twenty-seven was a shock to Jones and his brother, who happened to be at the colony at the time. They had known about her tumor and taken her for medical treatments that were supposed to have cured it. But like a doomed heroine from Norris or Dreiser, a child of the Depression whose parents died young, Mary Ann seemed fated to grow up alone in America and to die with her talents never realized.

Hearing of her death, Jones's Uncle Charlie immediately called on the United States marshal in Danville, Illinois, to investigate the circumstances of Mary Ann's death and to arrange for a coroner's inquest. The case was duly tried, and the jury ruled that she died of natural causes. Aware that his uncle's action was motivated by his dislike of Lowney Handy and a desire to discredit the colony, Jones did not at first react to it, but eventually he wrote a letter explaining the circumstances. He ended by saying, "I dont want to hear from you, and I shall not enter into a recriminatory debate with you or write you anything further."

Mary Ann was buried on June 8, 1952, and a copy of *From Here to Eternity* was placed beneath her pillow in the casket. Jones later dedicated *Some Came Running* to her memory.

Living in Marshall isolated Jones from the rest of the world, but his work was still widely disseminated throughout the country. Hardcover sales of *From Here to Eternity* would soon reach 500,000 copies in the United States, and New American Library brought out the paperback edition in 1952. In the first year alone, Jones earned $178,000 in royalties, three times the amount of his advance. Eventually, the novel sold well over five million copies in paperback.

The success of the film version of *From Here to Eternity*, released in the same year, not only contributed to these sales but also added to Jones's stature as a national celebrity. During the negotiations that preceded the sale of the rights to Columbia Pictures, Ned Brown, Jones's film agent, had arranged for Jones to be hired to write a treatment for the picture, and in the late spring of 1951, Jones and Lowney had gone to Hollywood, where they stayed modestly at a guest house on Vine Street. The next day, Jones called on Harry Cohn, the head of the studio, wearing an army T-shirt and jeans. From the first, they got on well: Jones described Cohn as "an undereducated self-made tycoon with a private barber, and he loves every minute of it."

Cohn was famous for being brash and aggressive, a man who churned out mediocre movies but who now and again liked to produce a serious film and who was proud of the Oscar statuettes lined up behind the desk in his office. He had a foul tongue, and when it was learned that he had bought *From Here to Eternity*, people asked, "Why should Harry want to buy a dirty book like that?" To which the answer was "He thinks everybody talks that way."

Cohn assigned Jones to work with his assistant Sylvan Sidney and with Eve Ettinger, the story editor, and to write a treatment that would avoid problems of language and situation that might arouse the hostility of the Breen Office, Hollywood's censorship bureau. Jones followed instructions, but so violated the spirit of his own book that Cohn found himself in the odd position of defending Jones's artistic reputation, protesting to Jones that he had "bastardized the book" and cleaned it up "without integrity or purpose."

Jones stayed on alone in Hollywood for a few weeks, but his heart was not in the work, and he returned to Illinois. Although he had agreed to work on the treatment during the summer, he wrote to Cohn that he was "not technically proficient enough" to work on it alone. "I am not a screen writer," he wrote when he withdrew from the project. He then sent Cohn a presentation copy of *From Here to Eternity*, inscribing it, "From one old fuck-up to another, no strings attached." At the bottom, he added, "Now for Christ's sake, *read* it!" because he knew that Cohn read only synopses.

To replace Jones, Cohn hired Daniel Taradash, who had made a reputation as co-author of a screenplay for Clifford Odets' *Golden Boy* and who volunteered his services because he knew Jones's novel. Taradash had already thought of ways to avoid difficulties that the book presented for filming, especially because the studio was eager to have the army's cooperation. Knowing that the stockade scene would surely upset the army, he suggested that it be omitted; Maggio's death would be sufficient to indicate the brutality. He also suggested ways to improve the dramatic quality of the story; he had Prewitt play taps after Maggio's death and interlaced the two love stories "so that there seemed a connection between them," even though there was none.

Once Taradash's treatment was completed, he and Buddy Adler, the film's producer, flew to Washington, where they successfully obtained the army's cooperation in their filming the movie at Schofield Barracks. Taradash then wrote the screenplay and sent a copy to Jones, who approved of it with only minor suggestions, among them that the ending should strike the right note, since it had taken him twenty or thirty revisions in the novel. The effect he wanted was of "life going on, people going on, Prew's death (so important to us and the audience) really nothing but a small ripple in a vast moving tide and current that stops for no man; really nothing, all this emotion, all this wasted energy."

The next step was the selection of a director, and at Taradash's suggestion, Fred Zinnemann was chosen. Well known for *High Noon,* he had also made a film called *Teresa,* which was about the army and seemed authentic. Zinnemann, Adler, Taradash, and Cohn were all involved in choosing the cast of the film. Burt Lancaster was their unanimous choice to play Warden, and Montgomery Clift was chosen for Prewitt. Jones had met Clift at Vance Bourjaily's house in New York and was so impressed with him that he wrote to Adler, suggesting him for the part; fortunately the others agreed to the idea. Eli Wallach was the original choice for Maggio, but he was under contract for another film, with Elia Kazan. In the meantime, Frank Sinatra, who was then in Africa filming *Mogambo,* sent telegrams offering his services, because he thought a role in *From Here to Eternity* would reverse the downward drift of his career. He was so eager for the role that he flew to Hollywood from Nairobi and agreed to play it for the minimum fee of $1000 a week. Joan Crawford was originally chosen for Karen but withdrew, and when Deborah Kerr's agent suggested her for the role, Harry Cohn said, "You stupid son of a bitch, get out of here." At the end of the day, he was still so outraged at the suggestion that he told Adler, Zinnemann, and Taradash about it. They all looked at one another and agreed that she was the perfect choice just because she was not a promiscuous type. Donna Reed was chosen for Lorene because she had performed so well in a screen test and had a certain propriety suitable for the part.

When the time came to start shooting the picture in Hollywood, Jones arranged to get a job working on another film based on a story called "The Circus," from Max Catto's *The Killing Frost.* For a guarantee of $20,000, he was employed by Norma Productions, a company controlled by Harold Hecht and Burt Lancaster. Although he worked conscientiously on the script, Jones felt he was in Hollywood mainly to be involved in the filming of *From Here to Eternity.*

Jones visited Zinnemann on the set and gave him special information about the prewar army and also technical advice. To an exceptional degree, *From Here to Eternity* excited those engaged in it, and Zinnemann was able to get first-rate performances from his actors because they all felt they were involved in an important project. Montgomery Clift took his role very seriously and talked to Jones at length about Prewitt. He rehearsed every scene privately in advance and carried a dog-eared copy of the novel with him, sometimes suggesting changes in dialogue that would better reflect Prewitt's character.

Off the set, Jones, Clift, and Frank Sinatra formed a threesome and stayed together at the Roosevelt Hotel on Hollywood Boulevard. Every night they went out together to a local Italian restaurant. "We would get very, very loaded," Jones later recalled. "After dinner and a lot more drinks, we would weave outside into the night and all sit down on the curb next to the lamppost. It became our lamppost and we'd mumble more nonsense to each other. We felt very close." Back at the hotel, they continued their drinking and were so rowdy that they were twice threatened with eviction. Like comrades in arms, they were constructive by day, destructive at night, seeking solace in alcohol and one another's company.

Feeling that their celebrity cut them off from ordinary human experience, they thought they were somehow being punished for their success. Moreover, they all had problems with women, and Montgomery Clift was a homosexual. Jones's friendship with Clift made others think that he was also a homosexual, and his habit of wearing Indian jewelry and tight jeans seemed to confirm the suspicion. When asked whether he and Clift had become intimate, Jones replied, "I would have had an affair with him, but he never asked me."

Jones was always open and even eager to talk about sex, and he liked giving the impression of having had more sexual experience than most people. It is almost certain that his remark about Clift was a put-on, for he enjoyed shocking other men by asking, in a matter-of-fact way, "Do you mean to say you've never sucked cock?" While it is not impossible that he had had an occasional homosexual experience as a young man, it is unlikely. Certainly he had had no such experiences while at Schofield Barracks, for homosexuals were immediately known by the other men and were socially segregated, which never happened to Jones. He was also too busy searching for a sympathetic woman to take an interest in homosexuality. His habit of talking knowingly about sex derived in all likelihood from his shyness and his sexual diffidence.

From Here to Eternity was completed in May, and Harry Cohn ordered the film to open on August 5 at the Capitol Theater in New

York. It was risky to open in midsummer with no air conditioning and most of the critics out of town, but Cohn sensed that people knew it was a special film. He took a full-page advertisement in the *New York Times* and for the first time in his life signed his name to it.

Nearly everywhere the movie received favorable reviews and was extraordinarily popular. In New York, the Capitol had to keep open round the clock to satisfy the demand for seats, closing only in the early morning to allow the janitors to clean the floors. Elsewhere in the country it was similarly successful. The film had cost Columbia $2.5 million, and by 1954, gross receipts reached $80 million. Coming at a time when the film industry was suffering from the competition of television, it showed that a serious and honest film could become a commercial success.

Jones was in Marshall when the film opened and was asked to go to Chicago to take part in the publicity campaign welcoming it there. He was so busy with *Some Came Running* that he sent a telegram saying he couldn't come. "I love you all," he said, "but please leave me alone." His earlier doubts about the film vanished with its success, and he was especially impressed by Clift, Sinatra, and Ernest Borgnine, who played Fatso, the sadistic stockade guard. It was not a *"truly* great film," he said, but "an immensely fine one."

The reception of the film, coming so soon after the extraordinary sales of the original novel, put Jones at the pinnacle of success as a young American novelist. It placed him, at the age of thirty-one, in a category of celebrity from which he would never be removed, for through the movie he became known to millions of people all over the world who had never read the book but who somehow felt they had. Knowing that *From Here to Eternity* was his story and his vision, they respected him for his courage and honesty in telling it. That was something Jones would never lose.

By the 1950s, the power of the movies had so increased that a successful film based on a novel not only would keep that book alive but would also help preserve the author's name. Without the film link, it is often difficult for a writer to be easily remembered as the author of a particular book. But ever afterward, Jones would be known as the author of *From Here to Eternity*, and it would be at once a benefit and a burden.

In late December, the New York film critics chose *From Here to Eternity* as the best movie of the year. Fred Zinnemann was cited as the best director, and Burt Lancaster as the best actor. This success was soon followed by the award of eight Oscars to *From Here to Eternity* by the American Academy of Motion Picture Arts and Sciences. The film itself was chosen as the best picture of the year, and Zinnemann was named best director. Daniel Taradash won an Oscar for his screenplay, Frank Sinatra was named best supporting actor, and Donna Reed best supporting actress. William Lyon won an award for his film editing and Burnett Guffey for cinematography. The film was also cited for its sound recording.

Despite the fame that came from the movie, Jones had no plans to leave Marshall. Indeed, he made it clear that he intended to stay there permanently by building a house for himself on the grounds of the Handy Colony. It is rare for a provincial writer to resist the temptations of cosmopolitan living after success has introduced him to a wider world, but Jones seemed to need the stability represented by Lowney's colony and the order and quiet that came from living in the country. He also had a profound nesting instinct, encouraged probably by his own unsettled childhood and his barracks life in the army.

The house would also be a physical monument to his self-sufficiency. He had now solved many of his problems by separating the different aspects of his life into compartments. He preserved his independence by living alone. He found intellectual companionship with Lowney, and obtained such sex as Lowney would not provide by visiting the prostitutes in Terre Haute.

In a similar way, the house reflected Jones's desire for orderliness. Having lived for so long in trailers, he had come to admire their compactness and neatness, so he duplicated these qualities in the house that he and Harry Handy designed. On the outside, it had no style, and was a curious mélange of white clapboard, maroon shingles, glass, and stone, but inside everything was as orderly as a ship.

The living room at the end of the house was two stories high, and the center wall was occupied by a stone fireplace flanked by numerous cabinets and showcases in which Jones displayed his collection of meerschaum pipes, Meissen china, toy soldiers, bowie knives, and Asian statuary. To one side stood a Stromberg-Carlson record player, to the other a table set for chess, and the floor was covered with Navaho rugs.

Bookcases lined the hall and filled the bedroom at the other end of the house, for by now Jones owned thirty-five hundred books. Two double beds filled the center of the bedroom, and on one side were specially designed cabinets containing Jones's coats and trousers, shoes, boots, and hats. On the other side, a standing bookcase formed an alcove, and there stood Jones's desk and filing cabinets.

In the kitchen everything was similarly fitted by hand; the blue-tiled bathroom, across the hall, was a plumber's paradise, with a pair of sinks, a toilet, and even a bidet in maroon porcelain. The lights were sunk into the walls and ceiling, and a shower stall enclosed by clouded glass etched with the figure of a naked woman stood in a corner.

Upstairs was a specially designed wooden cabinet where Jones kept his guns, and beyond that a large playroom containing a Ping-Pong table, a dart board, a shuffleboard, a punching bag, and other exercise machines. In a corner stood a bar with a secret compartment behind it where Jones kept his liquor. Four rag dolls that hung from the ceiling were presents from Lowney. "They're supposed to represent my ex-girl friends," Jones explained.

Outside was a barbecue and a garage where Jones stored his power tools. Everything in the house was functional and, since it cost $85,000, expensive. The woodwork was done by hand, and Jones installed an elaborate lighting system that allowed him to turn all the lights of the house on or off at once. He bought a set of silver from Denmark and laid out a miniature golf course. Clearly designed to make up for the deprivations of his youth, the establishment was an odd mixture of vulgarity and good taste. Above all, it showed that Jones had no fear of spending money. With the pleasure that comes to a man who earns his own money and is eager to enjoy himself, Jones bought what he wanted and what he could easily afford.

Once the house was completed and furnished, Jones settled down to a rigorous routine in order to move ahead with *Some Came Running*. Having slept naked in one of his two double beds, he would get up at five-thirty in the morning and take a shower and shave. He was very conscious of cleanliness and that is why he had a bidet. After shaving and chatting in French with a parakeet named Pierre, who lived in the bathroom, Jones made himself a cup of coffee and dressed. He wore jeans, a sweatshirt, and a baseball cap from Post 90 of the American Legion in Marshall.

To get ready for work, he read the paper and by six was at his desk. He would warm up by copying afresh what he had written the day before, in part to make revisions. But he found that the exercise also helped him sharpen his ear. He liked to listen to the words in his head and to get caught up in the rhythm of the language. If he found himself stuck in a sentence, he would have to start the process all over again so as to build up the necessary momentum to proceed. A day's output ranged from two to twenty pages.

By noon, he was finished for the day, "exhausted, wrung out." The writing involved a tremendous amount of energy, and he chain-smoked as he worked. "Sometimes I get concentrating so hard, somebody could stand behind me and I wouldn't know it."

Lunch would be preceded by a batch of dry martinis. Jones enjoyed making a ritual of his drinks and even had an atomizer for the vermouth so as not to use too much. While Jones drank alone, Lowney finished preparing a hot meal of meat and potatoes. They would eat together, and Jones would tell her about the morning's work. He confided in her about everything, and she would go over his typescript and comment on it. She was his immediate and initial audience, and everything he wrote was first directed to her. She was not a stylist, nor was she competent to discuss the nuances of writing, but she could tell if he fudged or misrepresented what she knew to be true, and she would take him to task for that.

After lunch, Jones would go to bed for an hour. Later in the afternoon, he would exercise, working out on a trampoline he had bought for the colony, practicing archery, or trimming the hedge. Sometimes he would take some of the members of the colony with him for a run around the Marshall High School track, and in fine weather he would join them at the swimming pond. Afterward, he might have a game of chess with one of the colonists. He had an expensive set, which he always had laid out on a board near the window in his living room, and he enjoyed the competition.

Living in his own house, he remained somewhat apart from the other colonists, however. On rainy days, he would work out upstairs in his game room or would spend the afternoon reading. He had a large collection of books and enjoyed burying himself in a subject. While working on *Some Came Running,* he read all he could find on Emily Dickinson, who partly inspired the character Gwen French. "She fascinates me," he said. "She had three, possibly four, love affairs and never slept with a man in her life." He also read the *Cambridge Mediaeval History,* especially those volumes depicting the end of the Roman Empire, and found many parallels to contemporary America.

At six, he had dinner, again prepared by Lowney. They would talk or he would listen to his records of Beethoven, Mozart, Ravel, Tchai-kowsky, or the jazz musician Django Reinhardt on the phonograph. By nine o'clock, he was tired and ready for bed. Jones kept to this routine seven days a week, varying it only on Saturday, with a trip to Terre Haute. Sometimes he would accompany Lowney and Harry Handy to the Marine Room of the Terre Haute House for dinner; at others, he would go alone or with a friend to visit the brothels. He also had a couple of girl friends in Marshall. He would invite them to his house, trying to make sure they were not seen by Lowney, who lived close by in her little cottage. Lowney always succeeded in pre-venting any permanent liaison by moving the colony south once the weather turned cold.

Jones's life was rigorously controlled and organized for the sole purpose of making him write. He was almost totally isolated. "I don't even write many letters," he said. "I get so sick of the typewriter once I'm through."

Yet he was hospitable to visitors. Late one morning in the spring of 1954, he heard a knocking on the door and went to find four sixteen-year-old schoolgirls, who said they would like to come in and talk. Jones welcomed them and asked them into the kitchen. He could tell that they were hungry, so he cooked them all steaks and began to question them about their school and their lives. One of the girls, who felt cooped up in her small town, could not understand why he had come back to Marshall after his first great success. "I can al-ways escape any time I want to," he replied. "The first break away is the important one." He seemed confident and self-assured, paying no attention to the black looks Lowney gave him as he spent the afternoon showing the girls the colony and demonstrating his exercise machines.

Occasionally the routine of the household was varied by visitors like Montgomery Clift and Shelby Foote, the novelist and Civil War historian Jones had first met at the National Book Award ceremonies in New York. Jones was fascinated by the Civil War and had a large collection of books on the subject. While at the Kennedy General Hospital in Memphis, he had taken notes on General Bedford Forrest, whose statue stands in that city and whom he considered one of the most talented soldiers in history.

Jones also took brief trips away from Marshall. In January of 1954, he spent a week in Chicago, where he was introduced by his friend Herman Kogan to the ballet. The Sadler's Wells company was in town, and Jones went nearly every night, fascinated by the dancers' physical prowess and grace. He had never before seen dance but immediately became an enthusiast and bought dozens of books on the subject. Through Kogan, he managed to meet the prima ballerina Svetlana Beriosova backstage after a performance and quickly decided to write a novel about the ballet with her as the heroine. Jones was so taken with Beriosova that two months later in New York he went to see her again in *The Nutcracker*. He was starved for music and art and also went to Carnegie Hall to hear Arthur Rubinstein play.

Jones's trip to New York in the spring of 1954 came about when he was summoned by his publishers to help prepare a defense against a lawsuit for $500,000 in damages that had been brought against Scribner's and Columbia Pictures. The plaintiff was Joseph A. Maggio of Brooklyn, who had been in Jones's F Company at Schofield Barracks and who asserted that the character Maggio in *From Here to Eternity* had been drawn from him without his permission. Jones admitted to Horace Manges, the Scribner's lawyer, that he had used Maggio's name, but claimed he was told that the real Maggio had been killed in action and that, in any event, the details of his character's life were entirely invented.

Jones planned to remain in New York until the trial was over. After the isolation of Illinois, he needed a change, and he determined to use the opportunity to improve his personal life. Socially and sexually, he considered it unsatisfactory. He had visited the prostitutes at Madame Rose's in Terre Haute, and had even enjoyed talking to them, but he had no real feelings for them. He was beginning to miss having any connections in his life; he was emotionally unsatisfied. When he went to New York, he didn't know how to get a girl, so he told his friend A. B. C. Whipple of *Time* that he would be glad to pay one of the researchers at the magazine if she would take a week off to have sex with him. He didn't understand how inappropriate such a request was in New York. But he quickly began to see that something was wrong with the way he organized his sex life. His friends Mailer, Styron, and Bourjaily were all married; they didn't go around with prostitutes. Nor did his single friends pay girls to go to bed with them.

Jones therefore decided to seek out a woman with whom he could have a more satisfying relationship. He followed up various "prospects" whose names he had been given and took them to dinner. Then he was introduced by a fellow writer, Jack Cassidy, to Faith Dane, a dancer and actress who was famous for an act in which she bent over and played a trumpet between her legs. When Jones telephoned her, she told him she was ill, but he persisted and went to her apartment with an armful of groceries. She was attractive and amusing, and she was touched by his kindness, but when he began to talk about the prostitutes he had known in Terre Haute, she felt that he had little use for women. She accompanied Jones, however, to literary parties, where he introduced her to Norman Mailer, John Marquand, Jr., and other writers he knew, and for a time he moved in with her.

Jones's prolonged stay meant that he would also have a chance to get to know some of the writers he had met on earlier visits. He was aware that literary journalists thought of him as belonging to the same group of postwar writers that John Aldridge had discussed in *After the Lost Generation*. Although Jones was not discussed in this book — *From Here to Eternity* was published after it — he objected to Aldridge's lumping together writers of his age under a common label. He also disputed Aldridge's notion that the writers of the 1950s lacked the resources to write powerfully of their own time. Pointing out that his times were neither better nor worse than other times, including the Elizabethan Age, he showed that great writers rise in every period. Because he believed, too, that individual effort was far more important than any group energy, Jones was suspicious of the ideas that groups tend to hold in common. For Jones, the only universal truth was that "there is no universal truth." Moreover, he thought that group thinking inevitably fostered rivalry and competition among the individuals involved and produced attitudes entirely inimical to art.

With Mailer, Jones picked up where they had left off when Mailer and his wife, Adele, visited him in Marshall two years earlier. There Jones had read some of Mailer's *The Deer Park* while Mailer read parts of *Some Came Running*, and each had nourished the other with encouragement. The encounter was revealing to Mailer, who wrote Jones, "I've got a little idea how hard it is for you to work at times, but it seemed to please you once when I told you I thought you were every bit a writer, and so I say it again. Every fucking pulse in you is a writer, and no matter how hard it comes, and how slow, nothing will stop you till you croak, although maybe you got to relax now and again, sort of. Anyway, just to tell you I love you a little, you fucking bully."

Jones was far from relaxed in New York. He was fervently in search of new experiences and eager to take everything in. He spent a weekend in the country with Whipple, staying up late and getting up early, fearful of missing anything. They played chess, and Jones became so intense when he won that he would shout, "I've got you, you son of a bitch!" When he lost, he would sulk. Visiting a class at Barnard College given by Hortense Calisher, whom he'd met through Burroughs Mitchell, he was intelligent and restrained with the students, but afterward, following a few drinks at the West End bar on Broadway, he began to boast of his achievements. Earlier, a journalist joked with him about having a name so easily confused with others', but Jones replied, "Don't worry. I'm the only James Jones anybody will ever remember."

Often he would go out to dinner with Mailer; sometimes Adele Mailer and Faith Dane came along, sometimes not. Mailer was hoping *The Deer Park* would make up for the bad reception of *Barbary Shore*, and both men needed to solidify their literary reputations after their initial successes. Despite Jones's disavowal of competitiveness, they were obviously rivals, but they accepted the idea that there was room for them both. Frequently they would go out with Micky Knox, an actor from New York Mailer had first met in Hollywood, and the three would play liar's poker, in which the players made up their hands according to the serial numbers of dollar bills. The game involved a good deal of bluffing and pretense, and Jones always lost. Knox and Mailer teased him so much about being a country boy that he began to think he was being taken by what Mailer called the Jewish Mafia.

They would stay up till two or three in the morning, going to parties and visiting bars along Eighth Avenue. William Styron would sometimes be with them, and they had a feeling of camaraderie, jostling and poking one another in friendly rivalry. Arm wrestling was in vogue, part of the masculine image they allowed to color their relationship. For a long time, Jones and Mailer did not pair off, but one night, egged on by Knox, they sat down across from each other with their elbows on the table. Mailer was about Jones's height and comparatively slight, but he was very strong in the shoulders and quickly pressed Jones's arm down so that his hand almost touched the table. Then, with a look that seemed to combine will power and hatred, Jones strained to hold firm and gradually pushed Mailer's hand back up until the two hands were again upright. The match was declared a draw, but to a degree it was a triumph for Jones to have come back from such near defeat. From then on, the two men always treated each other with some reserve, as if they both acknowledged how evenly matched they were.

In all, Jones remained in New York until the end of April 1954, when the case against Scribner's and Columbia Pictures was heard in Brooklyn Magistrates' Court and dismissed by the magistrate. He ruled that permission was not required in the use of a name for a fictional character when the name was not prominent and the character's actions do not resemble those of the individual whose name was used.

Although Jones had enjoyed his time in New York, he found the pace of city life exhausting. Back in Marshall, he wrote to John Hall Wheelock, with whom he had dined twice during his stay in the city, "Im feeling much better since getting home. Not drinking as much, nor staying up nearly so late, and getting some exercise. And working much better. I really got very frightened there in NY. I always do if I go for very long without working. I think I could really kill myself in about six months with the peculiar kind of rabid wildness I have. I never know when to stop a thing. So I have to run away."

He also wrote to Norman Mailer about the relationship between friendship and egoism, for he had come to think of New York as just an arena for contests between personalities. "The only friendship is frustrated friendship," he wrote, "like Millay's poem: Let me lie down and lean with my thirst and my hunger. Real friendship is that sudden, short, sharp, poignant-to-the-point-of-pain feeling that you suddenly and momentarily get when you are doing something else, and for the moment think of someone youd like to see but havent seen for a long time, and go on with what youre doing. Thats the only real friendship; but let it try to be satisfied, let it try to be explained, let those two people get together and stay together for three weeks each trying so hard to prove his friendship — where's your friendship gone?

"And anyway, it all hurts your work. And for people who cant understand that your work is more important than their friendship and get their feelings hurt, what can you say? You certainly cant explain it to them."

Mailer's long and difficult quest for a publisher for *The Deer Park*, which included seven rejections, prompted Jones to express his faith in Mailer. In a letter to Robert Cantwell, he wrote, "Someday hes going to explode on the world like a nova, with a classic." But in the meantime, perhaps justifying his own inclinations, he criticized Mailer to Burroughs Mitchell for devoting so much of his time and energy to politics and to his belief "that the world could be made into a just, good, equal place through politics." Within a year, Mailer would be even more politically involved as a columnist and part owner of *The Village Voice* in New York. Jones's bias was always against political action, so he challenged Mailer's belief "that people are basically good, kind, loving, generous, etc" on the ground that they were also "bad, unkind, hateful, selfish." Admitting that he had shared Mailer's proletarian bias during the 1930s, "this fighting for the underdog thing," he had now come to the conclusion that "the only thing that keeps an underdog from being a topdog is just a simple lack of means."

Settled into the quiet routine of Marshall, Jones was again in a world he could control. The daily timetable kept him going with his writing, and he took pleasure from such mild diversions as buying records at Paige's music store in Terre Haute or reading Gibbon's *The Decline and Fall of the Roman Empire* and Suetonius' *Lives of the Caesars*. They gave him perspective and allowed him to live according to what was most important to him. One Christmas he even bought a tree for the house and decorated it, "in spite of the hoots of derision from Lowney and Harry," and bought some presents to place under it.

"A martini or two for lunch, two or three (the limit) for supper. Always a big fire in the fireplace. It's a wonderful life," he told Mitchell, "and I love it." In the afternoons, he took up working in the garage, planning to build one bench for carpentry and another for ceramics. He also wanted power tools to make furniture with. "It's a hell of a lot of fun," he told Mailer, "and a power saw has no ego and doesnt get its feelings hurt so that it keeps you from thinking about your characters. And the main thing is, you can think about what youre going to write tomorrow all the time your hands are doing this job or that." Jones also spent time spraying the apple trees, weeding, and planting grass to build up new lawns. "Someday we'll have a beautiful place here," he wrote to Mailer. Moreover, staying home kept him on an even keel, because, as he said, "whenever I take time off I usually seem to be mostly getting drunk and ramming wildly after ass — and usually winding up by creating in myself some vague but terrible fear when I see my own insanity."

Socially, Marshall left almost everything to be desired. Jones went out on drinking bouts with Earl and Andy Turner, Lowney's brothers, and their escapades were a reversion to what he had known on overnight passes from Schofield Barracks. One night, they got so drunk that they threw cherry bombs and blew up the toilets of the bar they were drinking in. On another occasion, after Jones was finally persuaded to go home from a house he was visiting, he called from outside, "Help, I broke my leg!" When reached, he admitted that he was all right. "And now can I come back in for another drink?" he asked.

Apart from the visits to brothels, his sexual life continued as before. He yearned for love and warmth, but Lowney deliberately remained aloof, and Jones accepted this arrangement. He had come to believe her theory that since she did not love him physically with the same ardor that he loved her, he would become a great writer, "simply because in her love I can never be completely satisfied; as I could be in marrying some young thing and having children.

"Now, I could leave her and marry some domestic woman and get what I hunger for, the simple sexual social (and in a measure) spiritual love. But in doing so, in satisfying myself, I would lose greatness as a writer, simply because of being satisfied in life. I desire to be a great writer more than anything on earth; and because of that, would stay with her; deliberately seeking not to be satisfied in love."

As long as his work went well, this pact worked. It was the price Jones felt he had to pay to write *Some Came Running*. He had accepted Lowney's teachings apparently without much questioning and seemed to prefer the tranquillity of a limited life to the turmoil of a real relationship with another person. But Lowney also had to pay a price, and as she grew older, it was harder for her to do. As Jones's ambition was to be a successful writer, Lowney's was to be famous as a midwife to literature, bringing forth new writers. Unfortunately, except for Jones, she had little luck.

Not until 1955 did she succeed in placing the work of one of her colonists, Jerry Tschappat, whose novel *Never the Same Again* was published by Putnam's under the pseudonym of Gerald Tesch. Next came Edwin Daly's *Some Must Watch*, which was published by Scribner's, as was Tom Chamales' *Never So Few*. Chamales was the most gifted and persistent of the colonists, and his book was well received. He became a close friend of Jones's but had a violent streak that was his undoing. He died young in a fire in his hotel bedroom in Hollywood.

The work of these three writers was small return for the enormous amount of energy Lowney expended on her charges and on the publishers to whom she sent their novels. Jones, her most successful protégé, said that it was difficult to explain her usefulness to a young writer. "She never handles two guys alike," he said, "and never handles the same one alike twice in a row. And yet she infuses them with a confidence and enthusiasm, even when shes riding their ass, in a way that no one else can do. She gives them *belief*. And this belief, which is so hard to come by anywhere else, is why they all come back."

When applicants visited the colony, Lowney would interview them thoroughly. Generally she "took the failures," convinced they had something to say and were against the norms of society. She liked to have them come angry; then, as if leading them to a religious conversion, she would empty them of petty ambition, self-pity, and sensuality in the hope that, in a state of defeat, they would recognize their complicity with the world that angered them and be able to write about it honestly. She wrote long letters full of advice to the colonists. Some of what she said was sound, some of it half-crazy or at best naïve. Urging one colonist to copy out the Pearl Harbor scene in *From Here to Eternity*, she asked, "Did you ever notice how cold Jim wrote his best passages, the most emotional ones. This is a gimmick in writing that is invaluable." She told the same writer, a black, to ignore his racial origins. "Forget that you are a negro. Forget discrimination. You have never been discriminated against here." She told him to stick to the essence of his story: "negro blood has nothing to do with this. You must learn to write coldly and leave all that out . . . and then the greatness will be there."

When not encouraging her charges, she was berating publishers, writing long, semiliterate letters to editors in New York, who were always open to the possibility that another James Jones might turn up in Marshall. Citing an accumulation of grievances, she asked Burroughs Mitchell why she should "fight, work like a slave and let Scribner's and Hollywood walk off with all the cash." Shifting her line, she asked, "I don't see why my boys are discriminated against." Lowney frequently used capital letters for emphasis, and concluded her three-page letter with this message: "I AM GOING TO TEACH THE GREATEST WRITERS THAT AMERICA WILL PRODUCE IN THE NEXT 50 YEARS. YOU CAN GET ON MY BANDWAGON OR STAY OFF OF IT. IT MATTERS NOT TO ME." Mitchell later wrote of Lowney that "her belief in herself and what she could accomplish with her writers had the intensity of madness."

The more emphatic she became, the more she revealed her considerable ignorance of literature and her limited ideas about it. Her messianic complex, which became more evident as her efforts continued without success, made her ridiculous. A large woman, wearing trousers and a sweatshirt without a brassiere, she was increasingly on edge and, as Mitchell recalled, she "could explode into screaming strident obscenities."

In 1956, the poet David Ray, who was then a colonist, was caught with a copy of Proust, "which Lowney snatched from me, ripped up and threw away. 'I didn't tell you to read that,' she shouted. 'Your goddamned style's too intellectual and sissy-like as it is. Didn't I tell you to copy Dreiser? You're damned right I did. And why? Did you think about that? Did you? To get you out of that damned Proust style. That's one queer we don't read around here." During this diatribe, Lowney pronounced Proust as "Prowst"; other contraband authors were referred to as "Walter Stevens," "Kafkia," and "Die-land Thompson."

When three of Ray's friends from the University of Chicago visited him at the colony, Lowney brought them into her study and asked what writers they admired. One of them mentioned D. H. Lawrence, and Lowney bridled. "D. H. Lawrence was a queer, and that's why he died from T.B. — I know why people get T.B." When one of the visitors disagreed, she shouted, "Get out of here. You can't come in here with your goddamned intellectual claptrap and take up my time." She then pushed them out the door and speeded their exit from the colony by throwing bricks at them. They hurried off, but one of them was slow, and a brick hit him on the shoulder. "Lady," he implored, "I've got a sore foot, I can't run." Lowney threw another brick at him, so he ran.

A witness to the scene and a supporter of Lowney's, Jones said that he had "never laughed so hard" in his life; he added that he "heartily agreed with her action." But Lowney had never behaved toward Jones as she did to the colonists, and for his part Jones was an exceptionally loyal person. Appreciating her many years of support for him, he was hesitant to criticize her. Nevertheless, he could hardly ignore Lowney's erratic and even hysterical behavior. They also quarreled, mostly about money, and Jones threatened to withdraw financial support from the colony, complaining that she was profligate. For all her enthusiasm, Lowney allowed her overbearing manner, her impatience, and her violence to ruin the enterprise she most loved. Indirectly, she must have led Jones to reconsider the kind of life he had been living with her for ten years. It was a gradual process, but a real one.

Even with the organized pattern of his life, *Some Came Running* was not going well. At times the writing went so slowly that he would "work all damn morning on a single four or five line paragraph" and even then not get it right. He was haunted by doubts. "I live in fear, active, livid fear, undulating around me like a living constrictor." His difficulties arose mainly from a desire not to repeat himself. He now looked on *From Here to Eternity* as "a good adolescent book, but still an adolescent one," because he had accepted an optimistic view of life. Reading *The Fable,* a novel about World War I he considered sentimental, Jones railed at Faulkner for having "lost his bitterness. And without it he is ridiculous. I think he either became naturally complacent about life, or else lied himself into believing he was." He also approved of Gertrude Stein's description of Hemingway as "ninety percent Rotarian," adding that he "just is not a thinker." Jones mistrusted all religious and philosophical codes, because he thought they were a substitute for thought. "There should be room for nihilism," he said. "Life is tragic — after all, everybody dies. But Americans shy away from tragedy. They want happy endings."

Jones's ambition was to portray life as it is. He was scornful of false optimism and told Mitchell that he wanted *Some Came Running* "to do for the great American myth and illusion of romantic love what Cervantes did for the myth and illusion of chivalry."

Occasional distractions arose to relieve the monotony of work. He spent time in Terre Haute with a theatrical group that wanted to put on *The Stockade,* a play by Mark Appleman derived from *From Here to Eternity* that had a brief run in New York. He also took a trip to Kentucky to visit Lowney's cousins and was interested in the stories they told. This was the country from which his fictional character Prewitt had come. "There is something fascinating about those people's lives," he wrote; "the physical danger they live in as a matter of course. Everyone carries a knife. A great many still carry pistols, on occasion. Most of the actual danger comes from drunkenness, and that wild beating-out frustration that is inarticulate and wild, and is out of control because of being drunk. Its the same quality that so fascinated me about Prewitt."

He also received a request from Melvin Lasky in Berlin for an article on artistic freedom that he could publish in his magazine, *Der Monat.* Jones agreed, provided that his article not be used for partisan reasons. It was his first piece on a political subject, and in keeping with his belief in individualism, he attacked the worthlessness of propaganda and emphasized his belief that "the great growths and advancement of the human race, few as they may be, have never been brought about by masses moving together in one direction, but by the single man, lonely, unsure, beleaguered, working alone, and trembling in the face of the freedom it is always more comfortable to be without."

Lasky was also in correspondence with Mailer, who soon wrote Jones mainly to express a feeling of solidarity. "I remember when I read Eternity," he said. "I was sick with grippe at the time and I just got sicker. Because deep inside me I knew that no matter how I didn't want to like it, and how I leaped with pleasure at its faults, it was still just too fucking good, and I remember the still artist's voice in me saying, 'Get off your ass, Norman, there's big competition around.' But what the hell, I don't have to explain it to you. I think in a way Styron, you and me, are like a family. We're competitive with each other, and yet let one of the outsiders start to criticize and we go wild. And there's a reason for it, too. I think our books clear ground for one another."

Within the year, however, there was bad blood between Jones and Mailer because, listening to gossip by a disaffected Handy colonist in New York, Mailer learned that Jones's opinion of him was "now unprintable." He therefore wrote to Jones, warning him not to start a feud. Jones replied, chiding Mailer for listening to idle talk. But he was sufficiently touchy to add that, for his part, he understood that Mailer, Vance Bourjaily, and Ted Purdy, then Mailer's editor at Putnam's, were "getting ready to try and free me from the domination of Lowney Handy." In bringing their relationship into the open, Jones adopted a defensive tone, revealing his own sensitivity about it. He understood, he said, that Marshall, Illinois, was "a pigsty in its own little way," but that it was nothing compared to the New York literary world, "except that all the nails are manicured, and all the armpits and crotches more or less washed." He added, in sarcastic defense of his own habits, that though Mailer, Purdy, and Bourjaily "may have great will power and strength of character, I do not, and I need somebody to look after me and keep me from killing myself drinking and fucking, somebody who has some common sense, like Lowney, and also I need somebody to read over my stuff and tell me if it is good or not. Because I never know, like you and Vance and Purdy do."

The exchange touched a sensitive nerve, for it not only questioned Jones's compromise solution to his private life; it also threatened to undercut his intention to use *Some Came Running* as an attack on the notion of romantic love. Further, it increased his irritation with the colony and the neurotic behavior it seemed to foster. He even began to think of retreating further, of leaving Marshall for Kentucky, where he could buy land, dig a well, and build a log cabin. "Its a wonderful place," he told Mitchell, "and also Ill feel Ill have some place to go should the time ever come that I might lose this place."

Toward the end of 1955, Burroughs Mitchell visited Jones to discuss the nearly completed book. Ned Brown, his film agent, also came, with a proposal to offer film rights for *Some Came Running* through an auction. To maintain secrecy, Brown paid to have the whole manuscript retyped and mimeographed in Marshall. A limited and controlled number were to be sent on loan to the studios in Hollywood on an equal basis before publication, and the highest bid would be accepted. Brown was hoping for a sale in the region of $500,000.

As the end approached, the tension rose in Marshall. Reporters from *Time* and other magazines came for interviews. Jones was especially excited at the prospect of having a portion of his novel serialized in *Life*, as Hemingway's *The Old Man and the Sea* had been, but the project fell through. He had several attacks of nerves. "The whole thing is so big that it sometimes scares me," he wrote to Mitchell. "Not only in size, but in scope and spread and everything else." Jones imposed on himself a limit of two thousand typed pages, but as he progressed, he could tell that the book would be even longer.

"The pressure on me is getting terrific," he wrote, "almost more than I can stomach. Its much worse than the ending of Eternity, which I just sort of breezed through. Most of it is due to the fact that I know everybody is alerted to the end of this one, and know that all the barbs and hooks and knives and harpoons with which literary people love to score each other are being sharpened no doubt. There is no remedy for it, I guess, except to plug away my five or six hours every day and try to forget it the rest of the time."

He was thrown by a remark about the manuscript's needing revisions that Helen Mitchell made when she and her husband were in

Marshall. For a while, he pondered over it, and then he lashed out in a letter to Mitchell. "A few minor cuts here and there perhaps, like Eternity," he wrote. "And you remember you yourself told me in so many words that it needed no revision, major or minor. But I also remember that you told Helen: 'You talk too much.' As I say, Ive brooded on it a lot, Im running on a pretty thin ragged edge to get done, but that is no excuse for your lying to me." Mitchell sent him the required assurances, and Jones relaxed. "I've just finished proofing it this morning," he wrote, "and by God Im even kind of awed by it myself! I dont honestly, in my secret heart, believe Im that smart; or that good.

"I guess what really bothered me about that revision business is the fact that it scared me. You know? If the book really needed serious revision, when I myself did not think so, then I perforce must be blind and inadequate to my work, mustn't I, and thats what scared me. It leaves you feeling you dont know *anything*. But its really a terrific book — I think — you know it? Because if it did need revising, and I was wrong, then why hadn't *I* seen it?"

Finally, in December 1956, Jones finished the book. It had been a tremendous struggle, and during the last weeks before completing it, he lived, he said, "on nothing but gin and Miltown." *Life* sent a reporter and a photographer to record the event, and Jones picked up the twenty-three-hundred-page manuscript and held it for the camera. It was more than two feet thick, and Jones could barely hold it. "What I like is to feel the squared edges," he told the reporter. He was wearing jeans and a white T-shirt. "There's a certain moralism that drives me to write," he added. "I have to justify my existence."

7

✿

NEW YORK

ON THE DAY he arrived in New York to visit Scribner's and talk about his manuscript, Jones was ready for action. He had been invited to a cocktail party given by Harvey Breit of the *New York Times Book Review* at his apartment in the East Sixties, and he went there directly from the station, not bothering to stop at a hotel. He was wearing a rust-brown tweed suit bought at a country store, red socks, and heavy work shoes. There were a number of literary people at the party, but the one who interested Jones most was Budd Schulberg, who was already well known for his novels *What Makes Sammy Run?* and *The Disenchanted.* A burly man, interested in sports and politics, Schulberg attracted Jones because of his inner gentleness and sensitivity. Jones, in turn, strongly impressed Schulberg. "He was small but built large, with a barrel chest and a lantern jaw and the craggy face I would put on an ex-drill sergeant or tank-town middleweight." Although Jones looked like a country hick, Schulberg admired him for his lack of stylishness. "He didn't talk like the rest of us. His vocabulary was a string of four-letter words, and in the field of current literary gossip he was an ignoramus."

The cocktail party went on to nine-thirty, and afterward the two men went out and drank some more. When it was time to go home, Schulberg took Jones back to his apartment in the Sulgrave Hotel, on Park Avenue at Sixty-seventh Street. There they continued their talk. "I'm afraid I patronized him a little in my head," Schulberg later wrote. "He didn't talk theories, ideas, social stuff the way our crowd liked to do. He wasn't a do-gooder, a bleeding-heart, a seeker after social justice. He was a kind of literary hard-hat who talked facts, people, things, the everyday of human conflict. He didn't use phrases like 'the human condition.' It was refreshing. Most of my friends were used to worrying about the human condition. Jim talked about Jim and the people he had grown up with in Robinson.''

They talked all night, until, exhausted, Schulberg went to bed at dawn. A few hours later, he woke up to find Jones stretched out on the living room floor in jeans and an undershirt. They had breakfast and talked some more, exchanging their ideas about sexual relations, marriage, and love. Schulberg was impressed by Jones's fervor and honesty, and his loathing of the way people spent their lives lying to each other. Some of his views were primitive and naïve, but he was talking so intensely about his personal feelings that Schulberg felt he was already working himself out of his relationship with Lowney Handy, though he probably didn't yet realize it himself.

Later that day, Schulberg prepared to go out to dinner with his friend Faye Emerson. Jones asked if he could come along too. The directness of the appeal so disarmed Schulberg that he agreed, and after that, Jones was part of a threesome, with Schulberg and one of his girl friends. After a few days had passed, Schulberg decided to talk directly with his guest. "Jim," he asked, "what the hell's the matter with you?"

"I'm lonely."

"What are you looking for?" Schulberg asked.

"A woman," Jones answered. "I don't mean just for tonight. I'm tired of catting around."

"What kind of woman?"

"Well, she has to be interested in writers and writing, but don't give me one of those New York intellectual high-brows." He paused. "I'd like her to look like Marilyn Monroe."

It so happened that Schulberg knew someone who exactly filled Jones's requirements. Her name was Gloria Mosolino, known as Mos, and she came from Pottsville, Pennsylvania, which John O'Hara wrote about. Her uncle was the model for the bootlegger in O'Hara's *Appointment in Samarra*. Gloria herself had written a novel about growing up in Pottsville, but it had never been published. She had taken acting lessons in New York and, by extraordinary coincidence, had just finished working in *The Seven-Year Itch* as a stand-in for Marilyn Monroe. She was also one of Schulberg's girl friends, but when Jones asked to meet her, it was too late for Schulberg to renege on his promise to help Jones, so he phoned her.

"Will I like him?" asked Gloria.

"Mos," answered Schulberg, "take a deep breath, because that's what I'm doing. I've got a crazy feeling that you're going to marry him."

Jones moved out and took a room at the New Weston Hotel on Forty-ninth Street and Madison, but he was nearly two hours late for the date when he arrived at the Park Avenue brownstone where Gloria shared an apartment with two roommates. He was full of whiskey, which he had taken to fortify himself for their first meeting. They had dinner at a restaurant where there was a floor show, and the food sobered him up. But the first night was not a success. The next day, Gloria phoned some of her friends. "Guess who I went out with?" she asked. "James From Here to Eternity Jones!" Asked what he was like, she replied, "He was awful drunk."

Following their second date, she reported, "He was drunk, but I kind of like him."

And after the third, she said, "He drinks a lot, but he's fun and I'm in love and I'm going to marry him!"

Jones's reaction was even more direct. After their first evening together, he said, "I can't go out with you tomorrow, but after that, we have a date for life."

During this short stay in New York, the doubts Jones had begun to feel in Marshall about his emotional and sexual life had matured. Almost overnight, he discarded Lowney's theosophical teachings and the habits of more than a decade. The rush with which he fell in love with Gloria swept everything aside, and in the enthusiasm of the moment, he abandoned his bleak and suspicious views of women. He was bewitched. The golden girl he had dreamed of but could never find in all the lonely days and nights in Hawaii and in Memphis and in Robinson and Marshall was sitting beside him. The girl he had written about so romantically at Schofield Barracks, imagining himself with her on the beach while he watched the moon light the "golden glints" of her hair, was now quite literally in his arms. It had happened in a flash, and he walked about with springs in his shoes.

Gloria was an extraordinarily attractive young woman of twenty-seven, with a lithe and bosomy figure. She had a warm smile and lively sense of humor and enjoyed being irreverent. She would say shocking things about other people in a way that would always bring laughter. She adored parties, dancing, and men. She was attracted to famous people, especially if they were rich, and she wanted someone to look after her. Like Katherine (Scotty) MacGregor and Cecile

Gray, with whom she shared "the only tenement on Park Avenue," she was a born party girl and had lots of friends who were artists or in the theater. Often at gallery openings, she went to El Morocco, P. J. Clarke's, Sardi's, and the Colony. In addition to being physically stunning, Gloria was far more liberated than most women of her generation. "I was a writer-fucker," she recalled amiably, some years later. She and her friends were "freewheelers" who came to live in New York because they had "decided not to settle into suburbia with a boring husband."

Gloria had almost married a rich Venezuelan, who showered her with furs and dresses, but he was killed in an accident. Not long afterward, she met Jones. He took her to meet his literary friends, including John Steinbeck and his wife, Elaine, whom Jones had met in 1951. They hadn't always approved of Jones's girls, but when he brought Gloria to their apartment, he said, "This one you'll like," and they did. For her part, Gloria took Jones to Paul Stuart's to get some clothes. Always stylish herself and accustomed to friends who dressed well, she was determined to get rid of Jones's ugly suits, with their bold patterns and padded shoulders. He was only too glad to have his appearance improved, and when Budd Schulberg next saw him, he marveled at the transformation.

During the day, Jones worked on the manuscript of *Some Came Running* at Scribner's, but he and Gloria were together every night. They started going to less expensive restaurants, neighborhood places, getting to know each other, not quite understanding what was happening to them. They felt they were like Carole Lombard and Clark Gable or, at times, Hansel and Gretel lost in the forest.

As they talked, they drew each other out, exchanging their life stories. Their mutual sympathy was so extraordinary they couldn't quite believe it, and at a certain level were suspicious of each other. Jones's skepticism began to come back when he remembered Lowney's dictum that marriage was dangerous for an artist. Yet as they became better acquainted, they realized how much they had in common and how complementary they were. Both from small-town America, they had common feelings of social inferiority, Jones from his family's loss of money during the Depression, Gloria from her underworld background in Pottsville, which had provided wealth but no respectability. Yet Gloria had put her family's money to good use. When she graduated from Syracuse University, where she had become interested in writing, she knew instinctively that she belonged in New York. Jones's appearance on the scene suited her perfectly, for he was a celebrated author, and she valued the arts, especially literature. None of her other boy friends had achieved such fame. More important, she was attracted to him as a person. "He was beautiful and sexy and was my best friend," she said later. "He was also loyal and decent and could be very serious."

Sexually, she and Jones were also good for each other. After the long periods of frustration and repression Jones had lived through under Lowney's tutelage, Gloria gave him a sense of his own masculinity: he in turn confirmed her as a lady, not merely a frivolous playgirl who went from affair to affair. Also, Gloria's gaiety and sense of fun brought a whole new spirit into his life. He was essentially shy and withdrawn; she gave him people, laughter, and vitality. And he gave her a chance to be involved with a serious artist, the opportunity to contribute to something lasting in the world.

Within ten days of meeting, they talked of getting married, and Jones proposed to Gloria as they sat at a table in the back room of P. J. Clarke's. But he was not yet ready to act on his word. With the work finished at Scribner's, he returned to Marshall by himself. The next day he phoned Gloria in New York. "I think you better come out here," he said. They stayed together for a few days and then drove south. When they reached Florida, where Lowney Handy was, Jones put Gloria on the plane and sent her back to New York.

They had talked about Lowney, but Jones had avoided introducing the two women. He told Gloria that Lowney was nothing more than his foster mother, but Gloria suspected something more. Otherwise, why could they not say hello? Meanwhile, Jones had to confront Lowney by himself, and it was not easy. For fourteen years, she had dominated his life, taken care of him, and been his only constant and stable influence. He had treated her generously in return, giving her ten percent of his royalties and supporting the colony. But now he had to make a choice, and she wasn't just his foster mother. They had been lovers, but she was now fifty-three to his thirty-six. A passive man who disliked argument, Jones was afraid to tell Lowney about Gloria, and he was also afraid of changing his whole life, believing that there was at least some truth in Lowney's ideas about marriage. Perhaps his having fallen in love with Gloria *was* too good to be true.

When they finally spoke, Lowney was calm and matter-of-fact. Instead of berating him, she played on his doubts and insecurity, especially his fear of losing money. He had known Gloria for only three weeks. What did he know of her past? What if the marriage failed? Lowney told Jones that if they divorced, Gloria could claim half his earnings and win alimony payments for the rest of her life. She suggested that Jones ask Gloria to sign a marriage contract in which she agreed to make no claim on him should the marriage fail.

Back in New York, Gloria was disconsolate, imagining that she had lost him. She took to her bed and waited for the phone call that never seemed to come. When Jones finally called her and spoke to her about the marriage agreement, it was too much for her. She told him that her idea of marriage was to live with him for the rest of his life. She also told him what he could do with his marriage contract.

Jones thought this over and called her back. "I think you had better come down here," he said in his gravelly voice. Gloria later said that what most attracted her to Jones was his voice. "It was a cowboy's, like Gary Cooper's." There was no more mention of a marriage contract. He suggested they go to Haiti and get married. And he said nothing more about Lowney.

From Miami they went immediately to Port-au-Prince and took a room at the Hotel Oloffson, then in its prime as one of the most picturesque hotels in the Caribbean. Originally the private home of a president of Haiti, it was a gingerbread extravaganza standing in a garden full of palm trees and flowering plants. Roger Coster, the owner, who was a Frenchman of Russian origin, wanted his hotel to be the Greenwich Village of the tropics. But he had to cope with the political realities of the country. Asked by a reporter for an impartial view of Haiti, he replied, "Ze best view of 'aiti eez from ze terrasse of ze Gran' 'otel Oloffson." Queried as to whether he thought Haiti was a hotbed of political ferment, he answered, " 'ot bed, cold bed, zere are no beds in ze Caribbean more comfortable zan h'at ze Oloffson."

Jones and Gloria were immediately at home. It was a hotel for celebrities, and Coster named rooms for such visitors as Charles Addams, John Gielgud, and Graham Greene. Soon there was a James Jones Cottage, which Coster thought should perhaps be renamed "From Here to Maternity," since it had been the delivery room when the place was a hospital during World War I.

Jones and Gloria found congenial company in the crowd of Americans who sat around the pool or at the bar, among them Steve Kyle and his wife, Betty Comden, who wrote musical comedies with Adolph Green, and Ben Wolstein, a New York psychiatrist, and his wife, Irma, a painter. Tom Chamales was also there. They were all eager to be involved in the wedding. A license was procured from the *officier de l'état civil,* and the marriage was set to take place on February 27. As legal residents of Haiti, Coster and his wife agreed to be witnesses, as did a Haitian journalist and a beautician from the hotel.

As the hour for the ceremony drew near, Jones and Gloria became nervous. Wolstein spent about three hours walking around the hotel gardens and through the neighborhood, listening to Jones voice his doubts and feelings of guilt. He had been unfaithful to Lowney; would he be the same to Goria? Was he suited to any extended personal relationship?

Gloria was also concerned. In Florida, before traveling to Haiti, Jones had introduced her to some of the scuba divers he knew. There had been a lot of drinking and rowdiness, and Gloria had been unhappy, jotting down in her journal "fights" and "emotional turmoil." She was also apprehensive about their future, for she suspected that Lowney had been Jones's mistress, although he denied it. Wanting to believe him, however, she had agreed to the wedding, and now the moment was at hand.

Wearing white linen suits, Jones and Gloria stood before the Haitian official. Behind them, in the hotel garden, stood a crowd of onlookers that included their American friends. Some of them giggled at the French ceremony, which was drawn from the Napoleonic Code. Jones turned around and admonished them. "This is serious," he said.

The wedding reception began a honeymoon that was to extend their stay in Haiti to three months. They explored the island and Jones experimented with scuba diving along the shore. One night they went to a voodoo rite, in which the leader, under a spell, danced toward Jones with a machete, which he whirled round and round, getting closer and closer to Jones's chest. Considering it a test of nerves, Jones never moved. When the ceremony was over, his chest was untouched, but his back was bleeding from the scratches that Gloria, sitting behind him, had made while clutching at him.

In May, they returned to Miami from Haiti and drove to New York. For a while they stayed at Gloria's apartment, but the trip to Illinois could not be put off indefinitely. Because she was apprehensive about Lowney, Gloria invited some of her friends to visit her there.

At first there was no difficulty. Lowney was polite and correct, and Gloria had some guest beds installed in Jones's upstairs playroom. But as the inmates of the colony began to return for the summer season,

Lowney started to make trouble. Since she believed that her protégés should keep sex out of their minds, she forbade Gloria from using the swimming pool. The proximity of Lowney's house to Jones's also increased tensions. In her anger at Gloria's presence, Lowney began to throw out of her house the books and shoes and underwear that Jones had left there during his visits.

Gloria could not avoid seeing what their relationship had really been. She was not surprised, but she was upset that Jones continued to deny it and disturbed that he expected to continue seeing Lowney, if only for literary guidance. She was soon consoled by the arrival of her friends, however. They included her niece Kate Mosolino, then only a small girl, and Addie Herder, a painter, and Monique Gonthier, a French designer, whom she knew from New York. Then it began to rain, and continued until the grounds became flooded and the drinking water was polluted. With nothing to divert them, Monique and Addie would walk disconsolately into Marshall in search of a place to buy some wine.

One afternoon, while sitting in the living room with Kate, Gloria heard a loud crash. Lowney had just smashed through the screen door and was standing in the living room, beside herself with rage. "The only reason Jim married you," she shouted, "is that you're the best cocksucker in New York!" Gloria sent Kate out of the room, and then Lowney lunged at her with a bowie knife. Gloria and Lowney rolled around on the floor, scratching and punching, until Jones came in and separated them.

The next day, Jones and Gloria left Marshall. Even now, Jones had residual feelings for Lowney. He told Gloria that Lowney had been his mistress for years and even admitted having slept with her after he had asked Gloria to marry him. He told Gloria he could not get rid of his indebtedness to her — the "encouragement, advice and just plain raw fighting faith" that had made such a difference to his life. Nor could he forget that for fifteen years they had told each other everything, and Lowney had read everything he wrote, including his private notes and letters. He had allowed his inner passivity to guide him, turning a blind eye to Lowney's shortcomings. Now he had to absorb the shock of finding her crazed and violent. His life was in a shambles; the house he had built was destroyed and had to be abandoned because of his marriage. He was as bereft as he had been on the day he left Robinson by train to join the army and watched the figures of his parents fade into the distance.

For her part, Gloria was horrified by Jones's dishonesty in not telling her the truth about his relationship with Lowney. She had put all her trust in his truthfulness and now she was betrayed. She realized that, in a sly way, he had hoped to avoid reality by not saying anything. It was cowardly of him, and she berated him for his dishonesty.

Jones and Gloria drove away from Marshall without speaking. They were without destination, heading south. They stayed at cheap tourist cabins along the way, fighting, quarreling, hitting each other. Gloria would get out of the car and walk along the road alone; Jones would drive after her until she got into the car in silence. This went on for several days. It was the great crisis of their lives, for Gloria could not forgive him for betraying her by sleeping with Lowney after his marriage proposal. The more she brought up the matter, the more exasperated he became, knowing she was right but also aware that he had done it just to keep peace with Lowney.

They drove on, taking such comfort as they could from the flat landscape. Eventually, they turned east toward Cincinnati, where they began to talk calmly. But one subject was forbidden. "If you bring that up again," said Jones about Lowney, "I'll just leave." They also agreed they would go to New York to live. The crisis was now over. He had cut the cord. It was one of the most difficult periods of his life, a passage from one kind of living to another, but it was done, and there was no looking back.

Lowney remained in Marshall, trying to keep the colony alive by herself. Her health gradually deteriorated, however, and her behavior became more erratic as a result of the drugs she was prescribed. Without further literary successes to spur her on, she closed the colony in 1960. Her husband, Harry, died in 1963, and the following year she was found dead in the bedroom of her house. She was sixty years old. By this time, Jones had ceased to have any relationship with her. He acknowledged her early financial help but dismissed any literary contribution to his development as a writer.

Through Betty Comden, the Joneses were able to sublet a furnished apartment, on East Sixty-seventh Street between Lexington and Third Avenues, from an actor. The modern building, made of white brick, lacked architectural charm, but the apartment was on the top floor and had a small terrace. The front door opened onto a carpeted hallway, which led to a living room flooded with light from the terrace. Although the apartment contained no separate room where

Jones could work, he set up a desk in an alcove along the hall, and that became his study.

New York was invigorating, and after what they had been through, both of them responded to the city's magic. Down below, on the other side of Sixty-seventh Street, Jones could see a police station, a firehouse, a synagogue, and a community house, side by side, and he was fascinated by the variety of life they represented. He thought of writing a novel about New York.

Living in one of the most elegant parts of New York, with good shops and restaurants nearby, the Joneses found everything accessible. Soon they were caught up in social activities. *The Bells Are Ringing*, a new musical by Betty Comden and Adolph Green, had just opened, with Judy Holliday and Sydney Chaplin playing the lead roles, and the Joneses were invited to many of the parties connected with it. They met critics and musicians like Harold Clurman and Leonard Bernstein, and sometimes after the theater they would go to somebody's house to hear Frank Sinatra or Judy Garland sing. Almost every night they dined out and would go afterward to the Little Club or Goldie's, where there was music. On other evenings they would go to a big night club like the Copacabana to hear Sammy Davis and Lena Horne. But their favorite place to talk was the Oak Bar at the Plaza, and after an evening at the theater, they would have supper at the Algonquin or at Sardi's, across the street from where *The Bells Are Ringing* was playing.

Gloria was already at home in this world, and after the difficulties and insults she had endured in Marshall, she was delighted to introduce Jones to it. Together, she and Jones were a success: newly married, they were a golden pair, attractive and unjaded, full of life and unpretentious. Gloria adored the glamour of New York, and with charm and gaiety, and the help of her friends, she introduced Jones to the world of successful and interesting people.

The Joneses also went often to P. J. Clarke's, where he had proposed to her. On Third Avenue and Fifty-fifth Street, this old Irish saloon, owned by Danny Lavezzo, was a favorite meeting place for journalists, who enjoyed its paneled rooms, checkered tablecloths, straighforward cooking, and good drinks. The group that went there was lively and varied, and included Jack Whittaker the sports announcer; Charles Burke, a plainclothes detective; Edmund Trzcinski, the author of *Stalag 17*; Richard Burton; Ben Gazzara; and Budd

Schulberg. When a group of eight or ten people gathered, they would pull the tables together and talk about whatever was in the news: crime in East Harlem or Bedford-Stuyvesant, politics, sports, or the theater. As a celebrity, Jones was welcomed and taken seriously. Clarke's was like an informal club, an amiable forum where like-minded people could meet and talk, and what made it appealing to Jones was that it was free of the petty jealousies and rivalries that were so typical of purely literary gatherings. Norman Mailer and William Styron were now living in Connecticut, so Jones was seeing fewer writers than before his marriage. He found the world of the-ater, entertainment, and journalism more relaxing, because he didn't always have to be on his guard.

The Joneses' social activity gave their life an element of order inso-far as it distracted them from the differences that arose between them when they were alone. Although they were very much in love, they had both lived alone for a long time and were used to being indepen-dent. Their quarrels were caused not by essential differences between them but by willfulness, from having had their way for so long. Some-times Jones would do things that annoyed Gloria just to express his own identity.

When Tom Chamales came to New York, hoping to model his career on Jones's, the two men would go out drinking together. Chamales had a violent streak and usually carried a knife. Once, while out with Budd Schulberg, he picked a fight with a mild homo-sexual in a bar and smashed a heavy glass ashtray into his face, break-ing his nose and teeth and disfiguring him. Jones was both horrified and fascinated by Chamales' violence. It seemed to be a product of the same sort of rebelliousness he had characterized in Prewitt. He admired the independent spirit behind it and the physical courage it took to act in a lawless way, even though he knew it was immature. Conscious of the world's injustice, he could well understand the legit-imacy of a criminal response, just as Jean-Paul Sartre sympathized with Jean Genêt, the French playwright who spent years in reforma-tories and prisons. Rather than being critical, he felt protective to-ward Chamales, as he did toward the poet Delmore Schwartz, whom he also met in New York. He knew that both were driven mad by the pain of living. They were solitary and gifted men who were generally candid and friendly. But once they became upset by what Schwartz called the "ways of the fiendish world," they would find themselves "forced to be devious, suspicious, calculating." Jones helped them both when they were hospitalized and paid their bills. He recognized them as kindred spirits.

Gloria was afraid of violence and of Jones's attraction to it. She found it difficult to go along with his curiosity about human experience, regardless of the dangers involved. After his scuba diving in Florida and Haiti, Jones had become seriously interested in the sport. When, in late 1957, Percy Knauth of *Sports Illustrated* asked him to write an article on the subject, he therefore decided to take a week's trip to the Bahamas to gather material for the article. Scuba diving would later become a symbolic subject for Jones, but now he was just attracted by the physical and psychological challenge it presented. With a group of others, Jones and Gloria appeared on the dock at Fort Lauderdale to find that they were consigned to a filthy boat with airless cabins. They remedied their disappointment by having some drinks, and for the next week they traveled from island to island in an alcoholic stupor. During the day, Jones would terrify Gloria by donning a mask and flippers in order to dive below the surface of the water. At night, in port, the heavy drinking would resume and soon produce fist fights, raucous laughter, and brawls.

Gloria was deeply upset by the trip. She hated everything about it, the violence and the drinking, and she was also frightened for her husband. For a week, she and Jones quarreled so violently at dinner that most of the other passengers were convinced that their marriage was over. One said, cynically, "They do it for kicks." But each evening the storm would pass. Late one night, another passenger happened to glance through a skylight over the Joneses' cabin, and there they were, asleep with their arms around each other, like two little children.

To Gloria, her husband's behavior on the trip seemed a reversion to the loutish drunkenness of his bachelor days; to Jones, it was a renewal of the masculine camaraderie he had so long enjoyed. For some time, episodes like this would be a continuing feature of their marriage. They were upsetting and exhausting. They showed what each had to face if the marriage was to survive and also revealed the depth of their feelings for each other.

Soon after their return to New York from the Bahamas, Jones became involved in a second legal action taken by Joseph A. Maggio of Brooklyn against Columbia Pictures, Scribner's, and New American Library. This time Maggio alleged that he had been libeled in *From*

Here to Eternity and brought the case to civil court, hoping he could find a sympathetic jury and be awarded the $500,000 he asked in damages.

Harry Ander, Maggio's lawyer, sought to show that Jones had damaged Maggio, a member of Jones's F Company, by portraying a similarly named character as a hard-drinking gambler who rolled homosexuals. For the defense, Horace Manges decided it was first necessary to tell the jury how a book of fiction was actually written. He called Jones, who testified that he did not, as accused, copy biographical material from the files while working as assistant company clerk. He explained that his notes were personal and impressionistic and supplied only the raw material from which the fictional characters were drawn. Manges wore down the jury by reading them 250 pages of the novel and amused them by singing "Re-enlistment Blues" and the regimental song, "Oh, We Won't Come Back to Wahoo Any More."

Ander called two members of F Company to testify that the character Maggio was identical with the plaintiff, but after cross-examination, the case went against Maggio; Paul Slade, a photographer, revealed that far from being ashamed of his part in the book, Maggio wanted to "capitalize" on it. Frank Marshall, another witness for the defense and also a member of F Company, supported this contention. Asked why he had brought the case, Maggio said he wanted to put an end to the idea that he had been given a dishonorable discharge. By this time, Manges had succeeded in separating the Maggio in the courtroom from the Maggio in the book, so after eight days of hearing testimony, the jury retired for two hours and returned with a verdict of acquittal.

Newspaper accounts of the Maggio case were but part of the attention Jones was beginning to receive as the publication date of *Some Came Running* approached. The galleys were now available to reviewers and commentators, and gossip began to circulate about the quality of the book. After the great success of *From Here to Eternity*, Jones was on the line, and as he had predicted, a number of critics were eager to put him down.

He did not help his case by boasting about the book to a *Time* reporter. Jones gave the impression of believing the publicity that had been written about him and was quoted as saying, "It's not only longer than *War and Peace*, but it has more narrative pull. It's a great novel. It's the greatest novel we've had in America! What else have we got? *Look Homeward, Angel?* O.K. *U.S.A.?* Fair. Faulkner? *The Sound and the Fury* is his best, but not all that hot."

Jones salvaged some of his reputation by appearing with Gloria in a modest and charming fashion on Edward Murrow's "Person to Person" television show on CBS. One of the most popular programs of the day, featuring interviews with such notables as Harpo Marx, Mischa Elman, Sophia Loren, and Maurice Chevalier, it confirmed Jones's position as one of the few celebrities among contemporary novelists. Jones was interviewed in his apartment, and afterward gave a party to which, typically, he invited the film crew.

But the publicity didn't help, and on publication day the critics struck with a heavy hand. Granville Hicks commented on "how dull, how terribly dull" the book was and finished his review by saying that in "indulging his weaknesses for six years and in hundreds of thousands of words," Jones had "produced a monstrosity." Edmund Fuller commented that "if you like bad grammar, the grossest promiscuity, the most callous adultery, aggressive vulgarity, shoddy and befuddled philosophy, *Some Came Running* is your book. If you are looking for other things, look elsewhere." Concentrating on Jones's prose, the reviewer at *Time* observed that "Choctaw rather than English would appear to be his first language. Example: 'A person could actually kill themselves that way.' "

The flood of abuse was so unrelenting that the *New York Times Book Review* ran a special article on the book's critics, noting that nearly every reviewer mentioned the 1266 pages. Of the New York reviewers, it recorded that "one was courteous, one was kind, the rest attacked with various degrees of fierceness." To make matters worse, J. Donald Adams twice devoted his weekly column, "Speaking of Books," to attacking the publisher for bringing out the novel in the first place. In the first column, he wrote that "in justice to the author and to a patient reading public," *Some Came Running* "should never have seen the light of day." Adams criticized Jones for reveling "in a fatuous pride in being illiterate, standardless and faithless," and concluded by saying that the editors of "the great house of Scribner" were guilty of falling to the level of those houses which "lend their imprint to books of which they are secretly ashamed, but which offer a reasonable certainty of financial reward."

Jones was sufficiently stung by this article to draft a reply. "I will not attempt to defend *Some Came Running* to Mr. Adams," he wrote. "I will not attempt to defend this or any of my writing to any critics." But he protested the "mean and ugly attack" made by Adams in suggesting that Scribner's was ashamed to publish the book and did so only "to make money from a crashing best seller by means of sex sensationalism." Jones had the good sense not to send this letter to the *Times*, knowing that it is a writer's rule never to reply to a critic, but Adams required no goading to return to the subject two weeks later. By that time, the editors at Scribner's had made their displeasure known to him, but he continued to attack what he called Jones's "school of writing" for priding itself "on its illiteracy, its lack of moral standard and its inability to believe in anything but material well-being."

In fact, some of Scribner's editors had told Mitchell that they were unenthusiastic about the book, but he was mainly concerned about problems with obscenity. Together with Manges, Jones and Mitchell had gone over the questionable passages and resolved their difficulties. Length was not an issue, because Mitchell already knew it was a long book, but he was unsuccessful in trying to persuade Jones to give up "certain irritating mannerisms, like the many repeated adverbs." Later, Mitchell and Jones conceded that further cuts would have been useful, but small adjustments would not have moderated the book's bad reception.

In interviews given during the furor over *Some Came Running*, Jones was astonishingly calm about the personal viciousness of some of the attacks against him. Commenting patiently on his negative press, he said, "I don't think any of the reviewers really understood it. I don't think they tried." He pointed out what should have been obvious, that "the book is not autobiographical and I don't identify with Dave as a writer any more than I identify with Frank as a Peeping Tom." With some bitterness he added, "I object to being called the Neanderthal man of American literature. See, I wear shoes."

What is evident is that the critics, having been exposed to articles about Jones in his T-shirt and jeans, struggling to get his words down on paper with the help of Lowney Handy, began to think he really was the primitive he looked like in the photographs. The same publicity that brought him fame and attention was now bringing him ridicule. But Jones continued to insist that *"Some Came Running* is a better book than *From Here to Eternity*. I don't care what the reviewers say."

What then went wrong? From the first, Jones had a clear idea of what he wanted to do with the book. Drawing from his own experiences, he planned a story about a war veteran, Dave Hirsh, who returns to his native Midwestern town of Parkman, Illinois. Something of a rebel, he becomes an embarrassment to his elder brother, Frank, who lives by wholly materialistic values. Before the war, Dave had been a writer. He has no intention of continuing that profession in Parkman, but is successfully encouraged to do so by Gwen French, a single woman who gives him intellectual stimulation but will have nothing to do with him physically. Disappointed by her rebuff and by what he has seen of sexual careerism in middle-class Parkman, Dave decides to marry the town whore, Ginny, under the illusion that at least he can have a simple relationship with her. But he soon becomes bored with her sullen hostility to his work and decides to leave the town. On the road, he is accosted by Ginny's former husband, a former Marine Corps hero who is now a mental patient. In a fit of jealousy, he shoots Hirsh.

Despite its depressing conclusion, Jones intended *Some Came Running* to be a comic novel about modern love. In this novel, he said, nobody loves the actual person he thinks he is in love with; he does not even see him or her: "He loves the fictitious picture he has built up out of his own subconscious needs and has pasted across the figure of the beloved."

The situation is absurd but also pathetic, for the illusion of romantic love causes so much misery. Jones explained this failure of love to a journalist as the desire of everyone "to be loved by some other person more than that person loves himself. It's an insatiable greed in this country to be loved completely. It's not a joke to say that someone should love a person enough to be willing to die for them. They mean it literally and I find it horrifying."

Jones believed that most people wanted to be loved so that they could then appear as heroes in their own eyes as well as in the eyes of their lovers. He felt that all the trappings of modern society combined to further this egocentric notion. From the moment he was conscious enough to think of his own relationships, from his unloving childhood to his young manhood, Jones realized that his own experience of love supported this idea. He imagined that his failure as a lover was caused by his unheroic and unmanly bearing. "It took me a long time to feel that women liked me," he said. "I felt ugly and unattractive." Slight and with poor eyesight, he tried to build himself up to become muscular and strong, hoping to become a romantic hero. But then in wartime he found out what heroes were really like, or, rather, that heroism doesn't exist at all. For himself, Jones solved the problem when he moved in with Lowney Handy. She taught him to overcome his egocentricity and to give up any remaining romantic illusions. At least for a while, he accepted the idea that, for a mature person, "life is essentially a life of aloneness."

In *Some Came Running*, Jones wanted to show how the citizens of Parkman, Illinois, imitating the man in the Gospel according to Saint Mark who runs after Jesus in order to find the kingdom of heaven, take up their cross and run after romantic love, imagining it will answer all their problems. That is what he meant by his title. "What I was trying to do," he wrote, "was to write a 'romantic tragedy.' The Romantics, the modern Romantics, who believe that people only grow through pain, do not therefore believe in tragedy. They believe tragedy can be averted by growth. The Classicists, on the other hand, believe in tragedy, and the essence of tragedy is the fact that it is foreordained and cannot be avoided. Thus, a so-called Romantic novel cannot be a tragedy because it is not foreordained and growth is caused by the pain of suffering. I myself believe it is possible to believe in the idea of growth through pain, like the Romantics, and still believe in tragedy." In the novel, Jones resolves the apparent contradiction by having his central character, Dave, learn enough to abandon the illusion of romantic love, but at that very moment of attaining maturity, he is killed by forces he had set in motion when he was still immature.

A theme of this kind, even though tragic, could be treated in a comic manner with the gusto that eighteenth-century novelists brought to novels of amorous adventure, but *Some Came Running* has little of the light touch of *Tom Jones*. It is more like a nineteenth-century novel, infused with social consciousness and sympathy for the characters. The reader therefore does not know whether to take the story straight or to accept its basic absurdity. Jones shows how all of them, Dave, his businessman brother Frank, his intellectual and spiritual guide Gwen French, are mired down in illusions about romantic love. Mistrustful of human protestations of integrity, Jones has his characters change their ideas as they go along. Each one "does things which at first he had promised himself he would never do, and then rationalizes it into another personal integrity just as 'honorable.' " Some settle for comfort and materialism to avoid the pain, but no one is ever satisfied. In Jones's view, people go out of their way to make themselves unhappy so that they "can again feel the despair that needs love."

Jones's error in *Some Came Running* is one of conception, for his intentions are not clearly executed, and the scope of his book suggests a straight social study rather than a burlesque. Not by nature a satirist who could dispense with human folly in a brief story, Jones had too much feeling for the slow, drawn-out agony of his characters.

Half of the book's characters are reflections of middle-class prosperity; they are extensions of the materialists in Sinclair Lewis' *Babbitt* and not original contributions to literature. The other half, more sympathetically treated, are the losers, the lower-class individuals who reflect the Southern ease of the town. They are defeated by the circumstances of their lives, and Jones treats them with a sympathy and understanding that counters his original intention to treat them as absurd. Ginny, the town whore, Jones conceived of as being "little better than a high-grade animal," but she is also a warm and loving girl who comes to Dave Hirsh's rescue. She is bone-stupid and illiterate but touching in her goodhearted way.

Another character of the type, 'Bama Dillard, is shown to be a naturally good and decent man, despite his uncouth language and behavior. Unhappy in his marriage, he drifts around Parkman, but he is courteous and intelligent and unexpectedly well read. He is his own man, generous and kind, but he has a stupid self-destructive impulse that leads him to kill himself by drink.

Jones may have intended these lower-class individuals to be comic primitives, like some of Shakespeare's characters, but they evoke so much sympathy that they send out the wrong signals and interfere with the emotional responses Jones intended to elicit. In fact, Jones's success with these figures places him almost alone among American writers for treating lower-class characters as human beings and for giving them the dignity they deserve, without sentimentality.

The problems of conception in *Some Came Running* were made more difficult by Jones's experiments with language. Apart from idiosyncratic spelling and the omission of apostrophes and some other conventional punctuation, Jones used devices intended to break down the barrier that traditionally exists between the language of the narrator and the language of the characters. He believed that the abrupt change between colloquial dialogue and formal narrative was jolting. Wanting to bring his reader into the world he was writing about, he

tried to reproduce in storytelling the quasi-grammatical circumlocu-
tions he thought typical of Midwestern speech and thought. After a
direct quotation, he would therefore write narrative passages in the
same language as the preceding speaker, hoping to preserve the tone
of the dialogue. He was not consistent, however, and readers were
confused. Critics misread his intentions; finding narrative passages
written in a colloquial or semiliterate prose, they assumed that Jones
did not know how to write. Jones took full responsibility; to Shelby
Foote he wrote that "everything about that book was deliberate —
the heavy, involved style and syntax, as well as the loose sprawling
quality of the narrative — and all flaws are flaws of commission, all
done in an effort to reach a further expression. Where they fail, of
course they are flaws; where they don't, they're not." He explained
that his ambition was to reach beyond the understatement of writers
"who believe that to say something less subtly with one word is better
than saying it more subtly with three. Hemingway mined that vein
out. I'm after bigger bonanzas; Eldorado, if I can find it."

Jones's failure with *Some Came Running* was at least a failure of
commitment and ambition. He could have consolidated the achievement of *From Here to Eternity* by writing a modest novel that would
have allowed him to be respectfully considered a writer like all the
others. But he wanted to go forward, and although his techniques
were faulty, they enabled him to portray the feelings and beliefs of a
hitherto unrecorded segment of the American population. These
people are allowed to speak with an honesty and directness that, except in the work of Anderson, Wolfe, and Steinbeck, had hardly been
heard before. Instead of being revealed as grotesques or ethnic freaks,
they speak the idiom of America, with its limitations and its unexpected nobility.

Jones was surprisingly calm about the critical failure of the book,
partly because it sold well and therefore showed he had a popular following despite the critics. When he attended the National Book
Award ceremonies, he was attacked by a group of drunken critics
who wanted to know how he felt about producing such a "lemon" as
Some Came Running. Jones sat down with them and patiently explained what he had tried to do.

Although he would sometimes claim it was his best book, he also
admitted its shortcomings. "Somehow it got away from me," he said.
The fault lay mainly in his inability to see his work as others saw it, in
his failure to gauge his audience. It would prove to be a continuing

problem, especially when he was writing about civilian subjects, where he was less authoritative than with the military. With better guidance than what he received from Lowney and with the expert editorial direction that Burroughs Mitchell could have given him but probably was unable to once he was faced with the immensity of the project, Jones might have avoided his failures. But the long, isolated years of work had produced a single-minded absorption in the book that made him blind to the shortcomings of his methods.

The publication of *Some Came Running*, soon after his marriage to Gloria, was nevertheless a watershed for Jones. The two events were in many ways contradictory. In the concluding statement of the novel, Jones had Dave Hirsh realize "just how much he was, after all, alone — and would always be alone." There was "no way out of it; not through love, not through work, not through play, not through courage, not through fear. No way."

The contrast between this belief in isolation and his own marriage was not easy for him to resolve, but he tried to understand it by writing stories about his childhood, hoping perhaps to find there some clue that would throw light on his situation. Following the protracted work on *Some Came Running*, which he likened to "having t.b. or some such long term chronic ailment with a low-grade fever that takes a long time to cure," he compared his turn to short stories to "having a series of high-fever ailments in which the crisis comes soon and either passes or doesn't." Now in New York, Jones saw the Middle West with a vividness he had not felt since childhood, and he was drawn to "that beautiful, grim, frightening land- and spirit-locked part of the world."

The three stories he placed in this setting are among his best work. Each is about a small boy who grows up in a small town, where he lives under the pressure of adult control. All of them autobiographical, they are about shame, fear, embarrassment, and loneliness. "The Valentine," based on Jones's memory of giving a box of chocolates to Annis Skaggs at school in Robinson, is about a boy who dares to express his feelings for a girl only to have the other children ridicule him for his display of affection. "A Bottle of Cream" is about a young boy who drops the bottle he has been sent to fetch at the store. Terrified of being scolded, he is rescued by a kindly older boy, who buys him another bottle to take its place. In later years, the older boy turns into an habitual thief and jailbird, and the younger one wonders about the origins of crime and the nature of justice. "The Tennis Game" tells of a boy who likes to imagine himself in romantic situations. In the garage behind the house where his mother has sent him to work, he imagines that he is playing in the finals at Wimbledon and he goes through the motions of passing shots and the winning volley. Remembering that he had once been in a passage beside the garage with a little girl, he decides to go there to masturbate so that he can celebrate his victory. Just then his mother calls out to ask him what he is doing. "Playing," he replies, and she turns to her friends and says, "Oh, well, you know how children are. They're always playing some little game or other when they're by themselves."

During this period in New York, Jones also turned back to his army experiences as a source of material for fiction. In November of 1941, in anticipation of a Japanese attack, he had been sent with a detachment to Makapuu Point to install five fortified machine gun nests in the solid rock overlooking the beach. The soldiers worked in the face of a "hard-flowing wind that never stops howling" and lived in tents. Immediately after Pearl Harbor, Jones was stationed in this same place, where at night he sat behind a machine gun "staring into the dark toward Rabbit Island," waiting for the Japanese invasion. At the time, Jones still had a pistol that had been given him while he was on guard duty at Schofield Barracks, and he held on to it. His possession of the weapon was neither legal nor illegal; it was an accident, but he welcomed it as extra protection in case the Japanese actually arrived, with their much-feared samurai swords.

On one occasion, Jones was sent inland with a platoon to man a gun emplacement at Marconi Pass in the hills overlooking the coastline. A road led inland from a point halfway between Diamond Head and Hanauma Bay, and after passing a farm, the men had to climb up to the pass high in the steep green mountains of the interior. Jones began to write a story about this experience, and it grew to be a novella called *The Pistol.*

The central character is Pfc. Richard Mast, who has a pistol he is not authorized to have and which the other men in the detachment try to obtain, by purchase, bribery, or stealth. Mast succeeds in keeping it, and when the men reach the pass, they declare an unspoken truce, because the place is so beautiful that they feel safe. Soon, however, they begin to feel insecure again and fight for the pistol, which has a kind of magic power that will protect them. In the end, Mast is ordered to return the pistol to the supply sergeant who issued it. He accepts the order equably, realizing that there are no special protections in life; everyone is subject to the human condition.

Jones intended *The Pistol* to be "a strictly symbolical novel after the pattern of the European novel." The pistol represented personal salvation, but Jones also wanted it to contain some of the flavor of the "mythological history of the Old West," because he was interested in the lengths to which people would go "in killing, injuring, lying, cheating, hurting" to attain salvation of any kind, personal or otherwise. To preserve the symbolic quality of the story, Jones said he wanted "deliberately to remove the reader, to push him back a level from the action." This produced "too little of the actual experience of life" for his taste, he told Shelby Foote, but it made the book fun to write, "and easy, because it didn't really attempt to attack any of the really bigger problems."

Jones made sure that the symbolism was always subordinate to the story. The pistol stands for different things, and therefore the story does not become monotonous or predictable. The conflict is social, religious, political, and philosophical. The notion of a salvation offering protection against the inevitability of death is not only absurd; it provokes violence among others, who resent the unfair advantage that the so-called salvation provides.

The Pistol is a highly controlled piece of writing, and Jones intended it to be so. Although it was begun before the negative reviews of *Some Came Running* were published, he wanted to use it to prove that he could write a short novel in standard English. In his drafts, he consistently tightened the narrative so as to attain the denseness that symbolic prose should have. It was humiliating for a writer as serious and established as Jones to feel he had to go out of his way to prove his competence, but he did so and asked Burroughs Mitchell to read through the manuscript to make sure that it contained no errors of usage. *The Pistol* was perhaps the short and safe novel that would have followed *From Here to Eternity* had Jones been a cautious writer. As it is, it was a story that reflected the author's private concerns during the five weeks it took him to write it, and it served to make him ponder the contradictory impulses of his life.

By the time of their first Christmas together, the Joneses had started to consider what they would do with their lives. The sublet would soon expire, and Gloria was pregnant. It was time to settle down in some place that would suit them both. They had enjoyed living in New York and by now had numerous friends in the city. But a change was in the offing.

Christmas was spent with Rose and William Styron in New York, and the question of where to go next was in the air. Gloria had wanted to stay in New York, but Jones had suggested going out west to a place like Sheridan, Wyoming. He claimed that New York was not a good place for a writer. "Too many parties, too many things to do, too many distractions." A prose writer needs a daily rhythm for extended pieces of writing, and that was hard to establish in the city.

In the end, they decided to go to Europe rather than stay in the United States, because Jones wanted to write a novel about Django Reinhardt, the Gypsy jazz guitarist who had lived in France. During the early 1950s, many Americans had gone to live in Italy, France, and other countries, and the Styrons told the Joneses about their experiences in Paris and Rome during that time. At the end of the decade it was still cheaper to live abroad than in America, thanks to a good rate of exchange, and American residents abroad also had tax benefits. For the Joneses, living in Europe would give them the opportunity to use some of Jones's foreign royalties that had been blocked in Eastern Europe, notably Yugoslavia and Russia.

These were practical considerations. Personal reasons were more persuasive. Although Gloria had been to Europe, Jones had not, and he was eager to go. Jones later said they went "to travel and get a little culture. Culture with a capital C." There were vast areas of ignorance that needed attending to, and although Jones was never a dedicated tourist, he was interested in finding out what European civilization was really like.

In the spring of 1958, they began to take French lessons from Dolly Chareau, a tutor, who even got Jones to write stories in French. They bought luggage and collected the names of restaurants and hotels in the capital cities. The decision to go fit in well with Jones's professional needs and his growing unhappiness with New York. He had come to believe that New York was just a hotbed of literary coteries and self-promoters. The reception of *Some Came Running* showed him how hostile the critics could be to an outsider. Their failure to understand the book made him scorn their literary abilities, but his not having a university degree left him feeling ill at ease with them. The longer he remained in New York, the more he realized that the brotherhood he had felt toward other writers when he first arrived was an illusion.

What drove the point home was the deteriorating relationship with Norman Mailer. Memory of their quarrel while Jones was still in Illinois had not dissipated. Mailer told Jones "that deep in that crusty, fucking heart of yours you probably have the same kind of warmth for me that I have for you," but neither of them could leave well enough alone. In 1956, Mailer wrote to Jones, calling him a "dumb, benighted asshole of a writer," and told him to ignore gossip about Mailer's private life and to follow some of his own advice: "Do your own work, let me do mine, and have the sense to keep anybody from corrupting our natural respect for each other." Jones, in turn, told Mailer that he thought *The Deer Park* was "not a good book, and in fact isnt as good by far as 'Barbary' which I liked very much — when read as an allegory, and not as a novel, which of course it is not." Jones knew he wasn't being gentle. "Probably I'm hurting you. But this is honestly what I feel." Then he added, "I still believe there are great books in you. *Great* books. If you will ever get them out. But I certainly doubt very much youll ever do it while writing a fucking column for the *Village Voice.*"

The Joneses saw little of Mailer, because he and Adele were still living in Connecticut. But one night they met at a party given by Victor Weybright, who, as head of New American Library, was Jones's paperback publisher. It was a period when Mailer was drinking heavily and taking drugs. He had started the evening off badly by signing the guest book "To my fellow racketeer," a sentiment that Weybright didn't appreciate. Word spread through the party about Mailer's behavior, and in the meantime, Gloria and Adele had a contretemps. So when Mailer suggested that they all go out to dinner together, Jones declined. "We must be loyal to our wives," he said. It was a trivial matter, but it eliminated an opportunity for the men to heal their relationship.

Just before the Joneses left for Europe, they went to the hospital to see Rose Styron, who had just had her second child. There they learned that Mailer had wounded Styron by sending him an offensive letter. Jones's sympathy for Styron further alienated him from Mailer, but he had come to see that he and Mailer were no longer wholly in charge of their friendship. To some extent they were being manipulated by those who thought of them, in Mailer's words, as "rival corporations vying for attention in the literary market place." All this made Europe more attractive than ever.

Beyond the professional considerations of the trip abroad, there was the opportunity it would provide Gloria and Jones to get to know each other as individuals. Free of the New York social world, they would have the chance to come to terms with some of their difficulties and nourish the love that held them together. As celebrities, they would be in the public eye, and other people would compare them, probably negatively, with Scott and Zelda Fitzgerald, and accuse Jones of imitating Hemingway in Paris. But such matters were unimportant. On April 12, 1958, they sailed on board the French Line steamer the *Liberté*. Heading down the North River, they were on their own at last.

⇶ THREE ⇷

8

❦

PARIS

TRANSATLANTIC TRAVEL was still in its postwar heyday in the late 1950s, and the *Queen Mary*, the *Ile de France*, and the *Michelangelo* regularly plied the Atlantic, carrying Americans back and forth to Europe. The week required for the crossing was itself an introduction to the Continent; it gave passengers a taste of what was to come when they stepped ashore at Southampton, Le Havre, or Naples. As first-class passengers on the *Liberté*, the Joneses had the run of the elegant saloons of the upper decks, the grand ballroom, and the restaurant, where, in evening clothes, they would dine every night. During the day, they could walk on deck, go to the movies, swim in the pool, or read. There were cocktail lounges, dancing every night, and too much good food. Because he was a celebrity, Jones would be noticed, but the maître d'hôtel was accustomed to the famous and did not allow him to feel conspicuous. He concentrated on providing the quality of service and the joie de vivre for which the Compagnie Générale Transatlantique was noted.

The Joneses disembarked at Southampton on April 23, and after a weekend in the country, went up to London, where they stayed at the Stafford Hotel in St. James's Place, a narrow cul-de-sac a few steps from the offices of Collins, Jones's British publisher. They were in the center of West End club land, although they were less interested in Boodle's and White's than in the picturesque old shops like Locke's the hatter and Berry Bros., the wine merchants at the foot of the hill where St. James's Street runs into Pall Mall.

Soon they were invited to dinner by William Collins, who introduced him to other members of the publishing firm as well as to literary critics, journalists, and friends. They already had a number of other acquaintances living in London, among them John Marquand, Jr., Art Buchwald, Kenneth Tynan, and Elaine Dundy. At the time, Tynan was theater critic for the *Observer*, so they began going to plays and soon became familiar figures at such restaurants as Rules's and the White Tower, where theater and film people congregated. As the weather improved, they took boat trips on the Thames, and Jones even dressed up in a gray morning coat and top hat hired from Moss Bros. so that they could go to Ascot. They made excursions into the country to visit Oxford and Stratford, for Jones had a special interest in the Elizabethans. The visit to England was mainly motivated by his desire to see the world he had read about so widely in English literature. In addition to Shakespeare, he had read deeply in Dickens and Hardy, and was eager to see the landscape of their work.

Although Jones was out of his element and occasionally took refuge in playing the country boy, he made a pleasing impression on the people he met because of his modesty and genuine American quality. The Joneses were a refreshing couple who made it clear that they were having a wonderful time together. Sometimes, their encounters with the English produced unexpected results. A letter from Victor Weybright introducing them to the novelist Henry Green brought Jones and Gloria an invitation to dinner. "Green turned out to be a very paunchy, fat kind of stuffy Englishman," Jones recalled, "and his wife rather affected, though a very nice lady. But he was also deaf and you had to shout at him. So after we'd had dinner and gone into the living room to chat, he turned to his wife and said, 'Who did you say these people were?' "

After a month, the Joneses left to continue the trip they had planned to the Soviet Union, flying to Leningrad by way of Denmark. But on arriving in Copenhagen, Gloria discovered that she was in danger of having a miscarriage, so they flew directly back to London. The baby was lost, and Gloria, who had also developed an infection, had to enter the London Clinic. Jones, frightened and worried, visited her daily, once even getting into bed with her, much to the annoyance of the nurses.

During the hospitalization, he was much on his own and felt at sea. Although he accepted invitations, he was too shy to initiate meetings with others. Staying on by himself at the Stafford did not suit him, so he found a furnished flat at 61 Eaton Place, in the heart of Belgravia. An elegant quarter of London, with large white mansions, many of them embassies, it has pleasant streets for walking and is not far from

Sloane Square and its shops and hotels. Jones found a pub run by a man called Pat Kennedy and soon became a habitué of the place. He joined others in playing darts and found an easy level of conversation among the local people that he had missed at the dinner parties he attended with Gloria.

In July, when Gloria was fully recovered, her former roommate Cecile Gray arrived from New York, and they all decided to go together to Brussels to visit the World's Fair. From there they proceeded to Paris, where the Joneses looked for an apartment they could rent for a year. They were attracted especially to the Ile de la Cité and the Ile St. Louis because of their quietness and the openness of the views. "It's very beautiful," Jones wrote to his brother, Jeff, "the most beautiful city I have ever seen anywhere, or expect to see." The trees that lined the quais and the streets gave a feel of rural life that he had missed in Manhattan. "Partly because of the river I think," wrote Jones, "there is an openness about the city that you don't find in many other places."

Through an agency called the American in Paris, Gloria and Jones were lucky enough to find a sublet almost immediately on the Ile de la Cité. Located on the Quai aux Fleurs, it was on the floor above a crémerie with a view of the Right Bank that included the monumental Hôtel de Ville and the church of St. Gervais. It had only one bedroom, but they could watch the "barges loaded with everything from sand to oil to barrels of cognac" passing by their front door.

They were in the ancient heart of Paris. In front of the cathedral of Notre Dame was a plaque marked Kilometre Zéro, the point from which all distances in France are measured, and around the corner was a house with a sign saying that Abelard used to go there to meet Héloïse. Within easy distance were the art galleries along the Rue de Seine and bookshops along the Boulevard St. Germain. Jones and Gloria walked all over the Left Bank, having drinks in cafés and dinners in restaurants along the Rue St. André des Arts, afterward walking along the Rue Jacob to look at the shop windows full of porcelain and silver.

They were like innocents abroad, and the adventure of Paris drew them together. They were so in love that in restaurants they held hands at the table, but their artlessness little prepared them for another side of Parisian life. After dinner at the home of M. Nielson of the Presses de la Cité, Jones's French publisher, they realized how inadequate their French was and began to take more French lessons, this time from Hélène Veret, the agent who had found them their flat.

Paris in the late 1950s had changed a good deal from the early part of the decade, when it was flooded by young American writers like Peter Matthiessen, George Plimpton, and William Styron, who had gathered there to write and found *The Paris Review*. Jones belonged to a different generation from this group, whom Irwin Shaw called "literary hopefuls," many of them protected by "wealthy and benevolent parents on the other side of the Atlantic." Jones was older and established, and his arrival stirred up curiosity. Through friends from New York, he began to meet people, but because of language difficulties he did not become involved in the French literary community. He and Gloria "went through a period of pretty severe cultural shock" when they first arrived, Jones later recalled. "When the French talk fast, it's hard to follow." Through Mme. Georges Grüber, who was the daughter of the playwright Henry Bernstein and who ran a restaurant called Le Petit Pavé near the Rue de Rennes, which was much patronized by writers as well as such politicians as Pierre Mendès-France and François Mitterrand, they were introduced to Daniel Anselme, Tristan Tzara, the founder of the Dada movement, and Albert Camus, whom they also saw at a small place called the Village Bar around the corner from the Café des Deux Magots. Camus told Jones that *From Here to Eternity* was "a compendium of all American folklore." Another writer Jones met at the time was Romain Gary, who was later to marry the actress Jean Seberg. Gary had been with the French consulate in Los Angeles and knew English well.

Jones's failure to pay homage to Simone de Beauvoir and Jean-Paul Sartre, who were unquestionably the most prominent French writers of the time, and also regulars at the Brasserie Lipp and the Deux Magots, aroused some hostility. "I suppose I should have written a letter and gone to pay my respects," Jones later admitted. He claimed not to be interested in them, because they were so politically engaged. "Human themes are going to outlive political themes," he noted.

Jones made an effort to become familiar with new writing in France, even though he was hampered by his weak French. He read three stories and an article by Alain Robbe-Grillet in translation and told Burroughs Mitchell he thought they were "completely full of shit. That the French today think the novel is a second-rate form is only to me an indication of the great lack of vitality in all French writing, except that of a very few men." Jones felt that most young French writers were "totally emasculated by scholasticism" long before they became capable "of putting true human vitality into their work." He was more in tune with the great writers of the past, Balzac and Stendhal, whose work deeply influenced his own.

Mixing with French writers had never been one of Jones's reasons for going to France, but he welcomed the company of Irwin Shaw, who had lived in Paris for a long time. Well established before the war as a writer of seven plays, including *Bury the Dead,* Shaw had made his name as a fiction writer for *The New Yorker,* where such stories as "The Girls in Their Summer Dresses" were first published, and was now concentrating on novels. Both men were affected by "the permanent dark spots within the soul," Shaw's phrase for one of the consequences of serving in the army, and Jones knew and admired Shaw's war novel, *The Young Lions.* Shaw was now planning to move to Klosters, Switzerland, where he was having a house built, but he had a feeling for Paris that grew out of nearly a decade of knowing its people and neighborhoods. "It is summer or autumn or winter or spring," he wrote of Paris, "and it is sunny and raining and there is snow on the statues and bits of ice in the Seine and the trees are all in blossom and the swimmers are diving into the purified water in the wooden pools along the river banks and it is early in the morning and late at night and the President is giving a ball and the Garde Républicaine is out in breastplates and horsehair tails and the North Africans are rioting for autonomy and all the policemen have dents in their shining helmets."

A large, barrel-chested former football player with a prominent nose, blue eyes, and a warm smile, Shaw not only became a sort of godfather to Jones; he was also his best friend, the one writer with whom he could be most at ease. One day when Jones phoned to confirm a luncheon date, Shaw tried to put him off by saying he had had a bad morning of work. "If you don't have lunch with me," Jones answered, "I won't marry you."

Another writer important to Jones was James Baldwin, author of *Go Tell It on the Mountain,* who also spent a great deal of time in France. Jones thought highly of Baldwin's second novel, *Giovanni's Room,* and told Burroughs Mitchell it contained some "truly magnificent writing." The two men had suffered the humiliations of life in the lower reaches of society, Jones in the army, Baldwin in Harlem.

They even shared the same name, for Baldwin was illegitimate and had originally been named Jones. Baldwin respected Jones for not being a phony liberal, and Jones urged Baldwin to "forget all that nigger shit" if he wanted to write a real novel. He believed that in fiction human character was more important than ideas, including ideas about race. "People like you," Baldwin wrote Jones, "are very important to people like me and in this sad, bad world, very important period."

The novel with a Paris background that Jones planned to base on the life of Django Reinhardt had its seed in Jones's early interest in jazz. He had first heard recordings of Reinhardt's music in Robinson while writing *From Here to Eternity*. At that time he had lost the ability to be emotionally nourished by writing, because he had become so aware of literary technique. "Instead of long hours reading," he said, "I spend long hours listening to music. The world I have all but lost in reading by becoming a writer myself, I've regained in music."

Jones was especially attracted by the honesty of jazz. "Re-enlistment Blues," the song the soldiers compose in *From Here to Eternity*, is notable mainly for telling the truth about army life without pretenses of any kind. Jones appreciated the same honesty in Reinhardt's music and especially admired its accuracy of feeling — the "sharp erratic-explosive gypsy rhythms that cried over life while laughing at it, too fast for the ear to follow, too original for the mind to anticipate, too intricate for the memory to remember." This perfect expression seemed to come from something within the artist himself, and Jones admired this quality in the musicians he knew. He described Sidney Bechet, a large, placid-looking jazz pianist, as "one of the most potent, powerful people I have ever met. He did not look as though anything could bother him. He seemed to carry an atmosphere of peace and tranquillity around with him wherever he went."

Jones and Gloria spent a great many nights visiting the Mars Club, the Blue Note, and other jazz clubs where Django Reinhardt had played in order to pick up information about him. Reinhardt had lost two fingers while wandering through France in a Gypsy caravan and had been forced to adjust his style of playing to overcome this handicap. He learned to improvise and in the process became the first foreign musician to influence American jazz; he toured with Duke Ellington in 1946. At the Hot Club, where Reinhardt had often played before his death, in 1953, Jones interviewed his widow and brother, as well as many Americans who had known him and played with him. He also talked to Duke Ellington, Billie Holiday, and Lester Young. The more people he interviewed, the more confused he became. He heard all sorts of conflicting stories, and the only consistent thing he learned was that Django was "a really total individualist" and that "he played incredible, beautiful music."

The character of Django, as Jones conceived it in notes for a novel he intended to call *No Peace I Find,* was clearly based on his private concerns. The Django character is a consummate artist who still wonders, "Do I really have a capacity for great love? Or is the truth that I only pretend to give great love in order to *get* love?" He is tormented by his possible insincerity. At the same time, he is "terribly, terribly careful to be faithful to his wife. A former affair went wrong — one in which he was unfaithful — and from the very beginning. Does he hope, in his very immaculate faithfulness, to avoid his failure of love a 2nd time?" When he looks at women, he "mentally fucks them. But he never goes to the point of the physical. As if in desperation hoping this will save love. But then, what if his wife should be unfaithful to him! Well at least the loss of love would not be his fault, his guilt. But what of that? Love will still be *lost.*"

In the end, the Django character never really knows the nature of his capacity for love. "A celebrated, beloved, adored, admired man who still does not know if he has ever really loved greatly as he would like to do."

Continuing his exploration of the relationship between men and women, Jones now approached the subject from the point of view of one who was married. Clearly that status did not alter the basic tensions between the sexes, and he could use his own marriage as an example. Although he and Gloria loved each other deeply, they also had moments of open conflict. Each had strong beliefs and feelings and had no hesitation in expressing them. Once, while in London, Jones became so excited and pounded the wall with such force that he splattered blood all over the paint and had to have his hand bandaged. Another time, angered because he had to make extensive revisions, he banged his head against the wall so hard that he dislodged an expensive Picasso plate, which fell to the floor and broke. One day, Hélène Veret arrived for the French lesson at the Quai aux Fleurs and found Gloria sitting in the living room, surrounded by broken glass and smashed furniture and looking frightened. When the Irish writer Brendan Behan came to Paris, he went out with Jones for a wild night on the town, during which Jones danced naked on the quai. The episode became famous enough to be recorded in *Life* magazine, whose reporter stated that, in an excess of brotherly love, Behan addressed a gathering of blacks and Algerians in what they took to be a patronizing tone. "The *agents de police* averted mayhem," noted the correspondent, "but after it was all over, Jones, for reasons not detailed, went home and belted Goria, then went down to the Seine, removed his wedding ring and cast it into the waters forever. The next day he duly apologized, and they live quite happily."

Drunkenness contributed to this violence, but the principal cause seems to have been Jones's lack of ease with himself and a disappointment with his life that had lingered on despite his marriage. To what extent his erratic behavior was calculated or merely the product of lack of inhibition is hard to tell. Jones and his friends used a barracks language that surprised others not accustomed to it. Once at La Mediterranée, a seafood restaurant across from the Théâtre de l'Odéon, Jones was having dinner with a group that included Sydney Chaplin. The language soon became rough; words like *cunt* and *shit* were bandied about in loud voices. Finally a man came across from another table and said, stuffily, "If you don't mind, I happen to be with my wife." Before there was time for a reply, the man's wife came over and fetched him. "Come back and sit down, you asshole," she said.

Such instances may have stemmed from exuberance, but Jones could become genuinely angry with any woman he disliked, and he had no hesitation in calling such a person "a stupid cunt" or a "fucking overeducated bitch." Women who knew Jones dismissed his violent language as unimportant, merely a part of his earthy dislike of pretense; others were often shocked. One night he became so bored with a female guest at his table that he told her to shut up. She burst into tears, and Gloria told him to apologize. "I'm sorry," he said. Then after a pause, he added, "I said I was sorry, you fucking cunt, so shut up!"

Jones could also be physically vulgar, as if to celebrate his coarseness. To a degree, this was part of the exaggerated masculine front he sometimes put on with people he didn't know, but he occasionally farted and belched in public. This was bullying behavior, for no one would ever criticize him for it. Sometimes, usually with attractive women, he would display a physical crudeness that seemed a way of publicly acknowledging his unattractiveness. When he was introduced to a beautiful and delicate young Israeli actress, he responded by belching in her face. It was as though, in comparing her beauty and grace with his momentary idea of himself as a monster, he allowed his feelings of inferiority to manifest themselves.

After a year in Paris, Jones and Gloria rented a house in Portofino for the summer of 1959. They had taken a trip to Italy the preceding November and had bought a little Mercedes to drive to Florence, Venice, and Rome. Jones had thought about writing a novel with an Italian setting, but Rome disappointed him. "The atmosphere there is a sort of rural decadence," he said.

From Rome, they drove south to Anzio, where American troops had landed in 1944. A seaside resort dating back to the time of Nero and Caligula, it had been reduced to rubble by the fierce fighting between the Germans and the Americans. The long rows of white crosses in the American military cemetery were proof of how deadly the battle had been. "I talked to the man in charge of the caretaking for a while," Jones later recalled, "a red-bearded American who lived right there. No, not many people came, he said. It was too far away, and off the main tourist routes from Rome. And of course the local Italians had no reason to come there. But he liked to make sure the place was always well-kept, anyway. Sometimes it was hard, on the budget the U.S. government allotted him. But once in a while somebody might come by who had a relative buried there; or else someone like myself, who was just interested. I thanked him, and told him his caretaking was superb, which it was. What else was there to say? I got in my little car and drove back."

Portofino is a picturesque and popular small resort on the Italian Riviera between Rapallo and Genoa. The fishermen's port is crowded with boats, restaurants, and small hotels, but the Joneses' villa, owned by Jenny Graves, the daughter of the English poet Robert Graves, and called Il Casteletto, was built high on a promontory that protected the port from the sea. It was reached by a steep path leading up through flowering bushes and had a large living room and a terrace.

The Joneses enjoyed having guests who knew how to cope with Europe, and during the summer their visitors included Arnold Black, a composer Jones enjoyed playing chess with; Edmund Trzcinski, the writer; as well as Addie Herder and Monique Gonthier, who had visited Gloria in Marshall, Illinois, and whom she and Jones had met again in Paris; and Irma and Ben Wolstein from New York, who had been at their wedding in Haiti.

Every morning Jones got up at six o'clock to write. Usually he had a hangover, but he would plow on until his stint was done. Lunch was usually served on the terrace by the maid who came with the house, and in the afternoons, perhaps after a nap, Gloria and Jones would go down to the village to hire a sailboat or would drive into Santa Margherita or Rapallo. One reason for their choosing Portofino was that it was a good place for scuba diving. Jones obtained the necessary equipment, the rubber suit and the oxygen tanks, and went out with an instructor. The prospect of the dive frightened him; now it was Gloria who would tease him, and he would then go over the side. Jones was interested in diving partly because he wanted to master the technique. He was always fascinated by people who had practical skills or made things, and he enjoyed testing himself. For that purpose, he also took up sailing in Portofino. He had little natural grace, but he sailed correctly, as though he had learned to do it from a manual.

In the evenings, the Joneses would have drinks in the porticciolo, or little port, at La Grita, before having dinner at the Stella or the Delfina. Through Trzcinski, they had met a number of people living in the neighborhood, including an Italian prince who had a Chanel model as a girl friend. Jones invited them to dinner and also asked the scuba-diving instructor. At table, the prince ostentatiously snubbed the instructor. Jones, who had no patience with European social distinctions, became so enraged that Trzcinski told the model to take her prince away before there was trouble.

Life at the Joneses' was intense. They worked hard and played hard. One day, after the long steep climb up the hill from the port, Gloria noticed that Jones's lips had turned blue. She immediately ran down the hill to call the doctor, who soon arrived, took tests, and ordered injections for what he incorrectly diagnosed as a digestive problem. In fact, it was the first sign of the illness that would end Jones's life. The immediate problem, however, was how to administer the injections. Jones was the most capable person in the house, but he was the patient. Rex Harrison and his wife, the actress Kay Kendall, who lived in the neighborhood, came to the rescue. Harrison told Jones to lie face down on the living room couch and lower his bikini. He then gave him a tremendous slap on a buttock and shoved in the needle. So the injections continued. Asked about his method, Harrison explained, "I slapped him so he wouldn't feel the needle."

Jones was more upset by his illness than he let on. He did not understand what the diagnosis "digestive vertigo" meant, and although he was only thirty-eight, he was worried about himself. "This summer," he wrote Burroughs Mitchell, "seems to have been selected to point out to me that I am no longer a 'young' man. I find myself still staring in astonishment and wanting to say, 'But see here, you don't understand. This is me!' " Kay Kendall died that summer of leukemia, and Jones was further reminded of his own mortality. Recalling the doctor's first visit, he wrote, "I lay there believing I was on the way out — I was absolutely convinced of it. I guess I still haven't gotten entirely over that. My own eventual death is much closer to me now than it has ever been, even during the war."

The return to France soon cheered him up. He and Gloria had thought of moving elsewhere, but when they reached Paris, they changed their minds. "We suddenly discovered we were home. It had all seemed strange before. It no longer did."

They were soon back with friends, including Edwin Morgan, Joe Warfield, and Bob Mullen, a group of Americans, working in Paris, with whom Jones could relax. One night after having dinner with them at a restaurant near the Panthéon, Jones had an accident while driving home: he smashed into a stanchion in the Boulevard St. Michel. The men were taken to the hospital and the police asked questions. "I know you want me to say I was drunk," Jones said. "That's what you want, isn't it? O.K., I was drunk." This confession caused Jones to lose his license for a year.

The accident also cost Jones two weeks of work and made him feel foolish. Soon afterward came word of the death of Camus in a car crash, and Jones was shaken. "It's a terrible tragedy," he said. Coming so soon after his mysterious attack in Portofino, these accidents made Jones reconsider his habits. He was now approaching forty, and Gloria was pregnant again. It was time to settle down.

Their lease on the small apartment on the Ile de la Cité was coming to an end, and they knew they would have to move. Renting an apartment large enough for the baby would be expensive and would also require key money. The alternative was to buy a place, and that is what they decided to do, even though they realized that they would have to stay in Paris for about ten years to amortize the large outlay of capital.

They expected to move away from the river to a less expensive neighborhood, but they found an apartment nearby, on the Ile St. Louis. Just across a narrow bridge from the Ile de la Cité, it was in a five-story Art Nouveau building that was being renovated for apartments. The one the Joneses liked faced the Seine and cost $64,000, although Jones was ultimately able to buy it for less. To raise some of the money, they planned to sell the house in Marshall and to ask Scribner's for an advance on Jones's next book. The rest of the money would be borrowed. Jones was delighted with the prospect of living on the Ile St. Louis; he wrote to Burroughs Mitchell that it was "like a tiny village set down in the heart of Paris all by itself." The apartment faced south, which meant they were on the sunny side of the island. It was on the second floor, with the combined living room and dining room facing the quai. The other rooms were in a seventeenth-century building that was immediately adjacent and reached by a corridor.

Across the river, they could see the hill on which the Sorbonne was built, with the towers of St. Séverin, St. Etienne du Mont, and St. Julien le Pauvre outlined against the sky. At the summit of the hill stood the Panthéon, with its Classical dome and tombs of Jean-Jacques Rousseau, Victor Hugo, and Emile Zola. Although the Joneses' address was 10 Quai d'Orléans, their front door faced a narrow lane called Rue Budé, which led to the Rue St. Louis en l'Ile, where shops and restaurants were found. In the other direction, along the quai, was one of the most spectacular views in Paris, the flying buttresses of Notre Dame Cathedral seen through the leaves of the trees planted along the street. Upstream, the Pont de la Tournelle spanned the Seine, leading to the Rue Cardinal Lemoine and the Boulevard St. Germain. Near the corner, overlooking the river, were the windows of the famous Tour d'Argent restaurant.

The Ile St. Louis dates back to the end of the sixteenth century, when Henry IV had the notion of combining two empty islands, the Ile Notre Dame and the Ile des Vaches, into a single habitable island. The work of development was completed during the reign of Louis XIII, when houses of pleasing appearance were raised along the reinforced banks of the new island. In time, the island was the home of a number of characters famous in French history, among them the niece of Louis XIV. Although she was the richest heiress in Europe, she had no suitors, because she was so huge and ugly. Eventually she cornered the impoverished Comte de Lauzon and married him. Six years younger and seven inches shorter than La Grande Mademoiselle, the little count vented his rage at the fate that had brought him such marital infelicity by addressing her sarcastically as "Granddaughter of Henry IV" and by ordering her to take off his boots when he returned to the house.

Like most of the residents of the Ile, Gloria and Jones came to know its history and its famous residents, among them the Duc de Richelieu, grand-nephew of the cardinal and a military man of whom it was said that "he was husband to all wives except his own." Victor Hugo claimed that the island produced a "tristesse nerveuse" in those who ventured there, but Charles Baudelaire lived in the Hôtel de Lauzun for two years that were among the happiest of his life, thanks to the proximity of his black mistress, Jeanne Duval. Another resident of the Hôtel de Lauzun was Théophile Gautier, whose famous preface to the *Fleurs du Mal* helped establish Baudelaire's reputation. In more recent times, Ford Madox Ford, with the assistance of Ernest Hemingway, published *The Transatlantic Review* from a little office in the Quai de Béthune.

Jones was invigorated by the literary associations of Paris. "When the day's stint is done," he said, "I walk the streets with Stendhal, Proust, Rousseau and Voltaire. I stand under the arches of the Eiffel Tower and dream I'm in a pre-Zuni village at some prehistoric time. I feel lost in the primeval forest among the columns of Notre Dame. I get goosepimples just looking at the scene." Jones nourished his feelings for France by reading books like Victor Hugo's *Notre-Dame de Paris* and Balzac's *Père Goriot*, which he admired for their realistic scenes.

Once the papers for the apartment were signed, Jones hurried to ready it for occupancy. It had formerly been an office, so extensive remodeling had to be done. Jones took charge and extended his French vocabulary by supervising the carpenters as they installed cupboards and bookshelves throughout the apartment. In the meantime, he ordered his books to be shipped from Illinois. Eager to have furniture appropriate to the Ile St. Louis, he bought heavy Louis XIII chairs and cabinets, as well as a long refectory table and matching chairs with red velvet cushions.

Gloria was fearful of having another miscarriage, so she went to the hospital for observation and tests. The doctor ordered her to stay in bed at home for the remaining months of her pregnancy. Friends volunteered to help. Her former roommate Scotty MacGregor came from America, as did the Styrons and another New York friend, Vivienne Nearing. On August 5, Gloria was taken to the American Hospital for the delivery; Jones was by her side all the time and watched her give birth. Their baby girl was in perfect health, and they named her Kaylie Ann.

Jones was loving and attentive on the first day of Gloria's stay in the hospital, and delighted with his daughter. But after that, he vanished and did not come back. He had been so apprehensive that he was afraid that if he returned, he might break down from relief at seeing his wife and daughter alive and well, and thereby let her see how frightened he had been for her.

On the day Gloria and Kaylie were due to be discharged, Jones appeared at the hospital and took them home. The house was ready and they went straight to the Quai d'Orléans. When they arrived, he carried the baby gingerly, afraid that he might drop her. He was overcome by joy at her presence, and when he got used to having her around, he would hold her in his arms and dance with her through a whole number, gently embracing her.

In the new house, Jones took pleasure in domesticity. At the old apartment, there was no telephone, so he and Gloria were forced to run downstairs to the crémerie when someone called. But now they had a phone of their own, and Jones had his number listed in the Annuaire, where he identified himself as an *écrivain*.

Jones enjoyed doing household tasks, and explored the island's shops and cafés. He bought groceries at the Maison Forcellini, where he could get Italian salami and mortadella as well as Brolio Chianti. Across the street was a tablet erected to the memory of the 112 tenants of the house, forty of them small children, who had been deported in 1942 and died in German concentration camps. The sole survivor was Mme. Forcellini. "I make a point of reading that tablet every day," Jones said. "Depressing but good for the soul. The terrifying thing is that it can happen any time and in any country in the guise of morality."

Often Jones would go to lunch at the Brasserie de l'Ile in the Rue de Bellay, just a short walk from his apartment. The specialties were Alsatian dishes, like choucroute garnie and cassoulet. Outside were flowerpots full of geraniums, and inside the front door was the bar with a few tables, one of which Jones particularly liked because it gave him a view of the street. The main dining room was beyond, decorated with copper pots, German beer steins, and antlers. The first time Gloria went there with Jones, she said, "This is for us," and it became their favorite neighborhood restaurant. The patronne would hold Kaylie on her lap while her parents dined, and they would often bring house guests in for drinks in the evening. The chef was a German who had cooked for Rommel in the Afrika Korps. He was captured by the French, and once he saw Paris, he decided never to leave.

Jones liked the atmosphere of the island. It was warm and intimate, like the small Midwestern towns he had known. The Louisiens had a sense of their own identity and looked on the rest of Paris as a foreign place, the "mainland." Close by Jones's house was a long ramp that led down from the Quai d'Orléans to the river's edge. There, under the hanging branches of the trees, fishermen would stand, watching the Seine go by as they hoped for a catch, and women in black stockings would bend over to do their laundry. "They have lived all their life on the island, like their fathers and grandfathers before them," wrote Sir Anthony Glyn, long a resident of the Ile and a friend of the Joneses. "Many of them seem to be only about four feet high and they often have medieval names like Basseporte or Crêvecoeur."

Jones often wandered through the streets after lunch. Sometimes he would cross over to the Left Bank and walk up the Rue du Cardinal Lemoine, past hardware shops, garages, wine shops, and groceries, many of them run by Algerians. From there he would explore streets with literary associations. When Hemingway's *A Moveable Feast* was published, Jones spent three days visiting the places described, but when his tour was over, he said, "Hemingway's Paris doesn't exist. The book really isn't about Paris. It's about Hemingway. It shocked and horrified me, the egomania of the man. He was a swashbuckler who didn't swash his buckle or buckle his swash."

Like most writers of his generation, Jones had been under Hemingway's influence from the start. He admired *The Sun Also Rises* and the short stories for their technical proficiency, but Hemingway was less important to him than Wolfe or Fitzgerald, whom he said he could "take all the way, or at least nearly so." What troubled him about Hemingway was his lack of honesty, which in turn affected his personality as a writer. "Hemingway is just short on personality, that's all," Jones said. If a work doesn't ring true, it is worthless, and Jones gave as an example of Hemingway's weakness his failure "to account truthfully for how he can so easily have such a long, almost infinite, succession of Great Loves. A Great Love, a real one, is not transferable. I know that."

If Jones knew Hemingway's opinion of him, he never said so publicly. Charles Scribner had sent *From Here to Eternity* to Hemingway, imagining the older writer would be interested in a military novel by a younger man. He must have been surprised by the response: "It is not great no matter what they tell you. It has fine qualities and greater faults. It is much too long and much too bitching and his one fight, against the planes, at Pearl Harbor day is almost musical comedy. He has a genius for respecting the kitchen and he is a K.P. boy for keeps and for always. Things will catch up with him and he will probably commit suicide. Who could announce in his publicity in this year 1951 that 'he went over the hill' in 1944. That was a year in which many people were very busy doing their duty and in which many people died. To me he is an enormously skillful fuck-up and his book will do great damage to our country. Probably I should re-read it again to give you a truer answer. But I do not have to eat an entire bowl of scabs to know they are scabs; nor suck a boil to know it is a boil; nor swim through a river of snot to know it is snot. I hope he kills himself as soon as it does not damage your or his sales. If you give him a literary tea you might ask him to drain a bucket of snot and then suck the puss out of a dead nigger's ear."

Scribner's must have remonstrated, for shortly afterward Hemingway further explained his distaste for Jones. "The reason the Col. Jones got on nerves was that when I read the book I spotted him for a psycho and not a real soldier. Served time, sure, but not as a soldier. Then you saying he was and everybody saying how wonderful he was I thought I must be crazy to see something that I was absolutely sure of and it not be true. Then I saw the article about Jones and Lowny and one or the other's admission that he came back from Guadal 'a whimpering neurotic' and went over the hill because the Army would only give him one month leave and he wanted three and I stopped worrying." Hemingway then asked that references to his name be removed from the book and concluded with this wish: "All I hope is that you can make all the money in the world out of him before he takes the overdose of sleeping pills or whatever other exit he elects or is forced into. In the meantime, I wish him no luck at all and hope he goes out and hangs himself as soon as plausible."

These comments create more doubt about Hemingway than they do about Jones, but, in Irwin Shaw's words, Jones "grappled with the ghost of Hemingway all his life, excoriating him, mocking him, worried about what Hemingway meant to him. He knew from the beginning that he wanted to go beyond Hemingway, but I think he felt that to get there he had to retrace Hemingway's steps, at least part of the way."

There were strange parallels between their two lives. Both had been born in small Illinois towns, where they were sons of professional men — a doctor and a dentist — and had Christian Scientist mothers they despised. Both fathers committed suicide by shooting themselves. They both left Illinois never to return; both were involved with war; both made a display of their masculinity to prove themselves; both were discovered by Maxwell Perkins and published by Scribner's; both became international celebrities and lived in Paris. Jones was aware of this pattern of coincidences. He envied Hemingway his secure position in American literature and knew that his own was far less certain. This envy made him criticize Hemingway as Hemingway had criticized him. "Hemingway was a spectator at war," he said, "an ambulance driver or a correspondent. If you know you can get out, you stay. If you can't, you want to get out." He buttressed his opinion of Hemingway's war fiction by saying, "You know what *really* ruined Hemingway? It was the 2nd war, when all the boys found out what war was really like." In Venice, Jones and Gloria saw Hemingway walking across the Piazza San Marco. Gloria thought he looked lonely and suggested they go up and say hello, but Jones refused. Earlier, he had declined a publicity office suggestion that he and Hemingway be photographed together as two Scribner's authors. Asked why he had never met Hemingway, Jones answered, "I had the wisdom not to do it."

Jones knew that his life in Paris was less glamorous than Hemingway's had been in the 1920s. There were no groups comparable to those around Ford Madox Ford or James Joyce or Scott Fitzgerald who gathered at La Coupole or danced all night in a boite. In a sense, Jones had missed the boat: "My life's like that," he told his friend Martin Gabel. When Hemingway killed himself with a double-barreled shotgun in Idaho, Jones remembered his mean-spirited attacks on Gertrude Stein and Scott Fitzgerald for their sexual weaknesses. "Well, he finally got to suck those two cocks," he said. Upbraided for the remark, he laughed and dismissed the criticism as prudery. A year later he was asked who the best writer in America was now that Hemingway was dead. Jones "thought for a good ten seconds," wrote the interviewer, "his brow furrowed with the intensity of the search. 'Me,' he then said, and there wasn't a trace of vanity in his word."

To make sure they kept in touch with Irwin Shaw and his wife, Marian, the Joneses began to make a habit of visiting them in Klosters, taking a fortnight or a month off in winter for skiing in the Alps. Usually they stayed in one of the new apartments that had been built for skiers and took their meals at the Chesa Grischuna.

Skiers could take a gondola from Klosters to the top of the Gotschnagrat or, from Davos, take the cog railway to Weissfluhjoch. From there it was possible to ski for mile after mile down the gentle slopes of the Parsenn run, all the way back to Klosters. The speed and motion of skiing suited physical men like Jones and Shaw, as did "the sober joy" Shaw described, "especially for a city man, of merely stopping, breathing deeply of the cold winy air, and looking around at the white grandeur of the mountains spreading out to infinity."

Jones was not a proficient skier, never having had the necessary practice as a child, and one day in Klosters he was taken in hand by Peter Viertel, a writer and expert skier, who led him out to the beginners' slope, the Jacobshorn, in Davos. "This is rare for him," Jones wrote of Viertel, who was known for his fondness for women; "only girls!" Jones found it hard to relax and was tense when trying to learn the jump-turn while small children whizzed by him down the slope. On a later trip to Klosters, he saw injured skiers being brought down the mountainside by the ski patrol, who then bundled them off in ambulances to the hospital. It reminded him of the war, with the wounded lying in stretchers, and the equipment he had to put on was like the gear he had had to wear before going into battle. "I had a premonition," he later wrote of the next day's outing, "staring into the mirror of the men's john in the restaurant before going out to strap those things on me: would I still be in one piece by evening?" Then it happened. Coming down slowly, after making a turn, he fell over and tore a ligament at the very place that had bothered him for years when he was in the army. An ambulance took him to the hospital in Chur, where he was prepared for an operation.

The nurse was pretty and chatted with him amiably, but then came visitors from Klosters, assuring him that he'd soon be well and would be back on the hills next year without any trouble. "Go back next year?" he wondered. "I was just thinking a while ago, maybe the

Swiss might pass a law and let us all carry smallarms. Then we could shoot each other, too."

A much smaller resort than St. Moritz or Zermatt, Klosters had a comparatively intimate social life. After skiing, the visiting Hollywood actresses, Oxford undergraduates, French generals, and members of Parliament would gather around the fireplace for drinks in the bar of the Chesa Grischuna or the Silvretta. In addition to the Shaws, the Joneses knew a number of others in residence, who often included the agent Alain Bernheim, Peter Viertel and his wife, Deborah Kerr, and Enid Boulting, later the Countess of Hardwicke.

Jones's accident prolonged this visit to Switzerland, and when at length he climbed onto the train to return to Paris, he slipped and nearly fell. "You've broken the tip of your crutch," said his secretary, Kathryn Weissberger. Jones looked down at himself with mock horror. "My crotch? Now what have I done?" Back in Paris he put his skis in the corner of his study and placed the crutches beside them. He thought it fitting that they be there together.

By now, to help pay for the costs of expensive ski holidays and of his new apartment, Jones began to look for new film work with the help of Alain Bernheim, whom he had engaged to represent him as agent after first meeting him in Klosters. He had already some experience working on the dialogue of *The Longest Day*, a film Darryl Zanuck was producing about D-Day, June 6, 1944. The film was based on a book by Cornelius Ryan, who, together with Romain Gary, also worked on the script. To prepare himself, Jones took a tour of the site of the Normandy invasion, visiting the stretch of shore that ran from Utah Beach to Omaha Beach and on to Deauville and Le Havre. At Omaha Beach, where a thousand men had died in the initial assault, Jones climbed up on a bluff overlooking the shore. Summer cottages had since been built there, and he wondered what it must have been like to face German artillery and machine gun fire converging on the landing stage from left and right. "The terror and total confusion, men screaming or sinking silently under the water, tanks sinking as their crews died inside, landing craft going up as a direct hit took them, or grating ashore to discharge their live cargo into the already scrambled mess, officers trying to get their men together, medics trying to find shelter for the wounded, until out of the welter 'a certain desperate order began to emerge,' and men began to move toward the two bottleneck exits. I sat there until my friends began to yell at me from down below, and I fervently thanked God or Whomever that I had not been there."

Jones's work was limited for the most part to changing dialogue, but he felt much inhibited, because even such mild expletives as *damn* and *hell* were marked for deletion by the Johnson Office, now the censors in Hollywood. He was even more angry when the censors complained of the "excessive slaughter" in the film. "What the fuck do they think war is?" Jones demanded of Zanuck. "What did they think Omaha was if not a 'bloodbath'? Perhaps if we stop talking about war altogether, we can make everyone happier about having to undergo a good clean unbloody nuclear war." Jones was so exercised, he threatened to write a public letter to the *New York Times*. "I find it incredible that these ostriches can go on like they do, building fall-out bombshelters with one hand, and not allowing honesty in combat films on the other. And if they tell me that is what the American people want, I can only answer that they're full of bullshit!"

After Jones finished his work on the film, Zanuck wired to ask him for a further piece of dialogue. No longer interested in the project, Jones asked how much he was going to be paid. Zanuck offered him $15,000, so Jones changed a line written by an Englishman that originally read "I can't eat that bloody old box of tunny fish" to "I can't stand this damned old tuna fish."

Welcome additional money came when New American Library brought out the paperback edition of *Some Came Running*. Because of its great length, the novel was abridged, making nonsense of parts of the story. Nevertheless, in this form the book sold at the rate of over a million copies a month and went into eleven printings by 1972. These sales showed that Jones had established a following, people who would buy his work regardless of what the critics said.

The film version of *Some Came Running* appeared at the same time, and after going to a screening at an American army base near Paris, Jones remarked "that with their usual acumen, the Hollywood people have one by one, and piece by piece, accurately and fully reversed and subverted every single point I was trying to say about America and Americans."

The film had been made by Metro-Goldwyn-Mayer, based on a script by John Patrick and Arthur Sheekman, who had had to reduce the immense novel to a manageable story. Sol Siegel was the producer and Vincente Minnelli, noted for such films as *Gigi* and *An American in Paris*, directed the film. Frank Sinatra played Dave Hirsh, and the other lead roles were filled by Dean Martin and Shirley MacLaine.

The picture had been filmed on location in Madison, Indiana, a small town on the Ohio River halfway between Cincinnati and Louisville. The invasion of the M-G-M crew had set Madison agog, and Sinatra's noisy drinking, gambling, and dallying with imported whores upset the citizens. "I teach Sunday School," said one. "There are lots of Methodists here. What a terrible example that man set for our children."

Some Came Running had its première at the Paramount Hollywood Theater in Los Angeles and played at Radio City Music Hall in New York. Bosley Crowther of the *New York Times* gave it a polite review, but the film lacked drive. Dean Martin performed ably as 'Bama Dillard, and Shirley MacLaine brought the film to life with her interpretation of the stupid town whore, Ginny. Otherwise, it was a somewhat hollow and unconvincing film and made a far smaller impression than the movie of *From Here to Eternity.* It did not earn what Jones had hoped it would and added little to his reputation.

The favorable reception given *The Pistol,* however, encouraged Jones to return to the second part of the war trilogy he had planned from the time he realized that *From Here to Eternity* would have to stop with Pearl Harbor and would not contain combat material. David Dempsey in the *New York Times Book Review* noted with evident relief that "if nothing else," *The Pistol* "proves that James Jones can deal with moral abstractions as well as the personal vagaries that determine human conduct. It also demonstrates that he can write straightforward textbook English when he wants to." That was not the kind of English Jones wanted to write, but it was appropriate for the book he had in mind and was wiser for him to employ than the mannered language he had used in *Some Came Running.* He also abandoned forever the experiments with punctuation and spelling that had set the critics' teeth on edge.

Jones had begun writing *The Thin Red Line* in London and worked at it while in Paris and Portofino, but he was frequently interrupted by the events of his daily life, and did not finish it until 1961. In the ten years that had passed since the publication of *From Here to Eternity* Jones had matured as a writer and was prepared for a more realistic book than he would have written as an immediate sequel to his first book. He told Burroughs Mitchell that he wanted to use "as nearly as possible a completely objective style, and deal with only those things I have experienced myself, and those told me by men in my old company." While traveling throughout the West in his trailer, he had occasionally found old companions who told him what had happened to them on Guadalcanal after he left the island. In keeping with his desire for realism, Jones decided to base his fictional story of C-for-Charlie Company on the experiences of F Company of the 27th Infantry Regiment as it struggled to overcome Japanese opposition in such mountain outcrops as Sea Horse and Galloping Horse. Jones used these same places in his novel, giving them different names. He also based the company commander, Captain Stein, on his friend William Blatt, and he used many of the same characters who had appeared first in *From Here to Eternity*. Since Prewitt died in that book, Jones invented new names for characters with similar traits. Prewitt became Witt; Warden became Welsh; and Stark became Storm. Jones also gave the company clerk, Geoffrey Fife, a prominent role and thereby introduced an autobiographical element that was almost entirely absent in *From Here to Eternity*.

Originally, Jones had planned to have the combat passages in *The Thin Red Line* set off against short peacetime chapters that would create a contrast between the two kinds of life. Although he abandoned the idea, he wanted to present a truthful picture of warfare. "No book has ever really been written about combat in wartime with real honesty," he wrote Burroughs Mitchell. Either they emphasized the physically gruesome side of war, as the works of the First World War novelists did, or they stressed the mystique of bravery. "I think all are equally false," he said. Books whose characters admitted their terror he considered merely the reverse side of the bravery books. "Look how brave I was *not* to run when I was so scared."

As the title of his novel suggests, Jones thought of combat as a condition of acute and prolonged psychic tension that leads to madness. The soldiers in Kipling's "Tommy" are treated like dirt in the everyday army, but they are transformed into the "Thin red line of 'eroes / When the drums begin to roll." This social hypocrisy is only the beginning, for another aspect of the title is that "there's a thin red line between the sane and the mad."

In a later book, Jones quotes General Omar Bradley's comment on the infantry: "The rifleman trudges into battle knowing that statistics are stacked against his survival. He fights without promise of either reward or relief. After weeks or months in the line only a wound can offer him the comfort of safety, shelter and a bed. Sooner or later, unless victory comes, the chase must end on the litter or in the grave."

The only way to react to this condition is to crack up completely, or to laugh, which reflects another kind of madness. Jones had long wanted to deal with the absurdity of war in a comic fashion, and his first book, *They Shall Inherit the Laughter*, was an attempt to do that. It had failed because Jones found it impossible to establish the right tone. Aware of "the ridiculousness of grown men, straining to hide from each other how afraid they are," he nevertheless found it hard to get down on paper. Launched on *The Thin Red Line*, he realized it was "very painful to write even though I find myself laughing like hell over some scene or other." The best solution was to attempt a neutral tone and allow comic situations to emerge as naturally as they could.

Although *From Here to Eternity* was not a combat novel, Jones had been able to use an impassive comic tone in the bombing scene at Schofield Barracks, for which he was indebted to Stendhal. In *The Thin Red Line*, he was even more conscious of earlier fictional renderings of warfare. He admired the Waterloo scene in *The Charterhouse of Parma* for its picture of war as a complete absurdity. The battle rages on almost independent of its participants and with no one's knowing what is happening. Individual soldiers end up on the wrong side, and sometimes the battle even vanishes. This confusion forces the men to be wily or even treacherous in their efforts to survive. A vivid piece of comic writing, though not comic in tone or language, *The Charterhouse of Parma* is a burlesque of heroic attitudes toward courage. The battle of Borodino in Tolstoi's *War and Peace* has similar absurd instances in the midst of horrific slaughter. Kutuzov, the Russian commander, has no idea what is happening, and his commands simply confirm events that have already taken place. Napoleon wins the battle but loses the war. Jones wanted *The Thin Red Line* to go further than either of these books in emphasizing the absurdity of war while concentrating on the personal side of combat and on enlisted men rather than officers.

He had notes, for example, from his own experiences, which were in keeping with Stendhal's notion that courage was mainly a social impulse coming from a "fear of being ridiculous or cowardly in others' eyes." In the middle of a bombardment, Jones suddenly felt the need to urinate. He sat up, unbuttoned his fly, and urinated; then buttoned up and lay down again. "Even with death staring me in the face," he wrote, "I had to go through the whole customary procedure of urinating to keep from getting it on me. So strong was the early training of my childhood. At any moment I might be dead, but I could not just piss in my pants (which were already wet) or not even just lay down on my side to piss."

To capture the personal side of the war, Jones developed a special narrative technique. The story is told from the point of view of an omniscient narrator; but without breaking the rhythm of the narrative, Jones switches into the head of an individual soldier so that the reader has simultaneously an overall view and an intimate private view of what is happening. Jones considered the "injection of a subjective phrase" far less disruptive than stream of consciousness and used it to reveal an individual's feelings without disturbing the general story. "He had been appointed Acting Sergeant by an officer, by Bugger Stein himself, not by no fucking platoon sergeant like Keck. And about an hour before. And look who got command? You couldn't trust them no further than you could throw them by the ears, no more than you could trust the govermint itself to do something for you. Furiously, outraged, keeping his head well down, he stared at the motionless feet of Doll in front of him as if he wanted to bite them off."

The writing of *The Thin Red Line* took a lot out of Jones, for he had to relive the fears and terrors he had experienced in the army in order to get them down on paper. Writing alone in his study, he would take himself back to the horrors of the battlefield he had endured on Guadalcanal, the heat, the blood, the filth, and stench. Sometimes he would break down and weep while he was writing. When it came time to write the scene based on his killing of the Japanese soldier, he suffered especially, because he not only had to relive the experience emotionally, he also had to be accurate in order to get it right, physically re-enacting what he had done during his nightmarish struggle with his opponent. "It was very difficult," he later wrote. "I managed to get blind drunk and into all sorts of ridiculous positions."

The act of writing also led him to a new awareness of what war does to people. He felt that "the dead, frozen like flies in plastic, realized — at the moment of death when of course they stopped — that humanity must grow to feeling, to empathy, or become extinct. But the dead cannot speak." Jones wanted to speak for them, but he knew that no one would listen. "To remain alive with the knowledge of those that died," the living "could not accept, could not stomach, could not survive, the knowledge of themselves as less than human."

The novel with which *The Thin Red Line* must be compared is Ste-

phen Crane's *The Red Badge of Courage*, which for years was considered the best combat novel in American literature. Jones knew and
admired Crane's novel for its realism and unromantic attitude toward
warfare. Even though Crane had never been in a battle, he was able
to imagine the intimate details of war. He could therefore describe his
central character as being so caught up "in his intent hate" that he
"was almost alone, and was firing when all those near him had
ceased." The scene is psychologically sound in revealing the intense
mad feelings that killing can produce in otherwise normal people. But
Jones wanted to go further than Crane; he wanted to portray the
whole range of relationships among the soldiers themselves. He intended to trace lives in detail, to present the soldiers' often complex
and even wily motives for action, the strange sexual excitement that
comes from combat, their yearnings, and their exhaustion. For Jones,
the battlefield was a microcosm of a world gone mad, a world of men
who try to remain sane and preserve their humanity in spite of temptations to lose it. Jones's book is less concerned therefore than Crane's
is with proving a point about the nature of heroism; it is more ambitious in seeing warfare as an extension of human behavior. In its complexity and sustained energy, it achieves more than *The Red Badge of
Courage* does. *The Thin Red Line* succeeds because Jones combines so
well his general account of the campaign with his stories of the men.
At least thirty of the eighty-four named characters are clearly defined
as individuals, and as in Flaubert's *Salammbô*, they give a vivid sense
of how they are absorbed into mass actions, becoming killers while
trying to remain sensitive human beings. *The Thin Red Line* keeps the
pressure on all the way through. The smells, the heat, the strange
beauty, the noise and silence of Guadalcanal, are ever present; there
is no escape from the claustrophobia of war.

What takes the place of bravery or heroism in the middle of the
nightmare is comradeship and individual loyalty. In the face of imminent destruction, these qualities alone remain firm. Jones here puts his
finger on the paradox of the army and, by extension, of society as a
whole. Despite its terrible inhumanity, the army creates feelings of
pride and even joy. *The Thin Red Line* is therefore a natural extension
of the mixed feelings of love and hate that lay behind the writing of
From Here to Eternity.

Wanting to have Burroughs Mitchell's advice as he neared the end
of the book, Jones sailed with Gloria and Kaylie to New York on the
last crossing of the *Liberté* in November of 1961, and rented an apart-

ment on Seventy-sixth Street. It was a working visit, and he took the manuscript with him on a visit to Rose and William Styron in Roxbury, Connecticut. There he finally completed the book, placing and dating it at Styron's Acres, Thanksgiving Day, 1961.

To Jones's considerable relief, the novel was well received when it was published the following September. In a front-page review in the *New York Times Book Review*, Maxwell Geismar pointed out that, unlike many of his highly touted contemporaries, whose work was later to prove disappointing, Jones had "kept his integrity, his own version of life. And he proves his talent and his integrity once again in 'The Thin Red Line.'" In the daily *Times*, Orville Prescott also praised the book enthusiastically. "The news about this long and harrowing novel is that it is James Jones' best," he wrote. After referring to the "atrocious writing and embarrassing foolishness" of *Some Came Running*, Prescott noted that Jones had "picked himself up and had delighted his discouraged admirers" with *The Pistol*, adding that "the comeback he began then is now solidly achieved." Other reviewers were less charitable. *Time* claimed that *The Thin Red Line* merely confirmed the impression that Jones was a "one-shot author." In a survey of forty responses to the novel, the *New York Times Book Review* reported that fourteen were enthusiastic, nine were positive, eleven were moderately in favor, and six were negative.

Jones was pleased. "Almost all the major reviews were good," he wrote Romain Gary, "a great many of the smaller ones very damning. So far it seems to be selling well, but only time will tell if it will really make me money." He thought that authors had two careers quite different from each other. "One of them trying to write the goddamned things, and then a totally different one of sitting helplessly back and watching and waiting to see if it will make him enough money to live on," which, he added, "has nothing at all to do with the profession of trying to write a true, fairly honest book."

What encouraged Jones most was the response of other writers. When he first read the book, Romain Gary became so enthusiastic that he sent Jones a brief note: "I've read them all: you have not won a battle, you have won *the war*. It is a great victory. And I have never seen a writer fighting a battle with more dignity and honesty. Bravo, mon vieux!"

In a lecture on recent fiction at the Library of Congress, Saul Bellow commented on Jones's honesty in seeing how little value was placed on the life of the individual soldier. This "new idea cruelly assails the old," he said, "exposing its conventionality and emptiness. Young Fife, after he has gone the rugged course, kills like the rest, becomes quarrelsome, drinks and brawls, and casts off his hesitant, careful, and complaining childishness." Seymour Krim also praised Jones for facing the reality of modern warfare, calling him a "pioneer" and one "highly valued by those of us who know how originally you can change a previously held conception about a public experience. It is a rare role to have thrust upon one, distinguishing you from probably all the novelists of your generation."

Jones was pleased by this attention, for as he told Krim, "I get a little irritated at times about how little serious criticism has been written about me, my position in the hierarchy, and my work." But the statement that most touched him was a longer appreciation of the book that Romain Gary sent him after further thought, describing *The Thin Red Line* as "a realistic fable, symbolic without symbols, mythological and yet completely factual, a sort of Moby Dick without the white whale, deeply philosophical without any philosophizing whatsoever. The book belongs to that vein of poetical realism which is the rarest and to me most precious thing in the whole history of the novel; it is essentially an epic love poem about the human predicament and like all great books it leaves one with a feeling of wonder and hope."

Perhaps without realizing it, Gary touched on something that in his private life affected Jones fundamentally. The successful completion of *The Thin Red Line* restored his confidence and helped make his life more stable than it had been for some time. The value of hard work and the creative impulse fruitfully applied reduced the tensions that had marked the early phase of his marriage with Gloria. As they settled down together in the apartment in Paris, with Kaylie, they entered a new stage of their life, and the publication of *The Thin Red Line* confirmed it.

9

❦

THE AMERICAN ABROAD

"WHY WE GIVE a God damn what the reviewers think is something which, in the long run, escapes me," wrote William Styron to Jones in 1959, "but we do, even though they're practically all scoundrels." Styron wrote this just as his second novel, *Set This House on Fire*, was being published to unenthusiastic notices. He was not the only one of his generation to suffer from the public's response to his work. James Baldwin's *Giovanni's Room* was thought of as a retreat into self-pity; and after the failure of *The Deer Park*, Norman Mailer seemed to have reached the end of his road as a novelist and had turned to nonfiction.

For his part, Jones had been exposed to the whole range of literary judgment, from high praise to vilification, and he knew how useless it was to pay attention to it. What was far more important was to have a continuing friendship with other writers, people with similar experiences who could help preserve a sense of proportion, of balance and continuity. In France, there was no American writer he saw regularly, so he was delighted when Styron and his wife decided to join him and Gloria in sailing across the Atlantic from New York on the *France* after the completion of *The Thin Red Line* in 1961.

Over the preceding eight years, the two writers had become close friends and correspondents. Styron was still the junior partner but was pursuing his own career with energy. A tall, dark-haired, and elegant young man, he was, with Rose, a frequent visitor to Paris, and the Styrons' arrival was a cause for celebration. Jones and Styron enjoyed drinking and talking through the night, and once, along with James Baldwin, they decided to go out on the town. When dawn arrived, Baldwin retired to bed, but Jones and Styron kept on, discussing, over one more cognac, "life, love, literature, morality and sex."

By noon, they were at the Ritz Bar, still going strong; by three o'clock, after eighteen hours straight, they decided to return to the Ile St. Louis. "We went into the house," Styron recalled, "and the first thing I heard was a huge crash. Gloria had hurled a big teapot at both of us which missed Jim's head by an inch and shattered against the wall." Jones looked around in alarm, only to hear Gloria cry out, "If I ever lay eyes on you again, may God kill me, you drunken bum!"

Despite such outbursts, the Joneses and the Styrons spent the months of July and August 1965, together with their children, in a house they rented in Biarritz. The house, the Villa St. Georges, was set in a spacious garden but was some distance from the sea, so every day they would drive to the beach near the Hôtel Palais, where Peter Viertel and Deborah Kerr were staying. A former Marine Corps officer with service in the Pacific, Viertel had published several novels, including *White Hunter, Black Heart,* and had just won a prize for his screenplay of Hemingway's *The Old Man and the Sea.* He was an active man and organized excursions across the Spanish border to San Sebastian and Pamplona. These joint family holidays brought the families together and allowed Viertel, Jones, and Styron to talk at leisure.

Most of Jones's other encounters with writers were more sporadic and casual. Mary McCarthy and her husband, James West, arrived in Paris at about the same time as the Joneses did, and they quickly became good friends, going to each other's anniversary and birthday parties. Mary McCarthy found Jones uneducated, but she respected his sound judgment and good sense of human nature. He treated her respectfully. "I think he cleaned up his language when we were together," she said, "except when he forgot. I had the feeling he wanted to call me 'Ma'am.' " But she admired his intelligence. She once saw some galleys he had corrected and was impressed by how unerringly he cleared up problems.

From time to time, Jones met some American writers who lived in Montparnasse, among them Matthew Carney, a short story writer, and Daniel Spicehandler, a novelist. He encouraged them with their writing and tried to find them publishers. They and other friends would sometimes spend an evening at Jones's house, where they would stay up until three in the morning, "drinking and talking all sorts of bullshit, mostly literature."

When visitors came from New York, the Joneses often gave parties for them, like the one they gave Betty Comden and Adolph Green when they came to Paris for the opening of their film *Singin' in the Rain*. Another writer who came was Joseph Heller. Although they had not known each other then, Heller had been at New York University during the same time as Jones and had published his first story in the same issue of the *Atlantic* in which Jones made his debut. When *Catch*-22 appeared, Jones had praised it for its "weird comedy" and "its pathos for the tragic situation of the men," and he and Gloria took Heller out to dinner when he visited Paris. Afterward, they went on to a discothèque where they ran into the singer Hazel Scott, and from there they went on to another night club, where Ray Charles was playing. At five o'clock in the morning, they ended up at Les Halles for the traditional onion soup and more drinks, and there had a run-in with some Yugoslavs who had taken a shine to Gloria.

Such evenings on the town were typical of the Joneses' style of entertaining. Arthur Goodfriend, who was in Paris to write an article on Jones, was first taken to the Confucius, a Vietnamese restaurant on the Ile St. Louis, and afterward to Le Nuage, a psychedelic boite off the Boulevard St. Germain. "Every table was taken with the likes of Michelle Morgan, Belmondo, Antoine Blondin, Jeanne Moreau, Georges Pompidou, Darryl Zanuck, Sammy Davis and other fixtures of the trans-Atlantic jet set. The owner, Johnny Romero, a strapping Puerto Rican from Santurce, had come to Paris via Greenwich Village. He confided his secret for a successful bistro: 'There is no entertainment that can compete with clever conversation.' "

Yet another visitor was Thomas Berger, a Scribner's author whose novel *Crazy in Berlin* Jones liked, especially its characterization. Jones invited Berger and his wife to dinner, and they dined off pheasant and homemade sherbets. Everyone exclaimed over the food, but according to Berger, "Jones confessed that he served such things for the delectation of his guests, but when he consulted his own tastes, he would take meat'n'potatoes every time." On another evening, they dined out at Chez Allard. Returning after dinner to the house, Jones produced a box of Montecristo Numero Tres, the legendary cigar of pre-Castro Cuba, "enormous, torpedo-shaped, Zeus's smoke (but even for him only on feast days)." They both lighted up, refreshing themselves between puffs with some ancient Armagnac. For a few moments, they talked loftily about the unenlightened, who "sucked on paper tubes stuffed with rubbish-leaf," and then Berger was called out of the room. When he returned, he found that Jones had abandoned "the great butt of the Montecristo" in an ashtray and, "standing nearby, was puffing with obvious satisfaction on an American cigarette!" Berger was struck by Jones's courtesy in supplying what was expected of him and for his honesty in drinking and smoking what he really wanted.

One Paris visitor was unexpected, and when Jones saw him at the Club Rive Gauche, he was immobilized. "I really didn't know what to do," he told Burroughs Mitchell, "so I did nothing." At a table nearby, Norman Mailer was sitting with some friends. They all waved to Jones to join them, but instead he sat at the bar with Gloria. "Norman went to the john right past us and did not say anything to me and I didn't say anything to him."

This new chill in their relationship went back to 1959, when in an article for *Esquire* that was later included in his book *Advertisements for Myself,* Mailer undertook a critical survey of his contemporaries, including Truman Capote, Ralph Ellison, Vance Bourjaily, J. D. Salinger, and Paul Bowles, and denigrated all of them. Jones he treated the most generously, beginning his essay by writing that "the only one of my contemporaries who I felt had more talent than myself was James Jones. And he has also been the one writer of my time for whom I felt any love." He praised *From Here to Eternity* as "the best American novel since the war," but attacked *Some Came Running* for its length and "tiresome egotisms."

Jones was not irritated by the negative tone of some of Mailer's comments on himself, but he was angry with his dismissal of Styron's *Lie Down in Darkness* as "the prettiest novel of our generation" and of James Baldwin as being "too charming a writer to be major." Styron and Baldwin were at Jones's house when the book came out, and they discussed it with some vehemence. Jones approved of Mailer's honesty but was outraged by his giving the "authority of print to statements of ordinary gossiping talk. There is a considerable difference to me between saying these things during a drunken evening of discussion and putting them in a book which will be printed and sold with the dignity of literature." Jones believed that writers were part of a brotherhood and that they should support one another in public. Mailer believed that the level of literary criticism was so low in the United States that he was justified in speaking out.

Jones kept a copy of *Advertisements for Myself* in his living room, and when a writer who had been attacked visited him, he asked him to sign his name, with comments, on the page where Mailer's devastating judgment appeared. Saul Bellow signed the book and was surprised that Jones took the project so seriously.

By 1963, Mailer had further irritated Jones by writing a sequel to his early evaluations for *Esquire.* He began his article with a story about how, having got hold of a set of galleys of *Some Came Running,* Styron "would entertain a group of us by reading absurd passages of Jones' worst prose. I would laugh along with the rest, but I was a touch sick with myself," he wrote. Gay Talese had seen a tearsheet of the article at *Esquire* and mentioned it to Styron before it was published, so Styron immediately wrote Jones, admitting that he had read the passages. "I was quite nervous about you in those days — not knowing you, for one thing — and besides being exceedingly envious of someone who had muscled through with such prodigious energy that second-novel barrier." Jones dismissed the matter as a "tempest teapot hardly worth pissing in," and later, in an *Esquire* article of his own, he wondered "whether after all Norman, with his particular background, personality and gifts, was not cut out to be perhaps the greatest critic of our generation and not a novelist at all."

Mailer's analysis of *The Thin Red Line* was, however, curiously close to Jones's own view of the book. Mailer wrote that instead of wanting to be the greatest novelist who ever wrote, Jones had "apparently decided to settle for being a very good writer among other very good writers. The faults and barbarities of his style are gone. He is no longer the worst writer of prose ever to give intimations of greatness." The book was satisfying, but no more. "This is one time Jones should have written two thousand pages, not four hundred ninety-five. But then the underlying passion in this book is not to go for broke, but to promise the vested interests of the book reviews that he can write as good as anyone who writes a book review." Jones would have agreed in part with this assessment, for he admitted that *The Thin Red Line* "stays within the framework of already explored ground."

In order to earn extra money to help pay his expenses, Jones continued to exploit the possibilities of journalism and script writing. These gave him the opportunity to keep his name in the public eye and also allowed him to take advantage of what Europe had to offer. Asked by the *New York Times Book Review* to take part in a symposium on popularity, he used the occasion to explain what he set out to do as a writer. "How do you go about making the reader *experience,* really *live*, a given scene, instead of reading about experiencing and living said scene from a safe distance?" he asked. Admitting to breaking many rules of grammar and to including stylistic flaws, he explained that he did so to achieve a rhythm that would carry the emotional burden of what he was saying. He quoted Robert Frost's view that "no one can write a truly emotional sentence unless he has actually heard the sentence spoken" and applied the same principles of syllabic stress and rhythm to prose. "I would sacrifice everything dear or undear to achieve this," he said, adding that "in some small way, I think I have succeeded, and that's why people like my books."

Through Irwin Shaw, Jones acquired a literary agent to handle his translations and sale of his books in Europe. Her name was Hope Leresche, and Jones occasionally visited her in London to talk about his projects. In 1963, she took him to a performance of Joan Litlewood's *Oh, What a Lovely War*, which was performed in an East End theater. Staged as an old-fashioned musical review, with cheerful songs and dancing, it was a devastating attack on the lunacy of war. The songs and skits were drawn from official records of World War I, and the central figure is Field Marshal Sir Douglas Haig, who is pictured as being impervious to the death toll, praying only for victory "before the Americans arrive." Jones was so moved that he wept, and in an article he wrote for *Esquire* he mentioned an episode in which the first wounded soldiers return to Victoria Station. No one is there to meet them, so they march off, guiding their blind companions as best as they can. As they limp off stage, they begin to sing, "Pack up your troubles in your old kit bag and smile, smile smile." For Jones, the scene was "positively scalding." He hoped the review would be staged all over the world. "Not that it would do any good. Simply as a gesture."

Another *Esquire* article came from a trip to Pamplona taken later in the year with the Joneses' London friends, Kenneth Tynan and his wife, Elaine Dundy. Hemingway had made the festival famous through his description of the running of the bulls in *The Sun Also Rises*, and everywhere were scenes typical of "Don Ernesto." Jones wrote a spoof based on his own experiences of hanging out in bars with other Americans and meeting the famous bullfighter Antonio Ordoñez, who was so taken with Gloria that he bought her a bunch of balloons. Jones enjoyed taking in the scene and watching the brawls and drunkenness, but he also saw a side that Hemingway had ignored. From the first, he was conscious of the smell of Pamplona, which, he said, "seemed to be composed of street dust, cigar smoke, fried food, green olive oil, spilt red wine, and a distinct odor of shit." This last smell overcame the others, and in the conclusion of his article, which is really about Hemingway, he asks, "What had he done to us with his big masculine bullshit? What did it all mean? It meant people still have to have myths to live by, and if you built a better myth the world would beat a path to your door. It meant, to me, that very likely, for quite a while yet, there still would be heroes, great generals, and war."

Antonio Ordoñez was to appear in another piece Jones wrote in 1965 as the result of a commission he and Irwin Shaw received from *Playboy* for a pair of articles about a trip they took together in the south of France. The Joneses and the Shaws arranged to meet whenever they could, and four years earlier they had been in Yugoslavia during the summer. Shaw had sailed to Dubrovnik on board his yacht, and the Joneses came down by steamer from Venice to be with him. They stayed at the Hotel Argentina and took excursions along the Dalmatian coast. Jones loved the physical feel of the place. One day by the dock he found great links of seaweed gathered up. The others were repelled by the rank odor of the weed, but Jones pressed his face deep into the wet strands in order to savor their iodine smell and to experience the texture of the weeds.

When they met again on Shaw's yacht in the spring of 1965, Jones was attracted to the trip as an adventure and for his possible exposure to the excitement of danger. But at first, as they drove through the countryside from Juan les Pins to Antibes, Jones had other thoughts. He could not get the first lines of Scott Fitzgerald's *Tender Is the Night* out of his mind. The road passed by villas built into the hillside and pines and eucalyptus "spread greenly in the bright sun." The yacht, *Xantippe*, fifty-two feet overall, with its shining chrome and varnish, heightened such feelings of luxury and style, and as they sat in deck chairs on the afterdeck, Jones and Shaw agreed that "travel was a wonderful thing for a writer — the movement provides a sense of accomplishment, and since it makes it impossible to work, relieves the sense of guilt that always oppresses a writer when he is not at his typewriter."

They headed westward along the coast, intending to sail up the Rhône to Arles, to see the bullfights in the Roman arena. But the weather became blustery and cold and they had to disembark at the mouth of the river and take a taxi the rest of the way. The bullfights greatly engaged Jones's interest. Antonio Ordoñez, the main attraction, was famous as the premier matador of Spain. Jones was impressed by the emotional quality of his performance. "I think he, Ordoñez, personally and emotionally loved this bull he was about to kill, and by this very feeling made us love this bull too. This is what life is all about, he said to us. Bravery that always loses, as all bravery always loses, because in the end everything, everybody must die. And he made us believe it, and more, he made us *accept* it without rancor. For a little while, with a very pleasant melancholy sadness, I did not mind that I myself must eventually die."

Living in France exposed Jones to painting, and he soon became an enthusiastic buyer of works by many artists he knew and met. He and Gloria visited galleries along the Rue de Seine and the Rue Bonaparte, and through their American painter friends, notably Addie Herder, Donald Fink, Paul Jenkins, and his wife, Alice Baber, they kept abreast of new work.

Jones responded to painting through instinct. He was not at all trained in art history or technique, but he reacted to color and form much more readily than most writers do, without trying to formulate a literary response. One painter whose work he admired was Beauford Delaney, an American black who had lived in Paris for years and who was often destitute. Jones admired Delaney's generosity of spirit and lack of bitterness in the face of neglect. "He is so absolutely prodigal with color, shape, form, texture, with energy, with himself — as if none of these things might ever cease to be there for him to use," he wrote.

Sometimes Jones would be attracted by a color or form that struck a note in his memory. One painting of Delaney's he liked mainly because of its olive-green color, which he remembered was the same shade as the auditorium curtain in the Robinson High School. Another memory made him appreciate *Beachhead,* a canvas by Bernard Childs. Having fought in the Pacific, Childs portrayed the contrast between the brilliant blue sky and nature at its loveliest just before the bloody onslaught of a military invasion. Although the painting was abstract, Jones recognized that it expressed in another medium feelings similar to those he had had when he disembarked on Guadalcanal.

A similar echo of the past first attracted him to Alice Baber, who was brought up in a town forty miles north of Robinson and who painted in the bright red and orange colors of summer, which soon fade to the dark colors of winter. To Jones, this was a poignant gesture in the face of death, similar to the statement made by Delaney. Jones entitled the catalogue statement he wrote for Alice Baber's work "The Tragedy of Light," because light is not an independent quality but exists only through reflection. The light that gives color to nature can never be seen alone, so we can never sense it in its own terms. We yearn for light but can never possess it. It seems to be everything, yet in fact is nothing, and that is why it is tragic.

These themes were close to Jones's own work, but he was not looking for something familiar. Rather, he was looking for a new way of seeing reality. Often the perceptions revealed in another art form can be more persuasive than one's own, and Jones found in the work of Alexander Calder a vision that helped him in his own search for values. In October of 1963, Jones and Gloria were invited to visit Calder at his studio in Saché, just south of Tours. After dinner, they visited Calder's various studios, where he housed his immense stabiles and more delicate mobiles. Impressed by the "battered old workbench and jumble of tools," Jones knew he was with a genuine craftsman. But as they entered the high barnlike structure where the stabiles were kept, Jones was overcome. "In the gloom and moonlight I had the impression the future was finally falling in on me, as I have often dreamed it will someday. Behind me I heard my wife gasp. Soaring, looming black shapes and streaks circled and dived on me from above and from all sides. Off to my left, a squat fat silent chief of a commanding officer sat patiently waiting his chance at me. How did the Old Man know all he knew? Out of his own freedom, artistic sensibility and imagination he was showing me the real beauty of the future where such traits, and also things like himself, will no longer be tolerated to exist. How objective can one become?"

Calder's vision was terrifying and was extended in another building, where the mobiles were kept. There Jones saw them, "with their gay, seemingly simple, and yet curiously sorrowful colors, hanging everywhere indoors; and the larger ones can be seen across the grounds gently waving their various arms at you in the air." Like characters in a marionette theater or grotesques in a Fellini film, the mobiles have the same dependency that light has. The mobiles move only when the air moves.

For an exhibition catalogue of Calder's work, Jones wrote of the artist's daring willingness "to believe in a nonspace as well as in space." Painting and sculpture helped Jones see the world in a fresh way. "It may be that when the astronauts and cosmonauts, with their crude instruments, get far enough out into space to discover non-space," wrote Jones, "shove off for another solar system only to meet themselves coming back, they will find that Calder, with his peculiar cosmic, or universal, or Einsteinian view, call it what you will, working quietly and alone in Saché and Roxbury, will already have anticipated them, and stated their experiences."

Less emotionally rewarding than writing about Calder and other painters were the film treatments and scripts Jones wrote during the 1960s in Paris. Alain Bernheim could usually be counted on to find a project that would earn Jones from $30,000 to $50,000, and when his living expenses exceeded his normal income, he would take one on. One of the first jobs he took in 1963 was a treatment for a film to be called *Summer Project,* which is a silly story about a teen-age boy who, while home for the summer from his boarding school, decides to shoot down an airplane as a summer project. He finds an old Spitfire and shoots down a Lufthansa airliner as it crosses the United States, motivated by a desire to avenge his dead brother, who was shot down over Germany during the war. The film was apparently intended to be comic, but the story was so absurd that it collapsed, and despite Jones's efforts to give it some psychological plausibility, it came to nothing.

Jones also worked on a treatment for a motion picture called *Deaf Moore,* which was to be produced by Paul M. Heller. The story of a man, deafened in the Civil War, who decides to live a solitary life as a trapper in the West, it deals with the conflict between encroaching civilization and frontier self-sufficiency. Jones was attracted to writing about the West, but Deaf Moore is too unstable a character to be interesting, and the story rambles on without logic or feeling. Jones finished the treatment, but the film was never made.

Another project was proposed by a neighbor on the Ile St. Louis, Nicholas Ray, who was well known for a number of films he directed, including *Born to Be Bad, Rebel Without a Cause,* and *55 Days in Peking.* He had written a first draft of a script for a Western to be called *Under Western Eyes,* about a quarrel between two large landowners in the Southwest of 1870 that arises when one refuses the other permission to lead cattle over his land on the way to market. The story borrows heavily from *Hamlet* and includes fratricide, a daughter gone mad, an impetuous Laertes figure, and a bemused and hesitant hero.

Jones spent a great deal of time working on *Under Western Eyes,* both at the typewriter and in conference with Ray, who soon moved into Jones's apartment. He was interested in the work and told Burroughs Mitchell that it was "much *safer* too; it's not at all lonely-making, or terrifying, as writing a novel all alone." Jones finished the script and was paid, but the producers ran out of money and the film was never made. He had none of the guilt feelings that novelists often express when working on film scripts. It was professional work, and the money couldn't be denied. "I didn't make the rules," Jones wrote to Jeff, "and if I have to write movies every so often to make enough money to live the rest of my life at the expense of my novel writing, then that is Humanity's tough luck. They should have made a better system, and I don't mean Communism."

If his own film work was nonproductive, except for the money, the movie version of *The Thin Red Line* made little difference. It attracted even less attention than the film of *Some Came Running*, because the company that made it went bankrupt just as it was completed. Jones had written the original screenplay in 1962, but the script used was by Bernard Gordon. Philip Yordan, who was then producing many films in Europe, bought the rights for ACE Films and asked Andrew Marton to direct it. Marton had worked on Zanuck's *The Longest Day* and was experienced in finding European locations for films intended for other sites. He found an abandoned mine on a cliffside near Aranjuez, a city south of Madrid, that reproduced the mountainous terrain of Guadalcanal. For the swamp scenes, he flooded the city's park. Except for Keir Dullea and Jack Warden, who were brought over from America, the actors were drawn from the large pool of Americans then in Europe who were willing to work for very little.

The film received polite reviews and was praised for its fidelity to Jones's text. Jones himself, who received $40,000 for the rights, saw it in Paris. "It fails to substantiate the spirit of the book, as almost all films do, I think," he wrote to Burroughs Mitchell, "but I think in its own little way it's a very good war film." Among the letters Jones received about the film was one from a veteran, who told him it was "a crummy movie, one of the ten or so worst war movies ever made." He objected especially to the "foney psychological crap" and asked Jones to reimburse him for the $1.25 he had spent on his movie ticket. Jones replied succinctly: "Go and fuck yourself with your $1.25. And while I'm at it, I wish you'd learn how to spell phoney."

· · ·

In the midst of these projects, Jones and Gloria made a decision that changed their family life. When they were in Jamaica in 1962, they met a boy named Ambrose who was two years old, Kaylie's age, and had played with her on the beach. He was the foster child of an English couple; his real father was a Belgian nobleman, and he had been born out of wedlock. Within two years of meeting the Joneses in Jamaica, Ambrose's foster mother died, and the boy was sent to a nursery school in Switzerland. Remembering that the Joneses had liked Ambrose and that they had a daughter his age, the foster father approached Jones and Gloria to ask whether they would adopt the boy. They immediately agreed, because they liked Ambrose and knew that Gloria was unable to bear another child.

Although they were eager to act on their decision, the Joneses, as Americans, had to overcome a number of legal difficulties. Because of the low birthrate, the French government retained the right to assign children for adoption to childless French parents. Moreover, according to French law, a couple could not adopt a child if they already had a child of their own in the household. Despite these problems, Ambrose's mother signed him over to the Joneses, and he came to live with them at the Quai d'Orléans. For their part, the Joneses made it clear that Ambrose was to be their child, and Jones instructed his New York lawyer, Henry Hyde, to alter his will accordingly.

Still only three years old, the child had suffered a good deal. Twice abandoned, he was uncertain about his future. Jones reported to his brother that "the kids fight but no more than true brothers and sisters would at their age," and gradually the boy built up his confidence. It was not easy, however. One night while away on holiday, he woke up sick to his stomach and vomited in bed. Gloria's niece Kate heard him crying and went in to see what the matter was. "Don't beat me, don't beat me," he begged. It was a terrible moment, revealing what his early experiences must have been like. Gloria held him in her arms and gave him the love and warmth he so needed.

Ambrose had come with no possessions of his own except a small suitcase containing a few clothes and an album of photographs of his former life. He kept this suitcase very close to him so that he would have his belongings in case he were sent away again. Then one day he took the suitcase upstairs and gave it to Jones. He also said that he wanted to change his name to Jamie Jones.

Jamie's arrival inevitably made Jones remember his own unhappy childhood. He knew what children needed. On the occasion of Jamie's first Christmas on the Ile St. Louis, Jones wrote to his brother, "It is quite cold out, and the house looks nice with all the presents under the lighted tree. Christmas is really for kids and if I didn't have these two, I would never pay any attention to it. Still, it is fun to make one for them and one is impelled to remember the Christmases of one's own childhood. I find I have an overwhelming desire to make *secure* and unfearful Christmases for them, even though I know such a thing is impossible and a myth. I'm quite sure this is because my own Christmases as a kid were insecure and somehow never really happy."

Jamie's arrival brought into focus a gradual change that had been under way ever since Gloria and Jones moved into their new apartment with Kaylie. Parenthood and responsibility had begun to calm Jones, and although he was still rambunctious and an enthusiastic drinker, he was less wild and violent. Now in his mid-forties, he began to settle into a pattern of living that would last for nearly a decade. The presence of the children brought him closer to Gloria than ever before.

Animals also contributed to domesticity and were a part of the Joneses' family life from the time they moved to the Ile St. Louis. Two Abyssinian cats were always in residence, occupying chairs in the living room, and in 1962 they brought Sir Dog, a large Alsatian, home from the West Indies.

On Sundays, Jones often took the family on excursions to the country, driving along the Marne, for example, where they would stop for lunch and a swim or boat ride. The children took Jones out of himself and reminded him of human values. Unlike many writers, who devote nearly all of their energies to their work and become remote from the actual world, Jones spent much of his time helping his children and guiding them as they grew. Having been forced to face life as a penniless young man, he wanted to provide his children with the happiness and security he believed they should have.

These aims and responsibilities were costly, and Jones's living expenses continued to rise. In 1963, the owner of the ground-floor apartment at the Quai d'Orléans died, and Jones learned that the flat was for sale. It was expensive, but he knew that the opportunity to buy would probably never arise again, so he took it.

He and Gloria decided to convert most of the new apartment into living quarters for themselves, and Jones had a spiral staircase built to connect the children's bedrooms with the new study he was arranging at the top of the house. In the bedroom they installed an immense circular double bed with a velvet spread and in the bathroom a large sunken tub with a bridge over it. The wallpaper had a leopard skin design. It was, as Jones remarked, "the sexiest bathroom in Paris — if not in New York too. And that's what we want." Together with the bed, it was an avowal of their love for each other, the open physical pleasure they gave each other, and it also suited their offbeat Hollywood taste. It was uninhibited and unexpected, and they loved it. "Such bad taste," Gloria would joke when she showed it off to visitors, "but it's absolutely me!"

Jones's new study was spacious and intentionally distant from the main living quarters of the house. There he installed a desk, a swivel chair, a large double bed, and a bar, and stored all the books and papers he needed. Jones did not keep notebooks or journals in a regular way, but when engaged on a book, he would carry a small stenographer's notebook around in the leather shoulder bag he always wore when he went out. When he came across something that interested him, he would write it down in the notebook. It was always a slow process for him, since he did not write in script but printed his words in capital letters. His writing looked like a child's, and a friend in Robinson believed that his awkward penmanship may have derived from his having been forced to be right-handed as a child.

Jones went to his office every morning for his daily stint of work; the room gave him the privacy he needed for concentrated effort. Downstairs, Kathryn Weissberger handled his correspondence, household accounts and taxes, contracts and agreements, and typed clean drafts of his manuscripts.

The study was also an extension of Jones's personality. On the wall hung a large part of his knife collection, the bowies, hunting knives, and souvenir bayonets he had gathered over the years. He also kept his collection of guns in this room. His fascination with these weapons reflected both his youthful desire to assert his masculinity and his idea of art as a lethal game. He was fascinated by the elegance of the balanced knife and its latent power. What made art important was that it was dangerous. It required "the consciousness of immediate flux," he told Paul Jenkins, "the perpetual sensation of momentary chance. It's a big gamble. And that's why I love it."

The knives and guns reminded Jones that if art is to live, it must be fresh and spontaneous. It must deal with subjects that count, that make a difference between life and death. "The knife is man's first, and most basic, weapon," he wrote. "The way the hand curls around the hilt of a fine knife is almost as if the hand has its own experience and knowledge which antedates the conscious mind, its own appreciation which supersedes the mind's esthetic. The knife represents the most basic human danger, confrontation. And the exquisite, dangerous beauty of a beautifully made knife is heart-stopping, and next to impossible to describe."

Jones kept his guns and knives in perfect order, always cleaned and oiled. He admired carefully made objects and thought they deserved as much care and attention as any other work of art. And every morning of his adult life, he stood before the mirror and shaved himself with a straightedged razor.

Downstairs, the Jones household was dedicated to family life and sociability. It had become increasingly a place where people gathered for laughter and good times, and friends dropped by all through the day. The Joneses continued to be hospitable and their dinner parties were famous, starting with drinks served from an ancient wooden pulpit Jones had bought and converted into a bar.

From the time of Kaylie's birth, help was needed to run the house and entertain their guests, so the Joneses engaged some servants. Not accustomed to having help in the house, they preferred English-speaking employees. They first hired an Indian butler whose wife, an Englishwoman, did the cooking. Before long, difficulties arose. At dinner, Gloria would press a foot button to summon the butler to fill her guests' glasses, and the buzzing got on his nerves. One evening at a dinner party where the guests included James Baldwin, Nelson Algren, and the Styrons, the butler came in with the bottle, and instead of stopping when the glasses were filled, he continued to pour so that the wine spilled all over the table. Jones shouted at him to stop and asked him what he thought he was doing. As the guests mopped up the wine with their napkins, the butler replied, "You're a lousy writer!" Disconcerted, Jones replied, "Who do you like? C. P. Fucking Snow?" Without answering this question, the butler rushed from the room, saying that he was going to get a knife. Jones followed him and found the butler bleeding from a cut he had accidentally given himself with the sharp blade of one of Jones's knives. Jones bandaged him up and told him he would have to leave. The following morning, Jones looked out the window as the couple left by taxi. He noticed that the butler had taken with him an expensive umbrella Jones had bought in London.

Not long afterward French representatives of Interpol called on the Joneses and produced a letter of recommendation he had supposedly written on behalf of the couple. The stationery was Jones's, but the letter was forged. Evidently the couple had moved from place to place with false papers and were now under arrest for a series of robberies they had committed along the way.

To replace these servants, the Joneses hired a German woman, but she had to go after she cried out "Heil Hitler!" when the Christmas tree was lit. At the recommendation of the Bernheims, the Joneses eventually found two Portuguese maids, a mother and her daughter, who spoke French slowly and clearly. Silvinie did the cooking, and her daughter, Judith, looked after Kaylie and Jamie. They were warm and kind, and they soon settled into the orderly and tranquil domestic life of the Jones household.

Jones's main literary project after the successful completion of *The Thin Red Line* was a novel based on scuba diving that was published in 1967 under the title *Go to the Widow-Maker*. The favorable reception accorded *The Pistol* and *The Thin Red Line* had restored his confidence, and he now wanted to move into new territory, using the experience of undersea diving as a metaphor for his evolving views of masculine behavior and his exploration of love and of sexual relations between men and women.

Ever since his early experiences as a diver in Florida, on his honeymoon in Haiti, and even on the unpleasant excursion to the Bahamas, Jones found it a symbolically interesting and complex experience. At the simplest level, it was a challenge. He told Burroughs Mitchell that he was scared every time he went down. "But I love it just the same, perhaps particularly because of that very thing." From the professionals who helped teach him in Portofino and Dubrovnik, he began to think of scuba diving as one of the last remaining examples of individualism. "Basically, it's a desire to have to *live* a sort of dangerous life," he said, "where the percentages are not on your side. You're living in a dangerous element where there's new excitement all the time."

In Yugoslavia, he nearly had an accident when, after trying to bring up a Greek amphora from 110 feet down, he felt the pressure on his ears increase as he rose to the surface. "I had it drilled into me over and over again that diving problems must be solved down below," he later wrote, so even though his air tank was dangerously low, he dived back down five times before releasing enough pressure to allow him to reach the surface. Jones was attracted to the "adventurous challenge" of undersea diving, but it also taught him how to confront human and sexual problems and not run away from them, as so many do, believing they are conforming to some code of masculine values.

The strangeness of the undersea world could also throw light on human values. Diving is exhilarating because it breaks a barrier; it takes the diver into a new universe that has its own luminosity and feel. The water is clearer than it is near the shore, and its color is more vivid. The change from one level to another is abrupt, and unless the diver keeps in touch with the cord that is attached to the boat on the surface, he can lose his direction and become disoriented. Diving becomes more than a question of courage; it touches the nature of reality and of the human being's relation to his surroundings; it is rich material for literature.

Just as he responded to the strange vision of life he saw in Alexander Calder's sculpture, Jones found that diving sharpened his understanding of human experience. It reminded him of a recurrent childhood dream in which he floated through the air, drifting over the landscape like a god. Whenever he woke up, he would be overcome by a "feeling of sadness and loss," of fear he would never experience it again. Diving below the surface of the water, propelled by the slightest movement of his flippers and able to hang motionless, he felt he had experienced it all before. Lying on his stomach in the sand eighty feet below the surface, he had "the most powerful emotional experience" he had encountered as a diver. "All around me as far as I could see stretched the long deserted plain of sand. No living thing moved anywhere, and I was totally alone, more alone than I had ever been in my life, and yet not frighteningly so. There was no sound and nothing moved, and I looked around at all of it through my faceplate, breathing slowly and evenly to the singing of my regulator, and my childhood dream of floating effortlessly through the air came back over me again, more strongly than ever before. On my way back to the boat I picked up a big starfish and a nice large conch shell to give them in the boat, because I knew I could never tell them what I had just experienced, not and be understood."

The intense personal reaction to diving produced in those who experienced it a sort of brotherhood, a feeling of community among those who knew and understood it, and Jones wanted to explore that as well. In May of 1962, the Joneses, together with Judith and the family animals, flew to Montego Bay in Jamaica for a prolonged visit. They took a cottage at Lilliput Beach, just outside the town. It was a large and roomy house belonging to a doctor and stood right on the edge of the water. With a straw roof and a gazebo on stilts where outdoor meals could be served, it cost $250 in rent a month. Soon they were settled into a routine. "We go to bed around nine-thirty, read till eleven, get up at six," Jones wrote Burroughs Mitchell. "We step out of the front door and are swimming at once. Kaylie goes in three to four times a day and is getting brown already."

At the time of their visit, Jamaica had only recently become independent of Great Britain. The reality was not living up to the Jamaicans' dream of it, however, and the banana and sugar cane economy was as it had always been; tourism remained the main source of income. Among those hoping for a change were a group of religious fanatics called Rastafarians, who were noted for their hatred of foreigners, especially whites.

One day, when Gloria was about to drive Kaylie and Judith into the country outside of Montego Bay, she was stopped in the driveway by six members of the sect, who surrounded the car. Shouting, "We want to fuck you, white lady," and "Death to you, white lady," they approached with knives and tried to pull Gloria out of the car. She pressed down on the accelerator and escaped to the police station, but nothing was done about the episode. Jones was in Kingston when it occurred, and after he got back, he bought a gun, which he shot off from time to time to show that he was ready to repel boarders. Meanwhile Kaylie, who was just learning how to talk, went about saying, "Fuck you, white lady."

But normally, their life was tranquil, and they visited the Montego Bay Racquet Club and the Montego Bay Yacht Club, where Sir Bruce Tuck, who ran the agency through which they had found their house, obtained memberships for them. With the coming of autumn, the heat diminished, and Jones hired a boat so that he could take part in a local marlin tournament. He also presided over the opening of an exhibit of contemporary West Indian literature at the St. James Parish Library in Montego Bay.

Kingston seemed to be a better place than Montego Bay for scuba diving and spear fishing, so Jones went there to explore two small off-shore islands in search of material for his book. In November, he and Gloria took a trip to a nearby island, Grand Cayman, and were delighted by it. "You can hardly jump in the water without lighting on a fish," he reported. "It's much more primitive, and there are only about three decent hotels." He found a professional, with whom he went free diving down to sixty feet without an aqualung. The man told him that he was in the "upper bracket" of skin divers, which pleased him.

As always, Jones looked on experiences as challenges, but when he was invited to the Blue Lagoon near Port Antonio in Jamaica, he soon met his match. The property belonged to Robin Moore, the author of *The French Connection* and *The Green Berets,* who encouraged Jones to try to dive to the bottom of the 180-foot-deep lagoon. Moore knew of a ledge that was only eighteen feet below the surface, and he would swim down to it and resurface with a handful of dirt that he pretended had come from the bottom of the lagoon. Impressed, Jones responded to this challenge and dived down three times, returning "huffing, puffing and exhausted," as Moore recalled, very unhappy that he had been unable to reach the bottom, as Moore had done. Moore revealed his trick before Jones damaged himself, and Jones regained some of his esteem for his physical prowess.

Of this he had a good deal, for as Moore recalled, Jones always "wore the briefest of male bikinis and was apparently well-endowed and delighted to let people know it." One day he was visited by two dowagers who wanted him to teach their nephew how to write. Jones was somewhat indignant at their presumption but also amused to see how their eyes kept drifting down to his brief trunks. Finally, he called them "dirty old ladies" and walked away.

For Christmas, Betty Comden came for a visit with her husband, Steve Kyle, as did Addie Herder. In the evenings, they would go into Montego Bay for dinner and afterward to a night club or bar. Jones enjoyed talking with Betty Comden and sometimes read passages of his new book to her. He thought of her as a purist and called her "schoolteacher." Occasionally she would suggest a more graceful or clear way for him to express himself, but Jones would rarely accept her changes, even though he knew his writing was awkward.

Jones was a barfly and would talk to people for hours. Sometimes he would listen to bores until three or four in the morning, because he thought they provided useful material for his novel. In Montego Bay he did not meet many of the fellow scuba divers he hoped to include in his book and later had to rely on his earlier experience of them in the Bahamas, but he found much that was useful. He once hid behind a couch to listen to a couple having a marital squabble, because he wanted to make notes on what they said. He also encouraged visitors to dive with him. At one time, Gloria and Betty Comden were sitting in the boat, waiting for Jones and Kyle to surface, when Jones suddenly reappeared and grabbed his camera. "There's a shark down there," he sputtered, and disappeared. When he and Kyle came back up, he explained casually that he had wanted to take a picture of Kyle and the shark together.

Jamaica did not prove to be a good place in which to write. The time spent traveling and scuba diving robbed Jones of the tranquillity that is necessary for sustained prose. Returning to Paris in March 1963 by way of New York, on board the *United States,* Jones settled down to work on the novel that was to be drawn from his experiences in the Caribbean.

He had made extensive notes for the book and jotted down observations that suggest the impulse behind it. One he copied from a magazine: "Why do people skydive, skindive? Because they can commit suicide without paying the price." Another note read, "Why is he doing this? Reality? To find reality? Search out and discover a reality which all these past eight or ten years he had felt was missing from his life and from his work? Yes."

Go to the Widow-Maker is the story of a successful American playwright, Ron Grant, who falls in love with a beautiful New York actress, Lucky Vivendi. This leads him to break his relationship with his mistress, Carol Abernathy, who runs a theater in Indiana and has been his patron for years. Grant marries Lucky, and they go to Jamaica so that he can pursue his new interest in skin diving, which he has taken up to resolve doubts about his courage and masculinity. He falls in with a group of crude people, also diving enthusiasts, whose coarseness offends and bores Lucky. When Carol Abernathy arrives on the island, Grant devotes even more time to skin diving, partly to avoid her.

The tension between Lucky and Ron increases as each learns about love affairs the other has had before they met. Scuba diving also drives them apart because of its emphasis on physical prowess. But at the last moment, Grant comes to see how immaturely he has behaved.

He turns to Lucky with relief when he finally understands that her idea of love as a genuine connection between two frail human beings is worth far more than the vain posturings of masculinity.

The novel is a story of the conflict between individual fulfillment and love, between achievement and acceptance. The title is drawn from Rudyard Kipling's poem "Harp Song of the Dane Women," which questions the impulse men have to abandon the security of domestic life for an illusion that will kill them.

> What is a woman that you forsake her,
> And the hearth-fire and the home-acre,
> To go with the old grey Widow-maker?

Yet every year the fishermen leave their women and homes. They forget the "mirth, and talk at tables," and to prove they can do it, "drive out to where the storm-clouds swallow," and where danger is ever present.

Jones meant to populate his book with aggressive and successful men who are "really all hicks who act very commonplace. Most of them say fuck and shit in one sentence out of seven." Having met these people in Jamaica, Jones found them "curiously like a certain type of guy I knew in the Army, the guys who really *like* war; you know there are a lot of guys who really *liked* it; everybody didn't want to be back home." Although he envied their daring, Jones could see that "real heroes, guys who didn't care about risking their ass," were all stunted emotionally. "They all had some sexual hang-up. They were fags or they could only screw whores."

Yet the matter was not simple. Certainly cowardice is not preferable to bravery, and individual development is important. Jones wrote of his son, Jamie, "I want to teach my boy to be brave and strong, not to run away, to fight back when he has to. Yet I must admit that there is a paradox in my thinking. I also want my boy to be gentle. That's the goal I'm really striving for."

This paradox gives dramatic tension to Jones's portrayal of Ron Grant, but it is undone by his unintentionally making the central character so much like himself. Originally, Jones had rejected the idea of autobiographical fiction. "To make myself a protagonist!" he exclaimed to his brother, Jeff. "I'd flop miserably." He also said of other characters drawn from life, "They're not like anybody but themselves." At the same time, one of Jones's central beliefs was that a writer must not hold anything back, especially anything relating to himself. "Psychologically, I have always said that a good writer is somewhat comparable (on a different level) to a sexual pervert who has to expose himself in public. I think the greater the writer, the greater this self-exposure is in him."

In his early fiction, Jones kept himself out of his stories, though he based his fiction on his own experiences. As long as he kept the two apart, he was able to maintain an absolute objectivity about his characters, and that is what made them convincing. But beginning with *The Thin Red Line*, he allowed autobiography to seep in, and to a degree Geoffrey Fife becomes Jones's spokesman in the book. In *Go to the Widow-Maker*, the story is so closely autobiographical, with Ron Grant, Lucky Vivendi, and Carol Abernathy obviously derived from himself, Gloria, and Lowney Handy, that he blurred the impression he was aiming for. Had Jones been a withdrawn man, his autobiographical borrowings might have gone unnoticed, but since articles about him had been published in such national magazines as *Life* and *Esquire*, his private life was well known to the American public.

Ron Grant was also so like Jones in surface appearance and actions, and held so many notions Jones once believed in, that his views were taken as representing the author's. A careful reader could see that Jones meant to make a distinction between himself and his character, but their similarities outweighed Jones's attempts at irony. He had made the same error in *Some Came Running*, and readers had been badly confused. In *Go to the Widow-Maker*, he should have profited from that experience, but after two relatively cool and distant books, and with the confidence their success had given him, he wanted to plunge into his personal experiences and, by sparing nothing, produce the same intensity of feeling he had achieved in *From Here to Eternity*.

Jones had serious intentions with this novel. He wished to confront parts of his own life that needed to be resolved. He hoped in his writing to explore the conflict that had arisen between himself and Lowney and the guilt he felt about being unfaithful to her. He also wanted to examine the more basic conflict, which had plagued the early part of his marriage, between his bachelor's belief in a writer's need for independence and his love for Gloria.

"I'm trying to show," he said, "that the objective of man is to get rid of the animal functions. The best sex is not animal sex. A man gets a different level of sensation from different women. That isn't animal. The basic change in Grant, the real triumph in Grant, is in seeing the woman's viewpoint, in becoming humanized by Lucky's presence, by the influence of woman." Jones was greatly interested in Jack London's novel *The Star Rover*, and statements by the narrator of that book well represent Jones's own view: "Somehow I think that the story of man is the story of the love of woman." And, later, "More than far visions and the blood of life is woman to us, who, as lovers truly say, is more than all the world."

To make this point, Jones first had to examine the *lumpen* world of male America as he found it in the West Indies. Consisting mainly of self-made men, it is a world of sports, drinking, and crude language. The men have no interior lives and spend most of their time together. Their sexual lives are unsatisfactory and most of them are maladjusted. Either they cannot perform at all or dissociate feeling from sex and settle for sensation.

Jones was ambitious in wanting to get all of this material into the novel. "I'm scared because I am not sure I can do what I want to do with this book," he commented. "I bit off a lot to chew."

Jones's worries about the book were compounded by negotiations that were to lead to a change of publishers. For some while, he had been aware of the need for greater income from his writing and had spoken to his Paris agent, Alain Bernheim, about it. On a trip to New York, Bernheim, who was now associated with a New York agency, obtained an offer of a $150,000 advance for each of Jones's next two books. Jones turned this offer down out of loyalty to Scribner's, but the possibility of more money interested him.

At about the same time, he heard from Irwin Shaw that he had signed a contract with a new publishing house named Delacorte Press, which was to be the hardcover outlet of Dell Books, a large paperback publisher. By entering hardcover publishing, Dell stole a march on traditional houses, because it could offer paperback rights at the time the initial contract was signed. Moreover, it guaranteed its authors a hundred percent of paperback earnings, whereas the older houses split these earnings with their authors, taking half for themselves.

Donald Fine, who had formerly been in charge of the mass-market line at Dell, was put in charge of Delacorte, and he quickly set about obtaining the most popular literary novelists he could find. He was interested in Jones, and when he heard that Bernheim had reached a tentative agreement for Jones to sign a contract with Trident Press, a subsidiary of Simon and Schuster, he decided to try to get him for Dell.

He phoned Paris, but Jones told him he was committed elsewhere. Fine began to insist, so Jones hung up. Fine rang a second time, and once again Jones hung up. Although he had just been in the hospital with an ulcer, Fine flew to Paris, carrying a few bottles of medicine to soothe his stomach. The next time he phoned, Jones replied, "I thought I told you I was tied up."

"I know that," answered Fine. "I'm just calling to see whether you'd like to have lunch with me."

"Lunch? Where the hell are you?"

They were together for the next four days, with Fine tagging along to parties to which the Joneses were invited. On the wagon, Fine found the routine a strain, but Jones said he liked publishers who did not drink. They talked about growing up in the Middle West, for Fine was from Michigan; they talked about Norman Mailer, whom Fine had known at Harvard; they talked about Styron and about Fine's hopes for Delacorte. All the time, the Trident Press contract lay unsigned on a table in the living room. Finally, Jones picked it up and said to Fine, "Can you match this?" Fine placed a call to New York, and an agreement in principle was made.

For Jones, it was a difficult decision in many ways, especially because of his friendship with Burroughs Mitchell. Writing to ask for a release from the contract for *Go to the Widow-Maker,* Jones explained that he had not sought out a new publisher, but that he had been made "such a stupendous offer that I simply do not see how I can avoid looking into it further and, if it checks out with all that Bernheim has told me, accepting it." He told Mitchell that "this is probably the hardest letter I've ever had to write." Then, recalling, "all the lunches and the hours hanging around on the fifth floor," he wondered whether he could really make the change. "On the other hand, this is an offer that will give me total financial security for the entire rest of my life, plus the important fact that Gloria and the kids would be totally taken care of no matter when I died."

News of Jones's decision attracted a great deal of attention in the press and publishing community in New York. Charles Scribner said publicly that the parting was amicable, and in a sense it was, for some of the company's editors were privately unhappy with what they had seen of *Go to the Widow-Maker.* Burroughs Mitchell was shattered, however, and although he understood Jones's reasons, was sad to lose him. Other publishers were alarmed, and a meeting of the heads of such old, traditional houses as Knopf, Random House, Scribner's, Harper's, and Viking Press was held. Many who attended it were outraged at the prospect of losing their authors after nurturing them along, and several questioned the future of literature without the close connection of an educated editor and his author. It was clear that they were on the defensive.

The terms of the Delacorte contract stipulated that Jones would be paid $250,000 for the first novel, due on January 1, 1968, $250,000 for the second, due four years later, and $225,000 for the third, due in January of 1976, for a total of $725,000. The first book was to be *Go to the Widow-Maker;* the second would complete the trilogy begun with *From Here to Eternity;* the third was unspecified. Further advances were assured on sales of paperback editions beyond eighty thousand copies. Royalty rates for Delacorte Press editions were set at seventeen and a half percent on the first 110,000 copies sold and twenty percent thereafter, substantially more than what most writers then received.

These arrangements were modified extensively in negotiations between Jones's lawyers, Henry Hyde and his associate Robert Gluckman, and Dell representatives, notably Helen Meyer and Stephen Baer. To make use of provisions in the Internal Revenue Code, Hyde proposed that Jones become an employee of Dell and that his royalties take the form of salary. This was agreed to, and Jones was appointed foreign editor and given the task of scouting books for Delacorte Press. As a bona fide employee, Jones became eligible for company benefits, which included membership in the Dell health plan and coverage by the company's life insurance policy. Because of his later illness, these provisions were to be worth thousands of dollars. No contract of this kind had ever been made before; it provided extraordinary benefits. It would also affect Jones's literary life in many ways.

Jones had to go to New York twice for discussion of the final terms of the contract, and as the book neared completion, he decided to spend the summer of 1966 in East Hampton on Long Island so that he could go over the manuscript with Donald Fine. The family took a French cruise ship, the *Antilles,* to the West Indies, and Jones finished the novel while on board, dedicating it to Kaylie. The Joneses disembarked in Puerto Rico and stayed at a hotel that typified much of the growing mechanization and impersonality he disliked in America. "Even the chlorine in the pool is regulated by a computer," he noted. "They figure there are so many people in the hotel, then they figure what percentage of them are going to pee in the pool, so they load it up with chlorine accordingly. I hated the place."

Before he arrived in New York Jones pronounced himself satisfied with the book. "I sincerely feel that it is my best work up to now," he said, "and also that — having completed it — even if I were to drop dead tomorrow — I can say that, in fact, I have made myself one of the major novelists of my generation."

Before long, Donald Fine began to send sections of the manuscript marked up with his suggested changes. Jones wrote his reactions in the margins of the manuscript: "I disagree"; "It's humor, no change"; "You are rather stupid!" Jones was not unduly stubborn or defensive about his manuscript, but what often prevented a useful discussion was Fine's failure to understand Jones's intentions and Jones's assumption that he was being clear. Fine occasionally tried to improve Jones's prose, not realizing that the book had been written in an awkward way on purpose. After a while, the failure to communicate led them both to pass over sections in silence. Jones didn't mind, for he always remembered that in standing up for what he believed during discussions of *From Here to Eternity*, he had been proved right in the end.

When *Go to the Widow-Maker* was published the following spring, it received some of the worst notices Jones's novels were ever given. Josh Greenfield in the *New York Times Book Review* called it an "utter embarrassment" and predicted that it would be "the worst book by a good writer to be published this year." *Time* dismissed the book, in a notice weighted with word play, as "spillover Spillane combined with horrid Hemingway." Elsewhere in the country, the book was reviewed under such headings as "It's Tough Keeping Up with Jones," "Such Monumental Clumsiness," "James Jones' Worst," "Too Sexy, Too Long," and "James Jones Over the Hill." Even among sympathetic reviewers, the novel produced a good deal of soul searching, attempts to find out what had happened to a much-admired writer. In *The Atlantic*, Wilfrid Sheed called Jones the "king of the good-bad writers" and pointed out that his excesses required "a vulnerability to experience which many of his tight-faced competitors lack." Like many critics, Sheed completely misunderstood Jones's intentions. Gene Baro was one of the few to get the point, and he praised the book for its "calculated mode," stating that it was "like taking an exhausting holiday with the wrong people."

Jones was understandably upset by the critics' reaction, although he was far more disappointed than angry. Admitting "elements of self-doubt," he began to wonder after all "if maybe they're not right. I expected it with *Time* and *Newsweek*, and from all the dirty little hicky sex-starved hinterland papers, but the *New York Times* Sunday, *Herald Tribune* daily and our friend Fremont-Smith are all so universally damning that it really put me down for quite a while. I'm about resigned to becoming the Stendhal of my generation."

Even friends were no help. William Styron read the book in typescript and made suggestions for cuts, but his comments suggest he did not understand that Jones intended to ridicule his male characters by quoting them. Jones therefore pointed out that one of his methods had been borrowed from Ford Madox Ford's *Parade's End* and ended tartly by saying, "If you are so naive as to term my 'lapses' lapses, I am shocked. It's okay to criticize my method, but please do not call it a lapse."

Although John Thompson was one of the few reviewers to understand the book, and gave it a good notice in the *New York Review of Books,* he admitted in a letter to Jones that he hadn't understood it at first. "I didn't get the way the language works," he said, "and I have a sort of fear that maybe other people won't get it too."

Once again, Jones was fortunate that sales were not dependent on reviews; for some weeks, the book was on the best-seller list. Later, paperback sales were in excess of a million copies. Still, to have this bad reception, after Jones had so carefully staged a comeback following the failure of *Some Came Running,* was a disaster. He had put a lot into the book, and though he didn't let it show, he was shaken by what had happened. It was bad enough to have his book negatively reviewed, but to have it so completely misunderstood by nearly everyone naturally created doubts in his mind. How could he, after publishing four books, have misfired so completely with the fifth?

The trouble lay both with his conception of the book and the language he used. It was daring and, as it proved, risky to write about a class of people who were not only commonplace but boring. Unlike the enlisted men in *From Here to Eternity,* they had nothing to do but hang around bars and go out in boats, so Jones had trouble giving them fictional lives and interesting personalities. The sex sections failed in a different way. Intended to reveal mechanical attitudes to-

ward love, they were misinterpreted as representing what Jones was
in favor of. The extended sections on cunnilingus and fellatio made
imperceptive readers think that Jones was simply pandering to sensationalism.

Had Jones been a satirist, he might have treated this material with
some spirit, but his sympathies were so broad that he found admirable
characteristics even among the tedious men. A novelist who saw all
sides and refused to judge, he ended up being condemned himself.

Jones's difficulties with language also contributed to his problem.
Writing came hard to Jones. He would take an immensely long time
with his paragraphs and had no facility with language. Writing letters, he often became embroiled in syntactical and grammatical
errors. "Can you explain my stylistic flaws," he asked Burroughs
Mitchell, "which are frequent and annoying?" He had a good ear for
dialogue and colloquial English, but he was often verbose and repetitive in exposition and narrative. He loved adjectives and adverbs and
tended to use too many of them. Yet if he wished to, he could write
elegant and even witty prose, as he did in the novels written immediately after *Go to the Widow-Maker* and in his nonfiction.

The variations of style Jones employed suggest that his trouble may
have arisen from his not being firmly enough grounded in any one of
them to create a norm against which variations could be played. He
did not have a distinctive voice like Conrad or Flaubert. He had many
voices, and because he enjoyed playing roles, he chose different languages for the different parts he played.

No wonder that he had difficulties when playing with two or three
levels of diction and contrasting their effects. When Mary McCarthy
read his article about Hemingway and Pamplona, she complained of
the "wobbly diction." Jones gently explained that he was deliberately
putting side by side literary words and tough-guy words, upper-class
words and lower-class words, to achieve the effects he wanted. But he
didn't signal his intentions clearly enough to let readers know what he
was doing. "If one needs to explain these things," he conceded to
Mary McCarthy, "they haven't gotten across, obviously."

Luckily Jones now had financial stability, thanks to the new contract with Delacorte. Fortunately, he also had a loving family to
whom he could turn. He would need both as he faced the challenge
that the failure of *Go to the Widow-Maker* presented to his literary
reputation.

10

INTERNATIONAL CELEBRITY

IN THE EARLY EVENING, the guests began to arrive. Some came by taxi or in their own cars; others walked across the bridges that linked the Ile St. Louis to the rest of Paris. Inside the apartment, there was conversation and laughter as drinks were served from the pulpit bar. Some guests stood by the open balcony that faced the Seine and greeted friends as they came along the quai. It was Sunday night, and open house at the Joneses' was under way.

Gloria and Jones had begun to invite people in on Sundays because it was the maids' night off and they had to stay home to be with Kaylie and Jamie. Gloria wasn't a cook, but she enjoyed making spaghetti and a salad, and with lots of red wine and beer, it was easy to have an informal dinner party. Because it was so simple, they invited others, and they brought their friends. When James Baldwin's sister, Paula, came to Paris, she had a number of student friends in the Latin Quarter, and they were encouraged to come. The parties grew, a mixture of neighbors from the quai, like the actor Claude Dauphin and his wife, Ruda, who lived next door; friends from the fashion world, like Enid Hardwicke and Monique Gonthier; artists; journalists; film people; students; and even casual passersby the Joneses didn't know but welcomed along with the rest. Mostly they were Americans or French who could speak English.

After the bowls of spaghetti, Jones would turn on the record player and dancing would begin, often to the irritation of the neighbors. The police would come and Jones would pacify them with bottles of cognac. Most of the guests left by midnight, but some would stay on, and the drinking and conversation would continue, often until dawn.

The disappointment of *Go to the Widow-Maker* discouraged Jones;

he did not have the heart to begin a new project, and no one encouraged him to. He and Gloria went out a lot, and one night at the Club Rive Gauche they met a number of haughty young Americans, several of them the children of expatriate writers who had been famous in Paris during the 1920s. They made some disparaging remarks about Jones, and there was a fight. On another evening at the English Pub, off the Boulevard St. Germain, another group of young Americans came in while Jones and Gloria were sitting at the bar. They began to talk, and Gloria asked whether they recognized her husband, the author of the famous novel *From Here to Eternity.* No, they said, they'd never heard of the book or the author.

It was better to be in one's own house and entertain people there, to be close to the family. The Ile St. Louis was like a fortress, and Jones could make his own world there, as he had done in the attic in Robinson and in his playboy house in Marshall. He would bring the liveliness of the city to his living room and enjoy playing host to his version of *tout Paris.*

But Jones was never self-important at his own parties. He would stand in a corner, talking to one of the guests, or hover around a group, listening. He was shy and elusive, glad to hear a story, for everything interested him and was material. He would lean over the back of a chair or kneel beside the person sitting there, and talk quietly for a long time.

After a year or so, Jones instituted a new feature at the Sunday night parties by having a poker game after dinner. The game was not entirely for its own sake, however, but was a way to give a focus to the evening. Sunday nights at the Joneses' had lost their intimacy. Jones no longer knew who was coming; he was irritated by the drunks and by the freeloaders who came just for the food, and by the hippies grinding out their cigarettes on the rug. Sometimes people would arrive at two in the morning just for a drink, and Jones found that knives and art objects were missing. "I used to have to go around and buy back a lot of my stuff in the antique shops," he later recalled. He therefore put an end to these parties.

The poker games were continued, but only by invitation, and on Saturday nights. The guests were mainly from the neighborhood, old friends for the most part, like Bernie Frizell, the NBC correspondent who lived next door, Addie Herder, Jack Egle, Eileen Finletter, Eddie Morgan, and Harry Matthews. Irwin Shaw, now divorced and living with Bodil Nielsen, also came when they were in town. Usually seven or eight people would play, with a few of the other guests standing around to watch. Jones put on a cap with a visor and presided over the play like a sergeant major. He liked the competitive planning and bluffing, but he was cautious and steady, "a good mediocre player," as others described him. Mostly they played five- and seven-card stud, and because many of his friends were rich, Jones imposed certain limits on the betting. "We get more kick out of beating each other than we do making money out of it," he said.

The games were boisterous, with much shouting, and abuse poured on the heads of the winners. Gloria was impetuous and gambled with gusto; she could win a lot but could also lose recklessly, and this would annoy Jones. Once he got so angry that he threw the chip container down the stairs. Generally, the games would go on until two o'clock in the morning, but sometimes they would continue into the next day. One game went on for nearly three days. Jones knew that poker was an escape. "I think games are significant in people's lives because in a game everything is clearly defined. You've got the rules and a given period of time in which to play; you've got the boundaries and a beginning and an end." He thought that people were attracted to games because they wanted "to kid themselves, at least for a time, into thinking that *life* is a game; in order to forget that at the end of life there is nothing but a big blank wall."

Gloria was responsible for the social life of the household and handled the day's activities. A warm and gregarious person who hated to be alone, she made sure that people were always in the house. Ten Quai d'Orléans was never a salon — Mary McCarthy said it was more like a Western saloon — but it was designed to be a lively and cheerful place. Gloria wanted her children to be brought up in an intelligent household, and she wanted Jones to relax and have a good time after spending all day upstairs in his study.

Often the Joneses' parties were given for visitors from America who were in town — Senator Jacob Javits from New York, the economist John Kenneth Galbraith, the director Joshua Logan, the actress Lauren Bacall, the writers George Axelrod, Kurt Vonnegut, and Henry Miller, Helen Meyer from Dell, editors John Sargent from Doubleday and Herman Gollob from Atheneum, Henry Hyde, Gene Baro. With such guests, Gloria would also invite Paris friends: Mary McCarthy and James West; Janet Flanner, the *New Yorker*'s correspondent; Ellen Wright, the widow of Richard Wright and a literary agent; the Israeli ambassador, Walter Eytan, and his wife; Françoise

Sagan; Romain Gary and Jean Seberg; C. L. Sulzberger from the *New York Times;* Ambassador Sargent Shriver and his wife, Eunice; Carlos and Sylvia Fuentes.

They were lively and interesting parties, for Gloria knew how to put her guests at ease. No one was treated as more important than anyone else, and the atmosphere was relaxed and cordial. As Irwin Shaw said of Gloria, "She was the candle that kept the house alight."

Laughter always filled the house, and Gloria's malapropisms became famous. She once said of some students, "We'll have to breed some life into 'em." She also described a left-wing politician as a "rabble Communist." On another occasion, after a quarrel in the car that made Jones walk away and leave Gloria to drive home alone, she became so flustered that she couldn't get the motor to start. When a policeman arrived, she explained the situation by saying. *"Mon mari est en chaleur."* Surprised, the policeman helped her to get the car started and said, "Madame, you are very fortunate. I advise you to hurry home at once."

There were other moments of anger. Because Gloria was a disorganized housekeeper, Jones sometimes railed at her: Where was the food? There was nothing to drink. People were coming to dinner. And what the hell did she do around the house, anyway? To which she responded, echoing Irwin Shaw, "I light the candles."

Since talk at the dinner table was not primarily literary, Jones usually conversed with writers in his study. He would show them his knife collection and his "shit wall," where he pinned up mementoes. Tacked up near his desk was a list of troublesome words, and their meanings, so that he could distinguish between "effect" and "affect" and also remind himself of the meanings of "eminent," "immanent" and "imminent." Locked in his desk was a pornography collection he had gathered over the years. "It cheers me up when I feel low," he told John Thompson.

With his thick neck, broad shoulders, Western clothes, and turquoise bracelets, Jones was somewhat fierce-looking, but his husky voice, with its almost Southern tones, revealed his inner gentleness. He didn't talk much about his own contemporaries, except for Styron and Shaw, and was reticent about his own work. He spoke admiringly of Conrad and Kipling, whose work influenced him deeply, but he preferred to talk about ideas, such as responsibility and the nature of honesty. He was interested in visiting writers as people; he would ask them what they had done and try to find out whether they had paid their dues as human beings. He was quite open about himself. "Because I've made a lot of money, they think I'm no good," he told Leslie Garrett. "But I'm going to show them that I am good." In conversations with writers, he dropped his masculine pose. One night, after dinner with a young novelist, Michael Mewshaw, he said, "My God, I forgot to say 'fuck' once!"

Visits by Jewish writers from New York sometimes put him on guard, because he thought they might be in league with the critics who assailed his books. He intimated that Daniel Stern, who spent a year in Paris, was a "failed" writer, compared with himself, because the early success of *From Here to Eternity* meant that he was held to exceptionally high standards. Knowing that Herbert Gold had to teach for financial reasons, Jones would never ask him what he was writing but would inquire, "Where are you teaching?" When Stern brought Bernard Malamud to his house, Jones was more relaxed and flattering, acknowledging Malamud's genuine contribution to literature.

With young writers, Jones was extremely generous, both with encouragement and money. Walking across Paris, he would often stop off at an apartment where a young writer lived to leave a check. He was also a conscientious literary scout for Delacorte Press. He cast his net as wide as possible, keeping in touch with his London agent, Hope Leresche, and with Robert Knittle, his editor at Collins. For French books, he employed Eileen Finletter as a reader. Several of the books he recommended were written by young American novelists he knew in Paris, but despite his scrupulous reports to Donald Fine, none of the books he proposed was ever published by Delacorte.

Otherwise, Jones did not participate much in the literary life of Paris. Occasionally he read at the Shakespeare and Company bookshop, which had been founded by Sylvia Beach and Adrienne Monnier. He also knew Alice B. Toklas and met Thornton Wilder. Because there was no group or movement of writers in Paris, as there had been in the 1920s, he met other writers, such as William Saroyan, not on a regular basis but only occasionally, at dinner parties.

He did, however, respond to the famous "Questionnaire de Proust," invented by Proust and his friends in the 1920s as a spoof of literary solemnity, that was submitted to Jones by the newspaper *L'Express.* To the question "Where would you like to live?" he replied, "Paris, if Paris was a Caribbean island." As to what errors he most easily forgave, he answered, "Drunken arguments." His favorite fictional heroes were Stendhal's Fabrizio del Dongo and Julien Sorel; his favorite heroine was Hemingway's Jacob Barnes. The painter he most admired was Gustave Moreau; the musician, Mozart. As to his favorite quality, it was "sensitiveness." It was also his greatest fault, although he acknowledged his main characteristic as being "stubbornness." His ideal of happiness was to "make love to my wife without ever tiring and without any responsibilities." He had no favorite color: "Actually, I don't give a damn. Maybe the green of the trees, in spring." His favorite bird was the hummingbird and his favorite flower, "La femme, la femme, la femme." Asked about his favorite author, he replied, "I'm not conceited enough to answer that."

By the mid-sixties, the Joneses had established a pattern of travel on the Continent, going to Klosters in the winter and to Deauville or Trouville at Christmas or Easter. At Trouville they either took a house of their own or stayed at one owned by Françoise Sagan. They frequented the beaches, restaurants, and casinos and often stopped for a drink along the boardwalk. "Princes and countesses, starlets and polo players stroll by," wrote Milton Viorst of the Joneses' stay there, "many of them nodding in greeting. Claude Dauphin, the actor, who is a neighbor of the Joneses in Paris, sits down for coffee. Gradually the table fills and spills over, with the poker players of the night before, an old friend of Gloria's from New York, an American producer, a rich racehorse owner, somebody's mistress. Maurice Chevalier calls at the table to chat with Dauphin and to meet Jones."

Sometimes the Joneses would agree to meet friends somewhere for a weekend, as they did once at St. Tropez. The others included Ruda Dauphin, the film producer William Wilson, Monique Gonthier, and Françoise Sagan, and they met at a place on the beach called Club 55. For three days they were inseparable, talking, drinking, eating, and even swimming. With close friends, Jones could be full of energy, and his zest was infectious. In a holiday mood, he and the others said what they thought and became as intimate as people do on board ship. At five o'clock in the morning, after an all-night Saturday dinner, Wilson and Jones played the slot machines along the beach while Gloria found a combo with an accordionist to make music for them. They were all like-minded and had plenty of money. Like Scott Fitzgerald and Zelda, Jones and Gloria were recognized as celebrities and enjoyed it.

·   ·   ·

In the meantime, Delacorte had brought out a collection of Jones's short stories called *The Ice-Cream Headache*. Jones had made the selection during the first year of his contract, but the book was not planned for publication until 1968. It contained all but one of the stories he had written over the years, and most of them had been published in magazines. Of them all, Jones liked best the title story, which he had written "at a table in an open café on the Boulevard St. Germain." The street was choked with the dust of summer and Jones was reminded of "the fierce summers of Illinois" and felt himself transported there. Admittedly autobiographical and based on the Jones family history in Robinson, it is about a young boy's growing sexual awareness and the heavy weight of family social pressure that blunts it. Even intended kindnesses have a way of frustrating him. The grandfather gives the boy an ice cream just before he is supposed to meet a girl about whom he has had erotic fantasies, but it is so cold it makes him sick and prevents him from meeting her. "Was it to go on like this forever?" the boy wonders about his frustration, for it seems so like other disappointments he had endured in his life.

Jones once planned to write about his grandfather's generation in Robinson and the relationship among the four sons, whom he had forced to follow his will. The intensity of the story about the ice cream headache reveals such sharpness of detail and feeling that the project almost certainly would have suited his gifts. Jones neglected a rich vein in not writing that book, but perhaps the pain of returning to his childhood humiliations made him hesitant to write more about Robinson.

The Ice-Cream Headache received generally favorable reviews. It was not given the space that was normally allotted to Jones's novels, but the critics had an opportunity to judge his work calmly, free of the publicity that usually accompanied the launching of one of his larger books. In their understated way, the stories showed that, in the words of John Barkham, Jones was "no blowhard shadow-boxer but an artist at work." Moreover, the stories reminded readers of Jones's vital link to his roots. As John Thompson said in the *New York Times Book Review*, "Jones is incapable of anything but total loyalty to his own experience as a man, as an American, as a Middle Westerner, as a child of the Depression and of World War II, as the son of an American mother and, may heaven help us all, of an American father. The world that he and so many of us had to grow up in has been quite often enough a world that has taught us fear, awkwardness, mawkishness, vanity. Yet it is only from that same world and not from some other that we could hope to learn whatever there is of skill, courage, love or modesty."

Jones's unhappy memories of his own childhood made him want to be an attentive father; he knew the loneliness of having no one to turn to. He was especially gentle with Jamie. Once he jokingly punched him in the stomach and made him cry, and then fussed over him, explaining and apologizing. But generally he made light of family strife. When Jamie complained that Kaylie had bitten his ear, he just said, "Forget it," rather than make a moral issue of it.

At the table, Jones expressed concern about good manners and said that proper behavior was important. But then he would belch or say "fuck" and everyone would laugh. Sometimes, sitting contentedly with Gloria and the children, he would tell them about his war experiences and his time in the army. "You have no idea how lucky you are to be free of the horrors outside and to be living in this beautiful place," he would say. He was deeply moved and comforted by that fact, but he also knew they should welcome experience. Life is tragic because everybody dies, he would say, but in the meantime, you have to love. He gave his children no religious instruction to help them cope with blunt truths. "I hate kings and priests," he said. "They are the cause of most of the world's problems."

The children respected Jones for his lack of cant. He hid nothing from them even when they were young. Once when he and Kaylie were watching television together, Kaylie said of one of the people on the screen, "He loves her, doesn't he, Daddy?" Jones replied, "No, he just wants to screw her." Later in the program, by which time some family friends had arrived, another man appeared on the screen with the same girl. Kaylie said, "He just wants to screw her too, doesn't he, Daddy?"

Of the two children, Kaylie was the more precocious. If crossed, she could be inventive in getting revenge. Irritated by her cousin Kate Mosolino, she announced that she had seen her making love with one of the house guests. "He was lying on top of her," she said, "and there was all that heavy breathing." Kaylie went to a French lycée, the Ecole Active Bilingue, which was patronized mostly by Americans who wanted their children to know both French and English. She was bright but undisciplined. Her teachers reprimanded her for being "excessively talkative and inattentive in class," but also noted that "when she decides to get down to work, she will succeed." Jamie initially had trouble with languages, so he was sent to an American school in Auteuil named Pershing Hall. The Joneses made little effort to keep up with the social side of their children's schools; once Gloria, upset by a report about Kaylie, decided to go to her school to complain, but when she got to the school, she discovered she had gone to the wrong one.

To the children, Gloria and Jones were immensely glamorous, and they loved to watch them get dressed before going out. Although Jones generally went about the house in an old pair of jeans and a shirt, carrying his leather shoulder bag when he went out, he had collected an enormous wardrobe of clothes. The drawers were filled with ruffled shirts and American Indian jewelry, and the cupboards contained dozens of tailored suits and handmade shoes from London. On a night when he had to wear a dinner jacket, he would dress methodically, taking two hours in the process and fussing over which pair of cuff links to wear.

Jones was enchanted by his children and loved to read to them, especially books that made them understand that they were American. One of their favorites was E. B. White's *Stuart Little.* Jones could enter his children's lives with ease. One day he and Jamie were watching television in the bedroom when Rose Styron arrived from the airport. The maid let her in and she started to go downstairs. There she found them "sitting on the edge of the round fur-covered bed in full American cowboy outfits, both of them, with matching hats and boots, holsters, the works. They were two feet from the television set in which James Cagney was dancing 'Yankee Doodle Dandy.' They were singing along with it. They were so engrossed they didn't see me for a long time."

As Jamie grew older, Jones introduced him to his gun and knife collections and taught him to be careful and orderly. He showed him how to clean and oil the guns and even helped him make bullets with a little machine he kept in his study for the purpose. On Sundays, Jones would take the family to Camp Deloge, an American army base in Versailles, for pistol and skeet shooting. The painters Paul Jenkins and Alice Baber would sometimes come along, and while the men where in the shooting gallery, the wives would go on an excursion. On one of these, their Alsatian, Sir Dog, got caught up in a stag hunt. Frightened by the horns, he plunged into a nearby lake and was followed by all the French hounds, who abandoned the chase and leaped into the lake after him, to the considerable annoyance of the hunters.

Jones took his skeet shooting seriously and dressed up in a quasi-military uniform with patch pockets. He enjoyed competing with himself, trying to improve his score, and the visits to Camp Deloge were a reversion to his time in the army. Jones also enjoyed taking his children and their friends to see American movies. His favorites were Sam Peckinpah's *The Wild Bunch,* Fred Zinnemann's *High Noon,* and Erich von Stroheim's *Foolish Wives.* His favorite song was "Rain-drops Keep Falling on My Head" from the movie *Butch Cassidy and the Sundance Kid,* and whenever he heard that Budd Schulberg's *On the Waterfront* was in town, he would go to see it, loudly applauding when Gloria, who had a brief walk-on role, appeared on the screen. When he took Jamie to see a war film one day, Jamie asked, "Daddy, is that the war you made all of your money out of?"

For a long time, Jones had tried to make Jamie's adoption legal in France, and with the help of friends who asked André Malraux to intercede with General de Gaulle, some progress was made. But because difficulties still remained, Jones decided to go America for the necessary papers. Guided by Gloria's cousin William Mosolino, who was a lawyer in Pottsville, the Joneses planned to spend the summer of 1968 in Pennsylvania. While the formalities were arranged in the court, they lived in a rented house in Orwigsburg, a village in farming country outside of Pottsville.

The stay in rural Pennsylvania made Jones sharply aware of the contrast between American political style and what he had experienced in France. During the Depression, when he was living in Illinois, he had been politically alert, and for a short period had had revolutionary views. But following his experience in the army and his subsequent economic rise, he was skeptical of much of what he heard, especially from political commentators who criticized the system that had nurtured his own career. References to "the people" particularly annoyed him. "Nobody knows the people more or better than I," he wrote, "in all their snot and grime and stinking sweat, or loves each one more." He scoffed at political theorists who had "never been on the bum" nor "sweated it out with the dispossessed, the soldier."

Politics to Jones was just a struggle for power, one group trying to dominate another, and he had little patience with the oratory that accompanied it. What had the politicians done to prevent World War II? "In a democracy, people get the gangsters they deserve," he

wrote. Consequently, he never voted. "It's like voting for Tweedledum or Tweedledee. If I ever find a candidate who put his love for the
people and his desire to help people ahead of his own personal ambition, then I'd be willing to vote for him. But I've never seen it."

As early as 1959 he was so cynical about Fidel Castro's revolution-
aries that he predicted that within twenty years they would "repress
by force, and, if necessary, execution, any of their own people who
disagree with them." In Paris, he remained aloof from the Algerian
war for independence. "I didn't pay much attention to it," he said. "I
didn't feel it." Most of his friends opposed de Gaulle, but he thought
the Algerians would be worse off if they were independent.

Jones felt more at home with American issues and joined James
Baldwin and a number of other actors and writers at the American
embassy and registered their support of civil rights. He was shocked
by Kennedy's assassination, and he volunteered to work for Lyndon
Johnson's re-election, forcing himself to give a speech, despite his
nervousness. But Jones's involvement was personal and came from his
friendship for some of the Kennedys, notably Eunice and her husband, Sargent Shriver.

Beyond that, Jones was a constitutionalist. For him, the Declara-
tion of Independence "was — and is — a loud and lingering cry of
faith in humanity. An abiding faith that humanity *can* govern itself,
can regulate itself toward the good of all, can continue to grow in its
humanity." Jones's books suggest that the opposite was true, but the
pessimism of fiction is rarely articulated in actual life.

Living in France, where he was isolated from political activity, and
ignorant of the social attitudes of American youth during the 1960s,
Jones was unaware of the forces that were gathering in an attempt to
change society. He had been a rebel ten years earlier, wearing a
leather jacket and driving through the countryside on a motorcycle,
but he was unaffected by what came to be known as the "countercul-
ture." Allen Ginsberg's *Howl,* Jack Kerouac's *On the Road,* and Her-
mann Hesse's *Siddartha* did not influence him. Intellectually, he was a
product of the early 1950s, and like so many of his fellow American
novelists — Faulkner, Hemingway, John O'Hara, and Robert Penn
Warren — he was conservative, believing in human decency and individualism but considering political activism none of his business.

He was therefore wholly unprepared for the outburst of political
activity that overtook Paris and most of France with sudden violence
during the spring of 1968. On a May morning of that year, five hun-

dred French students occupied the great court of the Sorbonne to demand a change in conditions at the University of Paris. They protested the dehumanization of their lives by overcrowding and bad teaching. They were opposed to the technocratic emphasis in higher education; they wanted some emphasis on values. With France so prosperous, there was no excuse for the impersonality that alienated them from society.

The government's reaction to the students' action was to call in the riot police. Wearing long black cloaks weighted with lead, and wielding wooden truncheons, they acted with professional ruthlessness, smashing heads and jailing everyone arrested. The violence of the police shocked the French populace; it also united the students against the régime. They gathered in the streets, chanting, *"De-Gaulle Ass-ass-in!"* They wrote slogans on the walls of the Latin Quarter: "Be a Realist. Demand the Impossible," "Power to the Imagination," "Freedom Is the Consciousness of Our Desires." A general strike was called in support of the students, and mass demonstrations broke out in other parts of the country. Georges Pompidou, the prime minister, returned from a visit to Afghanistan to take charge.

By now, hundreds of students were gathered on the Left Bank, from the Carrefour St. Michel up the hill toward the Sorbonne and the Panthéon. At night they threw cobblestones at the long line of black-coated police blocking the streets, and for several days the air was filled with tear gas and the sound of conflict as the riot police chased students down the Rue Gay Lussac or toward the Place de la Contrescarpe.

In a diversionary tactic, the students seized the Théâtre de l'Odéon, which they turned into a headquarters for debate and discussion. Meanwhile, in the country and in the suburbs of Paris, the workers began to take over the factories. De Gaulle returned from a state visit to Rumania and spoke on the radio. *"La réforme, oui,"* he said; *"la chienlit, non."* Reform, yes; a shitty mess, no. His statement missed the point the students and factory workers were making, but it appealed to many in France who were genuinely frightened of social change and revolution. Food was running low; it was impossible to drive because the gasoline pumps were dry.

As the fighting continued, de Gaulle worked behind the scenes to create dissension between workers and students. He dissuaded his generals from attempting a coup d'état; he negotiated with the Communist unions for large pay increases. Finally he organized a counterdemonstration along the Champs Elysées so that the middle class could express its faith in order and compromise. Soon it was all over.

From the living room window of his house, Jones could look through his binoculars across the Seine to where the riots were taking place. At night the *ee-aw ee-aw* sound of the police sirens would carry down the hill from the Panthéon, and the smell of tear gas drifted as far as the Ile St. Louis, where, down the quai, a heavy police guard was assigned to defend Pompidou's residence. On the neighboring Ile de la Cité, police reserves were gathered, and Jones could see the Black Marias and ambulances crossing the bridges.

Almost every night Jones put on his tennis shoes and went out to explore with his friend Joe Warfield, who, he thought, was knowledgeable about the issues involved. They would cross over to the Boulevard St. Germain and then go in the most promising direction. "I thought it was fun," Jones later said. "I was enjoying it like everybody else." It was not dangerous, and he was not afraid. "Watching the students and the police was more like watching a ritual dance than anything else. The students would rush forwards and throw a few rocks and the police would sort of pause. It was like watching two cats. The one who has the power of movement, the other who moves away until the power of movement declines."

On principle, Gloria and most of her friends were sympathetic with the students, and Kaylie, then only eight, waved a red flag out the window and shouted slogans at the police passing below on their way to guard the prime minister. Several of Jones's friends dismissed the students as the spoiled children of the bourgeoisie, but Dennis Berry, whose father was a left-wing film producer, was deeply involved and took them seriously. Uncertain of the truth, Jones announced himself as being "cynical about both sides. I even felt sorry for the police." He thought the students "did it to blow off steam. Things were going too good. They just wanted a little change. And the students had no political plans. They wanted total anarchy. And after it was over, they all went back to school and now they're all in relatively bourgeois jobs with bourgeois families. There was very little intellectual thinking. It was an emotional explosion."

The only result that Jones could discern from the 1968 uprising was an increase in the number of police in the streets and more stringent regulations, especially in the Latin Quarter. But for a writer, it was very good material. "It's all given me an idea for a new, short novel," he told his brother within a month of the riots.

Jones and Gloria on a quai overlooking the Seine

In 1958, the Joneses settled in Paris in a small flat overlooking the Seine. The next year Jones bought a spacious apartment on the Ile St. Louis. There was a large living room, containing a refectory table, and a study for Jones. From the living room window they could look across the Pont de la Tournelle to the Left Bank, with the Tour d'Argent restaurant on the left.

Jones shooting at Camp Deloge, outside Paris

With Darryl Zanuck in France during the filming of *The Longest Day*, for which Jones wrote dialogue

William Styron and Irwin Shaw, shown here crossing a bridge in Paris, became Jones's closest friends among writers. They frequently visited the Joneses in Paris.

Michel Ginfray/Gamma Liaison

In the evening, they would gather in the living room, around the bar that Jones fashioned from a medieval pulpit. *Left to right:* Bodil Nielsen, Rose Styron, Irwin Shaw, Gloria Jones, William Styron.

On weekends, the Joneses had poker games with friends.

The Joneses soon became a part of the expatriate literary life of Paris. Jones is seated here with Sylvia Beach *(center)*, founder of the Shakespeare and Company bookshop of the 1920s, and with Thornton Wilder and Alice B. Toklas.

American Cultural Center

Mary McCarthy *(left center)* and her husband James West *(far right)* moved to Paris at about the same time the Joneses did.

William Saroyan, shown with Gloria Jones and the French actor Claude Dauphin, was also a resident of Paris for many years.

Kurt Vonnegut in Paris, 1972, with Jones, the cat Ramses, and Rita Reit, a well-known translator of American fiction into Russian

Lunch at the Brasserie Lipp, 1974. *Left to right:* Gloria Jones, Bodil Nielsen, James Jones, Lauren Bacall, Ann Buchwald, and (crouching) Irwin Shaw and Art Buchwald.

Marian and Irwin Shaw with the Joneses in the Place de la Concorde the night the 1968 student riots began

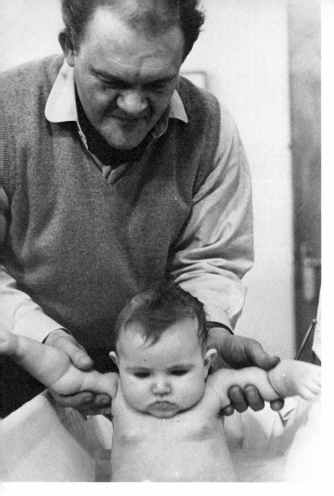

Jamie and Kaylie lead their parents up a staircase from the Seine, where fishermen and washerwomen gathered.

The Joneses' daughter, Kaylie, was born in 1960.

Jones's first car in France, a Mercedes convertible

The Jones family on one of the Bâteaux Mouches sightseeing boats on the Seine

Jones collected many things: paintings, porcelain, statuary, guns. He probably best liked the knife collection he kept in his study, for it combined beauty and danger, elements he admired in all art.

Jamie and Gloria in the apartment on the Ile St. Louis

Remembering the insecurities of his own childhood, Jones was an exceptionally attentive father and spent much time with Kaylie and Jamie. He enjoyed reading with them and playing chess, as he is shown doing with Jamie in the Paris apartment.

The Jones family, together with their Alsatian, Sir Dog, on the Quai d'Orléans outside their apartment on the Ile St. Louis, 1972

In 1973, Jones was asked by the *New York Times Magazine* to write about the last days of the Vietnam War. He is standing on the balcony of his hotel room in Saigon.

The Vietnam trip influenced Jones's decision to return to America. In 1974, the Joneses moved to Miami, where Jones took a position as writer-in-residence at Florida International University.

In 1975, the Joneses moved to Long Island and settled in Sagaponack, where they bought and remodeled an old farmhouse *(right)*. Other writers lived in the neighborhood, and soon Jones was friendly with a number of them. Jones is pictured *(above)* with John Knowles, Willie Morris, and Truman Capote in nearby Bridgehampton.

Kaylie Jones

At Elizabeth Fondaras' Quatorze Juillet party in East Hampton, Jones with Willie Morris and Irwin Shaw

Another writer in the neighborhood was Joseph Heller.

David Morris

Jones at a picnic in East Hampton in the baseball cap he often wore on Long Island

Gloria, Jamie, and Kaylie Jones at the *Whistle* party at the Seventh Regiment Armory, New York, 1978, the year after Jones died, at the age of fifty-five

Although Jones's contract with Delacorte called for the sequel to *The Thin Red Line* as the next book, Jones wrote to say that instead he would like to write what eventually became *The Merry Month of May*. By now, his editor, Donald Fine, had left Delacorte, and Jones was in the limbo to which so many other writers have been banished by the restless movement of editors from one New York publishing house to another. Now he learned that he was assigned to Ross Claiborne, Fine's successor, a man he hardly knew and who was of a very different temperament from himself. Jones felt he had no one to whom he could send his work and confide his hopes with the intimacy he had established with Maxwell Perkins and Burroughs Mitchell. Claiborne made no objections to Jones's plans, however, so he proceeded to gather material for the book.

For a man who compared politics to "one of those potentially dangerous, but generally just painful chronic diseases that you just have to put up with in your life," writing a book about political activity seems a perverse choice. But Jones was better able to cope with politics than he thought. When the American Center for Students and Artists, a private cultural organization in the Boulevard Raspail, became riven by politics because of the arrival of hippies and soldiers AWOL from Vietnam, Jones was asked to head an advisory committee to decide what the center should be involved in and what it should avoid. Jones was able to get the committee, a group of staid businessmen and left-wing intellectuals, to agree to a set of rational principles for the management of the center. He was immensely patient and hard-working; he talked to representatives from all sides, including the deserters, until the committee reached a consensus, which he described humorously for the Paris edition of the *Herald Tribune:* "No one is outlawed because he is over thirty and does not have long hair. It is even all right to wear a suit."

Jones was attracted to the subject because it got him out of the doldrums he had been in ever since the disastrous reception of *Go to the Widow-Maker.* He had started the last book of the war trilogy, but found it hard going; his heart was not in it. He also feared that the Vietnam War would kill interest in it. The Paris riots gave him an opportunity he could not resist, for having spent the last decade in a city that was no longer at the center of the world's stage, he suddenly found himself with a subject at his front door that would interest everyone, especially those who thought of it as presaging changes elsewhere around the world. A novel about the riots would also give him an opportunity to write about Paris; he could combine what he knew about Americans living abroad, the tenor of life as he saw it, with the events of 1968, using the riots as the background for a personal story.

To prepare himself, he collected news clippings from all the American newspapers and magazines he could find. These included the articles that Janet Flanner wrote for *The New Yorker* as well as features in the London papers. He made a file of French papers and magazines published during the events, such as *Le Nouvel Observateur*, and collected posters and fliers put out by those actively involved. These included *L'Enragé*, a leftist journal, pamphlets published by Action and Avant Garde Jeunesse, and a newspaper, called *The Second Front*, published by the International Union of American Deserters and Draft Resisters.

Jones also talked to Dennis Berry, who knew many students, and spoke at length to Angelo Quattrocchi, an Italian journalist, and Jill Neville, an English writer. Both later wrote of their experiences in Paris and were deeply involved with the Situationists, a group left of the official Marxists. They were in touch with people in "the street" who were eager to express their feelings about the psychological emptiness of the capitalist system.

When talking with these people and others, Jones tried to reduce everything to human terms and to avoid party slogans and labels. He had no other choice, for he was essentially ignorant of French life and saw the country only as an outsider. He had not mixed with the French nor steeped himself in modern French culture and literature, so he did not understand the nuances of French life, the family structure, the role of religion, or the educational system. Jones made no pretense of knowing about these subjects, but, not having been brought up in Europe, he could not understand the way in which everything is politicized and stands for something else. He was therefore unable to tell what was important and what was not.

Jones's solution to the problem was to go around it. As Hemingway had done in *The Sun Also Rises*, he chose as characters American expatriates living in Paris. He linked them to the Paris riots by involving them in two revolutions at once. One is the political and the other is sexual, and both are seen as childish. The story is about a conflict between generations, in which an idealistic and naïve son is opposed to his competent and cynical father. Basing his tale on the adventures of friends and acquaintances in Paris, Jones portrays the father, Harry Gallagher, a successful screenwriter, his son, Hill, and his wife and daughter, Louise and McKenna, as seeming to represent the ideal American family living abroad. But the two revolutions destroy that illusion. Hill falls in love with a liberated black girl named Samantha who likes to make love with a man and a woman à trois; he admires her for her race and her free spirit. But he is an ineffective idealist, a student film maker whose work is inept, and Samantha abandons him for his father, a libertine of long standing. Harry Gallagher becomes obsessed with her and eventually follows her when she goes to Rome. These relationships, played out against the background of the student revolution, end up by destroying the family, killing the wife, and making an orphan of the daughter.

Jones employs a passive narrator who watches the main characters act out their stories. Perhaps originally suggested by Conrad's Marlow, Fitzgerald's Nick Carroway, or even Hemingway's Jake Barnes, Jones's Jonathan James Hartley III seems most closely drawn from Dowell in Ford Madox Ford's *The Good Soldier*. Hartley speaks in an elegant manner that links him with the ideas and attitudes of the older generation, but he is also sympathetic toward the young, at least at first. The use of polished phrases may have been a deliberate effort by Jones to counter the charge of illiteracy that had again been leveled at him when *Go to the Widow-Maker* was published, but as the novel progresses, the language changes and becomes more colloquial.

Jones's uneven diction suggests that he underestimated the political differences between Harry and Hill. Sex is only part of their differences. The older man takes advantage of his son's inexperience and brushes aside Hill's idealism in order to gratify himself. Harry is a cynic who will even live off the yearnings of the young for his own professional advantage as a film maker; he dismisses their ideals as naïve. In *The Merry Month of May*, Jones does not deal with the political implications of this attitude; he does not take the politics of 1968 seriously, either because he did not understand them or, despite his research, was not truly interested in them.

Another book about the period, Jill Neville's *The Love-Germ*, reveals a side of the rioting that Jones left out. In this novel, the main characters see a slogan sprayed on a wall: the single word *"Jouissez!"* It means, one of them says, "come, spurt, spunk, let it out!" Beyond the sexual meaning, it also has the psychological and spiritual sense of making *life*, of refusing to be deflected from what makes life worth living. The older generation dismissed these aspirations as the prattle of spoiled youth, and in his novel, Jones seems to have gone along with them. His views resemble those of Harry Gallagher. His mistrust of politics appears to have blinded him to what the political language really meant — a desire, however innocent, for decent human relations, respect, and courtesy, rather than the mere efficiency of the system. In *The Merry Month of May,* Jones apparently missed the real point of his own story and settled for other people's explanations.

But Jones probably thought of the novel mainly as a portrayal of conflict, and he used Paris as a setting for this age-old struggle. Because of its history, Paris can reveal the never-ending paradox of beauty and destruction locked together, hope and despair side by side. Of Notre Dame, he wrote, "The old cathedral looked the same. That old stone barn, raised to tribal gods, has been sitting there on its haunches brooding over the bloodletting rituals of mankind for centuries. Beautiful and useless, it squatted over us all. With its highflung buttresses and stained windows, it was certainly a monument, to something or other. In the streets lots of children carried balloons."

When the novel was published, it was received with hostile and puzzled reviews. Some critics, like Daniel Stern in the *Village Voice* and Raymond Sokolov in the *New York Times Book Review,* praised the book, but many could not make out what Jones was up to and responded accordingly. The negative responses outweighed the positive ones, and even old friends fulminated. Maxwell Geismar in the *Chicago Sun-Times* called the novel a "melange of erratic personal journalism and distorted fictional romance," and Robert Kirsch in the *Los Angeles Times* attacked Jones as "the primitive American writer, trying to be chic and literary. And never quite making it." The reviewers' fury was most fully expressed by John Aldridge in *The Saturday Review,* who compared Jones unfavorably with Norman Mailer and stated that "the more Jones wrote, the more obvious it became that he had a thoroughly commonplace mind seemingly arrested forever at the level of his first adolescent ideas." This evaluation made it easy for Aldridge to see Jones as a man "who ladles up his rubbish, thinking it literate," and as one who can be assigned to "his rightful place in contemporary letters," in the company of Robert Ruark, Leon Uris, and Harold Robbins.

Once again, most of the fury seems to have been generated by the reviewers' failure to understand what Jones's intentions were, latching on to his descriptions of Samantha's sexual exploits and assuming that he approved of them, whereas his whole point was that they were destructive. The mannered voice of Hartley certainly should have been enough to make the critics aware that he was different from Jones, but few bothered to notice. It was easier and more comforting to assert that Jones was corrupted and cheap, had sold out to popular values, and was writing trash to pay for his expensive house on the Ile St. Louis. Jealousy and envy lay beneath many of these reviews, but there was little Jones could do about that. Perhaps *The Merry Month of May* inadvertently exploited popular prurience, but that was not his responsibility, either. The book was intended as a serious work of art, even if it didn't quite succeed.

Jones responded to the attacks with his usual stoicism. Probably he could reverse the trend if he wrote more war fiction of the kind that had made him famous twenty years earlier. But that would mean repeating himself. Perhaps if he stopped writing about American expatriates living expensively in Europe, he would make a better impression on American readers. But that was what he knew and where he lived. He had to follow his own course, taking his lumps like everybody else. He could take some solace in Mary McCarthy's approval of the atmosphere of the book, "the weather, and the long walks, and the way the fighting alternated with calm and ordinary pursuits, like sun and shade." She also got the point: "What I like best in the book are the Jamesian themes; I mean the old or middle-aged devouring the young and Americans feeding off France."

Despite this praise, Jones was still in the doldrums. He was tense, drank a lot, and was unhappy with himself. As if this were not enough, he discovered that he was not nearly so strong as he imagined himself to be.

The first sign of his illness since the misdiagnosed attack in 1959 appeared during the summer of 1970, while the Joneses were visiting the Styrons at their house on Martha's Vineyard in Massachusetts. It was a relaxing time, including a boat trip with John Hersey, laughter, and plenty of drinks.

Early one morning, Rose Styron heard a noise coming from downstairs. She quickly ran down and found Jones, lying prostrate on the living room rug, coughing and wheezing. He was very congested and seemed to be suffocating. The Styrons took him straight to the local hospital. Fortunately, Dr. Michael Herman, a heart specialist, was on the island, and he ordered Jones to be flown immediately to Boston. There, he was admitted to the Peter Bent Brigham Hospital, where he underwent tests and remained under Dr. Herman's observation for two weeks. The tests showed that Jones was suffering from cardiomyopathy, a disease of the heart muscle caused by a virus or by abuse of the physical system, usually by alcohol. It is the cardiac equivalent of cirrhosis of the liver; but unlike the liver, which to some extent can regenerate, the heart is permanently damaged. The impaired heart becomes enlarged as it exerts itself to perform its natural function, that of a pump, but because it is weakened, fluids accumulate in the body. Unless the disease is arrested, these fluids cannot be flushed out, and the patient usually succumbs to congestive heart failure.

At the time of Jones's illness, there was no mechanical cure for the disease. Heart transplants had not then been perfected. The progress of the disease could be halted, however. This required a rigid regimen, which included total abstinence from alcoholic drinks, no smoking, and the adherence to a salt-free diet, because salt retains fluid. Jones asked whether there might be a connection between his own ailment and his mother's early death from diabetes and was told that heredity played a minimal role in the disease. But his illness at Portofino was seen as an early manifestation of the disorder.

On his return to Paris in September, Jones began his new regimen under the direction of his French physician, Dr. Jean Dax. He gave up drinking liquor, though Dr. Dax permitted him to drink wine and smoke cigars. He instructed Jones to keep a notebook indicating his weight, hour of rising, amount of wine drunk and number of cigars smoked, his pulse, and the time of taking his medication. Jones kept these records for a number of years, and during that period, his weight went down from 165 to 154 pounds. He drank an average of three glasses of wine at lunch and four at dinner. He smoked six cigars a day.

Jones knew that drinking was bad for him. He had begun while still at high school in Robinson and had been drinking ever since. In the army, as in the small-town society of Robinson and Marshall, drinking was a way of life; it was a habitual part of American culture. As a strong and healthy man, he was able to get away with drinking because he did not suffer from bad hangovers and consequently could work the next day. But he also knew how destructive drinking was; it had ruined his father's dental practice and eventually driven him to suicide. In his writings, Jones expressed what he really felt about alcohol, even though he didn't live up to his own words. "We are a nation of drunkards," he wrote. "Really compulsive drunkards. Everyone knows this, but it is considered impolite to say so. I myself attribute this peculiarity to the fact that as a nation we are so repressed in our social and sexual lives."

Although Jones knew that drink turned him brutal and surly, he found it hard to stop. Moreover, he was so tense that drink was one of the few things that could relax him. Twenty years after the war, he was still affected by his combat experiences. Walking along the quai outside his house one day, he felt someone put his arms around him from behind. Only after Jones had tossed the man to the ground and was kneeling on him did he see that it was a friend. At Biarritz, he was knocked over by a wave and cried out, "I'm hit! I'm hit!" as though he had been wounded. In a theater in New York, he became so troubled by the war film he was watching that he left his seat and paced back and forth in the rear of the theater. Fortunately there were few people present, for Jones kept shouting to the actor on the screen, "Look out!" and "Watch where you're going!"

Even with the allowance of wine, it was not easy for Jones to stop drinking. He became bored by the repetitiousness of people's drunken conversations, the jokes that seem funny when you're drinking but fall flat when you're not. As an evening wore on, he would stand in a corner looking at the books on the shelf. "Aren't you ever going home?" he would ask. At times he would rebel against the regimen; not even fifty, he had to behave like an invalid. Walking past the pulpit bar in the living room, he would sometimes take a long swig from a bottle in a gesture of defiance. In New York, with friends at P. J. Clarke's, he would leave the table to go to the men's room and on the way stop at the bar to have a quick one. Chided for deluding himself into thinking he wasn't drinking, he would say, "I know, I know."

Even so, he certainly cut down on alcohol, and everyone remarked that he had changed for the better. He was not adhering exactly to what the American doctors had ordered, but he became more thoughtful, introspective, interesting. His language became less aggressive and violent, and he allowed his inner nature to come through.

His abstinence was all the more creditable because it came at a time when he was seriously worried about his career. In addition to receiving bad reviews for his recent fiction, he was hurt financially. He had hoped that *Go to the Widow-Maker* and *The Merry Month of May* would be made into films, but no solid offers were made. Partly he suffered from choosing subjects with foreign settings; he was also writing at a time when Hollywood was in a momentary decline. He would therefore be impatient if anyone dismissed the importance of reviews. "What do you know about this?" he demanded of one young man. "You've done nothing yet. Get your feet wet before you say anything. Get your feet wet!" When his friends the writer Allen Lewis and Paul Jenkins tried to console him, he cried out, "Do you know what this means? How am I supposed to live, and where's the money going to come from?"

It came from film scripts, and once again Jones took up various commissions, polishing dialogue or writing a treatment of a novel. Most of the projects were tawdry. One was about a hippie girl who goes to Malaya, where she gets stoned and takes part in a shaman's magic ceremonies. She then goes to sea with a European captain who rapes her, and goes blind. Jones and Dennis Berry wrote this treatment. No film ever came of it, nor was one made from *The Cage of the Puma*, which he wrote in collaboration with Paul Jenkins. Jones once wrote some notes for a script called "How Dolly Brought the Ice for the Drink She Forgot," which was about "the growth of deathing" and the "moral legitimacy of masochism." It may have been a spoof, based on his own experience as a film writer.

One project that interested Jones was a treatment of a detective story that was proposed to him by John Frankenheimer. Originally conceived with the title of *Hippy Murders*, it eventually became known as *A Touch of Danger*. Jones was promised $100,000 when the story was made into a film, with a partial earlier payment. He had confidence in the story and was sure the money would be forthcoming. He had jokingly named two rooms in his apartment the Darryl Zanuck Suite and the Nicholas Ray Suite, and he was sure there would be no trouble this time.

Unfortunately the money did not come through, so Jones decided to write a detective story from the treatment. He had long been attracted to the idea and took this opportunity to try his hand at it. To further the project, he decided to go to Greece, since it was the setting for the novel. He and the family had been to Greece once before, when they spent a month on Skiathos. There Jones read to the children every evening from a translation of the *Odyssey*.

This time they went to Spetsai, at the suggestion of Clement and Jessie Wood, who had become close friends in Paris. Clement Wood was a writer, and Jessie was the daughter of Louise de Vilmorin,

André Malraux's companion. They had a large household of children with whom Jamie and Kaylie were close friends. Spetsai had become fashionable with French and American residents of Paris. Just south of Athens, off the Peloponnesian Peninsula, it had lovely pine forests and honeysuckle vines along the roads, where only horse-drawn cabriolets went, since no cars were allowed. The center of the island's life was the port, where in the evening everyone gathered to sip ouzo and chew pistachio nuts before going to a taverna for dinner washed down by retsina.

On their first visit there, the Joneses took a house of their own and brought Carlos, their black Brazilian cook, with them. Carlos, who wore wigs, pretended to be a house guest, so when Gloria asked him to prepare a dinner party, he protested that he would be humiliated. Gloria served it herself. Later, in Paris, the Joneses discovered that Carlos went to parties in drag, wearing Gloria's evening dresses, and they had to part company.

The second year the Joneses went to Greece, they stayed with the Woods in their house and provided a boat, a large caïque in which they would go out for picnics and a swim. After working all morning, Jones enjoyed teaching the children how to dive and snorkel. Like a master sergeant with his company, he would organize everyone into activities. He set up chess tournaments and insisted that everyone play. The children tolerantly assumed that the purpose of the exercise was to have Jones win, which he usually did. He also helped stage a household play in which everyone took the part of somebody else in the group. The performance was taken seriously; there were rehearsals and costumes, and outside guests were invited. Wearing a dress and speaking in a high squeaky voice, Jones played one of Jessie's little nieces. Yet another enterprise was the publication of an annual house magazine called *L'Esperance*, in which everyone wrote about the summer's activities. Jones took his editorial responsibilities seriously, and patiently taught the children how to put down what they wanted to say.

Jones took great pleasure in the simple life and family spirit of Spetsai, and he made notes for *A Touch of Danger*. He was conscious of the differences between generations among the people vacationing on the island; in his novel he planned to deal with "an American man's aging and his unwillingness to accept it." This was a continuation of a theme in *The Merry Month of May*, and it was particularly appropriate to Spetsai, since there were a number of hippies there and many of the young smoked marijuana. Despite superficial differences, Jones thought the habits of the younger and older generations were much the same, marijuana replacing drink and promiscuity about the same. "The old 'virtues' are still pertinent," he noted.

Jones was motivated to write the book mainly for money. Some of his friends in Paris told him they thought he was wasting his energy, but working on a novel was certainly more worthwhile than writing film scripts or treatments. Moreover, he soon found himself being highly paid for it. Delacorte had offered $50,000 for the book, but in a chance meeting in London, Robert Knittle, Jones's editor at Collins, told Lee Barker of Doubleday about the novel, and he offered $250,000 for it. Jones obtained a release from Delacorte and accepted with relief an offer that would free him from many of his financial burdens and might lead to further earnings from film rights.

For many years an admirer of Raymond Chandler and Dashiell Hammett, Jones read a number of their books in preparation for his own novel. He hoped he could "knock off" a thriller quickly and even planned a series of detective stories with the same central character. He created a tough-guy detective, modeled on Sam Spade and Philip Marlowe, whom he called Lobo Davies, and equipped him with the moral standards of a "tough hard man who liked his work, and feels that whatever he does, he is doing it on the side of right. Otherwise he wouldn't do it. He has his own sense of honor as a man, and holds to it inflexibly."

Sent on holiday to a Greek island by a grateful employer, Lobo Davies soon falls into the world of foreign visitors, hippies, and drug dealers who are not above murder to attain their ends. He is hired by a glamorous countess who is being blackmailed, and he is so angered when a pretty girl called Sweet Marie is murdered that he vows to avenge her. Essentially a replay of Chandler and Hammett, the novel is nevertheless well conceived, with good structure and pacing. Writing detective novels requires special skills, and most novelists fail miserably when they try it. Jones's mastery of the form says much about his literary intelligence. *A Touch of Danger* is too long for its material, but it is imbued with the personality of Lobo, who sees humanity through sad eyes. "What a situation our race has got itself into," he thinks. "Condemned to separation. Not wanting to be separated. But having it. Hanging onto it for dear life. We would be laughable, if it didn't hurt so much."

Writing *A Touch of Danger* was not as easy as Jones thought it would be, however, and it took him much longer than he had anticipated. "I nearly killed myself finishing it up," he said. "I worked eight, ten and twelve hours a day for seven months."

On publication, the novel was not received with much enthusiasm. Anatole Broyard compared it favorably with a novel by Ross Macdonald that he covered in the same review in the *New York Times*; but generally it puzzled readers, who wondered why Jones had spent so much time on a novel that, though competent, contributed nothing new to literature and seemed a waste of his time and talent. "James Jones, come home!" wrote Hoke Norris in the *Chicago Sun-Times*. "Illinois and the Army still love you and still have that lamp in the window."

The novel irritated many of the residents of Spetsai, who thought they were ill used. Among these were some of the young people, who imagined that Lobo Davies' hard-boiled dismissal of their pretensions represented Jones's own opinions. One elderly gentleman, angered that James had used his wife as a model for a prominent character in the novel, told Clem Wood that he would have to challenge Jones to a duel. "I don't think he could respond," Wood replied. "He has a bad heart." His honor vindicated, the man was greatly relieved.

The old man's attitude may not have been far from Jones's own. He had written the book for money; there was no doubt about that. But he may also have felt that the best way to answer the critics of his recent works was to mock them by writing the trash they claimed he always wrote and, with bravura, show that he could write it with style and elegance. The pleasure he received from writing was his best solace. He told an interviewer that the sentence "All around us tall blue headlands stood out of the sea" was "one of the best lines I've ever written." Another, he liked even more: "We spent the whole day out." Explaining his intentions, he said, "The mood is below consciousness. I changed the sentence a dozen times. There's a whole picture of heat, sweat, weariness, of water, of loafing, and of the movement of the boat, without describing any of it. That's the kind of thing I take pleasure from, when it goes right."

During the early 1970s, the Joneses' social life began to change. Through the friends they made in Spetsai and Deauville, they became involved with a group of Americans living in Paris who had large private incomes and spent their time traveling, and living well. Jones was fascinated with them as a class. He admired their easy graciousness and their style, so different from that of the entertainers and writers he was accustomed to. Through the Woods he met Ethel de Croisset, a New Yorker by origin, who lived in an elegant house in the Seizième; another he knew was Elizabeth Weicker Fondaras, a neighbor on the Ile St. Louis. Many of the assumptions of the established rich irritated Jones, and he would quarrel openly with these women and others like them. He also surprised them by showing how well he knew them. He said of one woman they all knew well, and who appeared to be a dedicated spinster, that she was in fact the mistress of an important man, and he was right.

Gloria was especially attracted to these society women and soon was shopping with them and lunching at Fouquet's. Elizabeth Fondaras was keen about horseracing, and during the season she would invite Gloria and her friends to join her for lunch and an afternoon at St. Cloud or Auteuil. Gloria was also lent a box of her own and would get beautifully dressed for her outings. She used her poker earnings to bet. For his part, Jones joined the social world by becoming a member of the American Club in Paris and the Travellers Club on the Champs Elysées, though he rarely went there except in the company of a friend.

In this period, Jones became concerned about the money he and Gloria were spending, not only on horses but on living up to the standard of those who never had to think where their money came from. Their cars and chauffeurs, their Balmain and Dior dresses, were wonderfully elegant, but they required a large capital fund, which the Joneses did not possess.

Jones was odd about money, sometimes generous, sometimes close. Normally, he would give money freely whenever a needy person approached him, but he could also be surprisingly careful, as though fettered by the memory of childhood deprivation. When Irwin Shaw and Bodil Nielsen brought him Toblerone chocolate from Switzerland, he would hoard it in a locked cupboard and dole it out in small amounts to his children and friends. Once when he found that some of it was missing, he upbraided everyone, demanding that the culprit confess. He also placed an emblematic importance on money and possessions. If a guest used Jones's pen or cigarette lighter, he was made to think that he was being given a part of James Jones; everything he owned was a product of his labor. In the Bahamas, he bought an ugly fisherman's hat and wouldn't let anyone touch it. When Gloria took it off his head, he snatched it away from her, ran down the beach, and buried it in the sand.

As the Joneses' involvement with society increased, they narrowed their circle of friends. Jones's illness and the memory of the hordes who had come for spaghetti on Sunday nights made him prefer more intimate gatherings, and gradually a small group became regular visitors, almost an extension of the family. They included Monique Gonthier, Enid Hardwicke, Eileen Finletter, and the Woods. Genta Hawkins was a new friend. Sargent Shriver's assistant at the American embassy, she was the model for Sweet Marie in *A Touch of Danger*. She and Jones had long, intense conversations, usually about personal and sexual encounters. Jones was always interested in human behavior and preferred exploring it to making jokes. He also cared about his friends and would worry if they seemed to be in trouble. He had a knack for getting quickly to the essence of the subject. Whom he talked to didn't matter as long as he liked and trusted the person. Lauren Bacall, who was a close friend, noticed how philosophical and patient he was becoming. One night when she was upset about Jason Robards, then her husband, Jones urged her to relax. "Don't fuss," he said. "He's not going to change." Jones struck her as a deeply literary man who had higher standards than most of the people he associated with.

Age made no difference to Jones, and he made many friends among young people in Paris. One of these was Bobby Massie, the fifteen-year-old son of Robert Massie, author of *Nicholas and Alexandra*, who was then living in Paris. Bobby suffered from hemophilia, which so weakened him that he had to wear a brace. Jones accepted the disability without making a point of it and talked to Bobby about the Civil War and Vietnam, about childhood and moral choices, during their frequent lunches at the Brasserie. Jones took him seriously, as he did all people he cared about. Bobby admired Jones for overcoming the difficulties he had faced as a young man. "He knows what it is like to be different," he said.

Eugène Braun-Munk, an American-educated Hungarian nobleman who became Jones's French publisher, was also an intimate of the family. An amusing and eccentric man who wore elegant clothes and seemed affected, Braun-Munk had a warm and generous heart. He was at home in society and introduced the Joneses to many houses in Paris and Deauville. But when he took Jones to Geneva for a television interview, he discovered that the interviewer would not talk to Jones because of his allegedly conservative politics. Jones ignored the snub, knowing that Braun-Munk had to deal with the woman regularly. "Now we've got more time to do the things we want to do," he said.

Although Gore Vidal thought that Jones had unintentionally subscribed to a romantic ideal of Paris, creating a court around him that did little to nourish his real interests and talents, Jones knew the limitations of this world. When the young American novelist Jack Flam was invited to the Joneses' for Thanksgiving dinner, he looked at the large number of guests gathered at the apartment and asked whether Jones knew them all. "Yes, but I wish I didn't," he replied. "They're all the people I wanted to meet when I first arrived. But now?" And he shrugged his shoulders.

Jones and Flam used to walk through the streets in the afternoon. Jones was attracted to clochards, old bums, and knew a good many of them. They would not approach Jones unless they were desperate, for they knew his generosity; but when they were truly in need, they would come up, weeping and wringing their hands. Among them was a former concièrge from the Ile whom Jones had known for years and who was now an alcoholic. Jones would give him a hundred francs and try to cheer him up, but his own eyes would fill with tears. Passing a charcuterie, Jones would point to the sausages hanging in the window and say, "That's what this country is all about." He told Flam he liked to write about people like shoemakers or watchmakers who were proud of their métier. That was one of the reasons he enjoyed Balzac. He also opted for the rough-hewn word, preferring the crude way of expression, the way that was close to life. He was mistrustful of high gloss.

Aware of Jones's contribution to American letters and of his recent decline, several young writers urged him to forget about movie scripts and writing for money. They wanted him to return to his serious fiction. One of these, Neil Abercrombie, then a student traveling in Europe, encountered Jones walking down the Champs Elysées. A magazine article criticizing Jones's style of living had just been published in the United States, and Abercrombie was angry about it. On impulse, he went up to Jones and said, "Don't worry about those journalistic hacks. Just remember your readers. *From Here to Eternity* meant more to me than anything I've read, and you gave me that."

Jones was nonplussed, and Abercombie quickly said goodbye and disappeared into the crowd. Some time later, he screwed up enough courage to call on Jones on the Ile St. Louis. Jones said, "You gave me more energy by what you said than I've had in a long time. I've been writing on it for two weeks." They sat down to talk and Jones added, "I never get to meet a reader."

Emboldened by his reception, and observing Jones's style of living, Abercrombie urged him to give up the movie deals, the dinners at Maxim's. What Jones needed, said Abercrombie, was to get away, to take a trip like the one he himself was about to take, as a deck passenger on a ship from Marseille to Sicily. That way he would see how things really are.

Jones grew sarcastic. Did Abercrombie think he was going to change the world with his enthusiasm? If so, he was naïve. The same old corruption would rise again: nothing ever changes. Abercrombie glanced at Jones and thought he looked overweight and unwell. Jones had to admit that there was truth in what was being said about his work. He had received complaining letters. One had said, "Why don't you write what you know about? And why don't you go back to smoking five cent cigars. They're just as good as $5 cigars." Jones was irritated by the simplicity of the cigar comparison, but the point had been made, and he knew it.

There was no simple solution to the conundrum. Jones was caught in a bind. Naturally he wanted to write serious fiction, and he had faced the dilemma before: his solution was to honor the lives of his family as much as he respected his work. He had responsibilities, people depending on him; the memory of his own mean childhood made him determined to give Kaylie and Jamie what he had not known. The situation was becoming absurd. More and more of his time was spent in correspondence with film agents, lawyers, producers, publishers. He had to keep accurate financial statements, and he had to pay a secretary to look after the machinery of his business. He felt himself caught between two kinds of life. He had Pierre Cardin jackets, but he also wore cotton chino trousers. He didn't care anything about appearances, but he was torn between family responsibilities and personal yearnings. Life was a mixture of the two, and sometimes the compromise was too costly. It was a problem he would have to work out.

At least he knew that he was a novelist and that he must write. He would have agreed with William Saroyan when he said, "My job in Paris from the beginning has been to do my own work, because when a man reaches fifty, he knows he isn't forty, and he certainly isn't thirty, but he's still himself, and he still has his work, so is he going to do his work, or is he going to quit?"

Jones's curiosity and interests kept him going through these periods of doubt. He was also constantly sustained by what he read and saw. In Florence with the Woods, where he stayed at the house of his German publishers, the Fischers, he went to the Church of Santa Maria del Carmine to see the Masaccio frescoes. He was immensely struck by the vivid portraits of individual suffering and hardship he saw in such paintings as *The Healing of the Sick* and *The Expulsion from Eden.* He stood in front of them by the hour, studying every detail of the pictures in the Brancacci Chapel, deeply moved by what he saw and also wondering how he could apply this painter's technique to his own writing.

Once when he was ill, he spent two weeks reading such writers as Ford Madox Ford and Alain Fournier, the author of *Le Grand Meaulnes.* He also read through the complete works of Joseph Conrad, savoring the intimacy that comes with such deep involvement with a writer. Obsessed by the constant threat of war and violence, he read Clausewitz, and other writers on military theory, in the hope of discovering why war was such a recurrent part of life and why violence was ever present in human life.

The most convincing answers to these questions he found in Robert Ardrey's *African Genesis* and *The Territorial Imperative.* Ardrey, an anthropologist, appealed to Jones because of his unsentimental willingness to face facts. He shows that in prehistoric times the sudden expansion of the human brain, coupled with man's natural predatory instincts, produced a civilization in which the only constant feature was the universal desire to produce better weapons. Instead of throwing up his hands in horror at man's bloody nature, Ardrey explains that our civilization remains dependent on this impulse. Since another basic trait of animals and humans is the preservation of territory, the warlike instinct is necessary to preserve order. Knowing how quickly noncompetitive species become extinct, Ardrey writes, "I assert the first paradox, that our predatory animal origin represents for mankind its last best hope." We need the killing instinct to preserve society. The most dangerous course would be an appeal to conscience. It would be certain to fail, and the race would be soon reduced to an animalistic state.

Ardrey offers no hope except the race's instinct for order, but he observes that as weapons have proliferated and the predatory instinct has become more deadly, human nature has also changed. He points out that not long ago, human beings delighted in slavery, cannibalism, magic, and castration. Nothing prevents these from recurring today, he says, except the cumulative wisdom of society, which has conditioned men not to practice these things. "Our capacity for sacrifice, for altruism, for sympathy, for trust have evolved just as surely as the flatness of our feet, the muscularity of our buttocks, and the enlargement of our brains" in the long conflict between primates and animals that began in the savannahs of Africa. "Whether morality without territory is possible in man must remain as our final, unanswerable question," Ardrey concludes.

Jones responded to Ardrey's ideas because they were not one-sided or simplistic; they took into account the contradictions and paradoxes that Jones had noticed from the time he joined the army and found himself hating it and loving it at the same time. Ardrey was a realist who recognized human behavior for what it is and dealt with it accordingly. By continuously brooding over these problems, Jones, for all his seeming frivolity as a partygoing author on the beach at Deauville, continuously developed, emotionally and intellectually.

Some of the writing he did in Paris, especially *The Merry Month of May* and *A Touch of Danger*, seems opportunistic and a betrayal of his inner self. But despite the shortcomings of his work at this period, and despite the distracting social life, Jones kept in touch with what genuinely interested him about human nature, whether among rich or poor, young or old. He was dedicated always to an active exploration of life itself, and, in the end, this search nourished and invigorated him more than anything else.

One day when he was in Paris, Irwin Shaw invited a number of his fellow writers and artists to join him for lunch at a restaurant in the Bois de Boulogne. Jones was there, and among the others were Truman Capote, Gore Vidal, and William Saroyan. The conversation turned to their future lives and reputations, and Saroyan said, "When I die, I will go to heaven, and Saint Peter will meet me, and there will be choirs of angels to welcome me." This amiable statement was intended to put an end to an acrimonious squabble that had broken out between Jones and Vidal, in which each attacked the other's weaknesses. They were like an English setter and a bulldog, and there was no resolution in sight. Seeing that his remark had been insufficient, Saroyan spoke again. "Of all of us present here," he said, "the only one I'm sure will survive is this one." And he pointed to Jones.

→≫ FOUR ≪←

11

HOME TO AMERICA

HE WAS NERVOUS, even scared, for once again he was going into a battle zone, and anything could happen. The tropical air, with its smell of jasmine and frangipani, was pleasantly familiar, however, and reminded him of Guadalcanal and the New Hebrides, where he had been in the hospital. The cooking smells from the shacks of the poor recalled Hawaii. "A part of me seemed to be standing behind each next corner waiting to be reunited with the rest of me," he wrote in a notebook.

It was March 4, 1973, and Jones was in Saigon on assignment from the *New York Times Magazine* to cover the last days of American involvement in Vietnam after the accords to end the war had been signed in Paris. Robert Wool, the political editor of the magazine, wanted him to write a valedictory to that long conflict, to report what he saw from a novelist's point of view. He wanted "the sights and smells of the land."

Jones had a room at the Continental Palace in Saigon, which was where the newsmen stayed, and he thought of Somerset Maugham and Graham Greene, except that now the French patina of the city had been replaced by an American one. The prostitutes gathered on the hotel terrace looked too frail and delicate for the construction workers who were their clients. Alone, the men looked guilty, but Jones noted that when "two or more sat down together, their Protestant-Catholic, Christian American guilt was covered up with a kind of brutal raucous badinage and dirty-sounding laughter."

When he first told Wool on the phone from Paris that he would accept the assignment, Jones had no idea how much trouble he would be causing himself. Wool had told Jones that the *Times* office in Paris would help him get the necessary visas, but when he called there, he was repeatedly put off. On his own, he called at the two Vietnamese embassies. The mink-clad employees of the South Vietnamese embassy coldly received his application; at the North Vietnamese office, even with a letter of introduction from Mary McCarthy, he couldn't get past the front door. Five weeks went by without action.

Finally, he decided to play his trump card. In 1971, at a Thanksgiving lunch party in Paris, Jones had met General Frederick Weyand, who was then in Paris with Ambassador Henry Cabot Lodge for the peace talks. Jones learned that Weyand had commanded his old division, the 25th Tropical Lightning, and the two men hit it off. Now he was second in command of United States forces in Vietnam. Jones phoned Weyand's wife in Bangkok and asked what she could do to help him. On the following Monday, he had his visa. He went to the Paris office of the *Times* for expense money and tickets, and later noted that the look on the faces of the women who had done nothing for him "was worth at least twice the price of the call to Bangkok, perhaps more."

Although Gloria was worried that the trip might be dangerous, she did not object to his going. Jones told her that it would help him to get back in touch with the army, now that he was at work on *Whistle*, the last novel of his war trilogy. Moreover, at fifty-two, he knew this would probably be the last chance he would have for such an adventure. It was better than the freighter trip from Marseille to Palermo that Neil Abercrombie had proposed, and it made more sense. He flew to the Orient by way of Zürich, where he said goodbye to Gloria and the children, who were skiing at Klosters, and stopped for a day in Bangkok to see Arline Weyand.

Jones had arrived in Saigon equipped with maps of Vietnam and with pamphlets and documents representing both sides of the conflict. He hoped to see some prisoner exchanges, a Vietcong village, and perhaps evidence of a cease-fire violation. But flights to the north were fully booked, interpeters were unavailable, and once again the *Times* office could do little to help. Discouraged and lonely, Jones trudged the streets of Saigon, cluttered with piles of tomatoes and lettuce leaves rotting in the sun. Once again, he appealed to General Weyand, who wondered why he hadn't phoned earlier. The general sent his car and introduced Jones to Brigadier General Michael Healy, formerly of the Green Berets, who was now commanding II Corps as American troops were phased out and returned to the

United States. Healy took Jones north with him to Pleiku and arranged for helicopter visits to nearby fortified camps. At dinner with Healy's staff his first night in Pleiku, Jones made a brief speech and told the officers present that they didn't look as though they were "involved in a military-industrial conspiracy to take over the United States." He then offered around a box of Cuban cigars he had brought with him.

Though he was delighted with his good luck at having Healy's help, Jones was apprehensive about his adventures. Coming across a paperback copy of *The Thin Red Line,* he opened it at random to the song "Don't Monkey Around with Death," and had an unpleasant premonition. In his notebook, he wrote, "What the hell am I doing here?" After reaching Den Pak, he found out how dangerous the flight there had been. They hadn't been shot at, and General Healy explained that maybe the North Vietnamese "were just feeling in a good mood." The explanation gave Jones "a strangely chilling feeling. That it could just depend on that." Before leaving Saigon, he had typed a farewell letter to Gloria, admitting that he felt silly in writing it. "I've always loved you an awful lot," he wrote. "More than I've ever loved anything or anybody. Maybe my own work I've loved as much."

In the end, he saw everything he wanted to. He visited a Montagnard hospital, a leper colony, watched the funeral of the chief Bonze of Hué, took a tour of the delta region in the south, and watched a prisoner exchange. He found himself loving "the tropics as much as ever," but he was saddened while watching an exchange of Vietcong prisoners, who silently and grimly shed their uniforms at what should have been a joyful moment as they prepared to cross the line to the other side. Jones observed no sign of human feeling when they marched off. Instead, they shouted slogans, like "Down with the American imperialists and their Saigon puppets." Jones said he "suddenly felt very sorry for everybody."

The figure who impressed Jones most was General Healy. "You knew his aggressive physical courage was monumental," he wrote, "and that his nerves were absolute steel. But with Healy there was an added quality of unstated sadness, an overblanket of sorrow, about things." Healy took physical competence as a matter of course, but you "felt he had been born knowing that nothing could last forever. And he was quite willing to tell you that, if you asked him. But not unless you did."

Jones knew that because of his connections, his liberal friends would say, "Jones has gotten himself brainwashed by the army," but he figured he was no more influenced than Mary McCarthy was by the North Vietnamese. "Less probably. I knew how shitty the army could be." In Paris he had been aware of the many antiwar protests, but he believed that the North Vietnamese Communists were just as guilty of manipulation and atrocities as the Americans were. He also resented the assumption of moral superiority by many antiwar protestors. When Gloria helped organize her friends to buy an advertisement in the *Herald Tribune* that was signed by many prominent artists and writers in Paris, Jones refused to sign it. Gloria gave a party for all those who did, but Jones stayed upstairs in his office. His ancient doubts about political action and his study of such writers as Robert Ardrey prevented him from taking easy positions. He summarized his views of the war by saying, "They're shits and we're shits so we might as well be for us as for them."

One night in Saigon, before leaving Vietnam, Jones had dinner with a number of journalists. Frances FitzGerald was there, defending the Vietcong on the grounds that they had the people's interests at heart, whereas the government of South Vietnam did not. Jones agreed with her on the second point but had doubts about the first. His innate skepticism seems in the long run to have been justified. Recent scholars examining the records and observing the subsequent aggressiveness of the Hanoi régime have found a great deal of naïveté and wishful thinking among assertions, such as those made by Frances FitzGerald, that glamorized the Vietcong and "underestimated the role that North Vietnam played in leading the war in the South."

The *New York Times* editors may have expected Jones to write about American enlisted men during his trip to Vietnam, but most of the men had already been evacuated and returned to the United States. Those who remained were technical personnel, mainly officers and noncoms, supported by South Vietnamese troops. But Jones found a woman whose suffering moved him deeply and who seemed to stand, as private soldiers generally did in his fiction, for the meaningless torture of warfare. He saw her in the street, not far from his hotel. "Poor beaten woman holding scrawny baby," he jotted down in his notebook, "old musette bag hanging from her shoulder, leaning against store front grill, her face against it. Probably too hopeless and exhausted phys. and spiritually even to beg. I was so struck I stood and watched, then crossed the St. (Tu Do) and pressed 500 piasters in her hand. She just looked up at me pitifully. It seemed so little. I walked all the way back and gave her another and patted her shoulder. She just gave me the same look. I should have given her 5000." His last words on this country were "She was all of Vietnam to me."

In all, James remained in Vietnam for three weeks, the longest time he had ever been away from Gloria. "I love you forever," he wrote her. "You're so lovely, inside and out. I long to kiss you. Everywhere." Then he received a letter from Gloria saying that Henry Hyde had told her their tax returns had been examined and they owed $60,000 to the Internal Revenue Service. Jones was alarmed, and they decided to meet Hyde in New York.

On March 28, 1973, Jones boarded Pan Am flight 842 from Saigon to Honolulu. The plane stopped at Manila and Guam, and twelve hours and thirty minutes passed before it reached Hawaii. Most of the passengers stretched out over the empty seats, but Jones was too tense to sleep. As the plane came in over the west coast of Oahu, he picked out Mount Kaala and the Waianane Range. The plane flew along the shore, by Pearl Harbor and Hickam Field, and suddenly they were on the ground. Outside the airport, everything was unfamiliar, with six-lane freeways and skyscrapers. Jones had planned to stay at the Royal Hawaiian out on Waikiki, but it was full, so he got a room next door, on the twenty-fifth floor of the Sheraton. Down below, the pink baroque Royal Hawaiian looked like a doll's house, and at a distance, Diamond Head rose up, dark brown and massive in the clear air. Jones hadn't slept for twenty-four hours, but he was too excited to sleep. He showered and went downstairs to hire a car with a driver.

While waiting for the car, he strolled over to the Royal Hawaiian, which was the only building he recognized other than the Moana. The hotel gardens had been sold off for new buildings, and the Royal Hawaiian seemed cramped. He half-imagined he would see Prewitt and Maggio sitting on the curb, and when he went inside the hotel, with its black marble floors and deep pile rugs, he found it as it had always been. Jones looked at the shops and realized with a shock that he could afford what they had to sell.

When the driver asked him where he wanted to go, Jones hesitated, but then told him to drive to Wilhelmina Drive, a road that shoots straight up the mountainside. It is crisscrossed like a snake by Sierra Drive, and there he had imagined Alma's house, where Prewitt had stayed after killing Fatso. Down in the old part of town, where King Street and Hotel Street crossed Nuuanu Avenue, the sidewalks were empty and many of the buildings were boarded up. Wu Fat's Chinese restaurant was still there, but it was shabby and needed paint. The New Senator Hotel next door, where Alma had worked under the name of Lorene, was gone. The driver told Jones that there was more action out at Waikiki, and his taxi was available that night in case Jones wanted to pick up a hooker.

It was thirty years since he had been in Hawaii, and he had lost touch with everyone he had known. Tsuneko Ogure, the Japanese writing student who had been his friend at the university, was still in Hawaii, however, now married and called Scoops Kreger, and he had dinner with her the two nights he was in town. They reminisced about the old days, but she found him changed. The rebel soldier of 1942 was now pro-army and conservative.

The next day, Jones hired another car and drove out to Hanauma Bay, where his company had been posted after Pearl Harbor. Except that the road had been blacktopped, it was much the same, and he remembered where the command post had been and where Stark had set up his kitchen. His actual memories became confused with scenes in *From Here to Eternity,* and the characters merged in his mind. He went down to the beach and put on his trunks for a swim. Families with their children were playing in the sand. He lay on the grass to dry off. "Suddenly," he later wrote, "without any preparation at all, tears were behind my eyes. All that blood, all that sweat. How many men? Tears for thirty years, gone somewhere. Tears for a young idiotic boy in a 'gook' shirt and linen slacks."

In the afternoon, Jones drove up to Schofield Barracks. He had phoned ahead, and an official welcome was planned. As Joan Didion later remarked, just as Kilimanjaro belongs to Hemingway and Oxford, Mississippi, to William Faulkner, so "Schofield Barracks and much of Honolulu itself has always belonged for me to James Jones." Before meeting anyone, Jones wanted to look around by himself. He passed by the main flagpole, painted the same pure white, the infantry quadrangles he knew so intimately, and the building where he had seriously begun his education: "I knew every shelf on the inside of the Post Library." He felt he was going back in time, and when he drove out on the road to Kolekole pass, he was not sure whether it was he or Prewitt who had been forced to march up there twice with full field pack.

When he phoned the public relations office, he was introduced to the commanding general and shown around. He was shown the "new army." The vast halls of the barracks where beds had been lined up in rows were now broken up into separate rooms for three or four men. The stockade was a military police post; the "confinement facility" had been moved to Pearl Harbor. The next day he drove out to Makapuu Point, which he had used as a setting for *The Pistol* and for his story "The Way It Is." There, just before Pearl Harbor, his company had dug five pillboxes in the solid rock and floored and roofed them with concrete. Jones parked the car and stood in each of them, remembering. When he left the last one, he put his foot on the place where he had always stepped to climb out: "My foot still knew where it was." He started to take pictures but immediately realized how foolish that would be. "I felt I was bearing witness — bearing the witness I had come back to Hawaii to authenticate. But just exactly what it was — except a thumbing of my nose at time — I didn't know."

The return to Hawaii moved him deeply, for it meant the recapitulation of his whole life and made him understand what had happened to him in the intervening years. "I had come back hoping to meet a certain twenty-year-old boy," he wrote, "walking along Kalakaua Avenue, but I had not seen him."

In New York, the Joneses stayed at the Blackstone on East Fifty-eighth Street. Like a soldier returned from the war, Jones had a satchel full of souvenirs, pieces of ivory, and Thai silk blouses for Gloria and Kaylie. Irwin Shaw was at the hotel when Jones opened the bag and showed him a piece of shrapnel he had picked up. Shaw, perhaps finding the display in bad taste, tossed it back onto the table. "Yeah, a piece of shrapnel," he said.

Jones conferred immediately with Robert Wool at the *New York Times Magazine* about the articles and was eager to talk of his experiences. In all, he wrote five pieces, but by the time they were finished, the other editors had decided they should also cover authoritative political, economic, and social analyses. Jones had never been asked to include this material and was temperamentally unsuited to write it, so in the end the *Times* published only two of the articles but paid for them all. Jones sold two of the others elsewhere, and Helen Meyer offered to publish them all as a book, thereby easing the tax problems that Jones was discussing with Henry Hyde.

Jones finished the book within six months and reordered the material so that it would have narrative interest. He explained to Ross

Claiborne that he did not intend to portray the American army in the negative way it had been so widely described in the world press, and he was so honest and straightforward in his presentation of the facts that the book stirred up no protest among North Vietnam sympathizers. When it was published, it received universally favorable reviews, reflecting relief that Jones had returned to a subject that suited him.

The modest success of *Viet Journal* was a welcome change, for otherwise, as Henry Hyde pointed out, the Jones household would be in a somewhat precarious condition. Their style of living in Europe was not being matched by income, even with film money to help. They did not live extravagantly, but every month there was a deficit of one or two thousand dollars, and the cumulative effect was dangerous. Moreover, the very public life they led, traveling first class and entertaining generously, made it hard for Jones to work. He had long before rejected the somewhat monastic life that most writers live. Jones wanted to enjoy it to the full. Also, since everyone came to Paris, he did not enjoy the long periods of relative quiet and tranquillity that Irwin Shaw had in Klosters and William Styron had in Connecticut. Jones worked upstairs during the day, but almost every evening he rejoined the fast-tempoed life of a European capital.

The financial and social demands that Jones faced had begun to lower his standing in the literary stock market. Styron and Mailer were both moving into new territory and writing novels that engaged the interests of American readers. People read and discussed Styron's *The Confessions of Nat Turner* and Mailer's *An American Dream* and *Why Are We in Vietnam?* but Jones's novels stimulated little response, which undermined his critical position and harmed his future prospects. Even with his Delacorte contract, Jones was beginning to seem a good candidate for the kind of literary career Budd Schulberg outlined in *The Four Seasons of Success*, his study of Sinclair Lewis, Scott Fitzgerald, John Steinbeck, William Saroyan, and Nathanael West. All of these writers had begun with extraordinary success and ended up forgotten, embittered, and burned out. Jones not only seemed to be paying for the great success of *From Here to Eternity*, he had further contributed to his decline by writing books that damaged him.

This downward drift was made worse by changes in the tax laws that eliminated loopholes for writers living abroad. The exchange rate was no longer favorable to the dollar, and by 1970 France had become one of the most expensive countries in the world. Up till then,

Jones had been able to count on an income that ranged between $160,000 and $200,000 a year. In 1954 he had made $234,000 from sales of *From Here to Eternity* alone; in 1970 his projected total income was $181,000. Deducting $80,000 for purely literary expenses and $50,000 for taxes left him with a net income of approximately $50,000. It was a sizable sum, but fixed expenses soon ate it up.

Jones became increasingly worried by his financial condition. "What would happen if I could no longer take care of my wife and children?" he asked a friend. He began to fret about household costs and to be irritated by Gloria's expensive habits and racing losses. Fame had its price. He could enjoy knowing that the tour guides on the Bâteaux Mouches pointed out his house as belonging to the noted American author "Zham-es Chonz," but the strain of maintaining the position was beginning to show.

For some time, Jones had talked about returning to the United States to live, and he hoped that he could find a job as a writer-in-residence at an American university. Poets and novelists had been employed as university faculty members for many years, and the fiction and poetry workshops they taught had become established parts of the literature curriculum for gifted students. Robert Frost, Allen Tate, Archibald MacLeish, John Crowe Ransom, and Robert Penn Warren were among the first to take such positions; by the 1970s a great many universities not only employed writers as teachers but had full-scale writing programs offering degrees.

As early as 1965, Jones had been invited to teach at City College in New York and at the University of Connecticut. He turned down both offers, but in 1971 he began to correspond with young writers he knew at universities. One of them was the poet J. D. Reed, to whom he explained that he didn't want to teach in the East but preferred the West, with "its air and its expanses, and its outdoors." Two years later, he wrote Michael Mewshaw, who was then teaching in Texas, asking for his help and expressing a preference for Colorado. Mewshaw found that there was little interest in Jones among the universities he knew of. English departments at the better-known universities wanted a "literary" writer and were scornful of Jones as one who pandered to popular audiences. Nevertheless, Mewshaw had a friend, Harry Antrim, who had just taken the departmental chairmanship at a new university in Miami called Florida International University, so he wrote to him in Jones's behalf. By chance, Antrim was in Paris, and he called on Jones and found that he was genuinely interested. As a new university, Florida International had money to bring distinguished individuals to the campus, and Antrim was able to have Jones appointed to a part-time position as visiting professor and writer-in-residence for 1974–1975 at a salary of $27,500.

The thought of leaving Paris was distressing in many ways, but for some time Jones had spoken of having the children educated in the United States. Since the appointment was for only one year, he did not sell the apartment but sublet it to a Swiss family. Nevertheless, he knew that the move would become permanent. As the time approached for leaving, he saw how artificial his relationship to France had been. He had surrounded himself, he said, "with a sort of balloon, cushioning air," in which he could live and work. For seventeen years, he had been a tourist in Paris, and the way he spoke French revealed his relationship to the country. "His accent was disarming, and so was he," Lauren Bacall said of him, but as a writer, Jones knew that language was important and that he didn't belong. For a long time, it didn't matter, but gradually he became irritated with the French, frustrated by knowing them and not knowing them. He suffered from cultural loneliness. Asked by an interviewer about literary circles in Paris, he replied, "The best 'in' group there is has a membership of one." Jan Goenvic, the family chauffeur, who looked on Jones as a surrogate father, said that Jones's solitude went "way beyond friendlessness." He had come from nothing and done everything himself, and the greatest refuge in his life was his family. But beyond that there was nothing, especially in France.

Above all, Jones felt that France was "hidebound, burdened with history and tradition." Whenever he left France to go to America, he said, "I've felt as if a huge weight had been lifted off me." When it became known that he was leaving after so many years, he was interviewed, and, as reported, his comments seemed ungenerous to his host country. "I'm tired of living in France," he said. "I've always felt like an outsider." He added that "the United States is where it's all happening today, that's where the cultural revolution is really going on. Americans talk about how terrible things are in America. Well, I love it, it's moving." Later, he was to tell his students in Florida that one of the reasons he wanted to teach was to get back in touch with the youth of America.

The Joneses' friends were deeply upset to hear that they were leaving. Many realized that they would never return and that a phase of their lives was over. The charming habits of nearly two decades, the parties, the warm welcome for those casually dropping in at a friendly house, would now end.

Eugène Braun-Munk gave the Joneses a farewell party at a hotel; the room was decorated with wildflowers, and there was whiskey and caviar. He invited friends from all phases of the Joneses' life in Paris, from the early days to the present. The party was both happy and sad, for everyone knew an era was ending. Jones thanked Braun-Munk warmly and, using a word that was unlike him, said "it was a stunning party."

They sailed on the *France* on July 5, 1974, traveling cabin class, but by arrangement with the French Line, having the use of first class facilities, including the dining room. They were all there, the animals, Kaylie, and Jamie, with masses of luggage. For them all, it was the beginning of a new period in their lives.

They spent several weeks in East Hampton, staying in the guest house at Adolph Green and Phyllis Newman's place on Georgica Lane. They felt at home there, because they had already spent the summers of 1966 and 1970 on Long Island, when Jones had come to the United States to discuss the manuscripts of forthcoming books with his publishers. These trips had also reintroduced him to an America that was now rebelling against the social conformity and careerist ambitions described in the 1950s in such books as David Riesman's *The Lonely Crowd* and William H. Whyte's *The Organization Man.* Jones had sympathy with such feelings, but his experience of the 1968 Paris riots and of the drug culture he had encountered on the Greek island of Spetsai made him conservative, as had his money and his skepticism about politics.

Nevertheless, Jones was curious about America and eager to discover new signs of energy in the country. Long Island was a good place to go for this purpose, for though it was one of the oldest-settled parts of the country, it was neither isolated nor parochial. The first English settlement in what is now the township of East Hampton was a royal grant made to Lion Gardiner in 1639. By 1648, a group of settlers from Lynn in the Massachusetts Bay Colony decided to move to Long Island and bought thirty thousand acres from the Montauk Indians for a combination of odds and ends including twenty coats, twenty-four looking glasses, twenty-four hoes, twenty-four hatchets, and twenty-four knives, the whole valued at £30.

The new settlers had close links with New England and a strong Puritan character that was reflected in the town's architecture and in the strict morality imposed by the magistrates on behalf of the parish. In these respects it typified the oldest cultural strain in the country. The first house in East Hampton that the Joneses rented was on Further Lane, whose name recalls its rural origins. On the outskirts of the town, it was not far from the long sandy beach that stretches the whole length of Long Island from Brooklyn to Montauk. The land is gently rolling and flat, originally farmland but now broken up for large summer houses with spacious lawns. The Joneses had a number of friends living there, among them painters and writers who enjoyed its tranquillity but who were also tuned into the intellectual and artistic life of New York and the rest of the country.

Their earlier stays on Long Island had been somewhat boisterous, including a birthday party given for Kaylie in August of 1970. Jones had asked a group of Shinnecock Indians to come over from their reservation to dance for the children. Unfortunately, they arrived both late and drunk. Having trouble putting up the tent, they explained their difficulties by telling jokes to the children: "Teepee full of shit. Chief Bowels won't move." One Indian fell into the pool, and Gloria had to jump in to save him from drowning.

On another occasion, Ross Claiborne had invited Jones, Gloria, and some friends for a dinner to celebrate the completion of *The Merry Month of May*. Unfortunately, he chose a chichi restaurant in Amagansett, filled with crystal and bric-a-brac, that was run by a pair of prissy young men. They were given a large table in the center of the room, from which a noisy conversation began to erupt. Jones called out to a Parisian friend, "How do you say 'cocksucker' in French?" and the guests at neighboring tables were shocked. The owners protested, and Claiborne prevailed on his guests to leave after the main course.

Their present stay with the Greens was less turbulent and more pleasant. They would gather at the pool at noon for drinks, and Gloria would prepare the special salt-free hamburgers that Jones ate. The writer Willie Morris, who had been the editor of *Harper's Magazine* and who was to become one of Jones's best friends, was usually present, as were Muriel Murphy, a good friend of Gloria's, and Betty Comden and Steve Kyle. The Greens were struck by the Joneses' extraordinary vitality: life seemed to speed up, and they were constantly on the go. That summer the Joneses fell in love with Long Island and spoke of someday finding a house of their own there. In the evenings, the Greens sometimes showed movies on their projector, and Jones would weep at such films as *Gunga Din* and *The Four Feathers*. He also enjoyed reading poetry to the assembled guests. One of his favorite writers was Edna St. Vincent Millay, whose poems could move him to tears. His regimen made him conscious of death, but he was not maudlin. He believed in the future and suggested that Adolph Green plant some seedlings by his swimming pool so that he could watch them grow.

In August, the Joneses drove down to Florida in order to settle into their rented house and unpack the books and clothes that had been sent ahead from Paris. Jones and Gloria had flown over to Miami in the late winter to find a place to live and to choose schools for the children. Harry Antrim had suggested Coconut Grove, but they preferred Key Biscayne, an island across the bay from Miami that was reached by a long causeway. There they found a nondescript furnished ranch house on a quiet street and took it. Their neighbors included Richard Nixon and his friend Bebe Rebozo.

Jones had known Miami from the early 1940s, when he had gone to visit his brother after his discharge from the army. But in the intervening years, the city had changed a great deal. The old resort founded in 1895 by Henry Flagler, whose railroad brought rich Philadelphians and New Yorkers farther down the coast from Palm Beach, was now replaced by the mass tourism of Miami Beach, with its vulgar hotels and night clubs. Meanwhile, Miami itself had become a large international city, and by the time the Joneses moved there, it had absorbed thousands of Cubans who fled to the United States after Castro's revolution.

The house at 251 Island Drive was one of several similar structures set close together along the street. It had palm trees, a circular driveway, and a rock garden in front. A screened-in swimming pool stood in the back yard, and there the family spent most of the day, in bathing suits. Now fourteen years old, Kaylie had been enrolled in Coral Gables High School, and Jamie was to go to a private school named Ransome-Everglades. They would be picked up in the morning by bus and returned in the afternoon. Jones was a conscientious parent, so he took care to look after the children when they began their first days of school in America. There were rich children in the neighborhood, many of whom drank and took drugs. One night, a young friend of Kaylie's became so ill that she dragged him to her house. Jones made him vomit and gave him coffee, and then talked to him for a long time, trying to find out what had driven him to behave so suicid-

ally. On another night, a little boy knocked on the front door. He
had fallen off his bicycle and knocked out his front teeth. Jones got
out flashlights and everyone searched the gutter and the lawn for the
missing teeth. When they were found, Jones took the little boy to the
hospital to have them all put back in.

At the university, eager not to give the impression that he thought
himself too good for the drudgery of the English department, Jones
insisted on helping to register the students.

More students than he could accommodate expressed interest in his
workshop, so he set up two separate classes, one on Wednesday and
the other on Saturday, and read manuscripts to select the more promising students. Even so, he admitted thirty students to each of his
classes. Originally, Jones, like most writers, was skeptical about writing workshops, fearing that they would make students so self-con-
scious that they could not express themselves; he also did not think
fiction writing could be taught as a subject, because it "is an art which
has no definite set of rules." He therefore tried to make English 416C
and 499C as relaxed as possible. Wearing a safari jacket or a dark blue
sports shirt, khaki trousers, and loafers, he would tip his chair far
back, with his hands behind his head, and begin to talk. Yet beneath
the easy manner, he was nervous, and he perspired freely.

Jones began his first class by saying that the "best qualification you
can have for writing fiction is a private income." After the laugh, he
spoke of the importance of getting behind the façades of life to see
how people really live. "The most exciting story — to me — is the
one where a man with an overwhelming passion or dream takes on an
overwhelming obstacle to achieve it," he said. He then gave the students their first assignment, to write a thousand words on this scene:
"You are arriving at an airport. You will be met by your wife (husband, lover) whom you want to keep, but who you strongly suspect
has been sleeping with someone else while you've been away. What
are you going to do? If it's true, how will you handle it? If it isn't, how
will you find out — without offending?"

Wanting the students to read, Jones also assigned F. Scott Fitzgerald's *The Great Gatsby* and Hemingway's *The Sun Also Rises*, but
most of the time was devoted to the students' own work. When they
brought in stories, Jones would read them aloud to the class and ask
for comments from the others. He spoke less about technique than
about the human problems beneath each story. Jones did not believe
technical problems existed by themselves; they derived from some

failure on the part of the writer in conceiving the story. He urged the students to be frank and open, especially about the sexual lives of their characters.

After class, Jones would often go with two or three students to the Rathskeller to drink beer and talk informally. Joan Patterson, David Gelsanliter, and Sue Camacho he found especially promising, and he made private appointments with them in his office, where he kept a bottle of Almadén wine in the desk. When he found work he really liked, he would say, "That's fine." Often his teaching was indirect. He would invite a student for lunch before class and then talk about the people he had seen while driving about Miami in his Volkswagen. He had been struck by the sight of a pretty girl in cut-off jeans who was sweeping the street. He described her leg muscles as she swung the broom. "I would have liked to go to bed with her," he said. "The thing I like about teaching," he said afterward, "is that it makes you part of a community. Outside of New York, writers are not part of the community unless they have another function."

Teaching also gave Jones a platform, and the need to speak publicly made him pithy and epigrammatic:

"I am drawn to the haunted ones."

"Show me the sympathetic insurance man. Everyone suffers."

"The conviviality of men without women."

"The key is to catch the main character on the cusp of a change."

"Let the reader bring something to the story himself. It makes for delight."

"Hypocrisy is the grease which oils the wheels of civilization. As people grow older, they become too tired to be hypocritical."

"People's lives are unhappy because they do what other people do, or what they think they ought to do."

"Fighting is one of the ways up for a guy who can't make it any other way."

"Keep your first drafts."

"The middle class rejects anything that is dishonest. Thus they miss the whole language of the comman man — the rich texture of it."

"Find out what is read in the libraries."

"Each time you drive down the expressway, it's different."

"All of the people who leaped on Nixon — if their careers were checked out — would be dirty too."

"A lot of American girls have a built-in chaperone."

·　·　·

Every morning Jones rose early and began work in a study he had fixed up in the cellar of the house. He also took long walks along the beach to the lighthouse and back, sometimes stopping at a local bar, the Sands, where he had made friends; he preferred it to the expensive world of Key Biscayne.

Gloria was not a part of Jones's life with the students, and she began to dislike Florida. She had never wanted to leave Paris in the first place and felt she was stranded in an outpost, where there was nothing to do except cook and look after the house. There were no maids now. To give herself some company, she invited friends to visit, and their presence made life more tolerable. Irwin Shaw and Bodil Nielson came, as did Willie Morris, Betty Comden and Steve Kyle, and Stewart Richardson, a Doubleday editor who had taken an interest in Jones's work. Jones invited the writers to talk to his students. Meanwhile Gloria had discovered the horseraces at Hialeah and occasionally took her guests there, but Jones wasn't interested in going. "I don't like to be around rich people that much," he said.

The Joneses did have a few acquaintances in Miami and would occasionally go out to dinner with them. John Keasler, a journalist Jones had known in Illinois, was one; another was his student David Gelsanliter, who was also a journalist. Joan Patterson and her husband gave a dinner party for the Joneses, and they brought Willie Morris and Stewart Richardson with them. It was a lively party, but Gloria wanted to go home, so they left at eleven-thirty. Thinking Joan might have been hurt by their early departure, Jones phoned her later to apologize. "I didn't want to leave," he said.

The English department had planned to reappoint Jones for the following year but were unable to do so when it was learned that the university was overextended financially and would have to drop some courses. A group tried to raise funds for his salary from private sources but were unsuccessful. Jones was very disappointed, because he had enjoyed the year immensely; it had given him all he had looked for in returning to the United States. His health was good, the warm weather suited him, and he was working well. He was happier than he had been for years, productive and at ease. But now, with the lease expired and nothing to hold him to Florida, he prepared to take the family north.

Jones's energies were so high that during the short stay in Florida he had been able to complete the text of a book called *WWII*, for which he had interrupted his work on *Whistle*. This project arose after Eugène Braun-Munk, knowing of Jones's need of funds, introduced him to Robert Markel of Grosset and Dunlap in New York, who had just published an immensely successful picture-essay book by Norman Mailer called *Marilyn*. When Arthur Weithas, the former art editor of *Yank* magazine, approached Grosset and Dunlap to do a book on the art that came out of World War II, Markel immediately approached Jones to see whether he would write the text. Jones was delighted. "Of course I'll do it," he said.

When Jones met Weithas in New York, the two men hit it off, and Weithas called Jones "Jimbo." They took several trips to Washington, staying at a place named General Quarters, near the Pentagon, and began gathering material from the art collections in the archives of the army, navy, and air force, as well as from the Library of Congress. At the Pentagon one day, an officer who recognized Jones came up to him and said, "You saved the army by exposing its evils. You're one of my heroes." Jones was also pleased to have a leisurely talk with General Weyand, who was now the vice chief of staff of the United States Army.

While Weithas selected the illustrations, Jones began his research on the war, especially on the European front, of which he knew little. He consulted the twenty-volume Marshall Cavendish *Illustrated Encyclopedia of World War II* for facts and background reading. He had some problems of organization. He wanted to find a way of focusing the material so that in addition to giving a history of the war, he could make the book a personal narrative and comment on some of the issues that concerned him, such as the dropping of the atom bombs on Hiroshima and Nagasaki. Eventually he united these three strands — history, narrative, and commentary — in a discussion of the process he called "The Evolution of the Soldier."

As he looked at the pictures, Jones understood how hard it was to reconstruct what it felt like to be in the army. Memory blocks out what was frightening or painful, including the first part of a soldier's training, when he begins to lose a sense of his own identity. He learns that he is "the chattel of the society he serves and was born a member of. And is therefore as dispensable as the ships and guns and ammo he himself serves and dispenses." To reach this state, the soldier has to accept the idea "that his name is already written down in the rolls of the already dead." Only in this way can he function; otherwise he would be paralyzed by fear. Yet he must learn to accept anonymity, to realize that he is just a nameless cipher in mass statistics, "buried in some foreign land like a sack of rotten evil-smelling potatoes in a tin box for possible later disinterment and shipment home."

The next stage in the evolution of the soldier is, ironically, the rebirth of hope. Since it was evident, long before the fighting was over, that the Allies were going to win the war, many knew that they would survive after all. The conflict between this idea and the earlier acceptance of death led a good many to inflict wounds on themselves or to desert. The last stage was one that particularly interested Jones, since he was working on it in *Whistle*. Ceasing to be a soldier was as hard as becoming one. The returning veterans were like a race apart. They couldn't tell their wives what they had done and how they had treated the enemy. They took comfort in staying with their buddies, trying to preserve an esprit that was already fading. Many slept with naked bayonets or pistols under their pillows; some ended up in the psycho wards of veterans' hospitals. Whatever happened, they were scarred. They were part of a "generation of men who would walk into history looking backwards, with their backs to the sun, peering forever over their shoulders behind them, at their own lengthening shadows trailing across the earth. None of them would ever really get over it."

To launch the book, Grosset and Dunlap gave a big party on September 12, 1975, at the Sheraton Carlton Hotel in Washington. Many high military officials came, including General Alfred Gruenther and General Weyand, and so did a number of important political people, among them members of the Kennedy family, including Senator Edward Kennedy. Henry Kissinger was there, surrounded by Secret Service agents; and Averell Harriman, Bill Moyers, and Senator Eugene McCarthy came, too.

The affair was widely reported and was but one of many parties Jones would attend over the next weeks. Grosset and Dunlap arranged an intense series of interviews, and he appeared on the "Today Show," "Panorama," "NBC News," and many other programs. From New York, Jones traveled west on a series of trips that took him to Cleveland, Minneapolis, Pittsburgh, Chicago, Cincinnati, Detroit, San Francisco, and Los Angeles. He enjoyed them immensely, because he hadn't traveled in the United States for a long time and was glad to become acquainted with his own country again. Wherever he went, he was put up at the best hotels and taken everywhere by limousine. Interviews were only a part of his routine, for he also had to attend book lunches and receptions. Despite the bad reviews his recent books had received, Jones was a genuine celebrity. Everyone wanted to meet that man who had written *From Here to Eternity* and made such a deep impression on American life. *WWII* rekindled the association with the war, and many people his own age wanted to shake his hand and murmur something about their own days in the army or navy.

The attention was exhilarating, but the strain was enormous. Jones soon abandoned his diet. He couldn't control the amount of salt in his food, and he needed drinks to help him face the crowds. By the end of the tour, he looked gray and worn, and it took him a long time to recover his equilibrium. Jones made no objection to the trips, but he was to pay the bill later.

In June of 1975, following their year in Miami, the Joneses moved to Long Island, where they rented a house in Sagaponack, a small settlement on the outskirts of Bridgehampton. A large shingled house partly hidden by a high hedge, it stood on a wide tree-shaded street just below the combined post office and grocery store. *Sagaponack* means "the place where the greatest groundnuts grow." The oval graveyard at the foot of Sagg Main Street dates back to the seventeenth century, with Wilmots, Piersons, Stanboroughs, and Toppings buried there, generation after generation.

As in other parts of eastern Long Island, the people have a certain Yankee canniness reminiscent of early settlers, one of whom, a man by the name of Mulford, may have been typical. Angered by an unjust tax levied against whalers, he journeyed to London to complain to the king. Court officials blocked his advances, however, and one even picked his pocket while he waited. Mulford sewed some fishhooks into his pocket and returned the next day. This time the court official shrieked so loud when his fingers caught on the hooks that he was arrested. The matter reached the amused king, who admitted Mulford and granted his petition.

Life was tranquil and soothing in Sagaponack. Country roads with names like Parsonage Lane and Widow Gavitt's Road passed by old houses with elm trees out front, and the adjoining town of Bridgehampton served the Joneses' needs with De Petris' grocery shop and Bobby Van's bar and restaurant. Fishing boats sailed from the old fishing port of Sag Harbor to the north, and with potato fields and ponds full of Canada geese and wild duck, Sagaponack had the sort of rural feeling that suited Jones completely.

Not everyone was pleased that the Joneses had moved to Long Island; some feared they would import the style of life the press reported them as having led in Paris. At first, most of the Joneses' friends belonged to the group of people they knew when staying with the Greens in East Hampton. But as she had done in Paris, Gloria turned her house into a place where neighbors were always welcome, and her warmth and good humor soon won her many friends.

Jones was unconcerned about social matters; he was interested in finding out about village life. By now, Willie Morris was living permanently in Bridgehampton, so he took Jones under his wing and introduced him to local people. Morris, a Mississippian, was an exile from city life and liked emphasizing the "down home" qualities of small-town America. He delighted in the understatement of country farmers watching the city folk come out for the weekend. "What do you make of that?" says one with a glance at an exotic tourist. The other just shrugs his shoulders. "Yeah," says the first, "I thought so too."

Morris was comfortable and amusing to be with, and he and Jones became good friends. Morris was an excellent mimic, and on a day when the Joneses were having a dinner party, he phoned, pretending to be a county official, and announced that the water was to be turned off for twenty-four hours. If they wanted water, they should fill their empty bottles and their bathtubs. This they duly did, but somehow the water kept coming. On another morning, Jones picked up the phone to hear a voice say, "On behalf of the Union of Soviet Socialist Republics, I should like to invite you to our country to talk to the students about writing."

"Oh, go fuck off, Willie," said Jones.

There was a pause. "I beg your pardon."

"Look, I'm in the attic trying to work," Jones said before hanging up. "Just fuck off."

The next day there was another call from the Russian embassy in Washington, with reference to a strange individual who had answered the phone, but by now it was too complicated to explain, and the Russian trip never did take place.

The Joneses retaliated as best they could. Knowing that Morris was a casual housekeeper, Gloria went to his house, where she found a week's worth of dirty dishes piled in the sink. She filled a plastic bag with the food-encrusted plates and glasses and left it outside for the trash collector. When Morris came home, he soon discovered the reason for the uncommon neatness and rescued the plastic sack before it was carted away.

Bobby Van's, on the main street of Bridgehampton, soon became a gathering place for the writers and artists who had moved into the neighborhood over the years. With a long bar and paneled walls, Tiffany lamps and red-and-white-checkered tablecloths, it was like a local club or pub for everyone, including the farmers and townspeople. In time, the writers made a habit of going there for lunch, and Bobby Van set aside a table for them. Wilfrid Sheed saw Jones there often. "Silhouetted in the doorway, he looked like a statue of a GI — the eternal dogface who fights the world's wars and eats the world's shit; who dies and is forgotten and turns up right on time for the next one." Several of his new friends thought of him as a curiosity. To the cartoonist Charles Addams, "He was a guy with a baseball cap and a cigar." They went for a ride in one of Addams' antique cars, a Bugatti roadster, but it wasn't easy to converse. "A Bugatti is not a place where you can open your mouth to talk," Addams explained. "If you do, you may not be able to close it again." Kurt Vonnegut, a fellow Midwesterner who shared Jones's mistrust of New York critics, noticed that whenever Jones and Irwin Shaw got together, they loved to reminisce about the war, although Shaw did most of the talking. These lengthy conversations led Gloria to call World War II the "Hundred Years' War." Jones made a strong impression on whomever he met. Elaine Steinbeck thought he was forthright, a man of strong opinions, like her husband. To Muriel Murphy, he was like a sailor who might at any time stand up and dance to a hornpipe. His narrow waist helped give this impression, but he was also impish.

Gradually, Jones became friendly with other writers in the neighborhood: Truman Capote, who lived near the beach in Sagaponack, John Knowles, the author of *A Separate Peace* and other novels, who lived in Noyac, Joseph Heller, Peter Matthiessen, Shana Alexander. Matthiessen was impressed by Jones's seriousness as an artist and by the reading he had done on his own. He tried to work everything out for himself. Not having had a university education, he approached existential problems with a freshness others lacked. "He did the deep thinking for all of us," Matthiessen said, believing that his thorough examination of a subject was what made it more memorable than the work of other writers.

At parties, Jones was amiable, but as he had always done in Paris, he preferred to stand on the fringe of a group, listening. In 1975, he met Winston Groom, a young writer of fiction about the Vietnam War, and often spent a couple of hours with him in the afternoon, when the house was quiet, showing him how he could speed up his narrative by using indirect discourse. Jones very much enjoyed talking privately about writing, and while teaching in Miami had become accustomed to it. But at the dinner parties he attended at private houses on Long Island and at Bobby Van's, he was no longer with beginning writers who urged him to speak about writing in a serious way. Instead, he was among professionals of his own standing who, rather than talk about writing, would talk about anything else, usually money. Jones enjoyed the lively and amusing banter of his fellow writers, but he missed having a counselor like Burroughs Mitchell in whom he could confide his hopes and concerns. He was friendly with Helen Meyer and Ross Claiborne but never established intimacy with them. Instead, he began to feel indentured to Delacorte and thought of himself as a prisoner in a gilded cage. Jones had enjoyed working with Lee Barker at Doubleday, but shortly after *A Touch of Danger* was published, Barker died. Jones had subsequently established rapport with Stewart Richardson, and hoped that he might persuade Doubleday to buy up the Delacorte contract. He had much in common with Richardson, and Richardson could see how solitary Jones was, working in isolation. He needed somebody to talk to about his work, but it would have required so much money to match the Delacorte contract that Doubleday didn't even try.

Renting a house was intended to give Jones time to find a house to buy, for by now he had decided to sell the apartment in Paris and live permanently in the United States. Fortunately, he was able to find an old farmhouse on the same street in Sagaponack. It was built on a bluff and had a view of the farmlands below. A large shingled building with a high-pitched roof, it was comfortable and unpretentious and surrounded by old trees and bushes. The bedrooms were adequate, but the ground floor was cramped and needed to be expanded. Jones decided to build a new living room with a fireplace at the end and to add a porch that could be used in the summer. He also planned to add a sundeck on the upper floor, which could be reached directly from the bedroom he and Gloria chose for their own.

The house cost $150,000 and the extensions were sure to be costly, so Jones interrupted his work on *Whistle* to do a projected television series with his Long Island neighbor Robert Alan Aurthur. He had worked in similar fashion the year before, when with Paul Jarrico he collaborated on the script of *A Touch of Danger.* Richard Widmark and Oliver Ungar had agreed to produce the film, and since Jarrico was spending the summer in East Hampton, he and Jones would meet in Sagaponack to go over the script. The two men had little in common intellectually or politically, but they completed the work to their satisfaction. Then Ungar suddenly died, and the film was never made.

The Aurthur project interested Jones a good deal more, for it was intended as a series conceived in the manner of one of the British Broadcasting Company serials. Called *Home Front,* it was to be about those who did not go off to war but remained in America, making more money than ever by working in war industries and finding themselves liberated from the tedium of the peacetime Depression. Jones was attracted to it because of its similarity to the material of *Whistle.* Placing the story in a small city resembling Terre Haute, he was using a setting he thought typical of the "hysterical, frenetic gaiety" that came with the affluence created by the war industry. He remembered overhearing one munitions worker in Memphis saying, "If this son-of-a-bitching fucking war only lasts two more years, I'll have it made for life." Jones didn't want to write propaganda, but he wanted the proposed CBS series to give "a picture of life as it actually was, when all the boys didn't come marching home as heroes." Despite the work done and the confidence shown, the series was never made. Jones was disappointed, but he had been paid, so he accepted the decision with equanimity.

Although Jones preferred to remain at home in Sagaponack, he occasionally went into New York for conferences connected with his film work or books. On these occasions, he and Gloria usually had dinner at Elaine's on Second Avenue. When he first went there, Jones had little idea of its special quality as a restaurant much favored by novelists, playwrights, and journalists, but Elaine Kaufman, the owner, immediately gave him a warm welcome. Like the Brasserie in Paris, Bobby Van's in Bridgehampton, and P. J. Clarke's in New York, it was the sort of unpretentious place Jones liked, with its checkered tablecloths, familiar waiters, and good food. At Elaine's, he could also see old friends and keep up with such people as Jules Feiffer, Irwin Shaw, the critic John Thompson, Betty Comden, and Gay Talese.

On one visit there, Jones ran into Norman Mailer. They had not met since their silent encounter at Castel's in Paris, nor had they communicated. Nevertheless, their relationship went back over the years, and they had once been intimate. Finding Jones and Gloria sitting with the Styrons, Mailer was reminded of their old times together and went up to their table to say hello. Jones reacted in a hostile manner, accusing Mailer of belonging to the eastern intellectual establishment Jones so despised. Mailer, reverting to younger days, suggested they go outside to continue the conversation, but Jones replied, "My fighting days are over." Mailer had no idea of Jones's heart condition, and when he heard of it later, he was touched with sadness. The episode, he said, "was the story of my relationship with Jim."

In December of 1975, on the advice of Dr. Herman, who was continuing to monitor Jones's health, Jones went to see Dr. Eugene Teich in Huntington, Long Island, for a series of tests. Jones had not followed to the letter Dr. Herman's regimen and continued to drink wine with his meals. The amount he drank would not have been excessive for a healthy man, but it was dangerous for anyone suffering from cardiomyopathy. By 1975, he had begun to put on weight, a sign that fluids were gathering in his body because the heart was not functioning well.

On December 11, Willie Morris drove Jones to the hospital for the tests. He was in a resigned mood, but as they approached the hospital, he caught sight of a restaurant and bar called Glynn's Inn. Jones insisted that they stop, so they went in and drank a bottle of white wine. In the hospital, Jones underwent a series of tests which showed that his condition had deteriorated since his last examination by Dr. Herman. He was hospitalized and put on a strict regimen of salt-free food and given injections of vitamin B and thiamin. When he checked in, he weighed 164 pounds. Within ten days, he had lost nine pounds, mostly fluid.

Hearing that his brother had developed heart trouble, Jones tried to blame his illness on heredity, but Dr. Teich explained that Jeff had a different ailment. Jeff's son, Dr. Richard Jones, a Washington pediatrician concerned with infant alcoholism, believes that the only inherited element in the brothers' illnesses was the susceptibility to alcohol they inherited from their father. The onset of his illness had been gradual, and in moments of candor Jones accepted the blame. "I did it to myself," he admitted.

By Christmas, Jones was home with his family. Jamie and Kaylie were now students at the high school in East Hampton. Jones had

wanted them to experience American public education, and they had
both adjusted well, Kaylie acting in school plays and Jamie playing
football. Jones enjoyed being with his children and wanted to show
them as much of America as he could. During the spring vacation, he
and Willie Morris decided to take their two sons on a tour of Civil
War battle sites. They started out in Alexandria, Virginia, on Washington's birthday, and watched a parade from the balcony of Winston
Groom's house. The participants wore uniforms of the Revolutionary
War and the Civil War, and carried antique muskets and swords. The
next day, they made a private visit to the White House, arranged by
Groom through Vice President Nelson Rockefeller. Jones dressed up
for the occasion, but in the Rose Garden he stepped in a mess the dog
had made. "This sort of thing is always happening to me," he remarked as he tried to clean off his shoe.

In the early 1960s, on another visit to the capital, Jones had gone to
the Lincoln Memorial with William Styron. Jones admired Lincoln,
and he read the words of the Gettysburg Address, engraved on the
marble walls of the monument, with its reference to the "final resting
place for those who here gave their lives that that nation might live,"
and Lincoln's determination that "these dead shall not have died in
vain." When he had finished reading, he sighed and turned to Styron.
"What a beautiful crock of shit," he said.

Touring the battlefields, Morris and Jones told their sons about
Robert E. Lee and General Bedford Forrest, a barely literate officer
Jones considered the most brilliant of the war. But beyond the historical importance of battles and individuals was the fact of war itself,
and the threat it held for the two fifteen-year-old boys who were with
them.

Jones had already come to believe that war was vain, and that it
cast an irremovable blight on those who fought in it. *Whistle* was to
be a study of that change. At the same time, he realized that war was
sometimes the mechanism for the improvement of social conditions.
Moreover, the impulse for self-improvement that characterized
Americans was often generated by war. The stubborn individualism
of Americans, and of American soldiers in combat, was part of that
process and could not be denied. In addition to reading Robert Ardrey, Jones had studied Teilhard de Chardin on the future of mankind. He knew that in *The Phenomenon of Man* Teilhard stressed his
belief that the process of evolution was still in force today, and that
instead of becoming fragmented, the energies of nature were leading

toward convergence. Biological studies, he said, reveal "the *irreversible coherence* of all that exists." The eventual unity of the world that Teilhard foresaw would automatically eliminate war. But the question that remained was whether men were psychically capable of moving in that direction. And what would happen to the energies that lead to ends we now hold dear?

In acknowledging the two sides of what the Lincoln Memorial represented, the necessity of war and its evil consequences, Jones was trying to be realistic about human nature. He wanted to avoid both sentimentalism and pessimism. Neither alone was truthful. Jones hoped to present both the intense revulsion soldiers feel toward the military world and the persistent loyalty they have to their experiences.

He could not have chosen a more appropriate place for the setting of his novel than a military hospital. But it meant that the book would be about damaged people and damage itself, including psychological damage and the inability to love. Jones's illness sharpened his consciousness of damage, so he was able to make his book not only a war novel but a book about human relations in general.

As the third volume of the trilogy, *Whistle* had its origins in *They Shall Inherit the Laughter*, the novel Jones had discarded in order to write *From Here to Eternity*. It was originally to have been about the guilt some soldiers feel at not having suffered as much as some of the others. Jones then thought of the novel as a way of discussing the education of a professional soldier, but having treated that subject at length in *WWII*, he turned more immediately to how wounded men expressed themselves, and especially how they behaved while making love.

The writing of *WWII* reminded Jones of many episodes in the Kennedy General Hospital in Memphis, and they affected his conception of *Whistle*. Jones recalled "that there was a noticeable difference between the overseas combat men and the others. The combat men were clannish, and stayed pretty much by themselves, and there was this grim sort of iron-cold silence about them, except when they were in town and had a bottle in their hand. They made everybody else uncomfortable, and did not seem to care if they did nor not." In town, as Jones remembered from the Peabody Hotel, these same men threw themselves with hysterical abandon into the pursuit of pleasure. "Money was not much of a problem. Nor were women. There was always plenty of booze from somebody, and there were also unattached women at the hotel floor parties. You could always go to the Starlight Roof and find yourself a nice girl and dance with her a while and bring her down. Everybody screwed. Sometimes, it did not even matter if there were other people in the room or not, at the swirling kaleidoscopic parties. Couples would ensconce themselves in the bathrooms of suites and lock the door."

The lovemaking was energetic, but it was also affected by the war. The terrible wounds of the men made normal lovemaking difficult or impossible, and the girls' status as married women with men overseas made them fearful of having children. All they wanted was sex and excitement. Both men and women practiced oral sex, and because it was new to them, and upsetting, they talked about it.

In *Whistle*, Jones brought back the same characters he had used in his earlier war novels. Martin Winch is a reincarnation of Warden; Johnny Strange derives from Stark; Bobby Prell is Prewitt. A fourth character, Martin Landers, is drawn from Fife in *The Thin Red Line* and directly from Jones himself. On the hospital ship that brings them back from the South Pacific, and in the hospital in Luxor, which stands for Memphis, the four men establish a sense of brotherhood that derives entirely from their having been members of the same regimental company. The very military institution that turned their lives into a nightmare now gives them the only meaning they have. They are incapable of functioning in the outside world; they are perpetual alumni of the army and are incapacitated by that experience.

The men are very different from one another, but they are all doomed. The testing ground for their behavior is their relationship with women, and fellatio and cunnilingus soon become part of their lives. "They weren't shocked any more and they weren't innocent any more," Jones wrote. "All that had been burned off. And in being burned off had left behind a kind of ashy residue in them that carried the sour, bitter, acid smell of furnace cinders."

The decision to engage in oral sex troubled some of them. They feel liberated by the freedom of sexual contact and the removal of puritanical inhibitions. Denying that anything about the body is dirty, they also know that oral sex is a perversion of the principal function of sex, which is procreative. Strange believes that he has become "a pervert. A sexual pervert. From some deep well in him where he had never been, this thing had risen up and taken him over. In one fell swoop he had become an addict. And he didn't even care."

Sex soon becomes obsessional, for the war has killed the men's ability to have real feelings. None of them is capable of a lasting commitment toward a woman. All that remains is sensation, and, like a drug, it takes more and more from the men, leaving nothing but loyalty to their comrades, a loyalty formed in the place that marred them and that goes nowhere but backward. In the end, two of the four men commit suicide, one arranges to have himself killed in a barroom brawl, and the last ends up in a madhouse.

Whistle is a depressing tale, and as a story of wounded veterans, it is probably exaggerated, since no such extreme pattern of suicides emerged from returned veterans as a group. But Jones's point is that whatever happens, there is no real solution for those who have survived the combat zone; there are no happy endings, because the damage has already been done. In part Jones seems to have written the book for Jamie, "in the hope that he will never have to become the kind of man his father had to become in order to survive. It takes such a long time to get over."

In an unpublished prefatory note to *Whistle,* Jones wrote, "I can already feel the chilly arms of old age and her hooded lover closing around me." At that point, explanations become trite. All that remains is art, a vision of humanity. "Life is a loser's game from the first," he wrote. "You come into the world with nothing and you leave it with nothing. All that's been stated a million times." What then was left? Jones put it mildly but truthfully: "What interests me is the way different people handle this state of affairs."

After spending the summer in their rented house, the Joneses were able to move into their new house on Sagg Main Street in September. As usual, Jones was meticulous about the renovations that would make the downstairs spacious and attractive. He wished to preserve the Victorian feeling of the old farmhouse and supervised the cabinetmaking and the installation of bookshelves in the library. He even had the hand-carved designs on the old windows reproduced on the new ones.

In the meantime, the apartment in Paris was sold for a good price to a former American army sergeant, and Gloria went over to arrange for the shipment of furniture and belongings to the United States. It was a daunting prospect for her to close the house she had enjoyed for fifteen years. She had assumed that she would bring back only what was essential to the new house, but the difficulty of choosing was so great that Eugène Braun-Munk persuaded her to send everything in a container.

As a result, the pulpit bar was set up at one end of the living room, the paintings by Alice Baber, Paul Jenkins, Addie Herder, and Alexander Calder were hung, and the Greek amphorae from Yugoslavia were mounted in the hall, along with photographs of the family and of Jones's old F Company from Schofield Barracks. Inside the front door was a Paris salon that fit perfectly into an American farmhouse. The Louis XIII refectory table stood at one end of the long kitchen, looking as though it had been there forever, and upstairs went all the bedroom furniture, including the huge round bed.

Jones's study was in the attic. This room had already been transformed into a studio by the previous owners, so little needed to be done structurally. In the top of the house, as it had been in Paris, the workroom was painted white and was bright and cheerful, with views over the treetops. Jones's large desk stood in the middle of the room. A dictionary was on a stand nearby, and other reference books were within easy reach. Tables held collections of knives and souvenirs. Low shelves for books ran around the eaves, and in an alcove behind the desk was a built-in bed where Jones could lie down and rest. There were filing cabinets and memorabilia and sports equipment, a fencing set, a trombone, skin-diving equipment, and a samurai sword. It was like the upstairs room in Robinson, where as a little boy Jones had retreated with his toy soldiers and books.

Jones loved his new house, and one of his favorite moments of the day occurred in the early evening, when he sat on the porch overlooking the potato fields and trees to the west. In the summer, the light was soft, and all was quiet, as the lazy hum of insects slowly faded. Sitting in a white wicker chair, he would watch the sun set.

The new house made the Jones family stable again, and Château Spud, as Willie Morris christened it, soon became a place where friends gathered. After a day's work, Jones enjoyed an evening of sociability, although he found he had less energy than before. He still occasionally sipped white wine, but usually took grapefruit juice instead. One of the most noticeable effects of cardiomyopathy is shortness of breath, and after sitting at the table at a dinner party, he would sometimes have to lie down on the floor until his breathing became regular again. Having to do this exasperated him, and he would rail against his mother, blaming her for his disability. He was outspoken about his illness and made it plain that he did not want to die.

Nevertheless, he did not dwell on it. Sitting stiff and breathless in a chair, he seemed more surprised than worried. He was concerned about his family, fearing they would not be adequately provided for, but no one thought he was dangerously ill.

Sometimes he appeared to accept his fate calmly, and as he talked, he seemed, the painter Ellen Adler noted, like a "thin, pale wise man." Because of the pressure of work, he would stay for a long time upstairs in his study, but he was also beginning to withdraw from company. As he had so often taken walks along the Paris quais, so he would now go off by himself in the car to explore parts of Long Island he had not seen before.

Like Walt Whitman, attracted to "the salty shore and breeze and brine," he was drawn by the landscape. He would go down to the beach at Sagaponack to look at the surf crashing on the sand, but more often he visited the north shore. In Long Island Sound were many remote islands that attracted him, and he confided to friends some of the thoughts they inspired. One had an old fort on it that looked across toward Gardiner's Island. It was now a ruin, and he would walk along the shore by himself, thinking of the history of old wars and how the country had survived and mankind continued. He would also go to Orient Point, on the very end of the north fork of Long Island, and from the rocky, windswept beach look out over the water toward Plum Island. With the wind smacking him in the face, he would think of his own destiny.

> I will arise and go now, and go to Innisfree,
> And a small cabin build there, of clay and wattles made:
> Nine bean rows will I have there, a hive for the honey bee,
>   And live alone in the bee-loud glade.

These lines from W. B. Yeats's "The Lake Isle of Innisfree" were often on his mind, but he was not wholly submissive. He had long considered Edna St. Vincent Millay one of America's best poets, and she had often written angrily about death. Jones admired one of her poems, called "Dirge Without Music," which contains these lines:

> I am not resigned to the shutting away of loving
>   hearts in the hard ground.
> So it is, and so it will be, for it has been, time out of mind:
> Into the darkness they go, the wise and the lovely. Crowned
> With lilies and laurel they go; but I am not resigned.

With these thoughts continually on his mind, Jones became increasingly direct in talking to people. Asked to participate in the Southampton College Writing Conference, on July 16, 1976, along with Irwin Shaw, Richard Yates, James Farrell, and Budd Schulberg, he addressed the participants on the subject of "Creativity and Self-Exposure." In addition to looking outward to learn about people to write about, he said, the writer must also look deeply within himself. "Dostoievsky was able to *become* Raskolnikov," he said. "Become." Repeating his belief that writers are like exhibitionists, he urged his audience to concentrate on the "untellable parts" of a novel, on things that are never mentioned in polite society but are always there and are recognized with pleasure when discovered.

By the beginning of 1977, Jones was much more ill than was generally supposed. It was a hard winter, with more and more snow and cold weather than usual, and on the night of January 14, Jones suffered a severe attack of congestive heart failure. His heart was so enlarged and weak that it could not pump properly, and his lungs were filled with fluid. He risked dying by suffocation. Immediately the Bridgehampton volunteer ambulance service was called. The deep snow made it impossible for the vehicle to get up the steep driveway, so Jones had to be supported down the hill. The blizzard was so fierce that instead of taking him to Dr. Teich in Huntington, the ambulance crew drove to Southampton Hospital. By good fortune, Dr. William Diefenbach was on duty, and he admitted Jones to the coronary care unit of the hospital and immediately put him under observation. He was given intravenous medication and was supplied with oxygen so that he could breathe. His heart was beating at a rate of 120 to 150 times a minute, and his skin was drawn and sallow. In addition to cardiomyopathy, he was found to be suffering from hepatomegaly, an enlarged liver.

Gloria and the children were distraught, and Jamie was so frightened that he hardly dared come into the hospital room. The upper part of Jones's body was gaunt, but his feet and legs were swollen from retained fluids. When he learned that the nurse, Beryl Buchholz, known as Ben, was from Bridgehampton, he cheered up. If he complained, she would joke with him. "You may be in charge at home," she would say, "but here I'm the boss." He would salute and say, "Okay, Sarge." Sometimes he was moody, and Ben would speak to him more directly than his family and friends were able to do. He told her about his youth in Illinois and how much he had loved his father.

Sometimes he would weep and say, "It wasn't much of a childhood." He knew he was going to die.

In a corner room with good light for reading, Jones looked out the window at the trees. He did what he was told to do and gradually improved. The swelling went down, and he began to breathe normally. After almost three weeks, on February 2, he was discharged.

Jones was very weak, but with the reprieve granted him, he was determined to finish *Whistle*. Now, undoubtedly, he regretted the many times he had put the novel down to take up some other project. But apart from the financial needs of the moment, he had been superstitious about completing the book. It was the conclusion of the trilogy, and he believed that in finishing it, he might come to an end. He did not mean that he would have no subject left; he felt that he was going to die. He now faced the ironic possibility of dying before he finished the book. The delays had produced unexpected advantages, however. "Each time I put it aside it seemed to further refine itself," he wrote. "So that each time I had to begin all over again, working from material I thought was finished." This long period of gestation, which was accompanied by extensive reading and rereading of books like Joseph Conrad's *The Nigger of the 'Narcissus'*, Malcolm Lowry's *Under the Volcano*, and Ford Madox Ford's *Parade's End*, helped him produce a far richer book than he had first imagined.

When he began the novel, he was explicit about its purpose. "I want to make *everybody* guilty for war this time. Pacifists, too. They can't escape guilt either; by being C.O.'s or going to jail. Everybody is guilty for war." It followed that the soldiers' dream of a healing love was doomed from the start. "Love is used to create hate," he wrote. "This is the perversion of war. And the awareness of the perversion is the soldier's curse." But by the time he was writing the last part of *Whistle*, struggling to get the words down before he ceased to be present to write them, he told Willie Morris that he was surprised there was so little recrimination among the lovers in the novel. "I think it came out of me," he said, "the wartime situation. I didn't expect them to know the anguish of wartime love, but I understood it — the love, the patience — better than I thought I ever would. They were trying to understand themselves, against the cruelty."

Even before he was taken to the hospital in January, Jones had completed most of the novel and was well into the final section. Slowly recovering at home, he had strength to work only two or three hours a day. He ordered a moving staircase installed so that he could get up to his study.

Dr. Diefenbach visited him every week and seemed encouraged by his progress. Ben Buchholz came more regularly to give him shots for his liver disorder and some pills. Every time she came, he asked, "How do I look?" If he seemed better, she would tell him; if not, she would say, "About the same." He was easily discouraged. When he caught sight of himself in a mirror or looked at his emaciated arms, he would tell his nurse how strong he had been.

It was a trying period for the family. Kaylie and Jamie knew he was dying, and he thought it best to talk to them openly about it. "He told me that life was a great adventure," Kaylie later recalled, "and that death was one of those adventures. He said it was hard for kids, though, because we don't know anything about anything yet and we had to learn. So it's good we don't really feel about death. We have to be self-centered or otherwise we wouldn't survive."

Gloria also knew he was going to die but was so upset she couldn't talk about it. Once when Lauren Bacall came for a visit, she could see that Gloria was worried and nervous. Jones asked for some tea, and when Gloria came back with the tray, her hands were shaking so much that she knocked a cup off and it broke on the floor. Jones knew she was under stress; his illness made him understand the tenuousness of life. "It's all right, darling," he said. "It doesn't matter."

In late April, Gloria took Jones to New York to see Dr. Herman at Mount Sinai Hospital. He was given a series of tests, one of several which showed that the heart was functioning at about fifteen to twenty percent of normal capacity. Dr. Herman indicated to Gloria that the prognosis was bad, but he did not tell her how serious it was. He decided not to admit Jones to the hospital, because he knew the end was near and thought he would be better off in Southampton, near family and friends. Jones was so weak after the tests that Gloria had to take him out in a wheelchair. She was given no special instructions.

The next day, May 1, 1977, they returned to Sagaponack, and only then did Gloria realize that he was much more seriously ill than she had supposed. Ben Buchholz, who happened to be at the house, told Gloria that Jones should go immediately to the hospital. Muriel Murphy, who was also there, drove him to Southampton, and he was once again admitted to the coronary care unit, where Dr. Diefenbach gave him the full emergency treatment. By now, the disease had progressed further. He was very weak; his skin was almost orange in color, and he could hardly talk. He was given a sedative and went to sleep.

Gloria phoned Henry Hyde, Jones's lawyer. He flew out in a helicopter with Dr. William Foley of New York Hospital to see whether Jones should be transferred to the city. But when they saw him, they knew it was hopeless.

Jones was deeply concerned because he had not yet finished *Whistle*. He summoned Morris and said, "Willie, you're going to have to help me out, finish some details." He had already begun to dictate notes for the unfinished chapters into a tape recorder that Joseph Heller had given him. By now, Jones was very frail, and the poison in his liver confused his thinking. He could see visitors for only five minutes in the hour, and even that was a strain. Many of his friends began to gather around. William Styron came from Connecticut, and Peter Matthiessen also visited. Jones told him of a vision he had had during the night. He was in the center of a large bowl, like a French vegetable steamer that has leaves that close over whatever is being cooked. He was in the bottom of the steamer, and, one by one, the leaves began to close in on him. It grew darker, until there were only two or three that remained open. Jones struggled, fearful that it was all over, and gradually the leaves began to open, and the light poured in.

Outside the coronary care unit, the waiting room was by now full of well-wishers who wanted to show their concern and solidarity. They came and went, trying to comfort Gloria and the children. They brought in lobster and whiskey for their vigil. They tried to be as cheerful as possible. Knowing that *Whistle* remained unfinished, John Knowles told Gloria that perhaps it would go down in history like Schubert's Unfinished Symphony or Fitzgerald's *The Last Tycoon*. Gloria passed this on to Jones, and he said, "Go tell Jack Knowles to fuck himself."

As the days dragged on, the number of people in the waiting room increased, as did the confusion and drinking. When another of Jones's lawyers, Robert Gluckman, came out to consult from New York, he was horrified by what he saw. The nurses were also at their wits' end; Kaylie and Jamie were in a corner, hugging each other. At one point, Gloria came out of the coronary care unit, filled a paper cup with bourbon, and took it in to Jones. He sat bolt upright and ripped out all the intravenous tubes that were attached to him, including the oxygen supply to his nostrils. Dr. Diefenbach was furious.

Despite the stress, Willie Morris sat with Jones as long as he could, taking notes for the final chapters of *Whistle*. Jones spoke weakly into the tape recorder but wanted Morris to take his own notes in case anything was lost. He explained how the story was to end, how the four men ended their lives, as he, sitting on the edge of the bed to breathe better, was about to end his. It was an heroic effort, but without flourishes. When he was finished, he lay back on the bed and said, "God, I'm sleepy."

The next days had a fatalistic quality. Irwin Shaw flew in from Klosters to say goodbye; and when Peter Matthiessen came in for the same reason, Jones just gave him a wink. There was nothing else to say. He looked like a butterfly pinned on the pillow.

Jones asked for a copy of Yeats's "The Lake Isle of Innisfree" and read it to Gloria and Willie:

> I will arise and go now, for always night and day
> I hear lake water lapping with low sounds by the shore;
> While I stand on the roadway, or on the pavements gray,
>   I hear it in the deep heart's core.

On his last day, Dr. Diefenbach ordered morphine to ease him. In his confusion, Jones kept pulling out the support tubes. The pain was increasing, and he asked Ben Buchholz to rub his legs to reduce the discomfort. For a while he seemed better and lay back on the pillow. Then he opened his mouth to say something to the nurse, but before he could say more than her name, his head fell forward and he was dead. It was seven forty-five in the evening of May 9, 1977.

12

❦

EPILOGUE

WITHOUT THE SPIRIT that animated it, the house at Sagg Main seemed empty, populated only by ghosts and the stricken living. Fortunately for Gloria and the children, two old friends, Addie Herder and Bodil Nielsen, were on hand to help preserve the forms of normal life. It was not easy, however, and there was a good deal of drinking and grieving. Nor was the fact of Jones's death easy to accept. His presence continued to be felt everywhere in the house and to be bitterly missed. As Bodil Nielsen said, "He was loved in an extraordinary way by many people. He had been endlessly helpful to a great many and cared about them deeply."

Gloria was the most affected and enacted her grief like a Sicilian widow, cursing and drinking and weeping. Her grief was so great, she felt torn apart. Imagining that her life was over, she purged herself of all her feelings. Willie Morris feared that she might do herself in, so he lay down on the floor beside the couch where Gloria was sleeping. In the middle of the night, the phone rang and Gloria had to go and fetch the dog who had run away. She came back and lay down again without waking Morris. The seizure caused by her grief had passed: she had got it all out and was functioning again.

Irwin Shaw and Peter Matthiessen took charge of the funeral arrangements, which were to begin with a memorial service at the Bridgehampton Community House. A week was to pass before the service, but there was much to be done. For a man who had lived such a public life, Jones's departure could not be a small, hushed-up affair. Friends from Paris and California telephoned that they were coming, and with so many on hand proffering advice, an event of some consequence was inevitable.

The night before the service, as on many of the nights after his death, there was a gathering at the house. Earlier, there had been a dinner for Gloria, Irwin Shaw, Peter Matthiessen, Willie Morris, Helen Meyer, and the Styrons. Under the pressure of the next day's event, there was a good deal of drinking. William Styron called out, "Where is Jim? Where's Jim? He's up there in Innisfree." Gloria threw a drink at him. The next day, they all vowed to remain sober for the memorial at the Community House, a large Colonial structure facing the Montauk Highway that looked like an old New England church.

As the time approached for the service, Gloria began go grow nervous at the prospect of having to face so many people. When she announced that she wouldn't go, Bodil Nielsen picked up the newspaper and turned to the obituary page. "If you don't want to go to this one, we can go to another," she said. "Here's one that ought to do. It says he died with no relatives, so no one will know us."

When they reached the Community House, on edge and somewhat disoriented from the morning's drinking, Gloria and Bodil Nielsen were approached by a group of old men. They paid their respects and said they were members of the Pearl Harbor Survivors Association. "Survivors!" exploded Bodil Nielsen. "Nobody survived Pearl Harbor." They then swept into the hall, where by now some four hundred people were assembled.

The speakers stood in front of a backdrop of lilies and wild laurel, and Willie Morris began by speaking of Jones's gentleness. "He knew so much about human cruelty in all of its manifestations, but as a human being was so lacking in cruelty himself. He was deeply tender and caring." Irwin Shaw spoke of Jones's "unflinching honesty, his courage, his intelligence, his quirky, sly sense of humor, and his awesome dedication to work." William Styron, angered by Herbert Mitgang's obituary notice in the *New York Times* the day after Jones's death, which dwelt, with quotations, on the bad reviews his later books had received, used the occasion to attack the "voracious little barracudas" and "the literary magpies from the universities, book review hacks from Kansas City." The most moving parts of the service were Rose Styron's reading of "The Lake Isle of Innisfree" and the appearance of Kaylie, who read Edna Millay's "Dirge Without Music."

The ceremonies ended with Master Sergeant Patrick Mastroleo of the United States Army Band playing taps from the balcony. This gesture had been made possible by Senator Edward Kennedy, and the bugler was the most highly regarded in the army, having played at the funerals of three presidents.

After the famous notes faded out in the auditorium, about a hundred of those present went back to Château Spud, where drinks and food were provided. In addition to those who spoke at the service, they included Wilfrid Sheed, Budd Schulberg, Charles Addams, Shana Alexander, Truman Capote, John Knowles, Kurt Vonnegut, Eugène Braun-Munk, Warren Brandt, George Plimpton, Joseph Heller, John Lindsay, John Hearst, and Muriel Murphy. Gloria remained in her bedroom during most of the time, but came down occasionally to greet special guests.

The funeral took place the next day. Jones had originally stated that he wanted to be cremated and have his ashes buried at sea, preferably off the coast of Florida, but Irwin Shaw prevailed on the family to have him buried near his house. He also asked Peter Matthiessen, a long-time resident of Sagaponack, to approach the authorities and find out whether it would be possible to bury Jones in the old graveyard at the corner of Sagg Main and the Montauk Highway. Matthiessen explained that, although Jones had not long been a resident of the town, he had a special feeling for it and considered it his home. Permission was granted.

Some days before the burial ceremony, Shaw, Morris, and Matthiessen had driven to Southampton to pick up the ashes from Brockett's funeral home, and Shaw held the box on his lap as they returned to Sagaponack. They drove to Matthiessen's house. Upstairs was a Zen meditation room with a straw mat floor. The ashes were placed on a table, and after a brief service, they all went downstairs. Willie Morris played "Abide with Me" on the piano, and this proved too much for Shaw, who broke down and wept.

On the day of the funeral, they went to the graveyard, where Matthiessen had dug the hole in which the ashes were to be placed. It was a sunny day, and the air was full of the scent of spring flowers. About a dozen people were present, including the family. A Buddhist shawl held at its four corners by Kaylie, Jamie, Styron, and Morris was stretched over the hole, and the urn containing Jones's ashes was buried in it. Styron read Yeats's "Sailing to Byzantium," and Irwin Shaw stood by the grave for a moment. "Goodbye, Jim," he said. "The adventure is over."

In the next few days, tributes to Jones appeared in the press.

Styron's remarks at the memorial service were reprinted in *New York Magazine,* and the *New York Times Book Review* published a tribute by Shaw, in which he cited the four war novels as Jones's major contribution to literature. "Jones made his own war on cant and dishonesty," Shaw said. "From the stink of the battlefield and the barracks came a bracing, clear wind of truth." Meanwhile, a white marble gravestone was placed in the far corner of the burial ground where Jones's ashes lay. On it was inscribed JAMES JONES 1921–1977.

Among the decisions that had to be made at this time was what to do with the unfinished manuscript of *Whistle.* Even while Jones was still alive, a group of his friends, among them Morris, Shaw, Matthiessen, and Robert Aurthur, had gathered at a restaurant to discuss what was the best course. Proposals were made that Matthiessen or Morris finish the book from the notes that had been taken and recorded on tape. Shaw opposed this idea on the grounds that it presented a trap for whoever undertook the work. The critics would say he was a better writer than Jones or a worse one, and no useful purpose would be served. In the end, they agreed that Morris should simply edit the notes of the few remaining chapters and indicate how the book ended.

Morris and Gloria had meanwhile listened to the tape. "The machine went *crackle-crackle-crackle,*" Gloria later recalled. "We were terrified we were going to erase it. But then the first word, the first sentence, came out loud and clear. We managed to get it all down. Willie put it in order, edited it. Then we all read it. Kaylie said, 'Let's put it in the past tense,' and we decided that was the way it had to be; otherwise it would look fake."

The manuscript was duly sent to Delacorte Press. Helen Meyer had been afraid that an unfinished book would not sell enough copies to cover the large advance that had been paid for the work. But Jones really had finished the book, and all that remained were three chapters that functioned as an epilogue. Ross Claiborne asked Burroughs Mitchell to come out of retirement to edit the book, and he went to Sagaponack, where he sat at the poker table and read through the text, making the small corrections he knew Jones would have approved of.

To give the book the best possible send-off, Helen Meyer hired the Seventh Regiment Armory, on Park Avenue at Sixty-seventh Street, a block away from the building where Jones and Gloria had lived when they were first married. There she gave a large formal dinner party for nearly three hundred people. Set for Washington's birthday, February 22, 1978, it was intended to launch the book and also pay tribute to Jones's memory and to the military world that was his main subject. Gloria worked with Helen Meyer to make sure that it was a glamorous affair and helped prepare a list of the most important celebrities she could gather together from the literary, political, social, and entertainment worlds.

On the evening of the party, Gloria stood in a receiving line with Kaylie and Jamie to greet the guests as they arrived. In addition to close friends like Irwin Shaw, the Styrons, and their children, the writers who attended included Ralph Ellison, Norman Mailer, Elia Kazan, James Farrell, Theodore White, Gay Talese, and Arthur Schlesinger. Among the journalists and entertainers were Shirley MacLaine, Art Buchwald, Mike Nichols, Nora Ephron, Woody Allen, and Walter Cronkite; and representing society and public life were Jacqueline Kennedy Onassis, Patricia Lawford, Diana Vreeland, Sargent and Eunice Shriver, and John and Mary Lindsay.

After helping themselves to striped bass and beef Florentine at the buffet, the guests moved to the round tables they had been assigned to. "I gave each author a table with his friends," Gloria explained. "The rest were sort of scattered around." Some got rather widely scattered, among them Norman Mailer, Adolph Green, and Betty Comden. Because more people came than were expected, they ended up in an annex, which Art Buchwald dubbed "Tourist Class." Photographers were everywhere. One popular subject was the threesome who were responsible for *On the Waterfront*, the movie made by Budd Schulberg, Elia Kazan, and Sol Siegel.

A program of readings was arranged, with Irwin Shaw acting as toastmaster. Kevin McCarthy read the taps scene in *From Here to Eternity*, Lauren Bacall read from *The Thin Red Line*, and Martin Gabel read a passage from *Whistle*. Throughout the evening a trio played songs from the 1940s that were mentioned in the novels.

Many of the guests wondered what Jones would have thought of the party, assuming that he would not have taken one look and fled. Karen Lerner from ABC television offered a suggestion based on what happened the first time Jones went to Elaine's. "He had never heard of Elaine's," she said of the restaurant he eventually came to know so well. "He didn't even know he was at a bad table in the back of the room. But he had a ball."

Most of all, the party was a celebration of James Jones, now dead but alive in his new book. People came to pay homage to the man they knew and liked. Although few present had yet read the book, the evening also acknowledged the other side of Jones, the realistic and pessimistic side revealed in his fiction.

The two had always gone side by side and, because of their nature, were never reconciled. All that could be done was to encompass them, to make them both possible, alternately. All his life Jones had wanted to live fully, to experience everything a man could yearn for, to love and be loved, to create a family that would go on, after him, in health and intelligence. He loved his friends; he was full of gusto. Yet *Whistle* offers a bleak vision of reality. "I want to make everybody in the world groan with the inevitability of sorrow," he once jotted down on the back of an envelope.

The reviews of *Whistle* were generally favorable. Edmund Fuller in the *Wall Street Journal* cited it as "possibly his best work." Philip Caputo, the Vietnam War novelist, praised *Whistle* highly, stating that in trying to put down everything he knew about war and its meaning, Jones "had done it better than any other American writer I've read." Most reviewers wrote of *Whistle* in the context of his other war novels and while many acknowledged its power, they could not define it. As usual, they mistook his intentions, failing to distinguish the author from his characters. Despite the fears of the Delacorte editors that a posthumous book would not catch on but would be lost, in a period glutted with Vietnam novels, *Whistle* sold well and for a while was on the best-seller list. It more than earned back its advances and showed that Jones's public was always eager to hear from him on important subjects.

The four war novels are naturally about war, but they also record the four phases of life itself. They are about men who happen to be soldiers and the women who are their wives and girl friends. The setting may seem limited, but as Pablo Neruda once said, the most universal novel he knew of takes place in a small village on the plain of La Mancha. So Jones, in his four military novels, moves through the phases of life. First, in *From Here to Eternity*, come the dramatic encounters of youth, the first conflict of the individual with society, the struggle between freedom and order. In *The Pistol*, a more lyrical book, Jones examines the special joy and passion of individual existence as it appears in the fights and rivalry among the soldiers for the magic talisman of the gun that gives its owner special powers. It is a

novel about the illusion of young manhood and of human individu-
ality. *The Thin Red Line* is the next step, showing how the individual
becomes lost in the crowd, impersonalized, made to feel negligible.
These themes are drawn in a military setting, but they exist as truly in
the civilian world.

The final step occurs in *Whistle*, and this is the abandonment of
hope that comes with the realization that, for most people, the truth
about life is too much to bear. The four characters of *Whistle*, like the
Four Horsemen of the Apocalypse, step forth to present their vision,
crying out what was already said in the Book of Revelation: "How
long, O Lord, holy and true, dost thou not judge and avenge our blood
on them that dwell on the earth?" Jones's vision is as apocalyptic as
that of St. John the Divine, with his earthquakes and the great day of
wrath that he foretells. They are all corpses in the end.

Although his feelings were near the surface, always ready to brim
over, in his writing he believed only in the facts as he actually saw
them. "Feel with your eyes," he told his brother. Irwin Shaw, who
probably understood Jones better than anyone, said, "You had to
know him for a long time before getting to understand the various
paradoxical aspects of his character. He liked to play the rough old
soldier and use a soldier's gamy language, but he was a man of letters,
deeply involved in literature, and a great poem or an eloquent page of
prose would bring tears to his eyes. He was constantly worried about
money and the easiest touch for a friend in need or an old man down
on his luck. His vision of life was tragic, but when you were in a
movie theater with him and a scene struck him as funny, his loud, free
laughter rang out over all the other sounds in the hall."

Mary McCarthy sensed the same duality in him, the same tension.
"Death was his business," she wrote. "He lived with it as a writer and
as a man long before he came to grips with it in his immediate future.
No doubt it had something to do with having been a soldier; there
was something soldierly in him that kept him acquainted with death
and gave him a certain stubborn isolation from common concerns."
But the other, necessary, side to him was, as Mary McCarthy noted,
his marriage and closeness to Gloria, which in "making up a joint privacy, was essential and necessary to him; he must have made up his
mind on that score very quickly and stuck to it."

Jones's early death was universally mourned, but he had come full
circle and had rounded out his mission. In his last months, as he became frail and small, he reminded friends who had seen early pictures

of him of the delicate boy in glasses, growing up in Robinson. The books he wrote were also a product of this progression. They could not have been written by a young man; they needed the process of human maturity that he passed through in writing them. He was so sensitive, he had to adopt a masculine front to endure the life he led, but toward the end, he could express his feelings without shame, as he had done as a boy, but now with a very diffierent texture.

To reach that point, he needed the experience of his life as a man, as a living person, and not merely someone sitting for hours at a typewriter. His care for other people, his love for his children, his delight in guiding them, were also necessary for his maturity. "We try to live — and succeed at it — not only as if death were not an inevitability but also as if it were not a possibility daily," he wrote. "Yet it is only in the presence of death and its inevitable approach that life is understandable or even appreciateable. How unfortunate for us that only in the field of combat — only in war — where we contend in killing each other — are we able to achieve this necessary state."

NOTES

✿

INDEX

WRITTEN MATERIAL concerning James Jones's life has been obtained from four main sources. The largest collection of manuscripts, correspondence, business papers, and notes is deposited in the Humanities Research Center at the University of Texas in Austin. Most of this material relates to the latter part of Jones's life and was transferred to this collection by Jones's widow, Gloria Jones. Another important collection of manuscripts, notebooks, and letters, from an earlier time, was presented to Yale University by Jones himself in 1969 and is deposited in the Rare Book Collection of the Beinecke Library. The Princeton University Library possesses, as part of the Charles Scribner's Sons collection, the correspondence between Jones and various Scribner's editors, notably Maxwell Perkins, Burroughs Mitchell, and John Hall Wheelock. These letters trace Jones's development as a novelist from the very beginning of his professional life. The letters Jones wrote to his brother, G. W. Jones, known as Jeff, are in the possession of Dr. Richard Jones, Jeff's son. In addition to important letters, there are some early stories. The official records covering Jones's military service are preserved at the National Personnel Records Center in St. Louis and at the Veterans Administration office in St. Petersburg, Florida. Other smaller collections of letters and documents include correspondence and notes in the Robert Cantwell Collection at the University of Oregon and the private papers of Gloria Jones and Shelby Foote.

Few writers have preserved their documents as carefully as Jones did. Nothing of any possible value to future scholars or biographers was destroyed, so material for a remarkably complete picture of this writer has been preserved.

Four books about Jones have been published. *James Jones, A Checklist*, compiled by John R. Hopkins (1974), is a bibliography; Willie Morris' *James Jones: A Friendship* (1978) is a personal remembrance and memoir; James R. Giles's *James Jones* (1981) is a critical study of Jones's work; and

George Garrett's *James Jones* (1984) is a short illustrated biography. Each of these books contains much useful information. I also gathered a great deal of information from interviews with people who knew Jones at different stages of his life. In the introductory paragraphs to the notes for each chapter, I have given the names of the people to whom I spoke. I have not, however, indicated the source of each oral statement attributed to Jones or anyone else that has been passed on to me, because the only record and source for verification is in my notes. The only sources cited for individual quotation are those that appear in written form, whether in printed books or magazines or in manuscript.

For the sake of readability of the quotations cited in the text, I have very occasionally omitted a passage without indicating the omission by ellipses. In no instance does an omission materially affect the content of the statement. I have corrected obvious spelling errors, but I have preserved Jones's spelling and orthographic experiments, such as the dropping of apostrophes and the occasional short-cut spelling, such as "nite" for "night."

The principal sources of written material, as it appears in the notes, are abbreviated as follows:

Beinecke Library, Yale University	Yale
Humanities Research Center,	
University of Texas	Texas
Princeton University Library	Princeton
Collection of Dr. Richard Jones	R. Jones

The material at the Humanities Research Center in Texas had not yet been catalogued at the time I saw it, so I have not been able to provide details about the location of individual items in the collection.

⇶ PUBLICATIONS BY JAMES JONES ≪

BOOKS

From Here to Eternity, New York, Charles Scribner's Sons, 1951; London, Collins, 1952. Novel.

Some Came Running, New York, Charles Scribner's Sons, 1957; London, Collins, 1958. Novel.

The Pistol, New York, Charles Scribner's Sons, 1959; London, Collins, 1959. Novella.

The Thin Red Line, New York, Charles Scribner's Sons, 1962; London, Collins, 1963. Novel.

Go to the Widow-Maker, New York, Delacorte Press, 1967; London, Collins, 1967. Novel.

The Ice-Cream Headache and Other Stories, New York, Delacorte Press, 1967; London, Collins, 1968. Short stories.

The Merry Month of May, New York, Delacorte Press, 1971; London, Collins, 1971. Novel.

A *Touch of Danger*, New York, Doubleday and Company, 1973; Collins, 1973. Novel.

Viet Journal, New York, Delacorte Press, 1974. Nonfiction.

WWII, New York, Grosset and Dunlap, 1975. Nonfiction.

Whistle, New York, Delacorte Press, 1978; London, Collins, 1978. Novel.

STORIES

All of Jones's published stories are collected in *The Ice-Cream Headache and Other Stories* and are therefore not listed separately here. Most of them were first published in such magazines as *The Atlantic Monthly*, *Harper's*, *Esquire*, *Collier's*, *New World Writing*, and *Playboy*.

ARTICLES
(not including excerpts from books)

"James Jones," *New York Herald Tribune Book Review*, October 7, 1951.

"Living in a Trailer," *Holiday*, July 1952.

"Too Much Symbolism," *The Nation*, May 2, 1953.

"James Jones," *Twentieth Century Authors, First Supplement*, ed. Stanley Kunitz, New York, 1955.

"Marshall, Illinois," *Ford Times*, March 1957.

"Phony War Films," *The Saturday Evening Post*, March 30, 1963.

"Flippers! Gin! Weight Belt! Gin! Faceplate! Gin!" *Esquire*, June 1963.

"Letter Home: Sons of Hemingway" (Trip to Pamplona), *Esquire*, December 1963.

"Letter Home" (Visit to Alexander Calder's studio), *Esquire*, March 1964.

"Letter Home" (Klosters), *Esquire*, December 1964.

"Why They Invade the Sea," *New York Times Magazine*, March 14, 1965.

→» 1 «←

ROBINSON

Information concerning Jones's family and background came mainly from his wife, Gloria, and his children, Kaylie and Jamie. Stories about his childhood and parents were provided by Sally Jones, his brother's widow, and by Richard Jones, his nephew. Kaylie Jones and I also visited Robinson, Illinois, where we interviewed a great number of people who knew Jones's parents or were his classmates. Among the most informative were Rosemary Bahr and Annis Skaggs Fleming, who were school friends of Jones, and Vera Newlin, the former town librarian. Further information was provided by Ruby Abels, Thornton Bline, Robert Bonham, Inis Bussard, Jack Chamblin, Max Henry, Tinks Howe, Roscoe Kaley, Alta Dudley Mooney, Mary Moore, Wilma Nuttal, Leslie Seligman, Victor and Aggie Smith. Louise Lewis of the *Robinson Daily News* helped arrange the meetings.

For information about Robinson and Illinois, I consulted a number of regional histories and guides as well as the *History of Crawford and Clark Counties, Illinois,* edited by William Henry Perrin (Chicago, 1883), and *The History of Crawford County, Illinois,* published by the Crawford County Historical Society in 1981, which were provided by Annis Skaggs Fleming.

Page

3 "one of the Olympians": JJ to Maxwell Perkins, October 30, 1946; Princeton.

3 "which I know I shall never be free of": JJ, *New York Herald Tribune Book Review,* October 7, 1951.

6 "always an aristocrat": Radio interview, Bobby Van's, Bridgehampton, 1975; Texas.

7 "he wanted to get out of school quicker": JJ, quoted in Stanley Kunitz, *Twentieth Century Authors, First Supplement* (1955), p. 500.

8 "considered a great beauty locally": Ibid.

9 "hot emotions and broiling recriminations": Ibid., p. 501.

10 "We saw them kill the hogs": JJ to Mollie Haish, April 5, 1934; Yale.

11 "at least twenty times": JJ, "Interchapter," manuscript for *The Thin Red Line;* Yale.

11 "it had a great deal more to do": JJ, quoted in *Robinson Argus,* May 12, 1977.

12 "Without dough": John Dos Passos, quoted in Caroline Bird, *The Invisible Scar* (New York, 1960), p. 36.

12 "flipping pages of a magazine": JJ, notes for *Some Came Running;* Texas.

12 "She was also basically stupid": JJ to G. W. (Jeff) Jones, November 20, 1967; R. Jones.

13 "he was half tight": JJ to Charles Jones, January 6, 1944; Texas.

13 "never to tell anyone the truth": JJ, "Interchapter," manuscript for *The Thin Red Line;* Yale.

13 "I would sneak off": Ibid.

14 "I never made the squad": JJ to Jeff Jones, n.d.; R. Jones.

14 "was forced to fight for my pride": JJ to Maxwell Perkins, November 12, 1946; Princeton.

15 "My teeth would be chattering": JJ to Jeff Jones, June 25, 1940; Yale.

Page

15 "I of course was in love with her": JJ, "Whither Now, Frau?" manuscript; Texas.

15 "I was at a peculiar stage": Ibid.

16 "summer-deep greens": JJ, "Alice Baber and the Tragedy of Light," manuscript; Texas.

16 "considered them more neighborhood friends": JJ, quoted in Robert Bonham to JJ, May 6, 1975; Texas.

17 "all right for a guy to have a girl": JJ, "Whither Now, Frau?" manuscript; Texas.

17 "a steady boy friend": Ibid.

17 "Being class pres., Most Popular Boy": JJ to Jeff Jones, June 25, 1940; Yale.

17 "the guy that helped other kids": Ibid.

18 "sickness ran all through him": JJ, *The Ice-Cream Headache and Other Stories* (New York, 1967), p. 168.

18 "probably the only thing of value": Anonymous, interview of Jones in Florida, 1974–1975; Texas.

18 "Jim is quite a scrapper": "Notes 'n' Everything," Robinson Township High School, June 1939.

19 "very ephemeral": JJ, quoted in Kunitz, *Twentieth Century Authors*, p. 500.

20 "in the death throes of the depression": JJ, *New York Herald Tribune Book Review*, October 7, 1951.

20 "damned-fool kid": JJ to Jeff Jones, January 6, 1951; R. Jones. "Maybe I'll never see them again": Ibid.

-»> 2 «<-

SCHOFIELD BARRACKS, HAWAII

For background information about Jones's army career, I consulted a number of guidebooks and histories of Hawaii and of the 27th Infantry Regiment and the 25th Division to which he belonged. These include Melvin C. Walthall's *Lightning Forward* (1978), published by the 25th Division Association, and *The Bark* (1940 and 1941), an annual yearbook publication of the 27th Regiment. I have also used material provided by the curators of the museum at Schofield Barracks.

Much of what I learned about army life during the time of Jones's service came from Arthur Macedo, who provided information about army terms and practices, including details of training and living conditions, and gave me maps and other useful material.

The Office of the Chief of Public Affairs of the United States Army in New York opened the way for my investigation of army life in Hawaii and elsewhere. Through their good offices and the cooperation of numerous service organizations and publications, such as the 25th Infantry Division Association, the Pearl Harbor Survivors Association, *Army Times,* and *Army Magazine,* I located a number of individuals who belonged to Jones's army units. Frank Marshall and William Curran I met personally; others, whose names follow, talked to me on the telephone: Everest W. Capra, John Cloninger, Charles Earlywine, Joseph Forbes, Frank Grzebinski, Ray Jordan, John McKuin, Kenneth Nine, W. O. Williams, and Richard Yturralde.

Carl Stroven and Laura Schwartz Korn discussed with me Jones's experiences at the University of Hawaii. I also consulted Joan Didion and John Gregory Dunne, John Unterecker and Paul Pinkosh, Dr. Harry Arnold and Scoops Kreger, whose former name was Tsuneko Ogure.

Page

21 "could live better Inside": JJ, *From Here to Eternity* (New York, 1951), p. 8.

22 "This place is hell": JJ to Jeff Jones, December 8, 1939; Yale.

22 "They herd you around like cattle": JJ to Jeff Jones, n.d.; Yale.

22 "I've been quarantined": Ibid.

23 "While I was being examined": Ibid.

23 "Talk about sardines": JJ to Jeff Jones, telegram, n.d.; Yale.

23 "I met a swell girl": JJ to Jeff Jones, February 1, 1940; Yale.

24 "highest grade that he had seen": JJ to Jeff Jones, n.d.; Yale.

24 "kind of funny": Ibid.

24 "I didn't join the army to be a clerk": JJ to Jeff Jones, n.d.; Yale.

25 "I was born into the upper classes": JJ, *WWII* (New York, 1975), p. 71.

25 "I don't think I've ever seen": JJ to Jeff Jones; n.d.; Yale.

25 "about two out of every three people": JJ to Mollie Haish, n.d.; Yale.

25 "eyes as black as jet": Ibid.

25 "I don't like being broke": JJ to Jeff Jones, October 20, 1940; Yale.

26 "Getting my guts torn out by shrapnel": JJ to Jeff Jones, n.d.; Yale.

27 "one helluva swell guy": JJ to Jeff Jones, August 21, 1940; Yale.

29 "I love to drill with a rifle": JJ to Jeff Jones; n.d.; Yale.

32 "to escape out of life": Thomas Wolfe, *Look Homeward, Angel* (New York, 1947), p. 624.

32 "I, too, like Wolfe": JJ to Jeff Jones, May 1941; Yale.

32 "I had been a writer all my life": JJ, quoted in Kunitz, *Twentieth Century Authors,* p. 501.

32 "I hate myself and my dreams": JJ to Jeff Jones, n.d.; Yale.

33 "I think you have real ability, Jim": Ramon Jones to JJ, November 1, 1941; Texas.

Page

33 "Bad news, Jim": Ramon Jones to JJ, March 3, 1941; Texas.

33 "where I was alone": JJ to Jeff Jones, May 1941; Yale.

34 "In a land of fadeless day": Carrie Lee Brubaker to Mollie Haish, March 20, 1941; Texas.

34 "horror and revulsion": JJ, note card; Yale.

34 "She would sit in a chair": Ibid.

34 "the swellest, the grandest": Mary Ann Jones to JJ, February 4, 1942; Texas.

34 "Sometimes I'll lay awake at night": JJ to Virginia Moore, n.d.; Yale.

35 "years of agony and blackest despair": Ibid.

36 "lives alone with other men": Ibid.

37 "Did I ever tell you": JJ to Jeff Jones, n.d.; R. Jones.

37 "About all I do": JJ to Jeff Jones, May 1941; Yale.

37 "not favorably considered": JJ to Jeff Jones, n.d.; Yale.

38 "I'm working in the dark all the time": JJ to Jeff Jones, May 1941; Yale.

38 "Early that fateful morning": Intelligence Memo No. 10, January 2, 1942, by order of Major Tyer, Frank E. Stetson, 1st Lieut. Air Corps; Arthur Macedo.

39 "It was just another Sunday morning": JJ, "Note of December 7, 1941"; Yale.

39 "the explosions that began rumbling": *WWII*, p. 16.

39 "As he came abreast of us": Ibid.

39 "carrying messages for distraught officers": JJ, *Viet Journal* (New York, 1974), p. 251.

40 "three of the best friends I've had": JJ to Ramon Jones, January 21, 1942; Yale.

40 "I remember thinking": *WWII*, p. 25.

40 "with nothing but the machine guns": *Viet Journal*, p. 256.

41 "Dr. Jones was not in a condition": quoted in *Robinson Argus*, March 19, 1942.

42 "the last sentence in the first paragraph": JJ to Jeff Jones, March 22, 1942; Yale.

42 "life is like the sea": Ibid.

42 "Don't ever let anyone tell you": Ibid.

42 "Dad shot him *self*": JJ to Jeff Jones, April 3, 1942; Yale.

43 "The Joneses of Robinson": Ibid.

43 "to do something with my life": Anonymous interview of Jones in Florida, 1974–1975; Texas.

44 "The only trouble": JJ, "Whither Now, Frau?" manuscript; Texas.

Page

44 "But since he had been in the army": Quoted in JJ to Jeff Jones, n.d.;
   Yale.

45 "I could imagine myself in a heavy sea": JJ to Jeff Jones, n.d.; Yale.

45 "John T. Kolinowski, Seaman": JJ, "Of Seamen Sinking," manuscript;
   Yale.

45 "Did you ever read Robinson Jeffers": JJ to Jeff Jones, January 18,
   1942; Yale.

46 "I seem to have been born with the habit": JJ to Peggy Carson, September 18, 1942; Yale.

46 "nothing must ever come between me": JJ to Jeff Jones, November 3,
   1942; Yale.

46 "many women seem to like me": JJ, notebook entry, November 3,
   1942; Yale.

46 "Men go out and try to make women": JJ to Jeff Jones, June 25, 1940;
   Yale.

47 "I've always felt that my way": JJ to Jeff Jones, November 3, 1942;
   Yale.

47 "With their sun-blackened faces": *WWII*, p. 36.

48 "Our training was neither intensive nor complete": Ibid., p. 41.

48 "It's a rotten shame": Quoted in JJ to Jeff Jones, November 5, 1942;
   Yale.

48 "she was certain I wouldn't die": Ibid.

48 "with arms and legs burned off": JJ, notebook, November 18, 1942;
   Yale.

49 "more constant though less favorite pastime": *WWII*, p. 41.

49 "I might be dead in a month": JJ, "Whither Now, Frau?" manuscript;
   Texas.

49 "the wastes of the trackless Pacific": *WWII*, p. 41.

49 "what we had done at Schofield": Ibid.

⤖⤖ 3 ⤙⤙

GUADALCANAL

For information concerning the Guadalcanal campaign, I consulted several histories, notably Samuel E. Morison's *The Struggle for Guadalcanal*
(1964) and Melvin Walthall's *Lightning Forward,* which describes the
campaign from the point of view of the 25th Division. Newspaper accounts, such as William Hipple's "Yanks on Guadalcanal Fight Enemies
Besides Japs," *Kansas City Times,* March 24, 1943, were also useful for details of military life.

In *WWII,* Jones wrote about his own experiences in this campaign, and I
have quoted him where appropriate. I have also relied on the notes he kept

during combat and after, as well as on conversations with members of his company cited in the previous chapters, to whom the name of Hugh Milanese should be added. Jones's extensive correspondence with his brother, Jeff, adds to this account, as do the files of the National Personnel Records Center in St. Louis and Jones's full medical history, kindly provided by the Veterans Administration of St. Petersburg, Florida.

For information about Jones's experiences in Memphis and on leave in Miami Beach, I am indebted to Sally Jones and to Shelby Foote. Jack Warden also gave me valuable information about military hospitals.

Page

51 "I remember exactly how it looked": *WWII*, p. 48.

51 "bloody stinking hole": Samuel E. Morison, *The Struggle for Guadalcanal* (Boston, 1964), p. 4.

52 "Those of us already ashore": *WWII*, p. 49.

54 "I went where I was told to go": Ibid., p. 52.

54 "High ground before nightfall": J. Lawton Collins, quoted in Melvin C. Walthall, "Lightning Forward," history of the 25th Infantry Division, mimeograph; Texas.

54 "wounded in the head": Ibid.

55 "And that has always stayed with me": *WWII*, p. 91.

56 "When we began to dig": Ibid., p. 124.

56 "They will remain anonymous": Ibid.

56 "They had been initiated into a strange": Ibid., p. 88.

57 "a sort of instinctual dislike": Ibid., p. 86.

57 "commingled distaste, guilt and irritation": Ibid.

57 "It was the most godawful stuff": Ibid., p. 130.

58 "If it's as bad as what I just saw": Ibid., p. 139.

58 "He looked at me and grinned": Ibid.

58 "in the present from one day": JJ to Jeff Jones, February 19, 1943; Yale.

59 "into the belly of the nurse": Ibid.

59 "everybody that can is getting out": JJ, notebook, April 10, 1943; Yale.

59 "an unspoken feeling of comradeship": JJ, notebook, April 13, 1943; Yale.

59 "When anybody wearing ribbons": *WWII*, p. 61.

59 "The truth is I think we were very nearly a little crazy": Ibid.

60 "He can't hold his water": JJ, notebook, Yale.

60 "suffering immense pain": Ibid.

60 "Why in hell don't you just kill me": Ibid.

60 "If groaning or crying makes him feel better": JJ, notebook, April 13, 1943; Yale.

Page

60 "I stood on the upper deck": *WWII*, p. 139.

61 "Everywhere you looked you saw girls": JJ, notebook; Yale.

61 "did not laugh and smile": *WWII*, p. 146.

62 "It was a wild time then": JJ to Burroughs Mitchell, April 7, 1949; Princeton.

63 "Inside I was bored": JJ, notebook; Yale.

63 "He was never really drunk": Jeff Jones, "His Brother's Keeper," manuscript; Texas.

64 "Were you talking to me": Ibid.

64 "What the hell are you gawking at": Ibid.

64 "They went kill crazy": JJ, notebook, December 19, 1943; Yale.

64 "glossing over": JJ to Jeff Jones, n.d.; R. Jones.

65 "meaning vocab, grammar": JJ, notebook, September 29, 1943; Texas.

65 "belied by falseness underneath": Ibid.

65 "I pity the woman who ever falls in love": JJ, untitled manuscript; Yale.

65 "for someone to whom he might show": Ibid.

65 "Love Without Love": JJ, manuscript; Yale.

65 "My Epitaph": JJ, manuscript; Yale.

66 "I am in a hospital": JJ, untitled manuscript; Yale.

67 "I just stood there and looked at him": Lowney Handy, quoted in A. B. C. Whipple, "James Jones and His Angel," *Life*, May 7, 1952, p. 142.

67 "I am afraid the Army is killing": JJ, notebook, November 11, 1943; Texas.

68 "I caught the bus at midnight": JJ to Warren Wingfield, March 6, 1951; Yale.

68 "ideas, sentences, whole paragraphs": JJ to Jeff Jones, June 3, 1944; Yale.

68 "I'd write page after page": Ibid.

68 "I told them everything I could": Ibid.

69 "Feels he has done his share": Quoted in report "Chief Complaint — Condition on Admission — Previous Personal History," Medical Department, U.S. Army, Camp Campbell Station Hospital; Veterans Administration.

69 "acute depression": Quoted in report "Initial Summary, Working Diagnosis Sheet," Medical Department, U.S. Army, Camp Campbell Station Hospital; Veterans Administration.

69 "mood swings": Quoted in "Progress Notes, June 4, 1944," Medical

Page

Department, U.S. Army, Camp Campbell Station Hospital; Veterans Administration.

69 "psychoneurosis, mixed anxiety": Ibid.

69 "trapped and depressed": Quoted in "Consultation Request and Report," Medical Department, U.S. Army, June 7, 1944, W. L. Pugh, Captain, M.C.; Veterans Administration.

70 "for disability in line of duty": Certificate of Disability for Discharge, June 22, 1944; Veterans Administration.

70 "managed to get him out of the Army": Lowney Handy to Burroughs Mitchell, November 17, 1949; Princeton.

70 "I was unknown": Notebook for *WWII;* Texas.

⇶ 4 ⇜

THE SHINING DREAM

Much of the information in this chapter comes from notes and letters written by Jones to his brother, Jeff, and to his editors at Scribner's, Maxwell Perkins and Burroughs Mitchell. Informative letters were also written to Edward Weeks of *The Atlantic Monthly* and to Merle Miller and Frederick Lewis Allen of *Harper's Magazine.* In these magazines Jones published his first short stories.

Additional information came from talks with Annis Skaggs Fleming, with Ruth Aley, and with Arthur Pearlroth, who was a classmate of Jones's at New York University.

Page

73 "Of course, he knew the town": JJ, *Some Came Running* (New York, 1957), p. 3.

74 "a hero returned from the wars": JJ, notebook, November 11, 1943; Texas.

74 "sons of bitches": JJ, quoted in *Robinson Argus,* May 12, 1977.

74 "everybody lies about his life": JJ, notebook, Texas.

74 "trying to break me": JJ to Charles Jones, January 29, 1944; Texas.

75 "disregard the fact that I am a Jones": Ibid.

75 "could write so magnificently": Lowney Handy, quoted in JJ, notebook, November 11, 1943; Texas.

76 "spent all day in bed with Lowney": JJ, notebook, November 8, 1943; Texas.

77 "she subjected herself to me": JJ, notebook, November 11, 1943; Texas.

77 "a wonderful guy": Ibid.

77 "Lowney is an artist": JJ to Jeff Jones, December 4, 1944; Yale.

Page

77 "to furnish a haven": Lowney Handy, quoted in JJ to Jeff Jones, December 4, 1944; Yale.

77 "I am a natural": Ibid.

78 "No, if I can't see Perkins": JJ, quoted in Michael S. Lasky, "James Jones Has Come Home to *Whistle*," *Writer's Digest*, October 1976, p. 23.

80 "Why is it that this": JJ, "Backlash," manuscript; R. Jones.

80 "All fight for the same choice of heritage": JJ to Upton Sinclair, January 1948; Yale.

80 "No matter how much he drank": JJ, "Father, Dear Father, Come to Me," manuscript; Gloria Jones.

80 "Almost without exception": JJ, preface to Dan Morgenstern, *Jazz People*, manuscript, February 24, 1976; Texas.

81 "I remember how black discouraged you were": Claire Burch to JJ, February 14, 1951; Texas.

81 "the intolerable loneliness of New York": JJ, *New York Herald Tribune Book Review*, October 7, 1951, p. 8.

81 "The patient dislikes society": Special Neuropsychiatric Examination, James R. Jones, Veterans Administration Facility, Bay Pines, Florida, September 5, 1945; Veterans Administration.

82 "careless writing": Maxwell Aley to JJ, August 25, 1945; Yale.

82 "My transitions are too heavy": JJ to Jeff Jones, n.d.; R. Jones.

82 "I have always wanted to do a novel": JJ to Maxwell Perkins, February 10, 1946; Princeton.

82 "intense personal pride": Ibid.

82 "I'm putting myself in your hands": JJ to Maxwell Perkins, February 2, 1946; Princeton.

82 "I'm stumbling along": JJ to Maxwell Perkins, March 6, 1946; Princeton.

82 "that he could recall exactly how the light fell": Maxwell Perkins to JJ, March 27, 1946, quoted in John Hall Wheelock, *Editor to Author: The Letters of Maxwell E. Perkins* (Dunwoody, Georgia, 1977).

83 "Then just let the cards accumulate": Ibid.

83 "Having known a number of these men": JJ to Maxwell Perkins, January 15, 1946; Princeton.

83 "I do not know whether this book will sell": Maxwell Perkins to JJ, January 15, 1946; R. Jones.

83 "a social criminal": JJ to J. C. Donnell, May 10, 1955; Texas.

84 "the shining dream": JJ to Maxwell Perkins, October 30, 1946; Princeton.

84 "the little sword of your kid brother": JJ to Jeff Jones, n.d.; R. Jones.

84 "a sense of stability and security": JJ to Jeff Jones, n.d.; R. Jones.

Page

84 "I am learning gradually": JJ to Maxwell Perkins, October 30, 1946; Princeton.

84 "leaves out too much": Ibid.

84 "rather than real living persons": JJ to Maxwell Perkins, February 10, 1946; Princeton.

84 "Just as in music": JJ to Maxwell Perkins, June 2, 1946; Princeton.

85 "Emotionally, this story": JJ to Helen Stauble, April 16, 1949; Yale.

86 "because I like children": Ibid.

86 "Even if it's true": JJ, *The Ice-Cream Headache*, p. 13.

86 "to present life moving pictorially": JJ to Edward Weeks, January 24, 1948; Yale.

86 "Most every intelligent man": Ibid.

87 "I told you I would help you": Lowney Handy, letter undated and unsigned but by inference addressed to Jones, June 1944; Yale.

87 "a power which works in our lives": Henry N. Wieman, *The Source of Human Good* (Chicago, 1946), p. 116.

87 "whosoever will save his life": Matthew 16:25.

87 "Death is the secret of life": Paul Brunton, *The Secret Path* (London 1934), pp. 117.

87 "We must empty ourselves": Ibid., p. 122.

87 "*actually* become as hard inside": Jeff Jones to JJ, n.d., 1943; R. Jones.

88 "Before I could learn": JJ to Jeff Jones, n.d.; R. Jones.

88 "Several times I actually thought": Ibid.

88 "for about three or four seconds": Ibid.

88 "silently, mentally, concentrating": Ibid.

89 "I like sex": JJ to Jeff Jones, n.d.; R. Jones.

89 "breakfast served in bed": JJ, notebook; Texas.

89 "Love is the prime escape *from* reality": Ibid.

89 "You'll get over this": Ibid.

89 "I might very easily have killed": JJ to Jeff Jones, n.d.; R. Jones.

89 "Every sexual bout": Ibid.

90 "renounced society": JJ to Jeff Jones, n.d.; R. Jones.

90 "trying to associate Prewitt with myself": JJ to Jeff Jones, n.d., R. Jones.

90 "just put them together": Ibid.

90 "I have a fine place to work": JJ to Maxwell Perkins, June 23, 1947; Princeton.

90 "I sometimes despair of ever learning": JJ to Maxwell Perkins, April 9, 1946; Princeton.

90 "A deft man may toss his hat": Maxwell Perkins to JJ, Wheelock, *Editor to Author*, p. 299.

Page

90 "the development of a particular set of muscles": JJ to Jeff Jones, September 23, 1949; R. Jones.

90 "no one can help you": JJ to Lowney Handy, n.d.; R. Jones.

90 "I experienced such a feeling of joy": JJ, note cards; Yale.

91 "had learned things that Wolfe": Ibid.

91 "Jim Jones of Robinson, Ill.": Ibid.

91 "O lost, and by the wind grieved": JJ, quoted in Scott Berg, *Max Perkins* (New York, 1978), p. 451.

91 "was with Thomas Wolfe and not with me": Ibid., p. 450.

91 "I would prefer to work with one man": JJ to Burroughs Mitchell, quoted in Burroughs Mitchell, *The Education of an Editor* (New York, 1980), p. 59.

91 "I am learning things now": JJ to Peggy Carson, November 16, 1946; Yale.

91 "the need of a good big drunk": Ibid.

92 "I want to go through the Met": JJ to Burroughs Mitchell, November 1, 1948; Princeton.

92 "ability very quickly to establish": Burroughs Mitchell, *The Education of an Editor*, p. 62.

93 "I'm not looking forward to the trip": JJ to John Hall Wheelock, December 16, 1947; Princeton.

93 "drifts like dandelion seed": Ibid.

93 "Everybody drinks a lot down here": JJ, notes on Marathon; Yale.

93 "The same identical home": JJ, "Living in a Trailer," *Holiday*, July 1952, p. 74.

93 "closeness and intimacy": Ibid., p. 81.

93 "listening avidly to their tales": Ibid., p. 76.

94 "They are a stiff, proud": Ibid.

94 "curious sense of poignancy": Ibid., p. 81.

94 "I dread them": JJ to Dr. A. B. Chadwick, Veterans Administration, Chicago, Illinois, December 9, 1949; Veterans Administration.

94 "I am absolutely contented": JJ, quoted in a report by B. S. Buell, M.D., Neuropsychiatric Examination, October 28, 1949, Veterans Administration Hospital, Albuquerque, New Mexico; Veterans Administration.

94 "There are five stories here": JJ to Edward Weeks, September 21, 1947; Yale.

95 "I'd read about it, of course": Ibid.

95 "after the first flush of joyful disbelief": JJ, *The Ice-Cream Headache*, p. xiii.

95 "literary-cocktail-party stenographer": JJ to Merle Miller, April 22, 1948; Yale.

Page

95 "When I write 'it is' ": Ibid.

95 "Am I writing this for the *Ladies Home Journal*": Ibid.

96 "I have been puzzled by your letter": Frederick Lewis Allen to JJ, April 28, 1948; Yale.

96 "I work very slowly, and painfully": JJ, quoted in Burroughs Mitchell, *The Education of an Editor*, p. 60.

96 "It is not pleasant to be your own worst critic": Ibid.

96 "Life is plotless": JJ to Jeff Jones, September 23, 1949; R. Jones.

96 "I dont know and cant discover": JJ to Burroughs Mitchell, September 7, 1947; Princeton.

96 "write about something that happened": JJ to Burroughs Mitchell, January 20, 1948; Princeton.

96 "It's always the lonely ones": JJ to Burroughs Mitchell, May 6, 1948; Princeton.

97 "Nobody believes": Ibid.

97 "without romanticizing anything": John Hall Wheelock to JJ, December 3, 1947; Texas.

97 "Here is the *pièce de résistance*": JJ to Burroughs Mitchell, October 30, 1949; Princeton.

97 "I can't resist telling you": John Hall Wheelock to JJ, December 4, 1949; Texas.

98 "I am not over-enthusiastic": Lowney Handy to Burroughs Mitchell, November 17, 1949; Princeton.

98 "it turned out to be a veritable dump": JJ to Burroughs Mitchell, January 16, 1950; Princeton.

98 "They are not bitter at all": Ibid.

98 "I really feel very peculiar": JJ to Burroughs Mitchell, February 27, 1950; Princeton.

99 "Anyway, since this is such a great day": Ibid.

→» 5 «←

FROM HERE TO ETERNITY

Written documentation for this period of Jones's life comes mainly from his correspondence with his brother, Jeff, and with Burroughs Mitchell of Charles Scribner's Sons. There is also interesting correspondence with Robert Cantwell, B. W. Griffith, and Richard P. Adams, in which Jones discusses his own writings.

For Jones's experiences at the Handy Colony in Marshall, Illinois, I am indebted to John Bowers, with whom I talked and whose book, *The Colony* (1971), vividly describes the place. I also learned much from several of

Lowney Handy's relatives, notably her brothers Earl and Andy Turner, her niece Terry Crawford, and Belva Turner, Earl Turner's wife.

Others who gave me important information concerning this early period of Jones's professional life were Ruth Aley, Louis Auchincloss, Simon Michael Bessie, Vance Bourjaily, Hortense Calisher, Clifton Fadiman, Brendan Gill, Robert Knittle, Herbert Kogan, Norman Mailer, John P. Marquand, Jr., Budd Schulberg, Charles Scribner, Jr., William Styron, and A. B. C. Whipple.

Page

100 "excitement and delight": John Hall Wheelock to JJ, March 20, 1950; Texas.

100 "I am going to take the risk": Burroughs Mitchell to JJ, March 3, 1950; Texas.

100 "would lay the book open": Burroughs Mitchell to JJ, March 24, 1950; Texas.

100 "could make every cut": JJ to Lowney Handy, n.d.; R. Jones

101 "Officers are inclined": JJ to Burroughs Mitchell, March 29, 1950; Princeton.

101 "I saw that, with my own eyes": Ibid.

101 "That is one worry": JJ to Burroughs Mitchell, March 20, 1950; Princeton.

101 "hike bare-chested": JJ to Don Sackrider, n.d.; Yale.

102 "I'm just sweating the manuscript": JJ to Burroughs Mitchell, April 12, 1950; Princeton.

102 "modern Pompeii": JJ to Warren (last name unknown), February 28, 1950; Yale.

102 "All the people I can talk to": Ibid.

102 "I am hungry for the Middlewest": JJ to John Hall Wheelock, April 30, 1950; Yale.

102 "right now the greatest thing": JJ to Burroughs Mitchell, April 12, 1950; Princeton.

103 "elated and depressed": JJ to Burroughs Mitchell, August 10, 1950; Princeton.

103 "Surely, there is not anything": Ibid.

103 "one-way, two-way": JJ to Jeff Jones, October 3, 1950; Yale.

103 "I think they were pleased": Ibid.

103 "there were 259 fucks": Ibid.

103 "got tired of counting small words": Ibid.

104 "They all knock off": Ibid.

104 "curious combination": Ibid.

104 "I can safely say": Ibid.

104 "A prediction": *Publishers' Weekly*, December 16, 1950, cover.

Page

104 "and discovered me staring": JJ to Burroughs Mitchell, December 24, 1950; Princeton.

105 "reach something of the greatness": John Dos Passos to editorial department, Charles Scribner's Sons, December 22, 1950; Princeton.

105 "awful title": Norman Mailer to Burroughs Mitchell, December 21, 1950; Princeton.

105 "with the best of such American realists": Statement signed by Henry Seidel Canby, Clifton Fadiman, John P. Marquand, and Christopher Morley in the *Book-of-the-Month Club News*, republished in Scribner's advertisement for novel, tear sheet; Yale.

105 "I don't give a damn": JJ to Burroughs Mitchell, December 2, 1950; Princeton.

106 " 'From Here to Eternity' is the work": David Dempsey, "Tough and Tormented, This Was the Army to Mr. Jones," *New York Times Book Review*, February 25, 1952, p. 2.

106 "It's a damn good book": JJ to Jeff Jones, February 23, 1951; R. Jones.

106 "playing football on the beach": Ibid.

106 "since it was a piece of news": John P. Marquand to JJ, February 27, 1951; Yale.

107 "I have a horror": JJ to Marian Ives, November 8, 1950; Yale.

107 "youthful, earnest, spontaneous": Harvey Breit, *New York Times Book Review*, April 23, 1951, clipping; Texas.

107 "he was like a lonely rock": Wembley Bald, "Rough, Tough Jimmy Jones," *New York Post*, April 18, 1951.

108 "If you're not free": Ibid.

108 "an exceptionally high price": *New York Times,* March 6, 1951, clipping; Texas.

111 "was that the Army had an infallible way": JJ to B. W. Griffith, Jr., June 13, 1954; Texas.

112 "The first note was clear": JJ, *From Here to Eternity* (New York, 1951), p. 218.

113 "his realism turns to fantasy": J. Donald Adams, "Speaking of Books," *New York Times Book Review*, March 11, 1951, clipping; Texas.

113 "an immense moral scaffolding": John W. Aldridge, "Speaking of Books," *New York Times Book Review*, September 2, 1951, clipping; Texas.

116 "Lose that ego": Lowney Handy, quoted in John Bowers, *The Colony*, p. 33.

116 "A man who gets married," "An Artist must carry," "You think a woman," and "You think she's *romantic*": Ibid., pp. 32–33.

116 "We said fuck, shit": Ibid., p. 32.

Page

116 "When he ate": Ibid., p. 29.

118 "a direct reaction": JJ to Robert Cantwell, November 23, 1953; University of Oregon.

119 "We see each other for meals": JJ to Burroughs Mitchell, November 26, 1951; Princeton.

119 "It is hard, painful, unpleasant": Ibid.

119 "Doing lots of reading": Ibid.

120 "a novel of scope": *Christian Science Monitor*, January 30, 1952, clipping; Texas.

120 "seem to have a phobia": *Nashville Tennessean*, February 10, 1952, clipping; Texas.

121 "You can't have a tough master sergeant": JJ, quoted in *Life*, February 11, 1952, clipping; Texas.

121 "To see the Award": JJ to Kay Tower, January 29, 1959; Texas.

121 "an award to a professional": Ibid.

↦≫ 6 ≪↤

THE HANDY COLONY

Much of the information concerning Jones's stay in Marshall, Illinois, at the Handy Colony comes from letters and documents in the Jones collection at the Humanities Research Center of the University of Texas in Austin. Further information was gathered from his correspondence, especially with Ned Brown, Robert Cantwell, Harry Cohn, Shelby Foote, Jeff Jones, Norman Mailer, and Burroughs Mitchell.

I am also indebted to two written accounts, one by John Bowers in his book *The Colony*, the other an article by David Ray. Kaylie Jones and I visited the Handy Colony and learned much from conversations with Andy Turner, Earl and Belva Turner, and Terry Crawford.

For information about the filming of *From Here to Eternity*, I am greatly indebted to Daniel Taradash, who wrote the script and showed me a large amount of material he had gathered in the process, including letters from Jones. I also had helpful conversations with Robert Parrish and with Fred Zinnemann, who directed the film. Patricia Bosworth's biography of Montgomery Clift was also useful.

In addition, I spoke to a number of other people who knew Jones at this period of his life: Roger Angell, John Appleton, John Bowers, Hortense Calisher, Faith Dane, Stanley Finkel, Shelby Foote, Martin Gabel, John Keasler, Micky Knox, Herman Kogan, Morris Lebowitz, Norman Mailer, John Marquand, Jr., Helen Mitchell, David Ray, Katherine Shannon, Daniel Stern, William Styron, Ted Watts, and A. B. C. Whipple.

Page

123 "the perfect citizen": JJ to Maxwell Perkins, February 10, 1946; Princeton.

123 "explosive effect": JJ to Burroughs Mitchell, May 3, 1951; Princeton.

124 "a curious combination": JJ, "Marshall, Illinois," *Ford Times*, March 1947.

124 "my love for Lowney": JJ, note card; Yale.

124 "I think one of the main problems": JJ to Burroughs Mitchell, July 31, 1953; Princeton.

125 "I find, Mitch": JJ to Burroughs Mitchell, July 6, 1951; Princeton.

125 "I've been depressed": JJ to Burroughs Mitchell, November 9, 1957; Princeton.

125 "I'm working totally consciously": JJ to Robert Cantwell, September 3, 1955; University of Oregon.

126 "The intelligent writer": Ibid.

126 "No philosophy will ever": Ibid.

126 "to get *beneath* the soul": Ibid.

126 "Underneath the body": Ibid.

126 "If a man can *become* every character": JJ to Shelby Foote, April 9, 1952; Shelby Foote.

127 "in reality he didn't want to write": JJ to Edward Weeks, January 24, 1948; Yale.

128 "I dont want to hear from you": JJ to Charles Jones, October 16, 1956; Texas.

128 "an undereducated self-made tycoon": JJ to Burroughs Mitchell, May 3, 1951; Princeton.

129 "Why should Harry want to buy a dirty book": Bob Thomas, *King Cohn: The Life and Times of Harry Cohn* (New York, 1967), p. 308.

129 "bastardized the book": Harry Cohn to JJ, January 21, 1951; Yale.

129 "not technically proficient enough": JJ to Harry Cohn, July 4, 1951; Yale.

129 "so that there seemed a connection": JJ to Burroughs Mitchell, May 31, 1951; Princeton.

130 "life going on": JJ to Buddy Adler, December 30, 1952; Daniel Taradash.

130 "You stupid son of a bitch": Thomas, *King Cohn*, p. 311.

131 "We would get very, very loaded": JJ, quoted in Patricia Bosworth, *Montgomery Clift* (New York, 1978), p. 252.

131 "I would have had an affair": Ibid., p. 254.

132 "I love you all": JJ, quoted in "Male Garbo," *Variety*, n.d. (September 1953); Yale.

Page

132 *"truly* great film": JJ to Burroughs Mitchell, September 15, 1953; Princeton.

135 "exhausted, wrung out": JJ, quoted in unpublished interview, October 19, 1956.

135 "Sometimes I get concentrating": Ibid.

135 "She fascinates me": JJ, quoted in unpublished interview, December 5, 1956.

136 "I don't even write": JJ, quoted in unpublished interview, October 19, 1956.

138 "there is no universal truth": JJ to Burroughs Mitchell, December 4, 1951; Princeton.

138 "I've got a little idea": Norman Mailer to JJ, n.d.; Texas.

139 "Don't worry": JJ, quoted in John Keasler to Frank MacShane, June 4, 1983.

140 "Im feeling much better": JJ to John Hall Wheelock, May 11, 1954; Princeton.

140 "The only friendship": JJ to Norman Mailer, May 3, 1955; Texas.

140 "Someday hes going to explode": JJ to Robert Cantwell, September 3, 1955; Texas.

141 "that the world could be made": JJ to Burroughs Mitchell, January 27, 1955; Princeton.

141 "that people are basically good": JJ to Robert Cantwell, September 3, 1955; Texas.

141 "in spite of the hoots of derision": JJ to Burroughs Mitchell, December 18, 1954; Princeton.

141 "A martini or two for lunch": JJ to Burroughs Mitchell, January 17, 1955; Princeton.

141 "It's a hell of a lot of fun": JJ to Norman Mailer, May 3, 1955; Texas.

141 "Someday we'll have a beautiful place": Ibid.

141 "whenever I take time off": JJ to Burroughs Mitchell, January 17, 1955; Princeton.

142 "simply because in her love": JJ, note cards; Yale.

143 "She never handles two guys": JJ to Walter Minton, August 19, 1956; Texas.

143 "took the failures": Lowney Handy to J.W. (identity unknown), June 20, 1955; Texas.

143 "Did you ever notice": Lowney Handy to Charles Wright, January 11, 1956; Texas.

143 "Forget that you are a negro": Ibid.

143 "fight, work like a slave": Lowney Handy to Burroughs Mitchell, July 12, 1956; Texas.

Page

143 "her belief in herself": Burroughs Mitchell, *The Education of an Editor*, p. 68.

144 "could explode into screaming, strident obscenities": Ibid.

144 "which Lowney snatched from me": David Ray, "Mrs. Handy's Curious Colony," *Chicago Magazine*, September 1956, pp. 25–26.

144 "D. H. Lawrence was a queer": Lowney Handy, quoted in Ray, *Chicago Magazine*, September 1956, p. 26.

144 "never laughed so hard": JJ to Kenneth B. Hawkins, September 8, 1956; Texas.

145 "work all damn morning": JJ to Burroughs Mitchell, December 4, 1951; Princeton.

145 "a good adolescent book": Ibid.

145 "lost his bitterness": JJ to Burroughs Mitchell, January 27, 1955; Princeton.

145 "ninety percent Rotarian": JJ to Robert Cantwell, September 3, 1955; University of Oregon.

145 "There should be room": JJ, quoted in *Newsweek*, January 13, 1958, p. 89.

145 "to do for the great American myth": JJ to Burroughs Mitchell, January 17, 1955; Princeton.

145 "There is something fascinating": Ibid.

146 "the great growths and advancement": JJ, "The Writer and Freedom," manuscript; Texas.

146 "I remember when I read Eternity": Norman Mailer to JJ, August 29, 1955; Texas.

146 "now unprintable": Norman Mailer to JJ, February 29, 1956; Texas.

146 "getting ready to try and free me": JJ to Norman Mailer, March 5, 1956; Texas.

146 "a pigsty in its own little way": Ibid.

147 "Its a wonderful place": JJ to Burroughs Mitchell, September 2, 1956; Princeton.

147 "The whole thing is so big": JJ to Burroughs Mitchell, March 7, 1956; Princeton.

147 "The pressure on me": Ibid.

148 "A few minor cuts": JJ to Burroughs Mitchell, July 23, 1956; Princeton.

148 "I've just finished proofing": JJ to Burroughs Mitchell, September 12, 1956; Princeton.

148 "on nothing but gin and Miltown": JJ, quoted in *Life*, February 11, 1957, clipping; Texas.

148 "What I like is to feel": Ibid.

Page

149 "There's a certain moralism": JJ, quoted in unpublished interview, December 5, 1956.

⇢⟫ 7 ⟪⇠

NEW YORK

The move to New York brought Jones into the public eye more than ever before, and from this time until the end of his life, he was frequently interviewed. I have drawn heavily on these interviews, for they gradually seem to have replaced correspondence as a format in which he expressed his ideas on writing and other subjects. A number of unpublished interviews have also been used, most of them deposited with Jones's papers at the University of Texas.

From this point, Gloria Mosolino Jones became an integral part of Jones's life, and she was the source of an enormous amount of information and commentary on Jones's career and personality during the last twenty years of his life. Her contribution to this book was immeasurable.

In addition, the following individuals kindly contributed information for this chapter: Cecile Gray Bazelon, Charles Burke, Sydney Chaplin, Betty Comden, Shelby Foote, Stanley Frankel, Monique Gonthier, Adolph Green and Phyllis Newman, Jones Harris, Addie Herder, John Hersey, Percy Knauth, Daniel Lavezzo, Allen Lewis, Katherine MacGregor, Norman Mailer, John P. Marquand, Jr., Frank Marshall, Peter Matthiessen, David Ray, Budd Schulberg, Kate Soterity, Rose and William Styron, Edmund Trzcinski, Belva Turner, and Irma and Ben Wolstein.

Page

149 "He was small but built large": Budd Schulberg, "The Right-headed James Jones, 'True American Primitive,' " *Los Angeles Times Book Review*, January 19, 1977, p. 16.

149 "I'm afraid I patronized him": Ibid.

150 "Jim, what the hell's the matter": Ibid.

152 "I was a writer-fucker": Gloria Jones, quoted in Willie Morris, *James Jones: A Friendship* (New York, 1978), pp. 87–88.

154 "Ze best view": Roger Coster, quoted in John Kobler, "Haven for the Uninhibited," *Saturday Evening Post*, November 14, 1959, clipping; Texas.

154 " 'ot bed, cold bed": Roger Coster, *Saturday Evening Post*, November 14, 1959, clipping; Texas.

155 "fights": Gloria Jones, notebook; Texas.

156 "encouragement, advice and just plain": JJ to Burroughs Mitchell, May 5, 1949; Princeton.

159 "ways of the fiendish world": Delmore Schwartz to James Laughlin,

Page

May 8, 1951, quoted in Robert Phillips, *Letters of Delmore Schwartz* (New York, 1984), pp. 255–256.

161 "It's not only longer than *War and Peace*": JJ, quoted in *Time*, April 15, 1957, clipping; Texas.

162 "how dull, how terribly dull": Granville Hicks, "Critic's Ruling on New Novel by James Jones: 'Monstrosity,' " *Chicago Sun-Times*, January 12, 1958, clipping; Texas.

162 "if you like bad grammar": Edmund Fuller, "Jones' New Novel Takes Eternity to Read — plus $7.50," *Chicago Tribune*, January 12, 1958, clipping; Texas.

162 "Choctaw rather than English": *Time*, January 13, 1958, clipping; Texas.

162 "one was courteous": *New York Times Book Review*, January 26, 1958, clipping; Texas.

162 "in justice to the author": J. Donald Adams, "Speaking of Books," *New York Times Book Review*, January 26, 1958, clipping; Texas.

162 "I will not attempt to defend": JJ, draft for *New York Times Book Review*, n.d.; Texas.

163 "school of writing": J. Donald Adams, "Speaking of Books," *New York Times Book Review*, February 9, 1958, clipping; Texas.

163 "certain irritating mannerisms": Burroughs Mitchell, *Education of an Editor*, p. 73.

163 "I don't think any of the reviewers": JJ, quoted in Martha MacGregor, "Jones Answers His Critics," *New York Post*, January 19, 1958.

163 "*Some Came Running* is a better book": JJ, quoted in Art Buchwald, "Have You Seen Spring?" *New York Herald Tribune*, September 7, 1958.

164 "He loves the fictitious picture": JJ to Jeff Jones, n.d.; R. Jones.

164 "to be loved by some other person": JJ, quoted in MacGregor, *New York Post*, January 19, 1958.

165 "life is essentially a life of aloneness": JJ, quoted in unpublished interview, Southampton College; Texas.

165 "What I was trying to do": JJ to Faye Tinsley, November 4, 1959; Texas.

165 "does things which at first": Ibid.

166 "can again feel the despair that needs love": JJ, manuscript notes; Yale.

166 "little better than a high-grade animal": JJ to Faye Tinsley, November 4, 1959; Texas.

167 "everything about that book": JJ to Shelby Foote, June 8, 1959; Shelby Foote.

167 "who believe that to say": Ibid.

Page

168 "just how much he was": *Some Came Running*, p. 1230.

168 "having t.b. or some such": JJ, Introduction, *The Ice-Cream Headache*, p. xv.

168 "that beautiful, grim, frightening": Ibid, p. xiv.

169 "Playing": Ibid., p. 211.

169 "hard-flowing wind": JJ, *Viet Journal*, p. 255.

169 "staring into the dark toward Rabbit Island": Ibid., p. 256.

170 "a strictly symbolical novel": JJ, quoted in "Pessimistic James Jones Is Waiting for the Middle Ages," typescript, anonymous; Yale.

170 "mythological history of the Old West": Ibid.

170 "in killing, injuring, lying": JJ to Carl Jonas, March 29, 1962; Texas.

170 "deliberately to remove the reader": JJ to David S. Sanders, February 9, 1959; Texas.

170 "too little of the actual experience": JJ to Shelby Foote, June 8, 1959; Shelby Foote.

171 "Too many parties": JJ, quoted in Michael S. Lasky, "James Jones Has Come Home to *Whistle*," *Writers Digest*, October 1976, p. 26.

171 "to travel and get a little culture": JJ, quoted in interview, Paris, anonymous; Texas.

172 "that deep in that crusty": Norman Mailer to JJ, March 22, 1956; Texas.

172 "dumb, benighted asshole": Ibid.

172 "not a good book": JJ to Norman Mailer, March 31, 1956; Texas.

172 "Probably I'm hurting you": Ibid.

⇥⟫ 8 ⟪⇤

PARIS

For background on Paris during the years the Joneses lived there, I am grateful for a number of books devoted to the city, notably Irwin Shaw's *Paris! Paris!* (1976), Blake Ehrlich's *Paris on the Seine* (1962), Sir Anthony Glyn's *The Seine* (1967), and John Bainbridge's *Another Way of Living* (1968). Information about the Joneses in Paris was frequently reported in newspapers and magazines, and I have referred to them, too.

Jones's correspondence, except with Burroughs Mitchell, was curtailed or neglected because of his increasing need to write business letters. Nevertheless, there are important exchanges between Jones and Romain Gary, Seymour Krim, Irwin Shaw, and William Styron.

Most of the information in this chapter comes from conversations with those who knew Jones at the time: James Baldwin, Cecile Gray Bazelon,

Saul Bellow, Arnold Black, Sydney Chaplin, Thomas Curtis, Ruda Dauphin, Elaine Dundy, Eileen Finletter, Shelby Foote, Monique Gonthier, Georges Grüber, Leslie Hannon, Addie Herder, Henry Hyde, Gloria Jones, Robert Knittle, Seymour Krim, Katherine MacGregor, Vincente Minnelli, Edwin Morgan, Judy Atwell Mullen, George Plimpton, Norman Rosten, the late Irwin Shaw, Rose and William Styron, Edmund Trzcinski, Hélène Veret, Peter Viertel, Kathryn Weissberger, and Samuel White.

Page

178 "Green turned out": JJ, quoted in interview, Paris, manuscript; Texas.

179 "It's very beautiful": JJ to Jeff Jones, April 6, 1959; Texas.

179 "barges loaded with everything": Ibid.

180 "literary hopefuls": Irwin Shaw, "The Paris Review Notebook," *Paris Review*, no. 79, 1981, p. 377.

180 "went through a period": JJ, quoted in interview, Paris, manuscript; Texas.

180 "a compendium of all American folklore": Albert Camus, quoted in interview, Paris, manuscript; Texas.

180 "I suppose I should have written": JJ, quoted in John Dorscher, "James Jones," *Tropic*, Miami, January 5, 1975, p. 18; Texas.

180 "completely full of shit": JJ to Burroughs Mitchell, November 19, 1959; Texas.

181 "the permanent dark spots within the soul": Irwin Shaw, *Paris Review*, no. 79, 1981, p. 377.

181 "It is summer or autumn": Irwin Shaw, *Paris! Paris!* (New York, 1976), p. 42.

181 "truly magnificent writing": JJ to Burroughs Mitchell, December 2, 1959; Princeton.

182 "People like you": James Baldwin to JJ, n.d.; Texas.

182 "Instead of long hours reading": JJ, note card; Yale.

182 "sharp erratic-explosive gypsy rhythms": *From Here to Eternity*, p. 435.

182 "one of the most potent": JJ, "Jazz Preface," manuscript; Texas.

183 "a really total individualist": JJ, notes in manuscript of "No Peace I Find"; Texas.

183 "Do I really have a capacity": Ibid.

183 "A celebrated, beloved, adored": Ibid.

184 "The *agents de police*": Hugh Moffett, "Aging Heavy of the Paris Expatriates," *Life*, August 4, 1967, p. 32.

185 "The atmosphere": JJ, quoted in John Bainbridge, *Another Way of Living* (New York, 1968), p. 219.

185 "I talked to the man in charge": *WWII*, p. 137.

Page

187 "This summer": JJ to Burroughs Mitchell, September 14, 1959; Princeton.

187 "I lay there believing": Ibid.

187 "We suddenly discovered we were home": JJ, quoted in Bainbridge, *Another Way of Living*, p. 219.

187 "It's a terrible tragedy": JJ to Burroughs Mitchell, January 8, 1960; Texas.

188 "like a tiny village": JJ to Burroughs Mitchell, September 7, 1960; Texas.

189 "he was husband to all wives": Blake Ehrlich, *Paris on the Seine* (New York, 1962), p. 121.

189 "When the day's stint is done": JJ, quoted in Arthur Goodfriend, "The Cognoscenti Abroad — James Jones's Paris," *Saturday Review*, February 1, 1969, p. 36.

190 "I make a point of reading that tablet": Ibid.

191 "They have lived all their life": Sir Anthony Glyn, *The Seine* (New York, 1967), p. 83.

191 "Hemingway's Paris doesn't exist": JJ, quoted in Goodfriend, *Saturday Review*, February 1, 1969, p. 37.

191 "take all the way": JJ to Maxwell Perkins, October 21, 1946; Princeton.

191 "Hemingway is just short on personality": JJ to Warren (last name unknown), February 28, 1950; Yale.

191 "to account truthfully": JJ to Don Sackrider, n.d.; Yale.

192 "It is not great no matter": Ernest Hemingway to Charles Scribner, March 5, 1951, Carlos Baker, *Ernest Hemingway: Selected Letters, 1917–1961* (New York, 1981), p. 721.

192 "The reason the Col. Jones": Ernest Hemingway to Charles Scribner, April 11–12, 1951, Baker, *Selected Letters*, p. 723.

192 "grappled with the ghost of Hemingway": Irwin Shaw, quoted in Willie Morris, *James Jones: A Friendship*, p. 94.

193 "Hemingway was a spectator at war": JJ, quoted in interview, Florida International University, manuscript; Texas.

193 "You know what *really* ruined Hemingway": JJ, notes for *Some Came Running*; Texas.

193 "thought for a good ten seconds": Bob Considine, "On the Line: People, Places, Things," *New York Journal-American*, September 19, 1962.

194 "the sober joy": Irwin Shaw, "My Friends Don't Call Me the Unguided Missile for Nothing!" London *Daily Mail*, September 29, 1973.

194 "This is rare for him": JJ, notebook, January 7, 1964; Texas.

Page

194 "I had a premonition": JJ, "La Guerre en Suisse," manuscript for *Esquire* article; Texas.

194 "Go back next year": Ibid.

195 "The terror and total confusion": *WWII*, p. 163.

196 "excessive slaughter": JJ, "Phony War Films," *Saturday Evening Post*, March 30, 1963, p. 67.

196 "What the fuck do they think war is": JJ to Darryl Zanuck, October 23, 1961; Texas.

196 "I find it incredible": Ibid.

196 "that with their usual acumen": JJ to Victor Weybright, March 18, 1959; Texas.

197 "I teach Sunday School": quoted in "Frankie in Madison," *Time*, August 25, 1958, clipping; Texas.

197 "if nothing else": David Dempsey, "Not to Be Laid Down," *New York Times Book Review*, January 11, 1959, clipping; Texas.

197 "as nearly as possible": JJ to Burroughs Mitchell, February 17, 1959; Texas.

198 "No book has ever really been written about combat": Ibid.

198 "The rifleman trudges": Omar Bradley, quoted in *WWII*, p. 168.

199 "the ridiculousness of grown men": JJ to Shelby Foote, November 25, 1959; Shelby Foote.

199 "very painful to write": JJ to Burroughs Mitchell, May 10, 1959; Texas.

199 "fear of being ridiculous": JJ, quoting from Matthew Josephson's *Stendhal*, Notes for Combat Novel; Yale.

199 "Even with death staring": JJ, Notes for Combat Novel; Yale.

200 "injection of a subjective phrase": JJ to Seymour Krim, January 5, 1967; Texas.

200 "He had been appointed Acting Sergeant": JJ, *The Thin Red Line* (New York, 1962), p. 290.

200 "It was very difficult": JJ to Edmund Trzcinski, November 18, 1959; Yale.

200 "the dead, frozen like flies": JJ, statement written in office of Frank Loesser, n.d.; Arnold Black.

200 "To remain alive": Ibid.

201 "in his intent hate": Stephen Crane, *The Red Badge of Courage*, Chapter XVII.

202 "kept his integrity": Maxwell Geismar, "Numbly They Did the Necessary," *New York Times Book Review*, September 9, 1962, p. 1.

202 "The news about this long and harrowing novel": Orville Prescott, "Books of the Times," *New York Times*, September 17, 1962.

202 "one-shot author": *Time*, September 14, 1962, clipping; Texas.

Page

202 "Almost all the major reviews": JJ to Romain Gary, October 21, 1962; Texas.

202 "I've read them all": Romain Gary to JJ, October 9, 1961; Texas.

202 "new idea cruelly assails the old": Saul Bellow, "Recent American Fiction," lecture, Library of Congress, 1963.

203 "pioneer": Seymour Krim to JJ, May 5, 1963; Texas.

203 "I get a little irritated": JJ to Seymour Krim, January 5, 1967; Texas.

203 "a realistic fable": Romain Gary to JJ, April 22, 1962; Gloria Jones.

→» 9 «←

THE AMERICAN ABROAD

As the Joneses settled into living in Paris, they quickly extended their acquaintanceship. They met many Americans who lived in Paris as well as a smaller number of French, and they became acquainted with painters and other artists. They also traveled. Meanwhile, Jones wrote letters back to America, and his correspondence with Jeff Jones, Shelby Foote, Norman Mailer, Burroughs Mitchell, Irwin Shaw, and William Styron has been useful to me.

I have also relied on published and unpublished interviews with Jones and, above all, on talks with those who knew him at this time. I am indebted to the late Alice Baber, James Baldwin, Alain Bernheim, Gladys Berry, Arnold Black, Art Buchwald, the late Bernard Childs, Betty Comden, Silvinie and Judith Continho, Elaine Dundy, Donald Fine, Robert Gluckman, Arthur Goodfriend, Joseph Heller, Addie Herder, Henry Hyde, Paul Jenkins, Gloria Jones, Seymour Krim, Hope Leresche, Andrew Marton, Mary McCarthy, Helen Meyer, Arnold Newman, Elmore Richmond, Herbert Ruhm, Charles Scribner, Jr., the late Irwin Shaw, Kate Soterity, Daniel Spicehandler, Rose and William Styron, John Thompson, Jack Warden, Kathryn Weissberger. I also have made use of interesting letters from Thomas Berger and Robin Moore.

Page

204 "Why we give a God damn": William Styron to JJ, January 20, 1959; Texas.

204 "life, love, literature": William Styron, quoted in Willie Morris, *James Jones; A Friendship*, p. 128.

205 "We went into the house": Ibid.

205 "drinking and talking all sorts": JJ to Burroughs Mitchell, January 3, 1960; Texas.

206 "Every table was taken": Arthur Goodfriend, "The Cognoscenti

Page

Abroad — James Jones's Paris," *Saturday Review*, February 1, 1969, p. 38.

206 "Jones confessed that he served": Thomas Berger to Frank MacShane, August 29, 1982.

206 "enormous, torpedo-shaped": Ibid.

207 "I really didn't know what to do": JJ to Burroughs Mitchell, April 4, 1962; Yale.

207 "the only one of my contemporaries": Norman Mailer, *Advertisements for Myself* (New York, 1959), p. 463.

207 "the prettiest novel of our generation": Ibid., p. 465.

207 "too charming a writer to be major": Ibid., p. 471.

207 "authority of print": JJ to William Styron, January 8, 1960; Texas.

208 "would entertain a group of us": Norman Mailer, "Some Children of the Goddess," *Cannibals and Christians* (New York, 1966), p. 110. Originally published in *Esquire*, July 1963.

208 "I was quite nervous about you": William Styron to JJ, June 6, 1963; Texas.

208 "tempest teapot": JJ to William Styron, August 1, 1963; Texas.

208 "whether after all Norman": JJ, manuscript for *Esquire* article; Texas.

208 "apparently decided to settle": Norman Mailer, *Cannibals and Christians*, p. 113.

208 "stays within the framework": JJ to Shelby Foote, June 8, 1959; Shelby Foote.

208 "How do you go about making": JJ, "Why Are My Books Popular?" manuscript for *New York Times Book Review* article, 1962; Texas.

209 "no one can write a truly emotional": Ibid.

209 "before the Americans arrive": JJ, "Oh, What a Lousy Race," manuscript for *Esquire* article; Texas.

209 "Not that it would do any good": Ibid.

210 "seemed to be composed of street dust": JJ, "Sons of Hemingway, or Cigars, Fried Food and Red Wine," manuscript for *Esquire* article; Texas.

210 "spread greenly in the bright sun": JJ, "Arles Trip," manuscript; Texas.

210 "travel was a wonderful thing for a writer": Irwin Shaw, "Ships, Bells and the Wind from the North," manuscript; Texas.

211 "I think he, Ordoñez": JJ, "Arles Trip," manuscript; Texas.

211 "He is so absolutely prodigal": JJ, "Beaufort," manuscript; Texas.

212 "battered old workbench": JJ, "The Loom of the Future," manuscript; Texas.

212 "In the gloom and moonlight": Ibid.

Page

212 "with their gay, seemingly simple": Ibid.

212 "to believe in a nonspace": Ibid.

214 "much *safer* too": JJ to Burroughs Mitchell, September 2, 1963; Princeton.

214 "I didn't make the rules": JJ to Jeff Jones, May 7, 1964; R. Jones.

214 "It fails to substantiate": JJ to Burroughs Mitchell, May 28, 1964; Princeton.

214 "Go and fuck yourself": JJ to Frank Fahnestock, September 14, 1964; Texas.

215 "the kids fight": JJ to Jeff Jones, October 17, 1964; R. Jones.

216 "It is quite cold": JJ to Jeff Jones, December 23, 1964; R. Jones.

217 "the sexiest bathroom in Paris": JJ to Paul Heller, December 7, 1963; Texas.

217 "the consciousness of immediate flux": JJ, manuscript statement; Paul Jenkins.

218 "The knife is man's first, and most basic, weapon": JJ, foreword to *The Legend of D. E. Henry*, manuscript, November 19, 1973; Texas.

219 "But I love it just the same": JJ to Burroughs Mitchell, February 11, 1957; Princeton.

219 "Basically, it's a desire": James Jones and William Styron, "Two Writers Talk It Over," *Esquire*, July 1963, p. 57.

220 "I had it drilled into me": JJ, "The Skin Game," *King Magazine*, London, tearsheets; Texas.

220 "adventurous challenge": Ibid.

220 "feeling of sadness and loss": JJ, "Flippers! Gin! Weight Belt! Gin! Faceplate! Gin!" *Esquire*, January 1963, p. 129.

220 "the most powerful emotional experience": Ibid., p. 134.

221 "We go to bed": JJ to Burroughs Mitchell, n.d.; Princeton.

222 "You can hardly jump in the water": JJ to Burroughs Mitchell, November 10, 1962; Texas.

222 "huffing, puffing and exhausted": Robin Moore to Frank MacShane, February 3, 1983.

222 "wore the briefest of male bikinis": Ibid.

223 "Why do people skydive": Copied from Scott Slaughter, *Saturday Evening Post*, tearsheets; Texas.

223 "Why is he doing this": JJ, notes; Yale.

224 "really all hicks": JJ to Burroughs Mitchell, September 2, 1963; Princeton.

224 "curiously like a certain type": Ibid.

224 "real heroes": JJ, quoted in Milton Viorst, "James Jones and the Phony Intellectuals," *Esquire*, February 1968, p. 101.

224 "I want to teach my boy": Ibid.

Page

224 "To make myself a protagonist": JJ to Jeff Jones, n.d.; R. Jones.

224 "They're not like anybody but themselves": JJ, quoted in *Writers at Work: The Paris Review Interviews*, third series (New York, 1967), p. 241.

225 "Psychologically, I have always said": JJ to Leonard Greenberg, January 29, 1959; Texas.

225 "I'm trying to show": JJ, quoted in Viorst, *Esquire*, February 1968, p. 101.

226 "Somehow I think that the story of man": Jack London, *The Star Rover* (New York, 1919), p. 301.

226 "More than far visions": Ibid., p. 303.

226 "I'm scared because I am not sure": JJ, notebook, January 5, 1964; Texas.

227 "such a stupendous offer": JJ to Burroughs Mitchell, November 19, 1964; Princeton.

229 "Even the chlorine in the pool": JJ, quoted in Eve Tibby, "Place to Place, East Hampton: The Summer of James Jones," *Diplomat*, October 1966, p. 18.

229 "I sincerely feel": JJ to Burroughs Mitchell, June 20, 1966; Texas.

229 "I disagree": JJ on notes for manuscript of *Go to the Widow-Maker*; Yale.

229 "utter embarrassment": Josh Greenfield, "All the Brave Men," *New York Times Book Review*, April 2, 1967, p. 5.

229 "spillover Spillane": *Time*, April 7, 1967, clipping; Texas.

229 "king of the good-bad writers": Wilfrid Sheed, *Atlantic Monthly*, 1967, reprinted in *The Morning After* (New York, 1971), p. 23.

230 "calculated mode": Gene Baro, "Jones Tells How It Really Is in Malesville," *Life*, n.d., tearsheets; Texas.

230 "elements of self-doubt": JJ to Maxwell Geismar, May 18, 1967; Texas.

230 "If you are so naive": JJ to William Styron, November 24, 1966; Texas.

230 "I didn't get the way the language works": John Thompson to JJ, January 9, 1967; Texas.

231 "Can you explain my stylistic flaws": JJ to Burroughs Mitchell, November 10, 1962; Princeton.

231 "wobbly diction": Mary McCarthy, quoted in JJ to Mary McCarthy, July 26, 1963; Texas.

231 "If one needs to explain": JJ to Mary McCarthy, July 26, 1963; Texas.

⤳≫ 10 ⪡⪡

INTERNATIONAL CELEBRITY

Apart from newspaper reports, magazine articles, and reviews, and books on the 1968 Paris riots, notably Jill Neville's *The Love-Germ* (1969), and Angelo Quattrocchi's *The Beginning of the End* (1968), most of the information in this chapter came from interviews with the individuals involved in the story. I wish therefore to acknowledge the help of the following:

Neil Abercrombie, John Atherton, Lauren Bacall, Cecile Gray Bazelon, Eugène Braun-Munk, Charles Burke, Ross Claiborne, Ethel de Croisset, Ruda Dauphin, Jack Egle, Walter Eytan, Donald Fine, Eileen Finletter, Jack Flam, Elizabeth Fondaras, Bernard Frizell, Carlos Fuentes, Leslie Garrett, Herbert Gold, Herman Gollob, Monique Gonthier, the Countess of Hardwicke, Genta Hawkins, Addie Herder, Dr. Michael Herman, John Hersey, Henry Hyde, Paul Jenkins, Gloria Jones, Jamie Jones, Kaylie Jones, Robert Knittle, Bernard Malamud, Bobby Massie, Robert Massie, Harry Matthews, Edgar May, Mary McCarthy, Helen Meyer, Edwin Morgan, Bodil Nielsen, Henry Pillsbury, Angelo Quattrocchi, Françoise Sagan, the late Irwin Shaw, Sargent Shriver, Daniel Stern, William and Rose Styron, C. L. Sulzberger, John Thompson, William Wilson, Clement and Jessie Wood, Gore Vidal, Peter Viertel, Kurt Vonnegut.

Page

233 "I used to have to go around": JJ, quoted in anonymous interview, manuscript, Paris; Texas.

234 "We get more kick": Ibid.

234 "I think games are significant": JJ, quoted in *Writers at Work, The Paris Review Interviews*, pp. 249–250.

235 *"Mon mari est en chaleur"*: Gloria Jones, quoted in Viorst, *Esquire,* February 1968, p. 101.

236 "Where would you like to live": "Paris aux Caraibes, James Jones Répond au Questionnaire de Proust," *L'Express,* June 6, 1963.

237 "Princes and countesses": Viorst, *Esquire,* February 1968, p. 131.

238 "at a table in an open café": JJ, "My Best Story," introduction to an anthology to be edited by Rust Hills, manuscript; Texas.

238 "Was it to go on like this": *The Ice-Cream Headache,* p. 237.

238 "no blowhard": John Barkham, "James Jones Looks Better in Collection of Short Stories," syndicated review, Victoria, Texas, *Advocate,* March 24, 1968.

238 "Jones is incapable of anything but total loyalty": John Thompson, "American Gallery," *New York Times Book Review,* April 28, 1968, clipping; Texas.

Page

240 "excessively talkative": Translation of report from Ecole Bilingue; Texas.

240 "sitting on the edge": Rose Styron, quoted in Willie Morris, *James Jones: A Friendship*, p. 135.

241 "Nobody knows the people": JJ to Peggy Carson, November 16, 1946; Yale.

241 "never been on the bum": Ibid.

241 "In a democracy": JJ, note; Texas.

242 "It's like voting for Tweedledum": JJ, quoted in anonymous interview, Paris, manuscript; Texas.

242 "repress by force": JJ to Michael Dane Turner, February 28, 1959; Texas.

242 "I didn't pay much attention": JJ, quoted in anonymous interview, manuscript, Paris; Texas.

242 "was — and is — a loud": JJ, statement at children's party, American embassy, Paris, August 22, 1963; Texas.

244 "I thought it was fun": JJ, quoted in anonymous interview, manuscript, Paris; Texas.

244 "cynical about both sides": Ibid.

244 "It's all given me an idea": JJ to Jeff Jones, June 24, 1968; R. Jones.

245 "one of those potentially dangerous": JJ, quoted in "Comment," *New York Herald Tribune,* Paris edition, n.d., clipping; Texas.

245 "No one is outlawed": Ibid.

247 *"Jouissez"*: Jill Neville, *The Love-Germ* (London, 1969), p. 156.

248 "The old cathedral looked the same": JJ, *The Merry Month of May* (New York, 1971), p. 99.

248 "melange of erratic personal journalism": Maxwell Geismar, "The Struggle James Jones Misses Along the Seine," *Chicago Sun-Times,* February 14, 1971.

248 "the primitive American writer": Robert Kirsch, "Jones Unveils Exploration of Hemingway Country," *Los Angeles Times,* n.d., clipping; Texas.

248 "the more Jones wrote": John Aldridge, "Twosomes and Threesomes in Gay Paris," *Saturday Review,* February 13, 1971, p. 23.

249 "the weather, and the long walks": Mary McCarthy to JJ, February 15, 1971; Texas.

250 "We are a nation of drunkards": *The Ice-Cream Headache*, p. 172.

253 "an American man's aging": JJ, "Hippy Mystery Notes," September 20, 1971; Texas.

254 "The old 'virtues' ": Ibid.

254 "tough hard man": Ibid.

254 "What a situation": JJ, *A Touch of Danger* (New York, 1973), p. 297.

Page

255 "I nearly killed myself": JJ to Daniel Stern, November 9, 1972; Texas.

255 "James Jones, come home": Hoke Norris, "James Jones Come Home!" *Chicago Sun-Times*, June 3, 1973.

255 "All around us tall blue headlands": JJ, quoted in Cobey, "Writing," *Honolulu Advertiser*, May 1, 1973.

255 "We spent the whole day out": Ibid.

257 "He knows what it is like": Bobby Massie, quoted in Robert and Suzanne Massie, *Journey* (New York, 1975), p. 379.

260 "My job in Paris": William Saroyan, *Chance Meetings* (New York, 1978), p. 121.

260 "I assert the first paradox": Robert Ardrey, *African Genesis* (New York, 1961), p. 354.

261 "Our capacity for sacrifice": Robert Ardrey, *The Territorial Imperative* (New York, 1971), pp. 324–325.

≫ 11 ≪

HOME TO AMERICA

Information for this chapter has been gathered from many sources. For Jones's illness, I consulted his three American physicians, Dr. Michael Herman, Dr. Eugene Teich, and Dr. William Diefenbach, as well as Jones's nephew, Dr. Richard Jones. I also talked with Beryl Buchholz, who was the nurse in charge of Jones's care during his last illness at Southampton Hospital.

For information about Hawaii and for the courtesy shown me when I visited Schofield Barracks, I am indebted to the Office of the Chief of Public Relations of the Army in New York, as well as Lieutenant Colonel Noel Brady and Mr. McGill in Hawaii. For details concerning Jones's visit to Vietnam, I am obliged to General Frederick Weyand and his wife, Arline, and to Major General Michael Healy, both of the United States Army.

Others who provided information for this chapter include: Neil Abercrombie, Charles Addams, Ellen Adler, Shana Alexander, Harry Antrim, Lauren Bacall, Cecile Gray Bazelon and Irwin Bazelon, Eugène Braun-Munk, Jamie Bruce, Sue Camacho, Ross Claiborne, Betty Comden, Seymour Corenthal, Joan Didion, John Gregory Dunne, Judy Feiffer, Eileen Finletter, Elizabeth Fondaras, Betty Friedan, David Gelsanliter, Paul Gitlin, Robert Gluckman, Jan Goenvic, Adolph Green and Phyllis Newman, Winston Groom, Thomas Guinzburg, the Countess of Hardwicke, Joseph Heller, Addie Herder, Henry Hyde, Paul Jarrico, Paul Jenkins, Gloria Jones, Jamie Jones, Kaylie Jones, Elaine Kaufman, John Keasler, John Knowles, Scoops Kreger, Robert Markel, Peter Matthiessen, Norman

Mailer, Mary McCarthy, Helen Meyer, Michael Mewshaw, Willie Morris, Muriel Murphy, Bodil Nielsen, Sidney Offitt, Joan Patterson, David Pearce, George Plimpton, Peter Rand, Stewart Richardson, Elmore Richmond, Budd and Betsy Schulberg, the late Irwin Shaw, Wilfrid Sheed, Stephen Sheppard, Elaine Steinbeck, William and Rose Styron, Kathleen Tynan, Kurt Vonnegut and Jill Krementz, Elizabeth Vreeland, Jack Warden, Kathryn Weissberger, Arthur Weithas, Benjamin and Irma Wolstein, Clement and Jessie Wood, and Robert Wool.

Page

265 "A part of me": JJ, notes for *Viet Journal;* Texas.

265 "the sights and smells": Ibid.

265 "two or more sat down together": *Viet Journal* p. 31.

266 "was worth at least twice": Ibid., p. 20.

267 "involved in a military-industrial conspiracy": Ibid., p. 60.

267 "What the hell am I doing here": JJ, notes for *Viet Journal;* Texas.

267 "were just feeling in a good mood": *Viet Journal*, p. 184.

267 "a strangely chilling feeling": Ibid.

267 "I've always loved you": JJ to Gloria Jones, March 4, 1973; Texas.

267 "the tropics as much as ever": JJ, notes for *Viet Journal;* Texas.

267 "Down with the American imperialists": *Viet Journal*, p. 107.

267 "You knew his aggressive physical courage": Ibid., p. 87.

268 "Jones has gotten himself brainwashed": Ibid.

268 "underestimated the role that North Vietnam": Fox Butterfield, "The New Vietnam Scholarship," *New York Times Magazine*, February 3, 1984, p. 28.

268 "Poor beaten woman": JJ, notebook; Texas.

269 "She was all of Vietnam to me": *Viet Journal*, p. 233.

269 "I love you forever": JJ to Gloria Jones, March 7, 1973; Texas.

270 "Suddenly, without any preparation": *Viet Journal*, pp. 246–247.

270 "Schofield Barracks and much of Honolulu": Joan Didion, *The White Album* (New York, 1979), pp. 146–147.

270 "I knew every shelf": *Viet Journal*, p. 247.

271 "My foot still knew where it was": Ibid., p. 256.

271 "I felt I was bearing witness": Ibid.

271 "I had come back hoping,": Ibid., p. 257.

273 "its air and its expanses": JJ to J. D. Reed, September 13, 1971; Texas.

274 "with a sort of balloon": JJ, quoted in "Then and Now: The Expatriate Tradition," a round table discussion with Maria Jolas, Janet Flanner, James Jones, Virgil Thompson, tearsheets, p. 183; Texas.

274 "The best 'in' group": JJ, quoted in anonymous interview, Paris, manuscript; Texas.

Page

274 "hidebound, burdened with history": JJ, quoted in "Interviewing James Jones: Goodbye to All That," *Time*, June 17, 1974, p. 19.

274 "I've felt as if a huge weight": Ibid.

274 "I'm tired of living in France": JJ, quoted in Alice Moseby, "A Literary Expatriate Repatriates," *Washington Post*, February 25, 1974.

278 "is an art which has no definite set of rules": JJ to Wesley Hartley, October 27, 1959; Texas.

278 "best qualification you can have": JJ, notes for English 416; Texas.

278 "The most exciting story": Ibid.

278 "You are arriving at an airport": JJ, assignment sheet, English 416; Texas.

279 "The thing I like about teaching": JJ, quoted in Patricia Burstein, "Author James Jones Tries to Impart the Mysteries of 'Creative Writing,'" *People*, May 18, 1975, p. 44.

279 "I am drawn to the haunted ones" and following quotations: David Gelsanliter, "Remembering James Jones," *Writer's Yearbook* (1982), pp. 76, 77.

280 "I don't like to be around rich people": Ibid.

281 "the chattel of the society he serves": *WWII*, pp. 54–55.

281 "that his name is already": Ibid., p. 54.

281 "buried in some foreign land": Ibid., p. 256.

282 "generation of men": Ibid.

285 "Silhouetted in the doorway": Wilfrid Sheed, quoted in Willie Morris, *James Jones: A Friendship*, p. 190.

287 "hysterical, frenetic gaiety": JJ, background statement for *Home Front;* Texas.

287 "If this son-of-a-bitching fucking war": *WWII*, p. 82.

287 "a picture of life": JJ, quoted in Marilyn Beck, "Hollywood Hotline," Los Angeles newspaper, clipping, n.d.; Texas.

290 "the *irreversible coherence"*: Pierre Teilhard de Chardin, *The Phenomenon of Man* (New York, 1959), p. 217.

290 "that there was a noticeable difference": *WWII*, p. 146.

290 "Money was not much of a problem": Ibid., p. 148.

291 "They weren't shocked any more": JJ, *Whistle* (New York, 1978), p. 111.

291 "a pervert. A sexual pervert": Ibid., p. 277.

292 "in the hope that he will never": JJ, note; Texas.

292 "I can already feel the chilly arms": JJ, prefatory note for *Whistle*, manuscript; Texas.

294 "the salty shore and breeze": Walt Whitman, "Paumanock," from "Sands at Seventy," *Complete Poems and Selected Prose* (Boston, 1959), p. 351.

Page

294 "I will arise and go now," William Butler Yeats, "The Lake Isle of Innisfree," *Collected Poems* (New York, 1983), p. 39.

294 "I am not resigned": Edna St. Vincent Millay, *Collected Poems* (New York, 1956), pp. 240–241.

295 "Dostoievsky was able to *become* Raskolnikov": JJ, talk to Southampton College; Texas.

296 "Each time I put it aside": JJ, notebook for *Whistle;* Texas.

296 "I want to make *everybody* guilty": Ibid.

296 "I think it came out of me": JJ, quoted by Willie Morris in notes; Texas.

297 "He told me that life was a great adventure": Kaylie Jones, statement for Willie Morris; Gloria Jones.

→» 12 «←

EPILOGUE

Page

301 "He knew so much about human cruelty": Willie Morris, quoted in Alden Whitman, "James Jones Hailed by Friends at a Memorial Service," *New York Times,* May 16, 1977.

301 "unflinching honesty, his courage": Irwin Shaw, quoted in Alden Whitman, ibid.

301 "voracious little barracudas": William Styron, "A Friend's Farewell to James Jones," *New York Magazine,* June 6, 1977, p. 41.

303 "Jones made his own war on cant": Irwin Shaw, "James Jones, 1921–1977, *New York Times Book Review,* June 12, 1977, p. 34.

303 "The machine went *crackle*": Gloria Jones, statement for Willie Morris; Gloria Jones.

304 "I gave each author a table": Gloria Jones, quoted in Judy Klemsrud, "Party Hails Publication of Jones's Novel," *New York Times,* February 23, 1978.

304 "He had never heard of Elaine's": Karen Lerner, quoted in Rex Reed, "A Party for a New Book by an Old Friend," *New York Daily News,* February 25, 1978.

305 "I want to make everybody in the world groan": JJ to Jeff Jones, note on *Whistle;* Texas.

305 "possibly his best work": Edmund Fuller, "James Jones's Last and Possibly Best Work," *Wall Street Journal,* March 6, 1978.

305 "had done it better": Philip Caputo, "An Eloquent Farewell to Arms," *Chicago Tribune Book Review,* February 19, 1978, clipping; Texas.

306 "How long, O Lord": Revelation 6:10.

Page

306 "Feel with your eyes": JJ to Jeff Jones, n.d.; R. Jones.

306 "You had to know him": Irwin Shaw, *"Whistle,* reader's report," for Delacorte Press; Texas.

306 "Death was his business": Mary McCarthy to Gloria Jones, May 16, 1977; Texas.

307 "We try to live": JJ, note, writing ideas; Texas.

➤➤➤ INDEX ≪≪≪

⇶ ABOUT THE AUTHOR ⇷

Frank MacShane is the author of three other biographies, *The Life and Work of Ford Madox Ford, The Life of Raymond Chandler,* and *The Life of John O'Hara.* He has also edited eight books and has translated five others from Spanish. He is the director of the Translation Center at Columbia University, where he is also a professor in the School of the Arts. He lives in New York City.